SHAKESPEAREAN CRITICISM

Volume 7

KING JOHN AND HENRY VIII

KING JOHN AND HENRY VIII

Critical Essays

Edited by
FRANCES A. SHIRLEY

LONDON AND NEW YORK

First published in 1988

This edition first published in 2015
by Routledge
2 Park Square, Milton Park, Abingdon, Oxon, OX14 4RN

and by Routledge
711 Third Avenue, New York, NY 10017

Routledge is an imprint of the Taylor & Francis Group, an informa business

British Library Cataloguing in Publication Data
A catalogue record for this book is available from the British Library

ISBN: 978-1-138-84955-6 (Set)
eISBN: 978-1-315-72488-1 (Set)
ISBN: 978-1-138-85072-9 (Volume 7)
eISBN: 978-1-315-72456-0 (Volume 7)

Publisher's Note
The publisher has gone to great lengths to ensure the quality of this book but points out that some imperfections from the original may be apparent.

Disclaimer
The publisher has made every effort to trace copyright holders and would welcome correspondence from those they have been unable to trace.

KING JOHN and *HENRY VIII*
Critical Essays

Frances A. Shirley

GARLAND PUBLISHING, INC. • NEW YORK & LONDON
1988

Library of Congress Cataloging-in-Publication Data

King John, Henry VIII : critical essays

(Shakespearean criticism ; vol. 6)
1. Shakespeare, William, 1564–1616—Histories.
2. Shakespeare, William, 1564–1616. King John.
3. Shakespeare, William, 1564–1616. Henry VIII.
4. John, King of England, 1167?–1216, in fiction, drama, poetry, etc. 5. Henry VIII, King of England, 1491–1547, in fiction, drama, poetry, etc. I. Shirley, Frances A. II. Series.
PR2982.K53 1988 882.3'3 87-21187
ISBN 0-8240-8384-9 (alk. paper)

Printed on acid-free, 250-year-life paper
Manufactured in the United States of America

Contents

Part II: *Henry VIII*

King Henry VIII (Arthur Bourchier) confronts Cardinal Wolsey (Sir Herbert Beerbohm Tree) while Queen Katherine (Violet Vanbrugh) looks on from the dais. Tree's Production. Photo courtesy of the Harvard Theatre Collection.

General Editor's Preface

The Garland series is designed to bring together the best that has been written about Shakespeare's plays, both as dramatic literature and theatrical performance. With the exception of some early plays which are treated in related combinations, each volume is devoted to a single play to include the most influential historical criticism, the significant modern interpretations, and reviews of the most illuminating productions. The collections are intended as resource companions to the texts. The scholar, the student, the reader, the director, the actor, the audience, will find here the full range of critical opinion, scholarly debate, and popular taste. Much of the material reproduced has been extremely difficult for the casual reader to locate. Original volumes have long since been out of print; definitive articles have been buried in journals and editions now obscure; theatrical reviews are discarded with each day's newspaper.

"The best that has been written" about each play is the criterion for selection, and the volumes represent the collective wisdom of foremost Shakespearean scholars throughout the world. Each editor has had the freedom and responsibility to make accessible the most insightful criticism to date for his or her play. I express my gratitude to the team of international scholars who have accepted this challenge. One would like to say with Keats "that is all/Ye know on earth, and all ye need to know," but the universality of Shakespeare will stimulate new responses, yield fresh meanings, and lead new generations to richer understandings of human nature.

Generally the essays have been reproduced as they appeared originally. Some concessions in punctuation, spelling, and documentation have been made for the sake of conformity. In the case of excerpts, notes have been renumbered to clarify the references. A principle of the series, however, is to reproduce the full text, rather than excerpts, except for digressive material having no bearing on the subject.

Joseph G. Price

Introduction

King John and *Henry VIII* may at first glance seem an odd pairing. Although both are named for and deal with the reigns of English kings, and both take their material primarily from the chronicles, the differences are great. *King John* is relatively early, is predominantly military, and centers on a struggle for a tenuously held throne. There is no doubt that it is Shakespeare's work, although people have argued about its relationship to *The Troublesome Raigne of King John*, which has occasionally been regarded as a bad quarto. *Henry VIII* is one of Shakespeare's last works, is broadly domestic, and focuses on shifts in influence and position within an absolute monarch's court and household. For two centuries there have been doubts about authorship, with John Fletcher usually named as collaborator. The plays are not even linked by a sweep of events in the way that such dissimilar pieces as *Richard II* and *Richard III* are.

A number of factors, however, do draw the two works together. The English of Shakespeare's time saw a relationship between the two kings. John Bale, in his Protestant propaganda piece, *King Johan*, voices the position of those who considered Henry's break with Rome in the 1530s the completion of the struggle for independence that John began when he defied the Papal legates three centuries earlier. The Interpreter closes Act I with the reminder:

> This noble King John, as a faithful Moses,
> Withstood proud Pharaoh for his poor Israel;
> Minding to bring it out of the land of darkness.
> But the Egyptians did against him so rebel
> That his poor people did still in the desert dwell
> Till that Duke Josue [Joshua], which was our late King
> Henry,
> Clearly brought us into the land of milk and honey.[1]

More recently literary critics have frequently treated the plays in conjunction simply because neither is part of a tetralogy or immediately connected with the Wars of the Roses, although had Shakespeare written a play about Henry VII, *Henry VIII* would have become the conclusion of a sweeping treatment of English history from Richard II to the birth of Elizabeth. *King John* stands very much alone, dealing with the early 1200s although the Elizabethans saw parallels to their own time in the threat of foreign invasion and, more particularly, in the altercations of John and Pandulph, which seemed to presage Elizabeth's excommunication and Rome's absolving the English of any allegiance to her. Twentieth-century audiences may feel surprised that *King John* makes no mention of Magna Carta or that *Henry VIII* focuses on Katherine and relegates Anne Bullen to two speaking scenes and a coronation procession. Shakespeare, however, reflected contemporary interest by ignoring the signing of the great charter (a scene Tree inserted into his turn-of-the- century production) and focusing on John's other troubles with his barons and outside forces; and by concentrating on Queen Katherine and Cardinal Wolsey's falls from favor, and, by the end of the play, the hope for the Tudor era that is promised by the infant Elizabeth.

Neither work has been popular with scholarly writers and, in the later twentieth century, with producers. John Wilders mentions *John* once and *Henry VIII* five times in passing, while dwelling at length on the other history plays; E. M. W. Tillyard devotes a chapter to *King John*, but ignores *Henry VIII* while including *Macbeth* among the histories; Frank Kermode includes *Pericles* and *The Two Noble Kinsmen* in a treatment of the last plays but makes no mention of *Henry VIII*, which has similar authorial problems.[2] When they did write about the plays, essayists from the nineteenth century on tended to focus on a couple of issues for each, rather than trying to see the works as wholes. What is the relationship of *King John*, probably written in 1593 or 1594 and first printed in Folio in 1623, to the two parts of *The Troublesome Raigne*, which dates from 1591? Why has Shakespeare failed to make John the center of the play or at least provide a philosophical center, rather than letting the play almost become the Bastard Faulconbridge's by default? Who wrote which parts of *Henry VIII*, or could it possibly all be Shakespeare's? What is the effect of the pageantry or the emotional high points in a play that seems to be episodic?

Fortunately more recent critics have widened their perspectives on both plays. They have sought organizing principles for *King John* and seen many of the smaller details in *Henry VIII.* The output remains small, however, and frequently the essays have a retrospective quality. For both plays, they begin with a review of much that has gone before, in a way that is impossible for the more popular plays, where one can pick only a few articles to build on or disagree with. Even the small selection of essays reprinted in this volume, therefore, makes a reader familiar with a wide critical history.

In addition to critical trends in common, both plays have similar stage histories from the eighteenth century on. *Henry VIII* remained popular throughout the seventeenth century and John Downes traces the acting tradition in *Roscius Anglicanis*: "The part of the King was so right and justly done by Mr. Betterton, he being Instructed in it by Sir *William* [Davenant], who had it from Old Mr. *Lowen*, that had his Instructions from Mr. *Shakespeare* himself."[3] It has had a continuous stage history, while *King John* was not revived until 1737. In the eighteenth century, however, both plays became popular with leading actors and actresses, who kept them in their repertories year after year. John Philip Kemble and Sarah Siddons had great successes as John and Constance or Wolsey and Katherine. In the early twentieth century, Sir Herbert Beerbohm Tree produced lavish versions of both plays. The episodic quality and lack of focus that critics complain of may have made the works popular with actor-managers who needed to cut heavily to allow for the theatrical effects that were becoming increasingly popular, and who wanted their own roles to shine. In the twentieth century, spectacular Shakespearean productions whose pace is dictated by elaborate scenery have given way to fast-moving renditions with much fuller texts. Revivals of *King John* and *Henry VIII* are much less frequent, although occasionally a director, such as Tyrone Guthrie with *Henry VIII* or Douglas Seale with *King John*, will be involved in several productions. Many producers, however, feel that both plays are merely works that they are duty-bound to get through if they happen to be doing the histories or the entire canon in a theatre dedicated to Shakespeare. The great actors of today apparently do not yearn to play Wolsey or Faulconbridge, and audiences are not familiar with the plays in the way that they were in earlier centuries.

The essays in this collection sample the concerns that have been hinted at above. With one exception, they are arranged by play, and in each case the focus is first on productions and then on a range of other issues, including characters, imagery, textual problems, and themes. Of course the division between stage history and other critical approaches is not absolute. Professors Sprague and Byrne illuminate many points about character and theme that become apparent if one sees Shakespeare on stage. Eugene Waith reconsiders critical approaches to *King John* in light of what one learns from theatre history and popular responses to a play. Lee Bliss is aware of the pageantry and masque-like elements that go so well on stage though he focuses on the political aspects of *Henry VIII*. The earliest piece, by Francis Gentleman, talks generally about *King John* and then speaks of eighteenth century actors. The most recent essay, by Kristian Smidt, calls attention to the pageantry of *Henry VIII* before dismissing the purely theatrical and turning to themes.

The people whose views are collected here represent the critical approaches of their generation in many instances. Frequently the selection is part of a larger whole. William Hazlitt, like many in the nineteenth century, focuses on characters or on particular scenes which reveal characters most strikingly. These short pieces are part of a whole volume in which he picks out highlights and is quick to express a personal displeasure about characters he does not like. Caroline Spurgeon treats *King John* and *Henry VIII* in the same chapter and sees similarities and contrasts in the body imagery of the two plays. This excerpt is part of a much more complete study of Shakespeare's use of imagery that has inspired later writers to examine the effect of recurring image patterns. While many turned their attention to the details of the texts in the 1930s, Arthur Colby Sprague began his work on theatre history and the long tradition of stage business in Shakespeare's plays. Professor Sprague's chapter on *King John* is part of a book on the histories that follows other volumes in which he has created a sense of the performances of the past.

Because an occasional paragraph taken from a larger work is not an adequate representation, the selection does not include several of the most modern critical approaches to Shakespeare. Feminists have not yet dealt with Katherine or Constance except for passing reference, although a century and a half ago Anna Jameson devoted a chapter to each. Structuralists have not dealt with the works in any detail, although some of the most modern pieces reproduced here are concerned in a less specialized way with the structure of the plays. Marxists are still engrossed in parts of the canon that have been more thoroughly treated by others and which are more widely studied.

Many of the pieces on *King John* touch at some point on the problem of the title character, although they only occasionally compare the figure Shakespeare created with the man who appeared on stage in several other plays before and after 1592. Bale's play, revised early in Elizabeth's reign, is a moral interlude in style, with flat characters serving as vehicles for anti- Catholic propaganda. The anonymous *Troublesome Raigne,* more blatantly and comically anti-Catholic than *King John,* presents a less complex king than Shakespeare's. Three other plays show him in a semi-historical and even more unpleasant light. Munday's *The Downfall of Robert, Earl of Huntington,* and Chettle's *The Death of Robert Earl of Huntington,* both from around 1600, portray a tyrant, and *The Death* focuses on his unsuccessful approaches to Matilda (Maid Marian), whom he eventually has poisoned. In both works, there is a sense of England's suffering attempts to maintain old values under a selfish and cruel king. The same ground was later covered in Robert Davenport's *John and Matilda.* Given this climate of opinion, it is remarkable that Shakespeare is as restrained as he is, although certainly his John is an unpleasant figure without the fascination of Richard III's active villainy.

Actors have made something of the role, but of course find the Bastard Faulconbridge more appealing. Thomas Davies gives a hint of the problems encountered by David Garrick in one of the earlier eighteenth-century revivals where he and Thomas Sheridan were playing the male leads, and Garrick had one of his comparatively infrequent failures. William Hazlitt witnessed John Philip Kemble's far more successful production, although he finds the low-keyed, detatched rendition of the king less to his taste after seeing Kean's more flamboyant acting. These performances and many more are put into perspective by two recent pieces, the chapter by Arthur Colby Sprague and an essay by Eugene Waith which was published originally with a large number of illustrations. From these two we get not only a sense of critical problems, but also glimpses of many of the actors and actresses who helped make the play so popular in the nineteenth century. Waith, especially, by giving us a sense of the emotional appeal of different scenes, leads us to wonder if the desire to see a political design is of paramount importance.

Francis Gentleman, in the earliest excerpt reproduced here, shows the critical approach one often finds in the eighteenth century. He thinks in terms of the scenes he prefers, gives a bit of plot summary, and is quick to voice his outrage that John should resign his crown. There is a tone of moral disapproval as he thinks of John's dealing with Arthur. Hazlitt, commenting on the characters of Shakespeare's plays, also focuses on the scenes he finds best in a play he doesn't like and has put off until last among the histories.

In 1944, E. M. W. Tillyard published a volume on the history plays that became one of the standards for generations of students. The chapter on *King John* is a scholarly attempt to get at the cause of his dislike of the play, with its disjunction between John the man and John the patriotic English King standing up to foreign pressures. The relation of Shakespeare's play to *The Troublesome Raigne* is important, for Tillyard is focusing on a lack of coherence and proportion that resulted when Shakespeare compressed the two parts of *The Troublesome Raigne* into one, but developed the characters in ways Tillyard and others have found annoying.

Where Caroline Spurgeon focuses on a single type of imagery that runs through a play in her treatment of both *King John* and *Henry VIII*, and often tends to give lists rather than a wider interpretive treatment, James Calderwood looks at the tension and balance created by the use of two opposing ideas. In one of the most successful modern essays on the play, Calderwood examines "honour" and "commodity" as they are spoken of and practiced through the five acts. From the eighteenth century on, people have commented on the Bastard's set speech on commodity, and some have seen it as a key to his character, but only recently has it been viewed as helping determine the overall organization of the play. Adrien Bonjour also argues persuasively that the play is less poorly constructed than Tillyard believed. He welcomes its complexity and finds a pattern in the rising and falling curves of King John and the Bastard Faulconbridge's lives. Chaos, for him, is shaped by evolution.

The final two pieces in this section again treat the play more broadly. M. M. Reese takes stock of the long-standing concern with the lack of focal point, but is also one of the critics who notice the play's tone of cynicism and disillusionment, its lack of lyricism, and its view of political reality. Against these unpleasant aspects, there is the redeeming integrity of Constance and Arthur, and the development of the choric Bastard into a symbolic leading figure who balances the morally reprehensible king. Robert Smallwood is obligated by his role of editor to give a clear overview of the play and to provide comments on textual emendations, a summary of source material, and notes on words and lines. Only his Introduction to the New Penguin edition is reprinted here, but the whole volume is helpful to beginnner and experienced scholar alike. The commentary, in end notes, is twice the length of the text, and is enhanced by a geneological table, a list of textual emendation, and more work on the relationship of the play to *The Troublesome Raigne*. For those who want to go beyond this selection of essays, there is an extensive annotated bibliography, touching on most of the best work on the play from 1940 to 1974.

Just as *King John*'s apparent lack of a center and its relationship to *The Troublesome Raigne* continue to crop up, so do *Henry VIII*'s authorship problems. R. A. Foakes, in the excellent Arden Edition, argues convincingly for Shakespeare's sole authorship, although fairly representing the points made by Spedding and his successors. In a Postscript, written in 1962, he does give some credence to Cyrus Hoy's linguistic analysis, and like many modern writers on the play, wishes that the matter could be forgotten. Foakes points out a trend worth noting--that many of the critics who find the play badly constructed hunt a second author, while those who are sympathetic to it lean toward Shakespeare as sole playwright.[4] Although Foakes's Introduction is not reprinted here, it is rich in insights, and is supplemented by full bibliographical footnotes and by commentary conveniently placed at the bottom of the page, as well as by reproduction of selections from Shakespeare's sources.

The criticism that is reprinted here not only touches upon the most important aspects of the play and responses to it, but is also selected to complement some of the examples reproduced for *King John*. Rather than broader stage histories, for example, there are criticisms of two productions which are at opposite poles in the treatment of the play. Sir Henry Irving's staging was the culmination of a series of increasingly elaborate renditions of a play that had always been noted for its pageantry. George Villiers, making fun of stage business that has gotten out of hand, makes Bayes promise

> I'll show you the greatest scene that ever England saw—I mean not for words, for those I do not value but for state, show, and magnificence. In fine, I'll justify it to be as grand to the eye every whit, 'y gad, as that great scene in *Harry the Eight*—and grander too, 'y gad; for instead of two bishops I bring in here four cardinals.[5]

To make room for this popular pageantry, the fifth act was virtually eliminated, along with many other passages, and attention focused on Katherine and Wolsey. Irving's spectacular production opened in London in January 1892, and was brought to the United States two years later. Three reviews from Boston newspapers show the range of responses to a ruinously expensive interpretation with settings, properties, and costumes as close to the early 1500's as historical research could make them. We tend to think that the Victorians all relished this attempt at verisimilitude, but the anonymous reviewer for the *Evening Transcript* questions the principle, deciding that an appeal to the imagination would be more rewarding than Irving's infinite pains with details that can never add up to the real thing. He would probably have joined Muriel Byrne in classifying a Stratford production on a relatively bare stage as "realism" when conceptually it was far removed from Irving's. H. A. Clapp is more concerned with characterization, and notes the difficulty in having a Wolsey who must first be overweeningly proud and manipulative, and then a gentle and spiritual man. He gives a sense of Irving's strengths and weaknesses in the part, and is equally judicious in his comments about Ellen Terry and the supporting cast. William T. W. Ball, on the other hand, is totally in sympathy with this heavily cut production and impressed by the acting.

It was against such a stage tradition that Tyrone Guthrie produced the play several times in the decades before and after World War II. Muriel St. Clare Byrne's "descriptive analysis" of the 1949 version is a model of this sort of theatrical criticism. She gives a clear sense of the appropriately costumed play against its permanent set, with results that must have been far closer to the experience of the Jacobean playgoer than were Irving's. One theme of her review is the continuity that was evident in this relatively full presentation of the text, unimpeded with waits for set changes. An excerpt from a second article by Professor Byrne makes clear the way a single scene, well produced, can shed light on an entire play. She describes Katherine's trial scene, and points to its centrality to a play whose theme she considers the Tudor succession and the destruction of those who threaten it. The trial, in her view, has a reality in its quietness, as one sees emotion spending itself without reaching a fever pitch. Starting from this scene, Byrne sees the play as wholly by Shakespeare, the experienced author experimenting.

The authorship controversy apparently began with Richard Roderick in the mid-eighteenth century.[6] In 1850 James Spedding made a detailed analysis of the play and attributed ten of the seventeen scenes to Fletcher, along with Prologue, Epilogue, and part of III,ii. The piece was reprinted by the New Shakespeare Society in 1874 with letters of support, and scholarly arguments began in earnest. Marjorie Hope Nicholson pulled together the main theories in an essay that was the only notable American work on the play in 1922 and shows how central the authorship controversy had become. Although she reviews material on the sources, other plays on *Henry VIII*'s reign, and the Globe fire, she falls into the dangerous habit of postulating. She feels Shakespeare planned a play on "the buffets and rewards of fortune," but, unlike Byrne, she sees disunities in the text and a sentimentalizing hand blurring Shakespeare's original lines.

The structual problems that concern many scholars are ignored by Hazlitt and Anna Jameson. Like the nineteenth-century producers, they thought in terms of high points or a few leading characters. Hazlitt quotes much of Samuel Johnson's brief commentary on the play, which focused on Katherine, then concentrates on the unpleasant king. Mrs. Jameson, presaging feminist criticism, returns in great detail to Katherine, seeing an admirable dramatic character created from historical facts.[7] Truth is the basis of Katherine's character and the source of her understanding of and reactions to others. Mrs. Jameson defines a very different sort of truth from the political reality or attention to details that later writers have considered a cohesive factor in the play, but it provides a coherence for the character who at the beginning of the play seems secure despite her distrust of the powerful Wolsey, who endures the trial with a naturally simple manner, and who finally faces death with equanimity. Mrs. Jameson, like Professor Byrne, focuses on the trial scene and also feels that it is not to be compared with

Hermione's trial in *The Winter's Tale,* although many scholars have done so.

The three modern essays that round off this volume all seek to break away from the authorship controversy and find a way of dealing with the play's content. The long-standing accusation of inconsistency is not denied—Smidt's book is titled *Unconformities in Shakespeare's History Plays.* Like John, Henry is not a pleasant title character, and his actions are unpredictable. Sympathy and attention go to Katherine while she lives. The fifth act seems almost an afterthought, detailing Cranmer's downfall and most important for its prophecy about the newborn Elizabeth, who was in fact two when Katherine died.

Lee Bliss is correct in viewing the play as different in form from the conventional history plays. "Shifting perspectives" and conscious ambiguities keep characters and audience alike off balance. Public and private lives blend in confusing ways. There are visions and prophecies, but they are different in tone from the Bastard Faulconbridge's closing speech about England's strength. They are also different from the renewals and reconciliations of the romances. Central to Bliss's interpretation is Shakespeare's ability to create a "double view" of rising and falling movements, with Henry, the political figure, dominating a far-from-ideal world. Where Spurgeon had concentrated on images of the body, but seen very little symbolic significance, Bliss comments on the special emphasis on sickness, also noting suggestions of cyclical imagery in a play whose final hope is for the marvellous, idealized age of Elizabeth.

The chronological position of *Henry VIII,* well into King James's reign rather than of the Elizabethan period when chronicle histories were popular, has suggested some valid comparisons. The processions and masque-like elements, reminiscent of the romances, are far different in quality from the ceremonial occasions in *Richard II* or *Henry V*. F. W. Brownlow, however, like Byrne, believes that Shakespeare was still experimenting at the end of his career. Brownlow emphasizes the differences between *Henry VIII* and *The Tempest,* pointing to the ironies and worldliness that prevail in so many scenes, and form a counter point to Katherine's vision of angels. The subtitle, *All is True,* has an ironic ring to an audience trying to decide what can be believed and what is only the voice of expediency. Brownlow goes further into the irony, showing how, both obviously and subtly, it can give coherence to apparently disparate events.

The most recent essay, by Kristian Smidt, would shock past commentators, playgoers, and those involved with the recent BBC Television production, for it dismisses the pageantry as relatively insignificant. Smidt does not deny that the play is episodic or that ambiguities abound. But he uses these as the basis of an argument for more subtle relationships. Scenes that are at first glance disconnected become a carefully structured way of providing perspective on events and, more importantly, on characters.

Both plays reward close study, not because they are great masterpieces of the Shakespeare canon, but because they provide the opportunity to wrestle wth works that are less familiar and to have one's own insights without having to master volumes of critical writing to see what others have said. There are outstanding moments in both, there are distinctive and often richly drawn characters, and there are examples of the political realism and expedience that Shakespeare must have felt often underlie the actions of people in power. Both plays gain greatly on the stage, too, where good performances can reveal a vitality that may not be apparent to the reader. Although in the theatre one may miss the subtle ironies or the patterning of the confrontation of French and English forces before Angiers, or the pageantry that helps create an overall impression of Henry's court. In fact, on stage many of the problems so rightly pointed out by the scholars included here tend to be forgotten as the plays move quickly through the events of history that Shakespeare chooses and shapes.

NOTES

1. John Bale, *John, King of England*, ed. John S. Farmer, London: Early English Drama Society, 1907; reprint, New York: Barnes & Noble, 1966, pp. 233–224.
2. John Wilders, *The Lost Garden*, Totowa, N.J.: Rowman and Littlefield, 1978; E.M.W. Tillyard, *Shakespeare's History Plays*, New York: Macmillan, 1946; Frank Kermode, *Shakespeare: The Final Plays*, London: Longmans Green & Co., 1963.
3. John Downes, *Roscius Anglicanus*, ed. Montague Summers, London: The Fortune Press, n.d., p. 24.

4. *King Henry VIII*, ed. R.A. Foakes, London: Methuen & Co., Ltd., 1984, pp. xxvii–xxviii.
5. George Villiers, Duke of Buckingham, et al., *The Rehearsal*, in *British Dramatists From Dryden to Sheridan*, ed. George H. Nettleton and Arthur E. Case, Boston: Houghton Mifflin, 1939, V,i,1–8.
6. Richard Roderick, in *The Canons of Criticism and Glossary*, Sixth Edition, ed. Thomas Edwards. Roderick had left remarks to Edwards, who added them where appropriate to Warburton's edition of Shakespeare.
7. The fullest treatment of the historical sources Shakespeare used is found in Geoffrey Bullough, *Narrative and Dramatic Sources of Shakespeare*, Vol. IV, New York: Columbia University Press, 1962, which also includes sources for *King John*.

Part I
King John

Thomas Davies

From *Memoirs of the Life of David Garrick, Esq.*

In some select plays, Garrick and Sheridan joined their forces, in order to crowd the benches of the theatre; particularly in Horatio and Lothario in the Fair Penitent, and the King and the Bastard in Shakespeare's King John.

This play had been revived about the year 1743, nearly in its original state, to withstand an alteration and supposed improvement of it written by Colley Cibber; which, after it had lain dormant for some time in the hands of Mr. Fleetwood, the alterer, upon some disgust, withdrew. It was, however, acted at Covent-garden theatre with some success, notwithstanding its great inferiority to the old tragedy. Cibber was so little acquainted with the genius of Shakespeare that he melted down the Bastard Faulconbridge, which is one of the richest portraits of humour, to an almost insignificant dependent of the king. He was weak enough too, in extreme old age, to act the part of Cardinal Pandulph; but his voice, which was never either strong or pleasing, was by time rendered quite feeble and inarticulate. His deportment was much commended by some, who pretended to admire his majestic step and lofty carriage: to others his action appeared very affected, and most eminently insignificant. However, much ought to be pardoned on account of his very advanced age. Cibber did not know his own defect; he was at best a very imperfect and disagreeable speaker of tragedy, though he seemed to value himself much on his talent in the buskin. He reproached Mrs. Pritchard, who acted Lady Constance, for want of a tone, as he called it, though he granted she spoke with propriety and feeling.

Shakespeare's King John was played with great success at Drury-lane. The king was personated by Mr. Garrick with very great skill, and unusual energy of action; but it must be confessed that Mrs. Cibber, by an uncommon pathetic ardour in speaking, and a surprising dignity of action and deportment, threw every actor in the play at a great distance. This had a greater effect from her never having before attempted characters, where power of voice and action were so greatly requisite to express the passions of rage, anguish, and despair.

The tragedy had, on Mrs. Cibber's engagement at Covent-garden, been discontinued for several years at Drury-lane; but, soon after he returned to that theatre, in 1755, Mr. Garrick revived it. He then took the part of the Bastard, and gave the King to Mr. Mossop.

When the two principal characters of this tragedy were divided between Mr. Garrick and Mr. Sheridan, the former chose the King, and he actually consented that the Bastard should be Mr. Sheridan's part. Secretly he had determined to the contrary and, after making some apology to Mr. Sheridan, he endeavoured to persuade him to exchange parts; to which the latter was extremely averse: I know not for what reason; for, though he understood the sense and spirit of the part, yet there is in the Bastard Faulconbridge an exuberant wantonness of humour, and a romantic spirit of gallantry, which Mr. Sheridan could not assume. Nor could Mr. Garrick, with all his spirit and art, attain perfectly to the full exhibition of the character: he was so defective in the mechanical part of it, I mean height, look, and sinew, that he was obliged to search carefully for a proper actor to play his half brother, one with a consumptive look and a meagre form, to contrast and set off his own person; and, though in this he met with tolerable success, yet still there was a deficiency: nor did the speeches which related to the Bastard's manly form produce the desired effect.

It is but justice to the memory of Walker, who was the original actor of Macheath, to say, that he performed Shakespeare's Bastard in King John with such native humour, spirited action, and vigorous deportment, that, I think, no actor has, since his time, given an equal idea of the part.

Mr. Sheridan was, by continual solicitation of the manager, prevailed upon at last to take the part of King John; and, in this compliance, I think, he gained great advantage to himself: the deep tones of his voice, and the vehemence of his action, were well adapted to the turbulent and gloomy passions of John. In the scene with Hubert, in the third act, his representation of the anxiety and distress of a mind which strongly labours with, and yet is afraid to discover, a secret big with horror and death, was expressed with the feelings of one who is a master of the human heart. That accurate observer of the players' deficiencies, Churchill, could not withhold his approbabion of Sheridan's action in King John, though in his panegyric he threw some ludicrous strokes on his excesses in look and action. The play was acted several nights, and was honoured with the king's command.

Sheridan's success in King John heightened Garrick's jealousy, especially when he was informed, by a very intimate acquaintance, that the king was uncommonly pleased with that actor's representation of the part. This was a bitter cup; and, to make the draught still more unpalatable, upon his asking whether his majesty approved his playing the Bastard, he was told, without the least compliment paid to his action, it was imagined that the king thought the character was rather too bold in the drawing, and that the colouring was overcharged and glaring. Mr. Garrick, who had been so accustomed to applause, and who of all men living most sensibly felt the neglect of it, was greatly struck with a preference given to another, and which left him out of all consideration; and, though the boxes were taken for King John several nights successively, he would never after permit the play to be acted.

William Hazlitt

From *A View of the English Stage; or, A Series of Dramatic Criticisms*

Covent-Garden, Dec. 7, 1816

We wish we had never seen Mr. Kean. He has destroyed the Kemble religion; and it is the religion in which we were brought up. Never again shall we behold Mr. Kemble with the same pleasure that we did, nor see Mr. Kean with the same pleasure that we have seen Mr. Kemble formerly. We used to admire Mr. Kemble's figure and manner, and had no idea that there was any want of art or nature. We feel the force and nature of Mr. Kean's acting, but then we feel the want of Mr. Kemble's person. Thus an old and delightful prejudice is destroyed, and no new enthusiasm, no second idolatry comes to take its place. Thus, by degrees, knowledge robs us of pleasure, and the cold icy hand of experience freezes up the warm current of the imagination, and crusts it over with unfeeling criticism. The knowledge we acquire of various kinds of excellence, as successive opportunities present themselves, leads us to require a combination of them which we never find realized in any individual, and all the consolation for the disappointment of our fastidious expectations is in a sort of fond and doating retrospect of the past. It is possible indeed that the force of prejudice might often kindly step in to suspend the chilling effects of experience, and we might be able to see an old favourite by a voluntary forgetfulness of other things, as we saw him twenty years ago; but his friends take care to prevent this, and by provoking invidious comparisons, and crying up their idol as a model of abstract perfect, force us to be ill-natured in our own defence.

We went to see Mr. Kemble's King John, and he became the part so well, in costume, look, and gesture, that if left to ourselves, we could have gone to sleep over it, and dreamt that it was fine, and "when we waked, have cried to dream again." But we were told that it was really fine, as fine as Garrick as fine as Mrs. Siddons, as fine as Shakespeare; so we rubbed our eyes and kept a sharp look out, but we saw nothing but a deliberate intention on the part of Mr. Kemble to act the part finely. And so he did in a certain sense, but not by any means as Shakespeare wrote it, nor as it might be played. He did not harrow up the feelings, he did not electrify the sense: he did not enter into the nature of the part himself, nor consequently move others with terror or pity. The introduction to the scene with Hubert was certainly excellent: you saw instantly, and before a syllable was uttered, partly from the change of countenance, and partly from the arrangement of the scene, the purpose which had entered his mind to murder the young prince. But the remainder of this trying scene, though the execution was elaborate--painfully elaborate, and the outline well conceived, wanted the filling up, the true and master touches, the deep piercing heartfelt tones of nature. It was done well and skillfully, according to the book of arithmetic; but no more. Mr. Kemble, when he approaches Hubert to sound his disposition, puts on an insidious, insinuating, fawning aspect, and so he ought; but we think it should not be, though it was, that kind of wheedling smile, as if he was going to persuade him that the business he wished him to undertake was a mere jest; and his natural repugnance to it, an idle prejudice, that might be carried off by a certain pleasant drollery of eye and manner. Mr. Kemble's look, to our apprehension, was exactly as if he had just caught the eye of some person of his acquaintance in the boxes, and was trying to suppress a rising smile at the metamorphosis he had undergone since dinner. Again, he changes his voice three several times, in repeating the name of Hubert; and the changes might be fine, but they did not vibrate on our feelings; so we cannot tell. They appeared to us like a tragic voluntary. Through almost the whole scene this celebrated actor did not seem to feel the part itself as it was set down for him, but to be considering how he ought to feel it, or how he should express by rule and method what he did not feel. He was sometimes slow, and sometimes hurried: sometimes familiar, and sometimes solemn: but always with an evident design and determination to be so. The varying tide of passion did not appear to burst from the source of nature in his breast, but to be drawn from a theatrical leaden cistern, and then directed through certain conduit-pipes and artificial channels, to fill the audience with well regulated and harmless sympathy.

We are afraid, judging from the effects of this representation, that "man delight not us, nor woman neither": for we did not like Mr. O'Neill's Constance better, nor so well as Mr. Kemble's King John. This character, more than any other of Shakespeare's females, treads perhaps upon the verge of extravagance; the impatience of grief, combined with the violence of her temper, borders on insanity: her imagination grows light-headed. But still the boundary between poetry and phrensy is not passed: she is neither a virago nor mad. Miss O'Neill gave more of the vulgar than the poetical side of the character. She generally does so of late. Mr. Charles Kemble in the Bastard, had the "bulk, the threws, the sinews" of Falconbridge: would that he had had "the spirit" too. There was one speech which he gave well—"Could Sir Robert make this leg?" And suiting the action to the word, as well he might, it had a great effect upon the house.

Arthur Colby Sprague

From *Shakespeare's Histories*

Alleged Faults—Virtues—Appeal to National Prejudice—Archaeology—Parts to tempt Stars—John vs. Faulconbridge—Constance—Debatable Scenes—Hubert and Arthur—The Citizen of Angiers—*King John* and *The Troublesome Reign*—Commodity and Loyalty

One of the best productions of *King John* I have seen was at the Maddermarket Theatre, Norwich, in June 1959. Established some forty years ago by a disciple of William Poel's, the late Nugent Monck, this famous theatre has a stage modelled on Poel's adaptations of the Elizabethan stage. The actors are amateurs of wide experience with Shakespeare, all of whose plays have been given at the Maddermarket. In this *King John* the speaking of the verse was an immediate and sustained pleasure. The handsome young Constance, anonymous as were the rest of the cast, had the sincerity and disinterestedness one finds occasionally in very good amateur acting. She knew also how to treat the great tirades, making the lament beginning

> If thou that bid'st me be content wert grim
> Ugly, and sland'rous to thy mother's womb,

a well-controlled decrescendo as far as

> Of Nature's gifts thou mayst with lilies boast
> *And with the half-blown rose,*

which she spoke simply and without emphasis, as if stating the merest fact.[1] (It is only when Constance ceases to be articulate that she becomes a bore.) Poetry found expression in other ways

Reprinted from *Shakespeare's Histories* by Arthur Colby Sprague (1964), by permission of the author and The Society for Theatre Research.

as well. Turning away from realism, the producer, Mr. Ian Emmerson, used at times quite formal groupings (I recall one in which the Dauphin stood for a moment between Constance and Blanch, each kneeling and holding one of his hands). The battles were fought off-stage. The all-important last scene, in which if anywhere the play's meaning emerges, was impressive at many points. Monks in white cassocks passed above, chanting. Inconspicuous changes in lighting suggested the coming of day. The voice of the boy who played Prince Henry, beautifully contrasted with those of the men, sounded clear and poignant. Faulconbridge gave the closing lines their due importance, neither spouting them nor throwing them away. That even in such a sensitive production the history seemed a little fragmentary and incomplete must be admitted nonetheless. Perhaps, though I am reluctant to admit as much, this was inevitable.

Some of the objections formerly urged against *King John* have passed with the passing of time. Thus, it did not observe the unities. "Of all *Shakespear's* Plays," declared the author of *A Letter to Colley Cibber, Esq.* in 1745, "This is that which sins most against the Grand Unities of the Stage, *Time*, *Place* and *Action*."[2] James Kirkman, at the end of the eighteenth century, wrote that in the composition of this tragedy, Shakespeare disclaimed every idea of regularity, and had huddled such a series of historical events on the back of one another, as shame and the utmost stretch of probability."[3] The critic of the Boston *Emerald* (a few years later) had heard that Shakespeare's histories were not subject to the laws governing tragedy, but hesitated to go so far. Certainly the first two acts of the present history "jogged heavily" in performance, "and the last consisted of an interchange of striking and spiritless representation. . . . There is perhaps no other play, in which a good poet might exert his abilities to more advantage, than in alteration of *King John*."[4] Almost at mid-century, *The Theatrical Journal* was still saying that the fault of the play lay "in its defying all consistency in time and place."[5] Subsequent critics of the play's structure have proceeded against it without recourse to the rules.

Then there was the matter of indelicacy. Francis Gentleman, an over-refined critic of the seventeen-seventies, pointed out the offensive passages, most of them spoken by the Bastard. "Philip's blunt, sportive method of expression, tainted too with licentiousness, is abominable stuff for the ears and respectful decorum of royalty to be violated with." In particular Gentleman deplored the lines with which the first act ended, as "much more suitable to the bully of a brothel, than a person of good sense, good breeding, and real spirit," and, in the second act, the exchanges between the Bastard and Austria, "fitter for coalheavers than men of rank and education."[6] In Bell's Shakespeare (1773), which Gentleman edited, he went so far as to suggest that the omission of the whole first act would be no great loss; and the Reading schoolmaster, Dr. Valpy, in his adaptation of the play given (inconceivably) at Covent Garden, in the spring of 1803, omitted it. Indeed, when John Kemble substituted Shakespeare's original, during the next season, there were lively protests in *The Monthly Mirror* against the restoration. The first act ought, it was urged, to be "totally expunged" because of "indecencies which render it almost infamous for a modest family to be present at the performance."[7] (Dr. Valpy, I am convinced, had friends and influence.) In the eighteen-eighties Charles Flower in the Memorial Theatre Edition took satisfaction in having deleted the final episode in the act, that between Philip and Lady Faulconbridge, calling it "unnecessary as well as disagreeable."

Meanwhile, in a later issue of *The Monthly Mirror*, gratification had been expressed that "as now represented" (at Covent Garden, May 12, 1810), the play was "judiciously curtailed in several places, the *Billingsgate* scene between *Constance* and *Elinor*. . . and elsewhere."[8] This "Billingsgate scene" is best understood, perhaps, as a variation on the formal defiances before battle, so frequent on the Elizabethan stage—those, for instance, of Anthony and Octavius, Cassius and Brutus, in the last act of *Julius Caesar*. The homeliness of the exchanges in *King John* , which we welcome today—

> Elinor. Come to the grandam, child.
> Constance. Do, child! go to it grandam, child!
> Give grandam kingdom, and it grandam will
> Give it a plum, a cherry, and a fig—

would certainly have been embarrassing to spectators brought up on the neo-classical ideas of decorum. In Bell's Shakespeare the speeches were reduced almost to nothing. Phelps, however, at Sadler's Wells, towards the middle of the nineteenth century, wisely included "the vituperative conflict between the two queens."[9]

But if in some respects it is easier to enjoy *King John* than it once was, in others it is more difficult. Thus, with its Frenchmen, one or two of them sufficiently villainous, and Papal Legate, the play had an appeal, often exploited in the theatre, to national prejudice. At moments of stress it made good propaganda. Colley Cibber saw this when, in 1745, he adapted it under the expressive title *Papal Tyranny in the Reign of King John* , and Dr. Valpy, when he added patriotic speeches to it at the time of the Napoleonic danger. Then, indeed, the play flourished, for it was the time, too, of the Kembles. John Philip Kemble as the King was much admired, and he had his brother Charles beside him as Faulconbridge and his sister Mrs. Siddons as Constance. No later cast has equalled the one, say, of February 14, 1804.

That the French King can be played as a dignified and not unsympathetic character was happily demonstrated by Cyril Luckham at the Memorial Theatre in 1957. Lewis, the Dauphin, is more subtle. A villain before the play is finished, he overreaches himself and his treacherous practices are unsuccessful. The actor who would prepare us for the grim disclosures of Melun (in V,3) will find little to aid him in the Dauphin's own speeches. On the contrary, Lewis defies the cardinal-legate with spirit, and his grief after the French defeat looks forward to the desolation of Macbeth:

> There's nothing in this world can make me joy.
> Life is as tedious as a twice-told tale
> Vexing the dull ear of a drowsy man;
> And bitter shame hath spoil'd the sweet world's taste,
> That it yields naught but shame and bitterness.

To the Bastard, Lewis is no more still than "a beardless boy / A cockr'red silken wanton" (V,I,70), but in the school of Commodity he is making rapid progress.[10]

In John's defiance to Rome, Macready appears to have broken tradition by relating the speeches to character. So, at any rate, the sailor, actor, and lecturer, Charles Reece Pemberton, maintained in an essay first published in 1834. When Pemberton had seen this play earlier, with other actors in the role, "two regular peals of plaudit" had followed John's speaking of

> What earthly name to interrogators
> Can tax the free breath of a sacred king,

and the reply to Philip's

> Brother of England, you blaspheme in this,

a moment later.

> These two speeches have hitherto been used as appeals to a favourite Bullism—a swagger of independance and patriotism. And all the family have clapped their hands in laudation of John's boldness and energy, and their own: if they had looked beneath the surface they *might* have seen that of this patriotism, &c. there is not a breath in *King John* 's composition. . . .
>
> Mr. Macready threw into his manner and expression, the irritation of an aggrieved selfishness—his ire was birthed in a sense of encroachment on his privilege to tithe and tax—Shakespeare understood kings as well as he did Pandulfs, and knaves in humbler garb.11

And, on the other hand, this great actor made much of the few words which John utters as he watches the French King's face:

> The King is mov'd and answers not to this (III,i,217).

Pemberton speaks of "the *crushed* tone" in which Macready pronounced them; of the sense he conveyed of both apprehension and rage.

In 1823, as we have seen, archaeology triumphed on the English stage in Planche's production of *King John* [12] and archaeology, more or less happily mated with spectacle, was associated with the presentation of this play for almost a century to come. There was no work of Shakespeare's, Henry Morley wrote in 1852, which admitted, and indeed justified, "a magnificent arrangement of scene" to quite the same extent. "So mounted" (and Professor Morley was thinking of Macready's production as well as Charles Kean's), "we see in this play . . . a solid fragment of our English history. We see revived the rude chivalric grandeurs of the Middle Ages, the woes and wars of a half-barbarous time, in all its reckless splendour, selfish cruelty, and gloomy suffering."[13] Tree's production, in 1899, belongs to the end of the same tradition, one, it might be, already a little discredited. A *tableau vivant* showed what Shakespeare had so disappointingly failed to show, the signing of the Magna Charta. In the last scene, monks drew near, chanting ever louder, as the Bastard began his great speech; and their climactic "Amen" was so timed as to reinforce its concluding lines, while at the same moment the sun burst through the clouds. (H. Chance Newton was so carried away as to take the singers for an angel-chorus, who were presumably giving assurance as to the state of John's soul; an angel-chorus, in any case.)[14]

The attainment of historical propriety in the staging of Shakespeare's plays was still being greeted, a generation ago, with unmixed satisfaction: it was a manifestation of progress. Then came reaction. Today the observation of historical propriety in a play like *King John* is either ignored or taken for granted. It is no longer an end in itself. Thus a good, conservative critic, Miss Audrey Williamson, writes of George Devine's production in 1953 that it was hampered by scenic conditions: "and Morley's too-authentic reproduction of the ugliest, heaviest and funniest armour in any period of mediaeval history did no help."[15] As for spectacle, this is more modest than in the days of battle *tableaux* and swarming troops. But here economic realities are as much a factor as alterations in taste. Even supers, I am assured, have become abominably expensive.

We have seen that Shakespeare's histories owed much of their popularity in the theatre to patriotic sentiment and a fondness for archaeology and show. *King John* is a good example, and *King John* had tempting parts for star players as well. John himself has been better liked by actors than by critics. They, the critics, charge him with being weak and vacillating; bad, and not bad enough. Hudson, who treats him with particular severity, seems to have Queen Victoria in mind at one moment and Richard the Third at the next. John (alas!) was neither. "The idea of wearing the crown as a sacred trust from the nation never once enters his head," Hudson asserts, without much risk of contradiction. And then: "Nor is John less wanting in manly fortitude than in moral principle; he has not the courage even to be daringly and resolutely wicked."[16]

For the old tragedians John offered a change from Hamlet and Richard and the four or five other Shakespearian parts which they played so constantly. Though the role was lacking in sympathy or brilliance, it contained two, or it might be three, scenes of undeniable power. These were, it was agreed, the two scenes with Hubert (especially the first) and the surprising, lurid death.[17] Macready, viewing the character as a whole, brought out its moral interest. In his performance the scene in which John hints at the desirability of young Arthur's death was central. Hitherto, a Plantagenet "haught and martial in bearing, swift and bold in decision," he assumed from now on "something of the dogged, covert look, the bowed form, the stealthy gait of the assassin."[18] The transition was well conceived and skilfully executed. John, some thought, was the best of Macready's Shakespearian parts.

Yet across the path of a tragedian undertaking *King John* fell inevitably the shadow of the Bastard Faulconbridge. In any comparison between them John is at an enormous disadvantage. Faulconbridge is all that he is not, a character of boundless energy and charm. From the close of that first engaging soliloquy his relations with the audience are of the friendliest. John, on the contrary, is aloof, withdrawn, sharing no confidences with us. His repeated, half-incredulous, "What? mother dead," in the fourth act, is exceptional; the actor must do what he can with it. The flicker of remorse, just before,

> They burn in indignation. I repent
> There is no sure foundation set on blood,
> No certain life achiev'd by others' death,

is unlikely to win much sympathy for him.

In particular many a *King John* must have grudged Faulconbridge his final speech (the England speech) and have wondered whether nothing could be done about it. And in one or two obscure productions the Bastard seems actually to have had these lines removed from his part. A veteran Canadian critic, Hector Charlesworth, writing about the play in the Toronto *Globe and Mail*, September 6, 1941, recalled seeing Helena Modjeska as Constance, forty years before. She was thrilling despite her foreign accent. Her *King John*, R. D.

Maclean, "did an atrocious thing. He cut out the epilogue because it detracted from the interest of his own death scene. The Falconbridge of the production was a much finer actor. . . ."[19] That *King John* has ever gone so far as to speak the lines himself seems incredible. Surely they were too well known! Yet in one instance I am suspicious, though perhaps nothing more is involved than a bit of careless reporting. In Birmingham, during the summer of 1824, *The Theatrical John Bull* in its notice of a recent performance at the local theatre praised Young as *King John*:

> We never saw so pictorial a death. His last and best words were
>
> > "Nought shall make us rue
> > If England to itself do rest but true."
>
> An admirable finish; be it but prophetic![20]

I should add that the manager of the Birmingham theatre in 1824 was Alfred Bunn. And this Bunn, the infamous Mr. Bunn of Macready's Diary, was capable of anything.

In *The Green Room* (1880), a Christmas annual edited by Clement Scott, the old actor and teacher of acting Walter Lacy has stories to tell of his beginnings of the stage. He remembers Macready and especially Charles Kemble, John Philip's younger brother.

> In my pastoral days, when ambitious of playing the Bastard, the pivot of my success in after years, Charles Kemble gave me this invaluable hint, "Take care, Lacy, Faulconbridge is very near being a bully," and I might add, for the benefit of young actresses, Constance may easily degenerate into a virago.

Kemble himself had too much of the air of a courteous gentleman ever to be taken for a bully in the part, which he made very much his own.[21] The danger against which he warned Lacy persisted, even so. In 1866 it was suggested that the mere phrase the "bastard Faulconbridge" might have misled actors into coarsening the character: as if the son of Richard Coeur-de-lion were a very common swaggering sort of fellow![22]

The opposite danger—that Faulconbridge may "turn miraculously into a *preux chevalier* the moment the king's sword touches his shoulder—was pointed out by Gordon Crosse. He conceived of him as somewhat loutish and rustical at the beginning. Ralph Richardson was playing him so in 1931,[23] but the idea of development in the character had been grasped, seemingly, a long time before. George Henry Lewes, going to the Princess's Theatre in February 1852, did not expect much of Alfred Wigan as the Bastard and was surprised and delighted by acting that "was *the* acting of the piece" (Lewes had no compliments for poor Kean as *King John*).

> You may observe [he writes], that Falconbridge, who begins as a ribald, careless soldier, deepens into bitter irony when experience of the treachery of France has roused him, and, as the dark scenes of the play follow each other, he loses the gaiety of careless light-heartedness, and rises into personal consequence, till the conduct of affairs seems almost to reset with him. All these changes were broadly and truly marked by Wigan.[24]

This interpretation of the character may have some bearing on our understanding of the play as a whole, and I shall come back to it presently. Meanwhile, it should be noted that the Bastard's role is one in which failure on the stage though not unknown has been rare.[25]

Constance, on the other hand, is excessively difficult to act well. That Mrs. Cibber, Mrs. Siddons, and Helen Faucit greatly succeeded in the part is beyond question, and for a time it was highly thought of in the theatre. Not *King John* , Mrs. Inchbald wrote in 1808, but Constance is "the favourite part both of the poet and the audience"; and George Darley in his introduction to Cumberland's acting edition, a few years later, agreed: "the great charm" of the play was "the Lady Constance."

Mrs. Siddons herself in "Remarks" on the character of Constance printed in Campbell's biography, could think of no single role in all dramatic litrature more difficult to present. "Whether the majestic, the passionate, the tender Constance, has ever yet been, or ever will be, personated to the entire satisfaction of sound judgment and fine taste, I believe to be doubtful; for I believe it to be nearly impossible." There was, Mrs. Siddons points out, the completeness with which the part must be imagined, the unceasing concentration which it demands. And in a famous passage she tells of how she was accustomed to stand, with Arthur beside her, listening to the march, as the French and English powers entered Angiers to ratify the marriage contract between Lewis and the Lady Blanch: "because the sickening sounds of that march would usually cause the bitter tears of rage, disappointment, betrayed confidence, baffled ambition, and, above all, the agonizing feelings of maternal affection to gush into my eyes."[26] To a modern actress, the attempt at identification would be understandable. She would read with rather less patience, I am afraid, what Mrs. Siddons has to tell her about the voice and its modulation; the maintaining of "temperance" even in "these whirlwinds of the soul." A remark of Macready's comes to mind. Macready, grumbling "characteristically over the incompetence of Mrs. Sharpe as Constance, goes on to explain what was wanting: "it is because every line is so effective that common minds cannot rise from one level, and have not the skill by contrast and variety to give relish and effect without great effort.[27]

Constance as Mrs. Siddons conceived her, was "a lofty and proud spirit." It was only in the performances of later actresses that softening set in. George Fletcher in his *Studies of Shakespeare* (1947) praises Helen Faucit for her recognition that "*feeling*, not *pride*, is the mainspring of the character." From what he had been able to learn of her great predecessor "it was in gracefully commanding *force* that she so wonderfully excelled, and in the expression of *tenderness* that she was often felt to be deficient," whereas the "intimate association" of these qualities in Miss Faucit qualified her for "this arduous part—the most arduous, we believe, of all the Shakespearian female characters." In particular, she brought out through many delicate strokes the love of the Lady Constance for her son.

> Nothing could have been "more beautiful in itself, or more true to nature and the poet, than the graceful fondness with which, after throwing herself on the ground in the climax of her grief, she looks up, and raises her hand to play with the ringlets of her boy as he stands drooping over her."[28]

The Siddons tradition was passing. Mrs. Kean, according to G. H. Lewes, descended in the same role into an unpleasing sort of domesticity: it was a portrayal "stripped of all the elevation and grandeur of poetry."[29] But Constance herself was not much longer to be exempt from criticism. She had been much overpraised, Hudson wrote in 1872, as a consequence of the dazzling genius of Sarah Siddons: there was often in her speeches "a redundancy of rhetoric and verbal ingenuity."[30] Later still, at the turn of the century, came disparagements of the chracter by scholarly critics like Barrett Wendell and Brander Matthews, who found her guilty of rant;[31] while J. T. Grein pronounced her "great scene of woe" unplayable by any mere woman (it demanded, he thought, "a Titan").[32] Julia Neilson, who was then attempting the role, liked it nevertheless, and in her autobiography speaks of "the enormous emotion that gathers about each entrance and exit of Constance" and of the poignancy of certain of her lines.[33]

As with the chief characters in this play, so with certain scenes, their appeal has not been constant but has varied in accordance with the changing taste of the times. The fortunes of one scene in particular, that between Hubert and Arthur, might furnish the subject of a curious essay. Often, in deed, as with Hazlitt and William Winer, its praise has passed into rhapsody,[34] the single reservation likely to be granted being that it was possibly rather too harrowing for the sensibilities of "a modern audience." The critic of *The Sketch* wrote to this effect in reviewing Beerbohm Tree's production, adding a little surprisingly that "the two most painful scenes" in this play "follow immediately upon one another."[35] It was only in the nineteen-twenties that the blinding episode was seriously attacked. *The Times* then referred to it as "impossible"; Professor Charlton found that its long admired pathos and horror were those of melodrama; and James Agate breathed the dreaded word "sentimentality" in referring to Arthur.[36]

On another occasion, Agate took exception to the practice of assigning the part of Prince Henry to a young woman, remarking further that, "as Arthur Miss Ann Casson acted very well but looked like Robin Hood in a Christmas pantomime."37 A distinction exists between these two Shakespearian roles. Prince Henry has fewer than thirty lines to speak, in all, and though they deserve to be spoken well—the unforgettable

I am the cygnet to this pale faint swan

is among them—his part should be comfortably within a boy's powers. Except, in fact, when a company is seriously short-handed (and *King John* has only about half as many men's parts as *Henry V* and *2 Henry IV*), I can see no more excuse for an actress as Prince Henry than for an actress as Prince John in *I Henry IV* or as either of the little princes in *Richard III*. Arthur, on the other hand, with his poetic conceits and sudden simplicities, his sophistication and childishness, is a virtuoso role demanding of its performer a degree of technical skill beyond that, say, of the boy actors whom one remembers seeing at the Royal Shakespeare Theatre. The distinction is not, in any case, one of recent date. In London during the eighteenth century, Prince Henry rarely and Arthur usually went to young actresses.[38]

Hubert calls for both strength and unselfishness. His is a supporting part and one to be played *against*, as in the two great scenes with King John. Although it is he who describes picturesquely and at length the effect upon the common people of the supposed death of Arthur, as a rule he speaks curtly. It is for John or Arthur or the Bastard to be eloquent. Macready out of courtesy to Charles Mayne Young when that amiable tragedian chose John for his benefit peformance condescended to appear with him as Hubert (Young, he adds, "was most earnest in his acknowledgements to me, not only for acting the part, but for the manner in which, in his great scene, I placed myself upon the stage to give prominence to his effects").[39] George Frederick Cooke had been Hubert to Kemble's John, and it was remarked that he was "more anatomically fitted" for the character than other actors.[40] One recalls with appreciation the seamed and rocky face in the portraits. At Stratford, Connecticut, in 1956, a player of such obvious good nature was chosen for the part that there could be no doubt as to the outcome of his scene with Arthur. At the Memorial Theatre, a year later, Ron Haddrick was sufficiently threatening in appearance, and he brought out, most happily, it seemed to me, Hubert's devotion to the King. One effect, whether through the actor's timing or execution, was on this occasion almost lost. In *The Troublesome Reign of King John*, an earlier, or rival play about which I shall have something to say presently, Hubert at the beginning of the scene with Arthur tells the executioners what his signal will be for their return to blind the young Prince. But this signal, the words "God save the King," he gives almost immediately after Arthur's entrance. We are not kept waiting for it, and are not shocked when it comes.[41] In Shakespeare's *King John*, we are ready to hope that Hubert will be dissuaded from his purpose, that he will not give the signal, will never stamp. And when at last he does stamp we should be appalled.

So much for the scene between Hubert and Arthur which, when all is said, has a fair chance of prevailing in the theatre still. Another debatable scene, or sequence of scenes, political this time rather than domestic, is that "before Angiers" in Act II. The first time I saw *King John*, many years ago, it was performed in the parish house of the Church of the Transfiguration in New York, on a very small stage. The citizens of Angiers—there were two of them on this occasion—looming large above their wall, gazed down upon the adherents of Arthur and King John, the contending powers of France and England. The sense of foreshortening seemed in keeping, somehow, with the disclosure of a world governed wholly by self-interest, "commodity." What we saw gained in significance through its reduction in scale. A realistic approach was out of the question.

Yet it has been in the simplest terms of verisimilitude that this scene has sometimes been criticized. Thus, in the Folio (our only early text) there is one citizen, no more, who is presently referred to as "Hubert"—for no better reason, perhaps, than that the actor who played Hubert doubled the part. As this representative character, at Stratford, Connecticut, the late Whitford Kane gave his juniors a lesson in the art of listening, and his presence, grave and attentive but perfectly relaxed, lingers in the memory. To the critic of *The Theatrical Looker-On*, however, at Birmingham, in 1823, the appearance of this single citizen in the person of an actor named Thorne, was occasion for mirth.

> By-the-way, these *contentious citizens* were represented by THORNE *only*, who, we suppose, must have been their *Legislatorial Attorney*, or *Mayor* at the least. It was vastly amusing to seeing him sitting with his elbow resting on the town wall, looking as interesting as *Juliet* in the balcony, and talking to the two *Monarchs of France and England* with the most enviable ease and *sang froid*. . . . *John* appeals to "the brave citizens of *Angiers*,"

and there was no part of one to be seen, save and except THORNE'S nose poking over a wall.[42]

Today, when departures from actuality are no longer regarded as necessarily ridiculous, it is possible to view the stylized treatment of this scene with admiration.[43] And as if to add pungency, as well as to bring out meaning, the Bastard is present throughout: now conducting his own little affair with Austria towards it happy termination,[44] now criticizing the pompous style of the Citizen, or the conceitful style of the Dauphin; at last, railing in good set terms upon commodity, whom he flatly declares he will serve, too. The richness and raciness of his lines, it may be added, have no counter part in those of the "hardy wildehead, tough and venturous" who passes for him in *The Troublesome Reign of King John*

This somewhat stodgy and pedestrian drama is remarkably like *King John* in plot and sequence of scenes and remarkably unlike it in expression. Such verbal resemblances as exist between the plays are trivial. Since *The Troublesome Reign* is in two parts, it is longer than *King John* (though much less than twice as long) including, especially, a lively, ribald episode in which Faulconbridge is shown collecting money in the monasteries—and very corrupt monasteries they prove to be. For the author of this play, unlike the usual botchers-up of "bad quartos," has a serious point of view. John, as he sees him, is a champion of Protestantism, unsuccessful at the last only because of his own sinfulness. Not for him was it to "roote these Locusts from the face of earth"; not for him to tread down

the Strumpets pride,
That sits upon the chaire of *Babylon*.

The death of young Arthur weighs upon his soul.[45]

Until recently, *The Troublesome Reign of King John* was very generally accepted as Shakespeare's source. Its early date (it was published in 1591) seemed to rule out the possibility that it was anything else. Shakespeare's 'prentice powers were only beginning to be exerted in 1591; a *King John* was obviously beyond them. That the old chronology was too rigid, that some at least of the assumptions on which it rested were unwarranted by the facts, has become increasingly clear. Shakespeare's beginnings as a dramatist may very well belong to a time a good deal earlier than was supposed. Whether *King John* preceded, or, as I think, followed *The Troublesome Reign*, must be decided on the basis of internal evidence alone. And in a wisely speculative little book, *Marlowe and the Early Shakespeare*, Professor F. P. Wilson warns us that the internal evidence is either "reversible or inconclusive."[46]

What relationship existed between the two plays is important, none the less. Thus the attempts, not very auspicious in themselves, to discover precise topical significances in Shakespeare's drama must reckon with the embarrassing possibility that the same significances already existed in *The Troublesome Reign*. The general relevance to events in John's time became obvious after the papal sentence of excommunication against Elizabeth I. Holinshed, the year before the Armada, found the same meaning in them Shakespeare was to find:

> Here therefore we see the issue of domesticall or homebred broiles, the fruits of Uariance, the gaine that riseth of dissention, whereas no greater nor safer fortification can betide a land, than when the inhabitants are all alike minded. . . . From division and mutinies doo issue (as out of the Troiane Horsse) ruines of roialties, and decaies of communalties.[47]

Faulconbridge concludes, for the author of *The Troublesome Reign*:

> Let *England* liue but true within it selfe,
> And all the world can neuer wrong her State. . . .
>
> If *Englands* Peeres and people ioyne in one,
> Nor Pope, nor *Fraunce*, nor *Spaine* can doo them wrong.

Shakespeare's Faulconbridge strikes the same note, and as if empowered to do so, as if the whole history led up to this moment.

Earlier, beneath the walls of Angiers, the Bastard has discovered that men are ready to betray principle and good faith at the first whisper of self-interest, "Commodity." He makes no exceptions, not his own English King:[48]

> John, to Stop Arthur's title in the whole,
> Hath willingly departed with a part. . . .

The fact of betrayal is brought home to us by the bitter distress of Constance. It is not allowed to remain abstract. Then, with the arrival of Cardinal Pandulph, the new agreements are thrown over by the French. Increasingly, the progress of the play is through episodes which involve some conflict between loyalties. Poor little Blanch's love-and-honour scene, just before the beginning of the battle, is of this sort, as in its way is Hubert's scene with Arthur. For Hubert, as I suggested, is not to be confused with such creatures of tyrannical kings of James Tyrrel in *Richard III* or the assassins of Banquo in *Macbeth*.

Faulconbridge has long been absent from the stage when he returns at the end of the fourth act to find Arthur dead and Hubert suspected of the murder—

> Hubert's hand,
> The practice and the purpose of the King.

It is now the Bastard's turn to choose; but the terms of choice are not stated though they may be inferred.[49] Better to serve his King, even a *King John*, than to make one with those "discontents at home" who were joining the French! In Shakespeare's play, though not in *The Troublesome Reign*, the Bastard's political doctrines are acted upon, rather than expounded.

Two scenes later, Faulconbridge comes to the rebel lords bearing defiance to them and their young pretender. He makes no attempt to argue with them. The French he reminds of the terror which English arms have inspired in them; the nobles, he charges with the vilest ingratitude. At last, the Dauphin will hear him no further. "Strike up the drums," he orders. But Faulconbridge promises that their clamour will be echoed.

> Sound but another, and another shall,
> As loud as thine, rattle the welkin's ear
> And mock the deep-mouth'd thunder; for at hand
> (Not trusting to this halting legate here,

Whom he hath us'd rathr for sport than need)
Is warlike John; and in his forehead sits
A bare-ribb'd death. . . .

The words ring with courage and affirmation. On his lips, the King once more is "warlike John."

Shakespeare's play is not a tragedy and to approach it as such is unprofitable. John is not a tragic hero, nor is there any compelling reason why he should be. In a history, Constance and the Bastard have their rights, as well. Whether Shakespeare worked in the first instance from the chronicles or, as seems a good deal likelier, from the play published in 1591, he was more successful in bringing out meanings in these distant events than in shaping them into a plot. The Angiers sequences are interpreted realistically by Faulconbridge. Pandulph, with equal realism, looks forward to Arthur's death as inevitable from the moment of his capture. It will be a world for the Dauphin to bustle in! The earlier theme of Commodity is developing into one even more sombre. For answer, when the bad days of foreign invasion, Machiavellism, and civil war do indeed come, we have the loyalty of Faulconbridge to England and the Crown, a loyalty which the Elizabethan audience was asked to share. The closing lines of the play are admonitory as well as triumphant.[50]

King John on the stage needs style—and voices. It flourished in the days of the Kembles. Historical criticism has brought out the political significance of the later scenes, and recently we have been hearing almost as much about the Bastard and the Barons as about Constance, or Hubert and Arthur. As a result, the play stands higher than it did a generation or two ago. But this gain in estimation has been unaccompanied by the excitements of rediscovery, and there seem to be few readers or playgoers nowadays who do not prefer another tragic history, *Richard II*.

NOTES

1. For the Maddermarket Theater see especially Norman Marshall, *The Other Theatre*, London, 1947, pp. 92–97, and Nugent Monck, "The

Maddermarket Theatre and the Playing of Shakespeare," *Shakespeare Survey* 12 (1959).

2. Page 9. Cf. John Upton, *Critical Observations on Shakespeare*, London, 1746, p.70.
3. James Thomas Kirkman, *Memoirs of the Life of Charles Macklin*, London, 1799, I, 268. See Also Arthur Murphy, *Life of David Garrick*, London, 1801, I, 101.
4. II (1807), 135-137. The critic had seen the play given, with Fennel as King John , March 13.
5. November 5, 1842.
6. *The Dramatic Censor*, 2 vols., London, 1770, II, 155-157.
7. *The Monthly Mirror* for February 1804 (XVII, 133; see also, ibid., 120). The scene between Faulconbridge and his mother would have been hooted off the stage had the author not been Shakespeare (*Dramatic Magazine*, January 1, 1831).
8. N.S., VII, 390, 391.
9. *The Athenaeum*, February 3, 1849. For Macready's earlier restorations see C.H. Shattuck, ed., Macready's *King John* , Urbana, 1962, pp. 6, 25.
10. For this last point I am indebted to Audrey Williamson's fine paragraph on the Dauphin in *Old Vic Drama 2*, London [1957], p.150.
11. From *The Monthly Repository*, January and February, 1834, quoted in Pemberton's *Life and Literary Remains*, ed. John Fowler, London 1843, pp. 237, 238.
    Mr. Alan Wilkie, who gave *King John* frequently in Australia and elsewhere, early in the century, found John's defiance of the Pope one of the most effective moments in the play.
12. See above, page 4.
13. *The Journal of a London Playgoer*, London, etc., 1891, p. 30.
14. *The Sketch*, September 20, 1899 (Blinn Scrapbooks, Harvard Theatre Collection). See also *The Saturday Review*, September 30, 1899; *King John*, ed. G. C. Moore Smith, London, 1900, p. xliii; Julia Neilson, *This for Remembrance*, London, 1940, pp. 160, 161.
15. *Old Vic Drama 2*, p. 151, Miss M. St. Clare Byrne wants Elizabethan dress for the play ("Shakespeare Season," *Shakespeare Quarterly*, VIII [1957], 482).
16. *Shakespeare: His Life, Art, and Characters* (1872), quoted in *Furness Variorum Edition*, 558.
17. See, e.g., Gentleman, *Dramatic Censor*, II, 167; Genest, *Some Account of the English Stage*, VIII, 384; J. W. Cole, *Life of Charles Kean*, 2 vols., London, 1859, II, 27, 28; Margaret Webster, *Shakespeare Without Tears*, New York and London [1942], p.181.
18. Westland Marston, *Our Recent Actors*, Boston, 1888, 2 vols., I, 100 (cf. C. Cowden Clarke, *Shakespeare-Characters*, London, 1863, p.342).
19. Can this have been the "barbarous dismemberment" of the play made for Modjeska by William Winter, with the object of concentrating attention of Constance? (*Shakespeare on the Stage, Third Series*, p. 507). Maclean appeared in another mangled version, at the Columbia Theatre, Brooklyn (see *The Theatre*, May 1903, in the Blinn Scrapbooks, Harvard Theatre Collection).
20. I, 52 (July 10, 1824).

21. Leigh Hunt specifically notes Kemble's avoidance of a "preliminary bravado of gesture," a "flourish of fist," in the defiance of Austria (*Dramatic Essays*, ed., Archer and Lowe, p.109).
22. *The Athenaeum*, September 29, 1866. The reviewer goes on to praise Barry Sullivan's Faulconbridge, "a true gentleman and a soldier."
23. *Shakespearian Playgoing 1890-1952*, London [1953], p. 69.
24. *Dramatic Essays*, ed. Archer and Lowe, p. 182.
25. Charlton is exceptional among critics in disliking him. He writes of the Bastard's "utter immunity from every moral or decent scruple" and of his being qualified for political success by being "despicable" as a private individual (*Shakespeare, Politics and Politicians*, London, 1929, pp.10ff.).
26. Thomas Campbell, *Life of Mrs. Siddons*, London, 1834, 2 vols., I, 215, 220.
27. *Diaries*, ed. William Toynbee, I, 296.
28. Page 30. Fletcher's essay on the Lady Constance first appeared in *The Athenaeum*, February 11, 1843.
29. *Dramatic Essays*, ed., Archer and Lowe, pp. 180, 181. "Except in the hands of a fine artist," Marston writes, "Constance is apt to become either too sentimental or too shrewish" (*Our Recent Actors*, I, 128).
30. *Shakespeare: his Life, Art, and Characters*, quoted in Variorum Edition, p. 583.
31. *William Shakspere*, New York, 1894, pp. 139, 140; *Shakspere as a Playwright*, London, 1913, p. 98.
32. *Premières of the Year*, London, 1900, p. 68.
33. *This for Remembrance*, p. 161.
34. Winter, writing in 1916, called this episode, "of its pathetical order, unmatched and unmatchable" (3 *Shakespeare on the Stage*, p. 471.
35. E. F. S. in *The Sketch*, September 27, 1899 (in the Blinn Scrapbooks, Harvard Theatre Collection). How much was left, I wonder, of the concluding seventy-eight lines of Act III, following Constance's mad exit.
36. *The Times*, September 6, 1926; *Sunday Times*, September 5, 1926 (Victoria and Albert press cuttings); Charlton, *Shakespeare, Politics and Politicians*, pp. 8 ff.
37. *Brief Chronicles*, London [1943], p. 90, July 7, 1941.
38. See C. B. Hogan's invaluable *Shakespeare in the Theatre 1701–1800*. Percy Fitzgerald defends the use of actresses, as against children, in *Shakespearean Representation*, London, 1908, p. 101; Shaw had already condemned them ("Italian opera itself could go no further in folly"), *Our Theatres in the Nineties*, II, 289.
39. *Reminiscences*, ed. Pollock, 2 vols., London, 1875, I, 236.
40. John Williams, *The Dramatic Censor for the Year 1811*, p. 389. Phelps was another notable Hubert.
41. G. P. Baker, *The Development of Shakespeare as a Dramatist*, New York and London, 1907 (1916), pp. 155, 156.
42. II, 76 (July 21, 1823). *The Stratford-Upon-Avon Herald*, July 17, 1925, complained that Angiers could scarcely have depended for its defence upon "high walls and a few old people of pastoral aspect. . . . A hint, at least, of some soldiery in the background would have lent a greater realism to the picture."

43. See especially Tillyard, *Shakespeare's History Plays*, 232, and for the realistic approach, Charlton, *Shakespeare, Politics and Politicians*, pp. 8 ff.
44. The significance of Austria's lion's skin must often have been asked by puzzled actors at rehearsal. And since in *The Troublesome Reign of King John* this is fully explained, the possibility existed of lifting such obviously useful lines as, e.g.,

    My Fathers foe clad in my Fathers spoyle,
    A thousand furies kindle with reuendge. . . .

    Bell's acting edition of *King John* does in fact take over three or four speeches from the non-Shakespearian play, as had several eighteenth-century literary editions.
45. Praetorius Quarto, II, 37. As Miss Ruth Wallerstein writes, "The political instead of the religious side of the Pope's interference is emphasized" in Shakespeare's play (*King John in Fact and Fiction*, Philadelphia [1917], p.42).
46. Cambridge, 1943, p. 115. That *King John* is earlier than *The Troublesome Reign* is urged by Dr. Honigmann in the Arden Edition (1954). The incompleteness and obscurity of certain passages in *King John* might seem to imply hurried adaptation on Shakespeare's part.
47. Ed. 1587, III, 195.
48. See, however, Adrien Bonjour's excellent article, "The Road to Swinstead Abbey," *English Literary History*, December 1951. My view is close to that of John Palmer, *Political Characters of Shakespeare*, London, 1945, pp. 323 ff.
49. Cf. Tillyard, *Shakespeare's History Plays*, p. 225, Irving Ribner, *The English History Play in the Age of Shakespeare*, Princeton, 1957, p. 125, and M. St. C. Byrne in *Shakespeare Quarterly*, VIII (1957), 483, 484.
50. The muted rendering of these lines by Alec Clunes at the Memorial Theatre in 1957 was designed to bring out this admonitory side—the "if," as he explained, in them.

Eugene M. Waith

King John and the Drama of History

King John is a play which, in our time, there have been few to love and very few to see.[1] The notable revival of interest in Shakespeare's history plays has left it, along with *Henry VIII*, almost untouched on the Shakespearean bookshelf and rarely performed. A review in the London *Times* (11 March 1958) of a Marlowe Society production began: "There are plenty of good reasons why *King John* should be hazier in memory than almost any other of Shakespeare's histories."

One reason may be that the approach via Elizabethan historiography, largely responsible for this recent wave of interest in the histories, yields considerably lower dividends for *King John* than for the two tetralogies. E. M. W. Tillyard, for whom the play was "a wonderful affair, full of promise" but "uncertain of itself," emphasized the theme of rebellion and the theme of the true king.[2] Lily Bess Campbell saw *King John* , like the other history plays, as a "mirror of Elizabethan policy," and brought out the parallels between Arthur and Mary Stuart, between the rebellion of John's barons and the Northern Rebellion of 1571.[3] The authors of both of these influential books looked for the political meaning the plays might have had for an Elizabethan audience, and in general, presented them as plays of ideas. There is no doubt that Elizabethan historians saw parallels between their own times and various periods of the past, and it is reasonable to assume that such parallels interested Elizabethan audiences. As for us, the recognition of political themes makes the shape of plays like *Richard III* and *Richard II* much more readily understandable. Even when allowance is made for the qualifications of the historiographic approach proposed in the important recent studies that we might call

Reprinted from *Shakespeare Quarterly*, 29 (1978): 192–211,
with permission of *Shakespeare Quarterly*.

"revisionist," a grand design appears to underlie these plays and the tetralogies of which they are parts.[4] The design may be more complicated than we thought, but it is there.

It may, indeed, be there in *King John* as well, but when we compare Shakespeare's play with two other *King John* plays, that of Bale in the mid-sixteenth century, and *The Troublesome Reign of King John*, published in 1591,[5] we see that a political design is far *more* evident in them; as it is also in Colley Cibber's eighteenth-century adaptation, *Papal Tyranny in the Reign of King John*, and in Richard Valpy's *King John*, altered for performance by the boys of Reading School in 1800. In all these plays John is much more obviously the resister of papal influence who foreshadows Henry VIII or Elizabeth or both.

Oddly enough, what distinguishes Shakespeare's play from its predecessors as well as from later alterations is not only literary superiority but the obscuring of the Protestant and patriotic message or its relegation to second place. Cibber was surprised that Shakespeare "should have taken no more Fire" at the "flaming contest between his insolent *Holiness* and *King John*."[6] "It was this Coldness," he wrote, "That first incited me to inspirit his *King John* with a resentment that justly might become an *English* Monarch" (sig. A4). On Cibber's plans for alteration Medley, in Fielding's *Historical Register*, commented: "As Shakespeare is already good enough for people of taste, he must be altered to the palates of those who have none; and if you will grant that, who can be properer to alter him for the worse?"[7] No one doubts that *Papal Tyranny* was an alteration for the worse. What is important here is that it was an alteration intended to supply the clear political meaning that the original lacked.

Whether or not this deficiency accounts for earlier periods of unpopularity, the stage history of *King John* shows that our century is not the only one to have neglected the play. There is no record of its performance in the seventeenth nor in the early eighteenth century. The first revival, prompted (ironically) by rumors of Cibber's alteration, took place in February 1737 at Covent Garden. It was performed there seven more times that season and once at the Haymarket; then another eight times at Covent Garden over the next four seasons. Cibber, meanwhile, had been so daunted by the attacks of outraged Shakespeareans that he had withdrawn *Papal Tyranny* before performance. It was finally mounted at Covent Garden in February 1745, however, to capitalize on anti-Jacobite sentiments, whereupon Garrick put on Shakespeare's play at Drury Lane. During this season *Papal Tyranny* with Quin as King John and Mrs. Pritchard as Constance was performed eleven times, while the original play with Garrick as John and Mrs. Cibber as Constance was performed eight times. On six days the public could choose which *King John* to attend.

Though *Papal Tyranny* was given only once more, *King John* was frequently revived for over a hundred years, and in certain seasons, such as those of 1760–61, 1766–67, and 1817–18, there were rival productions at the two royal theatres in London. The greatest actors and actresses vied with each other in the principal roles. During the same period a very considerable number of performances took place in America. After the 1870s the play dropped out of sight once more. But in 1899 Beerbohm Tree mounted a spectacular production in London, after a single undistinguished performance at the Crystal Palace ten years before. Robert Mantell followed suit in Chicago and New York in 1907–08. With these revivals what might be called the ancien regime of *King John* productions seems to have ended.[8]

I propose to look at what attracted actors, managers, and audiences to *King John* when it was highly regarded and to ask whether the characteristic critical approaches of our century have been truly appropriate.

I

It is noteworthy that the comments on *King John* made during the period of its greatest popularity were usually on the characters of King John, Constance, the Bastard, Arthur, and Hubert; and again and again on certain scenes: the outrage of Constance at the accord between John and Philip of France, her grief after Arthur's capture, John's temptation of Hubert, little Arthur's pleading with Hubert, John's second interview with Hubert, and his agonizing death at Swinstead Abbey. Among early scholar-critics Theobald said that John "had that Turbulence and Grandeur of the Passions, that Inconstancy of Temper, that equal Mixture of Good and Ill, and that Series of Misfortunes consequent thereto, as might make him very fit for a Hero in a just Composition."[9] And Dr. Johnson, noting with pleasure the variety of incidents and characters, wrote: "The Lady's grief is very affecting, and the character of the *Bastard* contains that mixture of greatness and levity which this author delighted to exhibit."[10]

Mrs. Cibber showed one generation of theatregoers just how affecting the Lady's grief could be. Francis Gentleman in the 1770s and Thomas Davies a decade later agreed that she was by far the best interpreter of the role.[11] Her effect on her audiences can be gauged by Davies' statement that in her last speech the words "O Lord! my boy!" were uttered "with such an emphatical scream of agony as will never be forgotten by those who heard her" (I,55–56). According to Davies, only Mrs. Cibber was able to "utter, with the utmost harmony and propriety" all the succeeding emotions that Constance must display (p. 35). In Bell's 1774 edition of the play Act III is illustrated with an engraving of Mrs. Barry as Constance in a splendidly histrionic pose as she tears a veil from her headdress.[12] Beneath are Constance's lines: "I will not keep this form upon my head, / When there is such disorder in my wit." It is just before "O Lord! my boy!" Mrs. Barry's rendition of this speech may have prompted Francis Gentleman to write in a note for this same edition that the scene "grows rather too trying for refined sensations" (IV,37), for James Boaden later spoke of Mrs. Barry's ability to produce sounds almost "too terrible to enter human hearing."[13]

Davies wrote at the greatest length about Mrs. Cibber's Constance, but he also had praise for Walker (the original Macheath) as the Bastard (p. 15) and qualified praise for Quin's rendition of John's speeches to Hubert in the temptation scene (p. 53). No third act in any of Shakespeare's tragedies seemed to him so rich in scenes of pity and terror (p. 50).

Ther performances which elicited the comments quoted so far occurred in the years between 1737 and 1783. Toward the end of the latter year a worthy successor to Mrs. Cibber was found when Mrs. Siddons took the part of Constance; as *King John*, her brother, John Philip Kemble, outshone the previous interpreters, including Garrick, who never did the part to his own or anyone's complete satisfaction. For almost thirty years this remarkable team of John Philip Kemble and Mrs. Siddon, often with their brother Charles as the Bastard, played *King John* . Though we know that many critics found John Philip Kemble too artificial and too cold in the role of the King, Boaden in his *Memoirs of Mrs. Siddons* (p.59) wrote that Kemble had "in every spectator fairly substituted his own face and figure for the *picture sense* of King John" (an interesting term to which I shall return). In his *Memoirs of the Life of John Philip Kemble Esq.* he commented especially on "the great scene with Hubert," which he would select as the one scene most appropriate to Kemble, remembering "this noiseless horror, this muttered suggestion of slaughterous thought."[14] For his Mrs. Inchbald it was the death scene that stood out: "The genius of Kemble gleams terrific through the gloomy John. No auditor can hear him call for his "Kingdom's rivers to take their course / Through his burn'd bosom," and not feel for that moment parched with a scorching fever."[15]

Constance was one of Mrs. Siddons' most successful roles—for some critics her best. She achieved the majestic sorrow and the withering contempt demanded by the part; and as for the "piercing note of wild maternal agony" in her last scene, Boaden, comparing her with her predecessors, noted that while "the sharp shrillness of the organ itself will do something for an actress not highly intellectual," Constance "has meaning in her language," and that this was what Mrs. Siddons gave, rather than "an inarticulate *yell*, the grief of merely savage nature" (*Mrs. Siddons*, pp. 59, 52). Mrs. Inchbald made an extraordinary comment on Mrs. Siddons' command of histrionic technique in an earlier scene, where Constance flings herself on the ground at the news of the Anglo-French accord: "The following lines, uttered by Mrs. Siddons in Constance, "Here I and sorrow sit: / This is my throne, bid kings come bow to it," seem like a triumphant reference to her own potent skill in the delineation of woe" (p. 4). The power of the role and the power of the interpreter are fused in this perception of Mrs. Siddon's accomplishment. Boaden also spoke of the power of her rendering of this speech, and Mrs. Jameson, writing at about the same time of the character rather than the actress, said, "That which strikes us as the principal attribute of Constance is *power*—power of imagination, of will, of passion, of affection, of pride."[16] George Fletcher, who disagreed with Mrs. Jameson about the importance of pride in the character of Constance, considered Helen Faucit's impersonation superior because of her ability to convey the tenderness of Constance's feelings for Arthur. Mrs. Siddons, whom Fletcher had not seen, was said by some to have been deficient in this qualtiy.[17] For most of those who saw her, however, she remained the supreme Constance.

II

Several observations on these responses to *King John* are in order. The first one might be made on eighteenth- and nineteenth-century criticism of the performances of any Shakespeare play, but it has a special bearing on *King John*: critics then were accustomed to compare the renditions by several actors of a particular speech, as an opera critic would naturally compare, say, Nilson's Liebestod with Flagstad's. Though critics of Shakespeare today make such comparisons from time to time, they are rarely in the position of their predecessors of having seen the same play many times, acted by the gradually shifting casts of relatively stable companies. If the concentration on details encouraged by these circumstances moved critics to emphasize acting technique, it also enabled them to explore the impact and meaning of certain moments in a way that is not open to the viewer of a single performance. The critic tended to approach the play somewhat more in the manner of an actor, looking for what the text contained that might be effectively exploited.

The memoranda Mrs. Siddons left to her biographer, Thomas Campbell, illustrate perfectly such an approach. She regarded Constance as an extraordinary challenge. "I cannot indeed conceive, in the whole range of dramatic character, a greater difficulty than that of representing this grand creature," she wrote.[18] Keenly aware of the range of feelings that Constance must display, she fixed upon a unifying concept. Her idea of the character, she told Campbell, was "that of a lofty and proud spirit, associated with the most exquisite feelings of maternal tenderness, which is, in truth, the predominant feature of this interesting personage" (pp. 211–12). "Her gorgeous affliction, if such an expression is allowable, is of so sublime and so intense a character, that the personation of its grandeur, with the utterance of its rapid and astonishing eloquence, almost overwhelms the mind that meditated its realization, and utterly exhausts the frame which endeavors to express its agitations" (p. 225). To sustain the emotional intensity which this perfervid prose reflects, Mrs. Siddons found it necessary to leave the door of her dressing-room open when she was offstage so that she could concentrate on the distressing events onstage, "the terrible effects of which," as she said, she would have to represent. As she sat listening and thinking about the betrayal of her cause by

England and France, the sound of the march when the two armies enter Angiers would usually cause bitter tears to gush into her eyes (p. 215), and thus prepare her for her entrance in Act III, scene I: "Gone to be married! gone to swear a peace!"[19] For Campbell the result of these procedures was that she became "the embodied image of maternal love and intrepidity" (p. 209).

The accounts of Mrs. Siddons as Constance may well have inspired the scene in Henry James's *The Tragic Muse* where Sherringham listens to Miriam declaiming to her teacher: "He recognized one of the great tirades of Shakespeare's Constance and saw she had just begun the magnificent scene at the beginning of the third act of *King John*, in which the passionate, injured mother and widow sweeps in wild organ tones up and down the scale of her irony and wrath."[20] For James, as for Mrs. Inchbald, appreciation of technique and of the impersonated character coincide.

III

The reason why such an approach is especially appropriate for *King John* is that the play is notoriously episodic. Even well-disposed critics have doubted whether all the episodes hang together, and hostile critics have been sure they do not. One inference from the testimony so far considered is that the play lived, so to speak, from moment to moment, and that the effect of certain moments, especially with Mrs. Cibber or John Philip Kemble or Mrs. Siddons onstage, was overwhelming. The episodic structure loosened the bonds between one part of the story and another, releasing the moments to be valued for their individual dramatic impact. But it is also clear that Mrs. Siddons was concerned with continuity and coherence as well as with the individual moments. The coherence she strove for was emotional or psychological rather than narrative or thematic: the variety of passions displayed by Constance must be related to a "predominant feature," and the actress must stay in her part even when she was offstage, maintaining her relationship to the action in scenes where she did not appear. The play, thus conceived, was a carefully contrived sequence of intensely emotional scenes, revealing the mainsprings of the action in the characters of the principal personages.

If we return for a moment to twentieth-century academic criticism we see even more clearly how different was the approach I have been illustrating. For example, Miss Campbell, speaking of the dramatic gains seen in Shakespeare's reworking of this historical material says, "Perhaps the changes do make for dramatic gains, but if Shakespeare's play is considered as a history play, mirroring the great political problem of Elizabeth's reign, it is to the pattern of events in Elizabeth's reign rather than to dramatic genius that we must look for the explanation" (p. 136). Dover Wilson, who does not turn his back on dramatic values, nevertheless speaks in his introduction of the great concluding lines about England being true to itself as "the theme of the whole play," and of the Bastard, who speaks these words, as "the mouthpiece of the author" (Cambridge ed., p. lx). John Middleton Murry, like Dover Wilson, considers the Bastard the true hero of the play and says "His function is to embody England, to incorporate the English soul."[21]

Even critics who do not see the play as inculcating a political message seek to interpret it by finding its theme. Admirers—for despite its relative unpopularity, *King John* has had sympathetic and sensitive readers in our time—maintain that the theme, properly understood, explains the structure and characterization. In one of the best twentieth-century essays, Adrien Bonjour, charting the fall of the King and the rise of Falconbridge, finds that "the course of his twofold evolution illustrates the leading idea of the whole drama"—the importance of personal integrity.[22] James L. Calderwood bases a fine interpretation on "Commodity and Honour in *King John*."[23] Edward I. Berry says that "*King John* exploits history as a means of posing and resolving dramatically a specific political problem" (p. 113). Less sympathetic critics tend to blame the shortcomings of the play on the lack of a dominant theme or on Shakespeare's failure to take a consistent moral stand.[24] In the critical climate of this century it has seemed proper to ask first, "What is the play about?" L. C. Knights, in a very good essay, gives an answer with which it is easy to agree: ". . . it is a play about international politics, which are seen with complete realism through the eyes of the Bastard."[25]

Obviously, however, the earlier critics did not see it primarily as a play about international politics nor did the eyes and mouth of the Bastard seem to them to be Shakespeare's. He was a delightful character of a sort that Shakespeare drew well; he was rough, manly, intrepid, and humorous.[26] Hazlitt thought the character well chosen to relieve the poignant agony of suffering in the scenes with Constance.[27] For Mrs. Inchbald he was "one of the brightest testimonies of Shakespeare's comic power," and "Mr. C. Kemble personates this child of love as Shakespeare himself could wish" (p. 5). But if Charles Kemble's popular impersonation of the Bastard made him, as Charles Shattuck believes, rather too much of a gentleman and hero,[28] he was still seen as a less important character than Constance or John.

IV

The vast increase in the attention recently given to the Bastard and the corresponding drop in the attention to Constance are characteristic of a shift in sensibility which helps to explain modern attitudes toward *King John*. It is not only the concern with political themes that makes the Bastard a favorite, but a liking for his wry, satirical humor. His commodity speech and his flaunting of his bastardy strike a responsive chord, and even his patriotism, less appealing to some of our contemporaries, can be seen as tempered by an ironic view. Nothing tempers the passions of Constance; we turn away from her "gorgeous affliction" with a certain embarrrassment and impatience. An early instance of this sort of reaction may be found in a comment of A. B. Walkley's in his review of Beerbohm Tree's production: "The hysterical grief of Miss Julia Neilson's Constance seems overdone." He went on to say, "Mrs. Siddons used to shed real tears as Constance—at least so she said; but that was in the sentimental age. . . . I sometimes think Mrs. Siddons must have been what the Americans call 'a holy terror.'"[29]

In contemplating the modern suspicion of the sort of emotional appeal contained in the scenes with Constance or in the scene where the boy Arthur pleads with Hubert not to put out his eyes, we seem to confront an aspect of modern sensibility, though it is not clear that the same distrust of emotion applies to the opera, the film, or television. It may be that spectators come to Shakespearean plays, or all plays, with different expectations. It is curious, however, that the assault on the feelings made by such scenes is not altogether different from what Artaud and others have called for. And by those who do not favor the "theatre of cruelty," piercing screams have sometimes been regarded as a distinctively modern capitulation to raw sensationalism. However this may be, it appears that *King John* is not apt to convey all its dramatic riches to those who will not take Constance and Arthur to their bosoms.

Concern with emotional appeal is compatible with the emphasis of earlier critics on character rather than theme. And both were the logical products of certain ideas about dramatic composition and acting. Underlying the praise of particular eighteenth- and nineteenth-century performances is the assumption that Shakespeare's delineation of Constance, John, Arthur, and the rest is strikingly true to nature, and consequently that a good performance will touch the spectator with this truth. Davies praised an actress's performance for being "Natural and impassioned" (p. 9), and, speaking of Constance's last scene, said that "The grief, anguish, and despair of a *mother* are nowhere so *naturally* conceived and pathetically expressed as in Shakespeare's Constance" (p. 54; my emphasis). In the Modern Standard Drama edition of *King John* (1846), giving the text used by Macready and Charles Kean, Epes Sargent praised Shakespeare's transformation of *The Troublesome Reign* by saying that the historical incidents taken from the old chronicle "are rendered impressive by their being blended with evocations of human passion, which must always appeal to our sympathies because they must always be true to our nature."[30] Charles Kean himself, in a souvenir edition of the play after his production of it in 1858, wrote: "Shakespeare, with the inspiration of a genius, has converted the histories of several of our English kings into a series of dramatic poems, thereby impressing the imagination with living pictures of the Royal race, who in earlier days swayed the sceptre and ruled the destinies of this island." Poltical motives and public events, he said, were supplied by Holinshed, but "it is to his own consummate knowledge of human nature that we are indebted for the thoughts which find utterance in the person of each individual character."[31] Some twenty-five years later Richard Cumberland, dedicating *The Carmelite* to Mrs. Siddons, wrote: "The character of our Drama in its best examples is so close to Nature, that you, Madam, who are apt to give so perfect a reflection of her image, seem born for the elevation of the British stage. The Author, who shall write for you, must copy from no other model but Nature. . . ."[32]

Although there is nothing unusual about praise for truth to nature in characterization, one senses again a very different emphasis from that in most recent treatments of the play. Is it, once more, a matter of expectations? Turning back to Francis Gentleman, writing in Bell's 1774 edition of Shakespeare, we get certain hints of what these expectations were in his prefatory "Essay on Oratory." Gentleman is a useful witness for the very reason that he had nothing like the critical acumen of his great contemporary, Dr. Johnson, but as a moderately successful actor and playwright was thoroughly conversant with the theatre. He was also intelligent, sensible, and well-informed. In his "Essay on Oratory" he turns quickly to "stage delivery," which is more difficult than oratory proper because it includes more variety and more force of passion. "It requires the finest, and most significant feelings in the performer," he says, "to create, by sympathy, proper sensations in the audience" (I,22). "Sympathy" is the key word in this part of his essay. He calls it "that noble and almost peculiar sense of human nature," and quotes "the ingenious Dr. Smith" (that is, Adam Smith) in his *Theory of Moral Sentiments* as saying that sympathy arises from the view of emotions in another person (pp. 22–23). To create sympathy, then, is the actor's chief task. Imagination is the vehicle for conveying it to the heart; "that which the Theatre raises, is produced by the bold painting of the Poet's pen, aided by the natural and forcible talents of a good Actor" (p. 23). Gentleman then gives many examples of how the proper reading or declamation of certain lines (not all of them from plays) can create the desired effect. Under the heading "*Picture of deep* Diffident Cruelty, *from* Shakespeare" he quotes the lines of *King John* to Hubert when he is hinting that Arthur should be killed (pp. 43–44). In a note on this speech in the volume containing the play Gentleman says, "It is impossible for words to express, or imagination to paint, a finer representation of dubious cruelty, fearful to express itself, than this address of *John's* to *Hubert* exhibits: the hesitative circumlocution, with which he winds about his gloomy purpose, is highly natural, and the imagery exquisite. To do this scene justice, requires more judgment, than powers; a jealous eye, deep tone of voice, and cautious delivery, are the outlines of what it should be" (IV,33–34).

If it is up to actor to enable the spectator to respond emotionally, to Shakespeare's fine representation of "deep diffident cruelty," it is presumably the spectator's expectation that a good peformance of the play will bring about such a response. Gentleman's comparison of the actor to an orator, familiar enough to cause no astonishment, reinforces the impression that the peformance is thought of primarily in terms of the emotional responses it evokes, while his use of Adam Smith's theory of sympathy ties such responses to the spectacle of emotions displayed by others. When the spectator responds to a successful theatrical performance, he responds as he would if the actor's situation were actual rather than feigned, and in so responding the spectator behaves in a manner characteristic of human beings. Thus in two related ways, the portrayal of character and the response to this portrayal (though Gentleman does not say so), what happens in the theatre is a manifestation of nature.

V

Despite Charles Kean's implication that knowledge of human nature is more important than the historical information provided by chronicles, his productions of the play and the Macready production which inspired him are prime examples of staging influenced by the concern for historical accuracy that swept the nineteenth-century theatre. It affected plays of all sorts, by Shakespeare and others, but naturally had a special relevance to history plays. Macready's *King John* in 1842 showed what could be done. Kean followed with a New York production in 1846 and two London productions in 1852 and 1858.[33] These mid-nineteenth-century productions call our attention to two not wholly separable aspects of the play's appeal at that time: the lavish spectacle which theatres were increasingly able to provide and the recreation of a bygone age. How these attractions relate to the other qualities for which *King John* was admired is a question to which we shall have to return.

For Macready's production fourteen different scenes were designed by William Telbin. Though they were not the first to be done with great attention to historical accuracy, nothing on the scale of the *King John* sets had been seen. For the costumes Charles Hamilton Smith made use of Planché's notes on the historically correct designs he had executed for Charles Kemble's revival of the play nearly twenty years before. But the scenery and costumes, gorgeous as they were, did not by themselves constitute the spectacle on which every reviewer of Macready's production commented. The pageantry of court scenes and marching armies, the movement of large numbers of people across the stage, made it the equivalent of a Cecil B. DeMille extravaganza in the grand old days of film. Even the playbill reproduced in Charles Shattuck's edition gives some impression of Macready's staging. Instead of the unnamed and unnumbered "Lords, Ladies, Citizens of Angiers, Heralds, Officers, Soldiers, Messengers, and other Attendants" of a modern edition we find eight English lords, each assigned a name (though of course no lines), four or more unnamed English Barons, two unnamed Knights, seven named French lords, and such further supernumeraries as "Archbishop, Bishops, Mitred Abbots, Monks, Esquires, Standard-Bearers, Notarius Apostolicus, Crozier-Bearer, Knights-Hospitallers, Attendants, Citizens, Ladies," etc. (Shattuck, p. 45). The ground plan and added stage-directions for the first scene show how some of these actors were deployed. By Shattuck's count "there were fifty-nine persons on the stage" (p. 23) when *King John* spoke the opening lines. The throne room appeared to be a spacious and elegant hall with tapestried walls and a ceiling supported by hammer-beam oaken arches. John was seated on a blood-red throne on a dais beneath a blood-red canopy, with Queen Elinor at his right on a stool. The ground plan shows where each of the lords, ladies, and attendants was to stand, and the stage-directions added to the printed text, after describing the large circle formed in front of the throne, continue: "Norfolk, who is discovered in the act of speaking to the King, with 2 Knights and Herald with wand Exits Left, and returns immediately Left, ushering in French Herald, 6 French Barons, and Chatillon,—The circle divides, and the attention of all the Characters is given to the proceedings of the Embassy, who all bow to the King, on their entrance. A loud flourish of trumpet, kept up till King John ready to speak." (I have expanded contractions.) Here a static expository opening scene is made visually (and aurally) impressive and given movement even before the first words are spoken.

Act II, where the armies of Austria, France, and England meet before the gates of Angiers, brought eighty-eight people onstage in front of Telbin's impressive castle walls and his prospect of French landscape. With the withdrawal of the armies for the offstage battle (observed from the walls by the citizens of Angiers), their re-entrance, their regrouping as the proposal of marriage is discussed, and then their joint procession into the castle, the stage picture must have been almost constantly in motion. In intervals between the lines trumpets are called for more than ten times in addition to "wind instruments," "marches," "martial music," "noise of battle," "shouts," and "noise of gates opening." We recall that it was the marches of an earlier production on which Mrs. Siddons, in her dressing room, riveted her attention in order to prepare herself emotionally for Act III. That act, with the arrival of the papal legate and the offstage battle between the French and the English, provides more opportunities for pageantry, as do the last two acts. In Act V there were six settings, the last of which showed the orchard of Swinstead Abbey, illuminated by "Blue Mediums" to suggest moonlight.

It seems fair to ask whether the spectacle, comprised of scenery, costumes, and moving masses of actors, provided Shakespeare's play with an additional interest as both a theatrical experience and an exercise in historical recreation, or whether it was thought to enhance the effect of the scenes in which human nature was so strikingly manifested. That it was to some extent an "extra added attraction" can hardly be denied, especially when we note that so many of the most splendid scenes were ones to which critics of the play paid little or no attention. No doubt there is a serious danger that this sort of staging may swamp the play, but we have interesting testimony from Max Beerbohm that the contrary might be the case. He devoted the first part of his review of Beerbohm Tree's production to description of what took place onstage at several moments. Then he wrote: "Most of the points I have alluded to are, as you will have observed, points of 'business' and the stage management. For this I make no apology. I had never seen the play acted before, and I must confess that, reading it, I had found it insufferably tedious. I had found many beautiful pieces of poetry in it, but drama had seemed to me absolutely lacking. That was because I have not much imagination. . . . Therefore, when I go to a theatre and find that what bored me very much in the reading of it is a really fine play, I feel that I owe a great debt of gratitude to the management which has brought out the latent possibilities."[34] It must be added that these possibilities had doubtless been brought out on the Elizabethan stage too, though without the benefit of painted scenery. Even though the nineteenth-centruy productions were a special development, bringing with them their own hazards, the visual dimensions of the play, to which they did such ample justice, should never be disregarded in assessing its dramatic values.

A comment of Charles Kean's on Constance suggests how the sort of production that he and Macready staged might bring out the meaning he saw in certain portions of the play: "A lone woman stands in the midst of chivalry, encircled by the din of battle, the emblem of despair and ruined majesty" (p. vi). The gorgeous affliction" of Constance may have been heightened for the spectator by the visual contrast between her solitary figure and the comings and going of the French, Austrian, and English armies. The *Illustrated London News,* reviewing Macready's revival, printed a woodcut of the final scene with the comment: "We here present our readers with what we deem to be the most appropriate and effective grouping for scenic illustration—the last *tableau* of the tragedy. . . . *Hubert, Essex,* and *Prince Henry* are participators of the death-scene; and there is a bold grouping around, which places a splendid circle of caparisoned figures in constrast with the sweet and solemn distance—the beautiful orchard of the picturesque abbey of Swinstead beyond." The reviewer was explicit about the benefits of Macready's staging: "He wisely sees that the glorious pageantry which interweaves itself among the fine depictments and imaginings of the immortal bard give true and beautiful aid to the living stream of poetry." Illustration, he said, "Makes beautifully perfect the grand illusions of the play."[35]

VI

Pictures had a special fascination in this period of the early photographic experiments of Daguerre and Talbot. The word recurs frequently in dramatic criticism, whether or not it is a question of stage images. It will be recalled that Boaden believed Kemble to have "substituted his own face and figure for the picture sense of *King John,*" and that Kean credited Shakespeare with "impressing the imagination with living pictures of the Royal race. . . ." The *Illustrated London News,* which pointed to the contribution of pageantry and scenic illustration to the realization of Shakespeare's imaginative vision, made more general claims for the compatibility of art and poetry in its first issue, which appeared only five month before the review of Macready's *King John* . For the past ten years, the editor wrote, he had watched with admiration the progress of illustrative art. "it has given to fancy a new dwelling-place, to imagination a more prominent throne." Art, in the form of wood engraving, had, in fact, "become the bride of literature." "Even Shakespeare came to us clothed with a new beauty."[36]

We are thus reminded that Charles Knight's *Pictorial Edition of Shakespeare* had begun appearing about four years before Macready's revival. In his *Passages of a Working Life* Knight wrote: "Altogether it became necessary for me to look carefully at the plays, to see whether the aid of art might not be called in to add both to the information and enjoyment of the reader of Shakespeare, by representing the Realities upon which the imagination of the poet must have rested." He mentioned specifically architectural drawings "which imparted a character of truthfulness to many scenes, which upon the stage had in general been mere fanciful creations of the painter."[37] There can be no doubt that in the eyes of Macready and Charles Kean, Telbin's sets were to serve the same educational purpose of representing "reality"—the truth about the past. Again, the *Illustrated London News* offers a valuable sidelight. The first bound volume of the paper was published in January 1843, with a self-congratulatory preface asserting the value of an illustrated newspaper to historians. The example given is Sir Walter Scott. What would he have given for such a record of the life and times of Elizabeth? The historian of Victoria's reign will have the inestimable benefit of the *Illustrated London News*, which will "pour the lore of the Antiquarian into the scholar's yearning soul." A rousing sentence follows: "This volume is a work that history must keep" (pp. iii–iv). Illustration, whether on the page or on the stage, was not only a powerful stimulus of the imagination, and thus the "bride of literature," but was also the handmaid of historical truth.

VII

It is bound to strike us as curious that such historically faithful illustration as Telbin's sets and Smith's costumes for *King John* were what made "beautifully perfect the grand illusions of the play," but the paradox reflects more basic problems about the status of the play as a dramatization of history. We know, as did the nineteenth-century illustrators and actor managers, that much of *King John* is untrue to history—that the Bastard is largely a poetic invention, and that the confrontations of Constance and Arthur with their enemies and tormentors are heightened by contrivances of plot as well as by the speeches that Shakespeare (in this respect like some of the most famous historians) puts in their mouths. What makes their appeal to us most immediate is also what is least authentic.

Yet we also know that our responses to characters presented as historical differ from responses to avowedly fictional characters. "Historical writings," as Herbert Lindenberger says, "Make a greater pretense at engaging with reality than do writings whose fictiveness we accept from the start."[38] "*All is True*," the alternative title of *Henry VIII*, is the implicit claim of all history plays, and I believe that it does condition our responses even when we know that certain characters are quite unhistorical. There is powerful appeal in the very complexity of the process of history as it is presented in *King John* . We seem to see a reflection of the complexities of other periods, including our own, in which conflicting ambitions, good and bad luck, and mixtures of noble and despicable behavior have determined the fate of nations. The link with what we are willing to accept as true history is just strong enough to give us the sense that the events we are witnessing onstage helped to shape what followed, and hence that what these personages did or failed to do mattered greatly. Because they seem to be involved in the process of history they are at once authenticated and magnified.

To Hazlitt the intensified impression of reality in history plays was a disadvantage: "It gives soreness to our feelings of indignation or sympathy, when we know that in tracing the progress of sufferings and crimes, we are treading upon real ground. . ." (IV,306). His conclusion was a negative one: the playwright had better choose imaginary themes. But Hazlitt's testimoney to the special effect of historical material is nonetheless impressive. He seems to imply that truth to nature is given a disagreeably sharp edge by historical truth.

To further the illusion of veracity, historical costumes and sets must have been a powerful aid. For the reader of his souvenir edition of *King John,* Charles Kean even furnished a list of authorities for the costumes, thus tying the play to surviving monuments and manuscripts. To the extent that such devices helped to persuade audiences that all was true, they were far from being irrelevant. It was by encouraging the desired response that they were most likely to make "beautifully perfect the grand illusions of the play."

Now let us go one step further. If we say that, like historical settings and costumes, history itself can be used to further an illusion and therby elicit a certain response, the problems about the historicity of *King John* largely vanish. This is not to say that certain historical issues or certain periods of the past did not have intrinisic interest for Shakespeare and his audience. It is to suggest that these were not necessarily the principal interests of a history play then or later. We can be reasonably sure that they were not the principal interests for most of the witnesses I have summoned. In times of patriotic fervor there will be more people to feel as Heywood did about the glorius triumphs of Englishmen over foreign enemies. But much of the time even such stirring words as those which end the play—". . . nought shall make us rue, / If England to itself do rest but true"—may serve mainly to heighten the significance of the stories the play has presented of John, Constance, Arthur, Hubert, and the Bastard.

The case of the Bastard is especially telling. There is no doubt that this final patriotic speech of his is moving, as are his words to Hubert, picking up the dead body of Arthur: "How easy dost thou take all England up" (IV,iii,142). But what gives these speeches a large part of their special force is the fact that they are spoke by the cynical observer of international politics. His unexpectedly total commitment to the cause of his country is a *coup de théâtre* and it matters not one bit that he himself is a largely imaginary character. The mixture of greatness with levity, noticed by Dr. Johnson, is what makes him fascinating, and the historical context serves to provide him with the opportunity for greatness.

To refer to little Arthur as "all England" is a clear case of what Lindenberger calls "history as magnification" (see pp. 54–94). The pathos of his situation is infinitely heightened by our awareness of his symbolic and thematic significance. Chrles Kean said, "He is the centre from which every scene radiates: and in the spirit of retributive justice, the misfortunes of England appear as the consequent result of the wrongs inflicted by its unscrupulous monarch on his helpless nephew" (p. vi). This is an admirable statement of the connection between history and the emotional impact of Arthur's story.

To see history as instrumental in Shakespeare's creation of drama may further a more comprehensive effort to reorder our priorities in dramatic criticism. In the case of *King John* it may be that the tendency to look first for a pattern of ideas has kept us from understanding the power that critics once found in scene after scene. Perhaps if we are willing to alter somewhat the expectations we have cultivated, we too can feel that power, respond to "gorgeous affliction," and even be "parched with a scorching fever" at King John 's death.

NOTES

1. This article is a slightly revised version of the Fifth Annual Lecture at the 1977 meeting of the Shakespeare Association of America in New Orleans.
2. *Shakespeare's History Plays*, New York: Macmillan, 1946, pp. 221, 226, 233.
3. *Shakespeare's "Histories": Mirrors of Elizabethan Policy*, San Marino, Calif.: Huntington Library, 1947, pp. 142–143.
4. See, for example, Henry A. Kelly, *Divine Providence in the England of Shakespeare's Histories*, Cambridge: Harvard Univ. Press, 1970; David Riggs, *Shakespeare's Heroical Histories*, Cambridge,: Harvard Univ. Press, 1971; Robert Ornstein, *A Kingdom for a Stage: The Achievement of Shakespeare's History Plays*, Cambridge: Harvard Univ. Press, 1972; Moody E. Prior, *The Drama of Power*, Evanston, Ill.: Northwestern Univ. Press, 1973; Edward I. Berry, *Patterns of Decay: Shakespeare's Early Histories*, Charlottesville: Univ. Press of Virginia, 1975. Prior has an admirable *caveat* about critical reliance on such grand designs: "Shakespeare's genius is not, however, primarily theoretical; his insights into the ultimate nature of political thought and action reach us through his dramatic presentation of particular events and persons. . ." (p.12).
5. I accept the theory that this play preceded Shakespeare's and was by another author, though this is not the place to argue the case.
6. *Papal Tyranny in the Reign of King John*, London, 1745, sig. A3.
7. Ed. Wm. W. Appleton, Lincoln: Univ. of Nebraska Press, 1967, p. 44.
8. For eighteenth-century performances, see C. Beecher Hogan, *Shakespeare in the Theatre 1701–1800*, Oxford: Clarendon, 1952, I, 239–44; II, 319–33; and the relevant volumes of Emmett L. Avery et al., *The London Stage 1660–1800*, Carbondale: Southern Illinois Univ. Press, 1960–68. For a list of performances recorded by Genest and other performances in England and America in the nineteenth century, see the Variorum *King John*, ed. H. H. Furness, Philadelphia & London: Lippincott, 1919, pp. 656–60. See also Harold Child's stage history in the New Cambridge *King John*, ed. J. Dover Wilson, 2d. ed., 1954; rpt. Cambridge: Cambridge Univ. Press 1969, pp. lxiii–lxxix. Between 1737 and 1823, the year of Macready's first *King John*, the play was produced in London in 38 seasons, and sometimes in Edinburgh, Liverpool, Bristol, and Bath. During the next fifty years a writer for the *Illustrated London News* (23 Sept. 1899) counted "some twenty productions" in London, but none between 1873 and the Beerbohm

Tree revivals. The first American production occurred in 1768 and was followed by fourteen more before 1875.

9. *The Works of Shakespeare,* London, 1733 (i.e. 1734), III, 167.
10. *The Plays of William Shakespeare,* London, 1765, III, 503.
11. [Francis Gentleman], *The Dramatic Censor,* London, 1770, II, 171: Thomas Davies, *Dramatic Micellanies* [sic], London, 1783–84, I, 9, 35–36, 54–56.
12. *Bell's Edition of Shakespeare's Plays,* London, 1774, IV, facing p. 37.
13. *Memoirs of Mrs. Siddons,* London, 1827, p. 59.
14. London, 1825, pp. 133–34.
15. *The British Theatre,* London, 1808, I, *King John,* p.3.
16. Anna Jameson, *Characteristics of Women,* London, 1832, II, 215.
17. *Studies in Shakespeare,* London, 1847, pp. 27 ff.: Variorum ed., pp. 679–83.
18. Thomas Campbell, *Life of Mrs. Siddons,* London, 1834, I, 219.
19. My quotations from *King John* are taken from the New Cambridge edition.
20. 1890; rpt. London: Rupert Hart Davis, 1948, p. 260.
21. *Shakespeare,* London: J. Cape, 1936, p. 156.
22. "The Road to Swinstead Abbey: A Study of the Sense and Structure of *King John,*" *ELH,* 18 (1951), 271.
23. *University of Toronto Quarterly,* 29 (1960), 341–56; rpt. in *Shakespeare: The Histories,* ed., E. M. Waith (Englewood Cliffs, N.J.: Prentice Hall, 1965), pp. 85–101.
24. See Robert B. Pierce, *Shakespeare's History Plays: The Family and the State,* Columbus: Ohio State Univ. Press, 1971, p. 144; Ornstein, pp. 96–99.
25. *Some Shakespearean Themes,* London: Chatto & Windus, 1959, p. 38.
26. See, for example, Davies, p. 15.
27. *Characters of Shakespear's Plays* (1817), in *The Complete Works,* ed. P. P. Howe, London: Dent, 1930–34, IV, 311.
28. *William Charles Macready's King John,* ed. Charles H. Shattuck, Urbana: Univ. of Illinois Press, 1962, p. 51.
29. *The Speaker,* 30 Sept. 1899; quoted in New Variorum edition of *King John,* ed. H. H. Furness, Philadephia: Lippincott, 1919, p. 689.
30. *The Modern Standard Drama,* ed. Epes Sargent, #XXXV, New York, 1846, p. iii; in Vol. V, New York 1847.
31. *Shakespeare's Play of King John,* London 1858, p. v.
32. *The Carmelite,* London, 1784, p. iv.
33. About these major revivals we are fortunate to have voluminous information readily available in Charles Shattuck's splendid edition of Macready's *King John* .
34. *Saturday Review,* 30 Sept. 1899: quoted in New Variorum, pp. 687–88, where it is ascribed to G. B. Shaw.
35. 29 Oct. 1842, p. 392.
36. 14 May 1842, p. 1.
37. London, 1864–65, II, 284.
38. *Historical Drama,* Chicago: Univ. of Chicago Press, 1975, p. x.

[*Francis Gentleman*]

From *The Dramatic Censor or Critical Companion*

This play opens with peculiar dignity, being the royal audience of a French ambassador, whose very insolent address and arrogant demands, are replied to with such spirit as we wish British monarchs upon such an occasion may ever shew. From an observation made by the queen mother, upon Chatillion's departure, it appears, that the kindling flame of war has been lighted by Lady Constance, in favour of her son Prince Arthur, whose just title the queen seems to admit.

Robert Falconbridge, and his brother Philip, are introduced for King John's decision concerning a plea of birth-right, Robert urging bastardy against his brother. Philip's blunt, sportive method of expression, tainted too with licentiousness, is abominable stuff for the ears and respectful decorum of royalty to be violated with; however, from tracing some marks in his visage of that corrupt descent he seems to boast, after a slight altercation, the matter is settled thus; heritage of the paternal estate is granted to the legitimate brother, and Philip, with an invitation to join the warlike preparation, is knighted and confirmed in bastardy, by being ordered to take the royal name of Plantagenet.

After King John goes off, declaring his immediate intentions of invading France, our new made knight stays behind to meditate upon the change of his situation, which he does in a soliloquy of very quaint conceit, burthensome to an audience, because three-fourths of it is unintelligible to the general ear; and indeed, if not, is of very immaterial tendency. What ensues between this flighty blade and his mother, only serves to confirm what the king and queen took as fact, merely from apprehension.

We cannot think our author had any kind of reason for bringing Lady Falconbridge before an audience to confess her shame with such effrontery, therefore censure this scene highly; and are of opinion, that the last seven lines of this Act, spoken by the Bastard, are much more suitable to the bully of a brother, than a person of good sense, good breeding, and real spirit. This character might have been marked with oddity, as is evidently intended, without so much offence.

At the beginning of the second act, by poetical conveyance, we meet the French king and his powers before the walls of Angiers, where Constance and her son Arthur, yield him thanks for espousing their distressful cause. Upon the arrival of Chatillion, his master is informed not only of King John's warlike resolution, but that he has coursed him at the heels with such unaccountable expedition, as to be within the sound of beaten drums. We apprehend the play would have begun with much more propriety at this period, and there is not a single passage in the first act, save King John's reply to Chatillion, that could cause taste or judgment to lament the omission of it.

Upon meeting his brother of France, King John first utters peace, and then, on refusal, denounces war. To this the French monarch replies by arguments, in favour of Arthur's right; an altercation ensues, in which the ladies join, without seeming to have the least regard for essential delicacy; what passes between Austria and the Bastard also, is fitter for coalheavers than men of rank and education.

Upon a proposition of surrendering all his dominions in right of Arthur, John treats King Philip with contempt, but offers protection to the young prince; this brings on a fresh brawl between the ladies; at length, the citizens of Angiers being summoned to their walls by sound of trumpet, the two kings severally address them, denouncing threats on each side. Thus embarrassed, and equally endangered, the citizens very prudently intimate, that whoever proves strongest will prevail with them. This occasions immediate determination of a battle, for which purpose both kings go off. Here a scene of tumult, and what we may justly stile theatrical confusion, ensues, alarms! heralds! and a victory; after which the kings again meet, again debate, and still talk in a high strain, while Falconbridge flames between them with the spirit of Até.

After much controversy, to very little purpose, more than to gratify a disposition for talking, they agree to unite their powers against the resisting town; this sharpens the wits of the citizens, who, by way of palliating matters, propose a match between the Dauphin and Lady Blanche, a Spanish princess, nearly related to England; which matter being, like all other state marriages, concluded by sudden consent of parties, without any appeal to love, the gates of Angiers are thrown open, and our two kings enter in friendly terms. John promising to alleviate the pain such a coalition must give Constance, by creating young Arthur Duke of Bretagny, and giving him the Town of Angiers.

Here Falconbridge is again left alone to descant upon the late transactions, which he does with keen and just satire; there is a sort of word-catching in this soliloquy, some of the ideas are incumbered with superfluous expression, and the auditor's conception is fatigued with blameable obscurity; notwithstanding which faults, we allow it to contain useful thoughts and lamentable truths, respecting the influence interest has upon the highest as well as lowest characters of life.

In the first scene of the third act, as it has been rightly settled by the ablest editors, Constance appears, possessed of strong and natural resentment against the French monarch, for entering into pacific connections with her enemy King John; she rather rates Lord Salisbury for bringing her the news, and when he proposes her going into the royal presence, she replies with disdainful refusal, prostrating herself, and making the ground her throne, as she phrases it.

Just returned from the Dauphin's nuptials, the two kings encounter this monument of grief. Upon Philip's mention that so happy a day shall each annual return be kept a holy one, she rises, and vents her passion with much bitterness of expression; her widow's curse in the following terms is awfully nervous, and judiciously introduced by the author, as prophetic of what follows.

> Arm, arm ye heav'ns, against these perjur'd kings,
> A widow cries, be husband to me heav'n:
> Let not the hours of this ungodly day
> Wear out the day in peace, but ere sun set
> Set armèd discord 'twixt these perjur'd kings.

Her reproaches to boasting Austria are of a very stinging nature, and the Bastard's continuation of them sharpens their pointedness exceedingly. Mr. Pope, and other commentators, have added some lines to make the Bastard's behavior more justifiable; but, if we consider what passes in the second Act, we find that Falconbridge indulges a general blunt oddity, that even treads close upon the heels of majesty; indeed, mention of Austria's having killed his father, is very proper to lay the foundation of hearted resentment.

Pandulph, legate from the Pope, consequently in these days a mischief-making priest, here enters; and, in terms of peremptory demand, enquires why the then Archibishop of Canterbury was deprived of his fee: to this King John replies with very becoming independence of spirit, but we think in rather too harsh terms; dignity never sits with grace upon abuse. The thunderbolt of papal authority, excommunication, here issues from the enraged cardinal, who urges King Philip to support the church's quarrel against John; which, after some tolerable resistance, and some well principled arguments, he is at last persuaded to by the churchman's able sophistry. This occasions instantaneous declarations of hostility, and so very conveniently are both armies situated, that without a single line to give time for preparation, the battle joins. We apprehend that the cardinal and Constance might have been furnished with something to say, that would have been not only interesting but of use, to give some trace of probability to the time action.

After some martial flourishes, Falconbridge enters, as conqueror of Austria; we think the lion's skin as a trophy of honour worn by his father, should be worn by the Bastard through the remainder of the play. King John having taken Prince Arthur prisoner, commits him to the care of Hubert; here a few more alarms succeed, and the English monarch beats the French behind the scenes; after which he comes on with the Queen Mother, &c. orders Falconbridge to haste for England, there to raise against his coming taxes or contributions from the several orders of clergy.

We do not know any passage, in any piece, that can boast merit superior to the method King John takes of working Hubert to the destruction of Arthur. His diffidence, his soothing, his breaks, pauses, and distant hints, are most descriptive lines of nature in such a depraved state of agitation. What follows we think so rich a regale for poetical taste, that we should deem ourselves very blameable not to offer it to the reader's palate.

The sun is in the heav'n and the proud day
Attended with the pleasures of world,
Is all too wanton and too full of gawds
To grant me audience—if the *midnight* bell
Did with his iron tongue and brazen mouth,
Sound one unto the drowsy race of night:
If this same were a church-yard where we stand,
And thou possessed with a thousand wrongs:
Or if that surly spirit melancholly
Had *baked* thy blood, and made it heavy, thick;
Which else runs tickling up and down the veins,
Making that ideot laughter keep men's eyes,
And strain their cheeks to idle merriment;
A passion hateful to my purposes:
Or if that thou couldst see me without eyes,
Hear me without ears and make reply,
Without a tongue—using conceit alone—
Then in despight of broad-ey'd watchful day
I would into thy bosom pour my thoughts.

Notwithstanding the approbation we allow to that general excellence which distinguishes this speech, yet we cannot avoid remarking the two words distinguished by Italics. One o'clock in the *morning*, cannot with propriety be stiled the *midnight* bell—The word *solemn* would remove this objection—*Had baked thy blood*; to us it appears that melancholy is a cold, chilling disposition of mind; *baked* furnishes an idea of heat, therefore we would substitute *caked*, as more consonant to the meaning.

After King John has wrought up Hubert to his murderous purpose, and goes for England, the audience still remain in France, to hear Philip lament the effects of his late defeat; and Constance breath deep lamentation for the captivity of her son. The unhappy mother's plaints are extremely forceable and tender; yet, amongst many beauties, we must object to that speech wherein she speaks of the courtship of death, in such figurative extravagance. When Constance and the French king retire, Pandulph works on the Dauphin by some arguments of deep and probable policy, to retrieve his own honour and that of France, by undertaking the invasion of England; furnishing warm hopes of success from the internal disquiets of King John's government, especially those of the enraged clergy, plundered by that monarch's order—A most alarming circumstance to churchmen, who, notwithstanding they preach up contempt of this world, are peculiarly remarkable for coveting and holding fast its riches.

At the beginning of the fourth act, humanity encounters the painful circumstance of Hubert's commission to burn out Arthur's eyes, to prevent, by the Ottoman method, his succession or advancement to the throne; this scene, with respect to the young prince's part of it, does our author great credit; he has most happily traced nature, and has touched the tender feelings in a powerful manner, without straining them too much. Hubert's reluctance and pity are well described, the two characters impress an audience with compassion and esteem, insomuch, that tears of concern and satisfaction alternately flow.

When King John acquaints his peers with his second coronation, the Lords Salisbury and Pembroke express themselves in very free terms concerning that measure: the latter complains of Arthur's imprisonment, and claims his enlargement, which the monarch consents to, as supposing him dispatched. Here Hubert enters, and tells the king that his order has been fulfilled: when Salisbury and Pembroke are told of Arthur's death, they utter some expressions of vindictive discontent, and leave the king to consider his perturbed, ticklish situation. At this point of time a messenger enters, and increases his embarrassment, by an account of the French invasion, and his mother's death. The warlike operations of this play are conducted with astonishing rapidity, for King John, between the first and second acts, carried an army to France, which he landed before the French king heard of it; and between the third and fourth, the Dauphin lands a formidable power before the English know any thing of his approach. After Falconbridge is dispatched to sooth the discontented lords, Hubert re-enters, to acquaint the king of some prodigies which have appeared, and the popular confusion occasioned by Arthur's death; his description, particularly in the latter part, has singular merit. The guilty monarch's recriminating upon one he supposes a ready agent to his sanguine orders, is highly natural; the wicked always endeavour to lighten the oppressive load of a bad conscience, by throwing part of it upon another: Hubert's exculpation of himself comes favourably from the actor, but has more plausibility than truth; for his assertion of a mind free from the taint of any murderous thought, is contradicted by the readiness with which he understood and coincided with John's meaning; to have rendered him truly amiable, some passages might have been added to signify, that he only undertook the horrid charge to save young Arthur; at present he is left a very dubious or rather culpable character.

The unhappy young prince, raised to a state of desperation by his captivity, and other painful circumstances, appears on the battlements of his prison, and resolved upon attempting an escape; but by the fall puts an end to his life. The discontented English peers going to meet the Dauphin now enter, and are accosted by Falconbridge with message from the king, which they receive with haughty terms. Upon seeing Arthur's body, their wrath grows more enflamed, and a solemn vow of vengeance is entered into.

Hubert, with a second message from the king, and intelligence that the prince is alive, comes in, when a warm altercation ensues; being shewn the corpse of Arthur, Hubert pathetically asserts his own innocence, yet cannot gain credit from the lords, who openly avouch their design of joining the Dauphin: even Falconbridge seems struck with Arthur's fate, and speaks his doubts of Hubert. The picture he draws of the reigning political confusion is nervous and striking and merits being offered to the reader, but that we have already exceeded in the play the proposed limits of quotations.

At the beginning of the fifth act, we meet an incident utterly disgraceful to English annals, King John's resignation of his crown, and receiving it from Pandulph, as a mean dependancy on the Pope. His situation might politically require such a concession, but any man of even tolerable spirit would have rather died than shame an exalted station so basely; in return for the English monarch's submission, the cardinal goes to stop the Dauphin's hostile operations. Here the Bastard enters with intelligence that seems to stagger John, whose embarrassment gives Falconbridge an opportunity of remonstrating with great spirit and fire, especially against Pandulph's palliative commission; his arguments so far prevail, that he receives the royal authority to repel force by force.

In the next scene a solemn compact is entered into between the Dauphin and the English lords. Upon the cardinal's appearance, and the communication of his pacific disposition, the prince, with very becoming judgment and spirit, declines being propertied by the churchman; who considers no further than as circumstances relate to his master the Pope. During this parley, Falconbridge demands conference, in which he supports with soldierly demeanour, the dignity of his king and native land; however, he loses the gentleman in some of his remarks, particularly where he poorly and indelicately puns upon the beating of drums; bluntness and rudeness are very distinct operations of temper; good sense approves the first, but condemns the last.

A battle here ensues, during which King John appears, labouring under a heavy indisposition. Some tidings of great importance are brought by a messenger, but though of a favourable king, the sick monarch cannot relish them, but desires to be conveyed to Swinstead Abbey.

We are now conveyed to the French camp, where we meet Salisbury, Pembroke, &c. in a state of surprize, at the strength, number, and success of King John's arms; to fill them with more astonishment and confusion, Melun, a French count, who has received his death's wound, acquaints them with the Dauphin's design of cutting off all the revolters who have joined him, in case of victory; this determines them upon an immediate return to their allegiance, of which the Dauphin is informed, as well as of the fate his expected supplies have met, of being wrecked upon the Goodwin Sands; however, he bears up with resolution, and determines to stand the issue of another battle.

A scene merely expletive, occurs between Falconbridge and Hubert, which is, and we think with justice, generally omitted in representations; however, Hubert's account of the king's being poisoned, should be retained, and might come well enough from Salisbury or Pembroke, just before John's entrance.

We have now brought royalty to the last thread of life, and are sorry to be under the necesssity of observing, that our author has not displayed his usual force of genius in what the expiring monarch says; his speeches are too figurative for one in great pain, and are otherwise far too short of the circumstance; he resigns his breath too in a manner very unfavourable for stage action; though a most abandoned politician, not one pang of a guilty conscience is mentioned, which even in the midst of distraction, seldom fails to shew itself.

The king no more, Falconbridge, with commendable spirit, urges union of forces, to expel the Dauphin and his invading powers; however, it appears, that losses and disappointments have obliged that prince to concur in Pandulph's pacific plan, which the English lords and prince Henry seem ready to admit. This draws our piece to a conclusion, and the whole is summed up with this excellent and truly British remark, uttered by Falconbridge,

> Come, the three corners of the world in arms,
> And we shall shock them!—nought shall make us rue
> If England to itself do prove but true.

In writing this play, Shakespeare disclaimed every idea of regularity, and has huddled such series of historical events on the back of one another, as shame the utmost stretch of probability; his muse travels lightning winged, being here, there, and every where, in the space of a few minutes. We are by no means advocates for that pinching limitation which so disadvantageously fetters modern composition; imagination will indulge several trespasses of liberty, but must be offended when all the bounds of conception are arbitrarily trodden under foot.

In point of characters King John is a very disagreeable picture of royalty; ambitious and cruel; not void of spirit in the field, yet irresolute and mean in adversity; covetous, overbearing and impolitic; from what we can observe, totally unprincipled; strongly tainted with the opposite appellations which often meet, fool and knave; during his life we have nothing to admire, at his fall nothing to pity.

There is no capital character within our knowledge of more inequality; the greater part of what he has to say is a heavy yoke on the shoulders of an actor. His two scenes with Hubert are indeed masterly, and do the author credit; like charity they may served to cover a multitude of sins; the dying scene is not favourable to action.

Mr. Quin was the first we remember to see figure away in royal John; and, as in most of his tragedy undertakings, he lumbered through the part in a painful manner; growled some passages, bellowed others, and chaunted the rest. Mr. Churchill has sneered at Mr. Mossop for brow-beating the French king; had he seen and remembered the gentleman under consideration, he would have thought the poor tame monarch in danger of being swallowed up alive by his voracious brother of England. Mr. Sheridan has, no doubt, impaired as his faculties are at present, very striking merit, where he is working Hubert to the murder of the prince; his utterance and attendant looks are highly picturesque. We allow him to be also deserving of praise where he upbraids Hubert with so readily obeying his bloody orders; but in the other scenes of the four first acts, low as they are, he sinks beneath them; in dying, he overacts to a degree of particular offence.

Mr. Mossop, whom we have been obliged to find fault with upon several occasions, here deserves our warmest praise, and we are happy to give it him. That stiffness and premeditate method which, in other characters, took off from his great powers and good conception, being less visible in his King John. The rays of glowing merit here broke upon us unclouded and dazzling; where the author's genius soared aloft, he kept pace with equal wing; where Shakespeare flagged, he bore him up; wherefore, we are venturous enough to affirm, that no performer ever made more of good and bad materials mingled together, than Mr. Mossop did in this play. Mr. Powell was too boyish, he wanted weight and depth of expression to excel in John.

Of the chip-in-pottage French king, we shall say nothing, as no actor can make any thing of him; nor can his son, for the like reason, deserve much notice. However, we remember two performers that are worth mention, one Mr. Lacy, who did in the Dauphin [more] than criticism had any right to expect; and Mr. The. Cibber, who was undoubtedly the veriest bantam-cock of tragedy that ever crowed, strutted, and flapped its wings on a stage.

The Cardinal is a very well drawn churchman of those times, subtle, proud, irascible; rather prone to promote than prevent public calamites, where his master's interest seems concerned; a mere politician, not incumbered with delicacy of principle, or the feelings of humanity; he is not in favour of the actor, yet appeared very respectable in Mr. Havard's performance of him, no other person strikes our recollection.

The Bastard is a character of great peculiarity, bold, spirited, free—indeed too free spoken; he utters many noble sentiments, and performs brave actions; but in several places descends to keep attention from drowsing, at the expence of all due decorum; and what is very disgraceful to serious composition, causes the weaker part of an audience to laugh at some very weak, punning conceits.

Mr. Ryan had some merit in this part, by no means equal to what he shewed in many others. The unhappy impediment of his utterance being more conspicuous in it than usual.

Mr. Sheridan has apologized for it, but from what we have already said concerning his executive abilities, the reader may easily judge how very unlike the character he must be. Mr. Holland was too stiff, and made too much use of his strong lungs. Mr. Smith is pretty and spirited, but wants weight and bluntness. We have seen one Mr. Fleeetwood appear in it this season, at the Haymarket, with every fault of Mr. Holland improved, and all his strokes of merit diminished.

If ever Mr. Garrick's figure made against him, it was in this part; he struck out some lights and beauties which we never discovered in the performance of any other person, but there was a certain petitness which rather shrunk the character, and cut short the usual excellence of this truly great actor. Upon the whole, we are obliged to declare, that our idea of the Bastard and Shakespeare's meaning, to our knowledge, has never been properly filled. Mr. Barry, for external appearance and general execution, comes nearest the point. This remark may serve to shew, that though we greatly admire, and have hitherto warmly praised our English Roscius, we are not so idolatrously fond of his extensive merit, as to think him always foremost in the race of fame.

Hubert, though upon the whole an agreeable agent, is by no means an estimable personage; he appears in a very recommendatory light, and savours representation where there are any tolerable feelings. Messrs. Sparks and Berry did him very considerable justice, and Mr. Bensley has exhibited him with deserved approbation; we cannot say so much for Mr. Gibson. At the Haymarket, Mr. Gentleman has passed muster, as not having misconceived or ill expressed the part; but we cannot, as a public performer, congratulate him much on the happiness of his figure or features.

Prince Arthur is a very amiable and interesting character of the drama; we have seen it done affectingly by several children, whose names we forget; however recollect being particularly pleased with Miss Reynolds, now Mrs. Saunders, some twenty years since.

Who did the revolting lords has entirely escaped our memory, except at Mr. Foote's, this summer, and those gentlemen who personated them there may wish to be forgot also.

Every one of the female characters are too contemptible for notice except Constance; she indeed seems to have been an object of great concern with the author, and very seldom fails to make a deep impression upon the audience; her circumstances are peculiarly calculated to strike the feeling heart; dull, very dull must that sensation be which is not affected with the distress of a tender parent, expressed in such pathetic, forceable terms; even Mrs. Woffington, who, from dissonance of tones might be called the screech-owl of tragedy, drew many tears in this part; to which her elegant figure and adequate deportment did not a little contribute. A fine woman robed with grief, is a leading object of pity.

Mrs. Cibber, in the whole scope of her great excellence, never shewed her tragic feelings and expression to more advantage than in Constance; there was a natural tendencey to melancholly in her features, which heightened in action and became so true an index of a woe-fraught mind, that with the assistance of her nightingale voice, she became irresistable; and almost obliged us to forget every other character in raptured contemplation of her merit.

Mrs. Bellamy fell far, very far short of the forementioned lady, and cathedralized the unhappy princess offensively. Mrs. Yates and Mrs. Barry, have both powerful capabilities for the part, but can never justly hope to equal their great predecessor Mrs. Cibber, who must be always remembered with pleasure and regret by all persons of taste, who had the happiness to shed the sacrifice of tears at the shrine of her melting powers. Mrs. Phillippina Burton was indescribably deplorable.

The shameful irregularity of the plot we have already remarked; in the characters there is variety. The Bastard is an original and pleasing oddity, though somewhat upon the extravaganza; the language is bold, flowing, and where it ought to be, pathetic; yet in many places too figurative, obscure and turgid. As to moral, there seems to be no other deduction but this; that King John's crimes having merited his fate, the justice of providential dispensation is thereby vindicated. This play wants much alteration to make it quite agreeable on the stage, and is at present we think a better reading than acting piece.

Before we dismisss this tragedy, permit us to offer a short anecdote related by a gentleman who saw it performed at Portsmouth last war. The French party coming on with white cockades, a zealous tar shouts from the gallery, Harkee, you Mr. Mounseers, strike the white flags out of your hats, or b— my eyes, but I'll bombard you. A general laugh went through the house, but the actors deeming it merely a transient joke, took no notice; upon which, our enraged son of Neptune gave the word fire, and immediately half a dozen apples few, which worked the desired effect; three cheers ensued, and this incident diffused such a spirit through the house, that during the rest of the play loud huzza's attended the exits and entrances of King John's party, while King Philip and the Dauphin, notwithstanding the polite removal of their cockades, sustained many rough strokes of sea wit.

William Hazlitt

From *Characters of Shakespeare's Plays*

King John is the last of the historical plays we shall have to speak of; and we are not sorry that it is. If we are to indulge our imaginations, we had rather do it upon an imaginary theme; if we are to find subjects for the exercise of our pity and terror, we prefer seeking them in fictitious danger and fictitious distress. It gives a *soreness* to our feelings of indignation or sympathy, when we know that in tracing the progress of sufferings and crimes, we are treading upon real ground, and recollect that the poet's "dream" *denoted a foregone conclusion*—irrevocable ills, not conjured up by the fancy, but placed beyond the reach of poetical justice. That the treachery of King John, the death of Arthur, the grief of Constance, had a real truth in history, sharpens the sense of pain, while it hangs a leaden weight on the heart and the imagination. Something whispers us that we have no right to make a mock of calamities like these, or to turn the truth of things into the puppet and plaything of our fancies. "To consider thus" may be "to consider too curiously"; but still we think that the actual truth of the particular events, in proportion as we are conscious of it, is a drawback on the pleasure as well as the dignity of tragedy.

King John has all the beauties of language and all the richness of the imagination to relieve the painfulness of the subject. The character of *King John* himself is kept pretty much in the back ground; it is only marked in by comparatively slight indications. The crimes he is tempted to commit are such as are thrust upon him rather by circumstances and opportunity than of his own seeking: he is here represented as more cowardly than cruel, and as more contemptible than odious. The play embraces only a part of his history. There are, however, few characters on the stage that excite more disgust and loathing. He has not intellectual grandeur or strength of character to shield him from the indignation which his immediate conduct provokes: he stands naked and defenceless, in that respect, to the worst we can think of him: and besides, we are impelled to put the very worst construction on his meanness and cruelty by the tender picture of the beauty and helplessness of the object of it, as well as by the frantic and heart-rending pleadings of maternal despair. We do not forgive him the death of Arthur because he had too late revoked his doom and tried to prevent it, and perhaps because he has himself repented of his black design, our *moral sense* gains courage to hate him the more for it. We take him at his word, and think his purposes must be odious indeed, when he himself shrinks back from them. The scene in which *King John* suggests to Hubert the design of murdering his nephew, is a master-piece of dramatic skill, but it is still inferior, very inferior to the scene between Hubert and Arthur, when the latter learns the orders to put out his eyes. If anything ever was penned, heart-piercing, mixing the extremes of terror and pity, of that which shocks and that which soothes the mind, it is this scene. [Here Hazlitt quotes IV,i in its entirety.]

(Arthur's) death afterwards, when he throws himself from his prison walls, excited the utmost pity for his innocence and friendless situation, and well justifies the exaggerated denunciations of Falconbridge to Hubert, whom he suspects wrongfully of the deed.

> There is not yet so ugly a fiend of hell
> As thou shalt be, if thou did'st kill this child.
> —If thou did'st but consent
> To this most cruel act, do but despair:
> And if thou want'st a cord, the smallest thread
> That ever spider twisted from her womb
> Will strangle thee: a rush will be a beam
> To hang thee on: or would'st thou drown thyself,
> Put but a little water in a spoon,
> And it shall be as all the ocean,
> Enough to stifle such a villain up.

The excess of maternal tenderness rendered desperate by the fickleness of friends and the injustice of fortune, and made stronger in will, in proportion to the want of all other power, was never more finely expressed than in Constance. The dignity of her answer to King Philip, when she refuses to accompany his messenger, "To me and to the state of my great grief, let kings assemble," her indignant reproach to Austria for deserting her cause, her invocation to death, "that love of misery," however fine and spirited, all yield to the beauty of the passage, where, her passion subsiding into tenderness, she addresses the Cardinal in these words:—

> O father Cardinal, I have heard you say
> That we shall see and know our friends in heav'n;
> If that be, I shall see my boy again,
> For since the birth of Cain, the first male child;
> To him that did but yesterday suspire,
> There was not such a gracious creature born.
> But now ill canker-sorrow eat my bud,
> And chase the native beauty from his cheek,
> And he will look as hollow as a ghost,
> As dim and meagre as an ague's fit,
> And so he'll die; and rising so again,
> When I shall meet him in the court of heav'n
> I shall not know him; therefore never, never
> Must I behold my pretty Arthur more,
> K. PHILIP. You are as fond of grief as of your child.
> CONSTANCE. Grief fills the room up of my absent child:
> Lies in his bed, walks up and down with me;
> Puts on his pretty looks, repeats his words,
> Remembers me of all his gracious parts;
> Stuffs out his vacant garments with his form;
> Then have I reason to be fond of grief.

The contrast between the mild resignation of Queen Katherine to her own wrongs, and the wild uncontrollable affliction of Constance for the wrongs which she sustains as a mother, is no less naturally conceived than it is ably sustained throughout these two wonderful characters.

The accompaniment of the comic character of the Bastard was well chosen to relieve the poignant agony of suffering, and the cold, cowardly policy of behavior in the principal characters of this play. Its spirit, invention, volubility of tongue, and forwardness in action, are unbounded. *Aliquando sufflaminandus erat*, says Ben Jonson of Shakespeare. But we should be sorry if Ben Jonson had been his licenser. We prefer the heedless magnanimity of his wit infinitely to all Jonson's laborious caution. The character of the Bastard's comic humor is the same in essence as that of other comic characters in Shakespeare; they always run on with good things, and are never exhausted; they are always daring and successful. They have words at will and a flow of wit, like a flow of animal spirits. The difference between Falconbridge and the others is that he is a soldier, and brings his wit to bear upon action, is courageous with his sword as well as tongue, and stimulates his gallantry by his jokes, his enemies feeling the sharpness of his blows and the sting of his sarcasms at the same time. Among his happiest sallies are his descanting on the composition of his own person, his invective against "commodity, tickling commodity," and his expression of contempt for the Archduke of Austria, who had killed his father, which begins in jest but ends in serious earnest. His conduct at the siege of Angiers shows that his resources were not confined to verbal retorts. The same exposure of the policy of courts and camps, of kings, nobles, priests, and cardinals, takes place here as in the other plays we have gone through, and we shall not go into a disgusting repetition.

This, like the other plays taken from English history, is written in a remarkably smooth and flowing style, very different from some of the tragedies—*Macbeth*, for instance. The passages consist of a series of single lines, not running into one another. This peculiarity in the versification, which is most common in the three parts of *Henry VI*, has been assigned as a reason why those plays were not written by Shakespeare. But the same structure of verse occurs in his other undoubted plays, as in *Richard II* and in *King John*. The following are instances:—

> That daughter there of Spain, the lady Blanch,
> Is near to England; look upon the years
> Of Lewis the dauphin, and that lovely maid.
> If lusty love should go in quest of beauty,
> Where should he find it fairer than in Blanch?
> If zealous love should go in search of virtue,
> Where should he find it purer than in Blanch?
>
> If love ambitious sought a match of birth,
> Whose veins bound richer blood than lady Blanch?
> Such as she is, in beauty, virtue, birth,
> Is the young dauphin every way complete:
> If not complete of, say he is not she;
> And she wants nothing, to name want,
> If want it be not, that she is not he.

He is the half part of a blessed man,
Left to be finished by such as she;
And she a fair divided excellence,
Whose fulness of perfection lies in him.
O, two such silver currents, when they join,
Do glorify the banks that bound them in:
And two such shores to two such streams made one,
Two such controlling bounds, shall you be the kings,
To these two princes, if you marry them.

Another instance, which is certainly very happy as an example of the simple enumeration of a number of particulars, is Salisbury's remonstrance against the second crowning of the king.

Therefore to be possessed with doubled pomp,
To guard a title that was rich before;
To gild refined gold, to paint the lily,
To throw a perfume on the violet,
To smooth the ice, to add another hue
Unto the rainbow, or with taper light
To seek the beauteous eye of heav'n to garnish
Is wasteful and ridiculous excess.

E. M. W. Tillyard

From *Shakespeare's History Plays*

The study (and perhaps the appreciation) of *King John* is complicated by the survival of a play clearly related to it, the *Troublesome Reign of King John*, published in two parts in the year 1591. The two plays are very close in construction, but their intentions are quite different. Nor are the verbal likenesses very many. The *Troublesome Reign* is a Chronicle Play exploiting the frivolity and the treachery of the French and picturing John as a king more good than bad, the righteous champion of Protestantism against papal tyranny yet not virtuous enough to be God's agent of definitive reformation. It derives from Holinshed, who admits that John's contemporaries thought very ill of him but who puts down that ill opinion to clerical prejudice. Holinshed sums up by saying:

> The man had a princely heart in him and wanted nothing but faithful subjects to have assisted him in revenging such wrongs as were done and offered by the French king and others.[1]

Shakespeare's play is but mildly Protestant in tone and shows no extreme hostility to the French. On the political side it treats of the character of the true king but goes against Holinshed in quite denying John a princely heart; it also treats of the theory of loyalty and when it is lawful to rebel against the reigning king. On the dramatic side it shows Shakespeare bursting out in a kind of creative energy new and unconnected with the History Play. In construction the *Troublesome Reign* is better balanced than *King John*. Shakespeare huddles together and fails to motivate properly the events of the last third of his play. In the *Troublesome Reign* things happen evenly and in good proportion. It is interesting that the first part of the *Troublesome Reign* corresponds to two-thirds of Shakespeare's play and the whole of the second part to only the last third. Thus a massive scene in the *Troublesome Reign* (II.3) of nearly three hundred lines, showing the solemn banding of the English nobles against John at Bury St. Edmunds, is, as a scene, quite omitted in Shakespeare. Finely as the *Troublesome Reign* is plotted, its language is queer and fitful. There is a good deal of competently dignified verse, some amazing pieces of rant, prose passages suggesting garbled and abbreviated verse, pieces of really imaginative writing, a competent scene of knockabout in a monastery alien in tone to the rest of the play, and again and again solid and sensible writing dropping into verse that does not sound too bad and yet which does not quite make full sense.

The common opinion is that Shakespeare took the disposition of his material from the old play and rewrote it in his own language, with a different intention, and with transformed characters. Alexander sought to put the debt the other way round, but Dover Wilson has quite disposed of this endeavour. Nevertheless as an authentic, consistent, and self-supporting composition the *Troublesome Reign* cannot pass. The masterly construction is quite at odds with the heterogeneous execution. It is worth considering a third alternative.[2]

Courthope in his essay mentioned above (p. 134) may be nearer the truth when he made Shakespeare the author of both plays. Relying on the principle (too often ignored) that structure and character matter more than verbal detail, he joins the *Troublesome Reign* to the *Contention of the two famous Houses of York and Lancaster* and the *True Tragedy of Richard Duke of York* and accounts for them as the original Shakespearean versions of the accepted Shakespearean plays to which they are related. No dramatist but Shakespeare, he thought, had the power to marshal his material as it is marshalled in the *Troublesome Reign* :

> In the energy and dignity of the State debates, the life of the incidents, the variety and contrast of the characters, and the power of conceiving the onward movement of a great historical action, there is a quality of dramatic

> workmanship exhibited in the play quite above the genius of Peele, Greene, or even Marlowe. . . . The represention of mental conflict is a marked feature of *The Troublesome Raigne*. . . . If we assume Shakespeare to have been the sole author of *The Troublesome Raigne*, we credit him with a drama doubtless crude, ill-constructed, full of obvious imitation, such as might be expected from a dramatist of small experience, but yet containing more of the elements of greatness than any historic play which had yet been produced on the English stage.[3]

Courthope, as was pointed out above, was nearer the truth about the *Contention* and the *True Tragedy* than almost all the contemporary experts. He may well be nearer the truth, and in a similar fashion, over the *Troublesome Reign*. In other words, as the *Contention* and the *True Tragedy* have turned out to be bad quartos of *2 and 3 Henry VI*, so may the *Troublesome Reign* turn out to be a bad quarto (though perhaps in a different way bad) not of *King John* as we have it but of an early play by Shakespeare on the same theme. This play would then be the original both of the *Troublesome Reign* and of *King John*: the form keeping on the whole the fine construction of the original but garbling the execution and inserting an alien scene; the latter following but impairing the construction and altering the intention and some of the characterisation of its original.

That Shakespeare wrote and revised an early *John* cannot be proved; but I find the supposition best able to explain the facts. If he wrote it, he probably did so near the time of *I Henry VI*, for there is much in *King John* that suggests this play. Both plays deal with French deceit, both contain long scenes of siege-warfare in France. I noted how like the Bastard's were some of the remarks by Talbot and Joan. Shakespeare's first picture of the Bastard would have been one of a much simpler loyalty and would have been close to Talbot. The details of his character are derived principally from the character of Dunois, Bastard of Orleans, as described by Hall. Now Dunois occurs in *I Henry VI*, and Shakespeare used Hall as well as Holinshed for the play. So his own Bastard Falconbridge is drawn from the material of *I Henry VI*. It looks too as if in *I Henry VI* Shakespeare had the material of *King John* in mind, for he makes Talbot say before Rouen:

> And I, as sure as English Henry lives
> And as his father here was conqueror,
> As sure as in this late betrayed town
> Great Cordelion's heart was buried. . . .[4]

Like *I Henry VI* the *Troublesome Reign* abounds in classical reference, while the norm of its verse in places which do not seem corrupt, could well pass in *I Henry VI*: for instance the lines that close the play,

> Thus England's peace begins in Henry's reign
> And bloody wars are clos'd with happy league.
> Let England live but true within itself,
> And all the world can never wrong her state.
> Lewis, thou shalt be bravely shipt to France,
> For never Frenchman got of English ground
> The twentieth part that thou hast conquered.
> Dauphin, thy hand! To Worcester we will march:
> Lords all, lay hands to bear your sovereign
> With obsequies of honour to his grave.
> If England's peers and people join in one,
> Not Pope, nor France, nor Spain can do them wrong.

It is usually thought that the *Troublesome Reign* was published in two parts by an unscrupulous publisher wishing to get double profits out of his buyers and using the precedent of the two parts of *Tamburlaine*. But it may well be that he was merely reproducing in abbreviated and garbled form the two genuine parts of Shakespeare's early play.

The matters thus far treated in this chapter are not such as I wish to include in a book of this kind, but they may really help us to understand why *King John* should be so badly proportioned. In rewriting old matter Shakespeare could not avoid expanding in certain ways. Thus the difficulty of effective compression of two parts of a play (each the length of a normal play) into a single unit would be very great. He coped with it initially, but even so was left with a great residue of matter which he had to compress so drastically as to leave scrappy, unemphatic, and poorly motivated.

I turn now to *King John*, as we have it, apart from its previous history; the play as Shakespeare left it, probably in 1594, to be printed for the first time in the first folio.[5]

Though in earnestness and width of political interest *King John* cannot compete with the historical tetralogy it succeeded, it does dwell on certain specific political themes with powerful effect; and through wonderful innovations of character and language. Shakespeare troubles less with what I have called his official self but in redress allows the spontaneous powers of his imagination a freer, if fitful, effusion.

One sign of this diminished earnestness is that there is much less of the cosmic lore which had been abundant in the tetralogy, while the chief example of it is given a new, ironic, turn. True to the ordinary tradition are the references to the sun setting on the battle-field in Act Five, which duplicate *King John*'s decline into sickness and death. Shortly after Pembroke has said that "*King John* sore sick hath left the field," comes these lines from Melun:

> But even this night, whose black contagious breath
> Already smokes about the burning crest
> Of the old feeble and day-wearied sun. . .[6]

where "contagious" (suggesting sickness) and the sun combine to indicate the King's present sickness through poison. And in the next scene Lewis unconsciously refers to the coming death-struggle in John when he opens it with

> The sun of heaven methought was loth to set.[7]

Early in the play, before Angiers, John develops the correspondence between the human body and the body politic by putting the different parts of Angiers in anatomical terms with gates standing for eyes, walls for waist, and the shaking of the walls by the siege for a fever shaking the whole body. But none of these references has the elaboration of the Bastard's account of the god Commodity, or Self-Interest, and his interference in the world's course. Commodity is a "sly devil" who upsets the great and godlike principle of Order:

> Commodity, the bias of the wrold,
> The world, who of itself is peised well,
> Made to run even upon even ground.
> Till this advantage, this vile-drawing bias,
> This sway of motion, this Commodity,

> Makes it take head from all indifferency,
> From all direction, purpose, course, intent:
> And this same bias, this Commodity,
> This bawd, this broker, this all-changing Word. . .[8]

Commodity has undone God's work by corrupting the world created in the shape of a perfect sphere turning true into a bowl with its bias running crooked. "Direction, purpose, course, intent" are all attributes of "Degree" and anticipate the list in Ulysses's speech on Degree in *Troilus and Cressida,*

> Insisture course proportion season form
> Office and custom.

When Shakespeare calls Commodity "this all-changing Word" he means what Pope meant at the end of the *Dunciad* when he spoke of Dullness quenching light by her "uncreating word." As God himself had created the world through the Word, the second person of the Trinity, so Commodity is the vile "Word" undoing the great act of creation. And this theological reference is clinched when the Bastard a few lines later brings in the familiar ambiguity of the word *angel* as both coin and heavenly ministrant:

> Not that I have the power to clutch my hand,
> When his fair angels would salute my palm.[9]

Commodity used his angels or gold coins to corrupt the holy ends which God's angels have been promoting. Hitherto Shakespeare had used his cosmic lore with traditional and official solemnity; now he has become more sophisticated and, while remaining serious, can use it for subtle ends. The Bastard ironically hails this dubious gospel so fitting on the surface to his own dubious begetting. Yet all the time he is more kingly than the real king, the true upholder of the great principle of Degree.

As there is little cosmic lore so is there little reflection on the great motives of history. John's greatest crime, his inciting Hubert to kill Arthur, seems to contribute much less to his humiliations than does his own unstable character. This is a great change from the earlier tetralogy, and especially *Richard III*, where crime and punishment are so conscientiously connected. Thus in this play it comes as a slight shock when Salisbury refers to the great processes of history. Knowing John to be near death he says to Prince Henry,

> Be of good comfort, prince; for you are born
> To set a form upon that indigest
> Which he hath left so shapeless and so rude.[10]

The same is true when Constance uses the current doctrine of the sins of the royal grandparent being visited on the grandchild, to assail Eleanor. Speaking of Arthur she says:

> This is thy eld'st son's son,
> Infortunate in nothing but in thee:
> Thy sins are visited in this poor child;
> The canon of the law is laid on him
> Being but the second generation
> Removed from thy sin-conceiving womb.[11]

The specific political problems the play deal with are, in ascending order of importance, the succession, the ethics of rebellion, and the kingly character.

The succession does not count for much, though it may well have provided the original motive for Shakespeare's single excursions into English history outside the limits of Hall. John is plainly weak in his title, as his mother bluntly tells him near the opening of the play:

> *John*. Our strong possession and our right for us.
> *Eleanor*. Your strong possession much more than your right,
> Or else it must go wrong with you and me:
> So much my conscience whispers in your ear,
> Which none but heaven and you and I shall hear.[12]

But the theme of a guity conscience over the title is but faintly pursued. True, John guiltily evades the question when attacked by Lewis, saying

> Doth not the crown of England prove the king?[13]

But once again we conclude that it is John's defective character, not his defective title, that ruins him. After dealing at length with the titles of York and Lancaster Shakespeare may well have wearied of this theme.

It is otherwise with the theme of rebellion and strife, which must have had an uncommon hold on Shakespeare's imagination and which is one of the main means of giving the play a certain unity.

First he gives it great prominence by putting it several times in terms of the same metaphor: that of a river bursting out of its banks. The metaphor was not Shakespeare's invention but public property. For instance, the author of the *True Tragedy of Richard III* compares the abuses of the commonwealth to the waters of the Nile overflowing their banks. It is interesting too that in the Shakespearean passage of *Sir Thomas More* More speaking of the mob says,

> Whiles they are o'er the bank of their obedience
> Thus will they bear down all things.[14]

In *King John* the metaphor does not always stand for political rebellion. Standing for any kind of unbridled excess, it does finally narrow itself to the excess of sedition and with a powerful, culminating effect. John, arguing with Philip before Angiers, likens his legitimate course of action to a stream which if Philip interposes an unlawful obstacle, will cause floods and havoc. Later, the Citizen of Angiers, urging the two kings to a league, gives the contrary picture comparing their prospective unity to two rivers joined, flowing peaceably and glorifying the banks by which they flow. Constance, still incredulous of the league and the end of her hopes for Arthur, asks Salisbury, who has given the news,

> Why holds thine eye that lamentable rheum,
> Like a proud river peering o'er its bounds?[15]

John begging Pandulph to quell the civil war he has raised calls it

> This inundation of mistemper'd humour,[16]

where the word *inundation* shows that as well as the humours of the body Shakespeare is thinking of the waves of a flood. Thus it is that when the revolting lords through the mouth of

Salisbury use the same metaphor to express their return to the king, it comes with powerful effect, catching up and crowning what has gone before:

> We will untread the steps of damned flight
> And like a bated and retired flood,
> Leaving our rankness and irregular course,
> Stoop low within those bounds we have o'erlook'd
> And calmly run on in obedience
> Even to our ocean, to our great King John.[17]

But if Shakespeare conveys through this repeated metaphor that sedition and repentance of it are main themes of the play, he commits at first sight a gross inconsistency when he compares John to an ocean and calls him a great king; for John had been behaving very meanly indeed. It will be best to explain this inconsistency before saying more about the doctrine of rebellion; and to do this means examining the character of John.

Dowden noted the "show of kingly strength and dignity in which John is clothed in the earlier scenes of the play" and interpreted it as "no more than a poor pretence of true regal strength and honour."[18] But it is most unlikely that an Elizabethan audience, hearing John defy the French king through his ambassador Chatillon—

> Be thou as lightning in the eyes of France;
> For, ere thou canst report I will be there,
> The thunder of my cannon shall be heard—[19]

or administer excellent justice to the brothers Falconbridge, or oppose the alien interference of the Pope, thought of him as hypocritically assuming a part. Instead they would have treated him somewhat as they would have treated Enobarbus when he described Anthony meeting Cleopatra on the Cydnus. Far from being troubled that Enobarbus should utter an ecstatic passage of verse quite alien to his nature, they would willingly have turned him into a choric character capable of any sort of utterance and have allowed him to resume his individual function when the speech was over. Similarly John is not strictly himself when he is face to face with a Frenchman but An English King, bound to behave with seemly defiance and not to let down the dignity of the English crown. It is just so that Cymbeline's wicked queen behaved to the Roman ambassador; speaking to them she ceased to be a wicked woman and a witch from a fairytale and turned into A British Queen. I noted the same thing happening to Queen Eleanor in Peele's *Edward I* (p. 104). We need not therefore be surprised if John is sometimes a conventionally dignified monarch and at others a mean and treacherous man, realistically portrayed. Thus, when Pembroke repents of sedition, it is to the anointed King of England, not to the bad King John that he vows allegiance. The King of England was indeed the ocean, rightfully claiming the tribute of all the rivers flowing into it.

I turn to the problem of when rebellion may be allowed. This is the theme of the play's culminating and best scene: Act Four Scene Three—where Arthur dies after jumping from the battlements, and first the seditious nobles, next the Bastard, and then Hubert find his body. The behavior of the nobles and of the Bastard is sharply contrasted. Finding Arthur dead, Pembroke Salisbury and Bigot conclude, on the mere fact of his death, that John was guilty; and they betray the levity of their reasoning by the extravagance of their sentiments.

> *Sal.* This is the very top,
> The height, the crest, or crest unto the crest,
> of Murder's arms: this is the bloodiest shame,
> The wildest savagery, the vilest stroke,
> That every wall-eyed wrath or staring rage
> Presented to the tears of soft remorse.
> *Pem.* All murders past do stand excus'd in this:
> And this, so sole and so unmatchable,
> Shall give a holiness, a purity,
> To the yet unbegotten sin of times;
> And prove a deadly bloodshed but a jest,
> Exampled by this heinous spectacle.

To which, with a self-restraint and effort of reason sharply opposed to the facile passions of the nobles, the Bastard adds:

> It is a damned and a bloody work;
> The graceless action of a heavy hand,
> If that it be the work of any hand.[20]

Here the single word *graceless,* meaning beyond the scope of Divine Grace, is a more tremendous indictment than all the noble's hyperboles, but one which the speaker refuses to invoke till he knows the truth. Certain that John is guilty, the nobles decide that rebellion is the virtuous course of action; and when Hubert enters, it is only the Bastard's intervention that stops them killing him as John's agent. It is when the nobles have gone and the need to balance their levity has been removed that the struggle in the Bastard's mind begins, that the problem of rebellion is set forth in its acutest and most distracting form. Appearances are all against Hubert, and if against him against his master; and violent suspicion excites the Bastard to speak poetry the sincere violence of which constrasts superbly with Salisbury's and Pembroke's rhetorical extravagances quoted above:

> If thou didst but consent
> To this most cruel act, do but despair;
> and if thou want'st a cord, the smallest thread
> That ever spider twisted from her womb
> Will serve to strangle thee; a rush will be a beam
> To hang thee on; or wouldst thou drown thyself,
> Put but a little water in a spoon
> And it shall be as all the ocean,
> Enough to stile such a villain up.
> I do suspect thee very grievously.[21]

Hubert protests his innocence. But, still deeply suspicious, the Bastard has forced on him the terrible choice between sedition and serving a usurper or at least a discredited king. Speaking to Hubert and pointing to Arthur's body, he says:

> Go, bear him in thine arms.
> I am amaz'd, methinks, and lost my way
> Among the thorns and dangers of this world.
> How easy dost thou take all England up!
> From forth this morsel of dead royalty
> The life, the right and truth of all this realm
> Is fled to heaven; and England now is left
> To tug and scramble and to part by the teeth
> The unow'd interest of proud-swelling state.
> Now for the bare-pick'd bone of majesty

> Doth dogged war bristle his angry crest
> And snarleth in the gentle eyes of peace:
> Now powers from home and discontents at home
> Meet in one line; and vast confusion waits,
> As doth a raven on a sick-fall'n beast,
> The imminent decay of wrested pomp.
> Now happy he whose cloak and ceinture can
> Hold out this tempest. Bear away that child
> And follow me with speed. I'll to the king.
> A thousand businesses are brief in hand,
> And heaven itself doth frown upon the land.[22]

These doubts, affecting a man who has a natural bent for action, are very moving. Hitherto the Bastard has needed to do no more than serve his master faithfully. Now he is forced to consider the whole case of Arthur. He admits Arthur's right to the throne; he suspects John of murder; he knows that the credit of the land has fallen far. He has to decide between the sin of sedition and the dishonour of serving a bad master. With superb strength and swiftness he makes his choice once and for all and turns from perplexities to the "thousand businesses" of the king.

What the Bastard has actually decided is that, though bad, John is not a tyrant as was Richard III. And he has decided right. It was better to acquiesce in John's rule, bad though it was, hoping that God would turn the king's heart to good and knowing that the sin of sedition would merely cause God to intensify the punishment, already merited, the country was in process of enduring. By his firmness the Bastard prevents the country from collapsing before the French, and God showed his forgiveness by uniting it very shortly under Henry III.

It is typical of the play that in this high place of the action the Bastard uses no cosmic lore. He could so easily have compared the distractions in his own microcosm to those in the body politic, as Brutus did in *Julius Caesar*. He prefers the undignified metaphor of dogs quarrelling over a bone, and the homely one, easily understood in an England unenclosed and still widely overgrown with scrub, of a man gone astray in a wilderness of thorn-bushes.

And, last of the political themes, there is that of the true king. It seems that Shakespeare was apt to speculate on him all through his career. We have seen how in *2 Henry VI* he measured both Humphrey of Gloucester and York by an imagined ideal and found them wanting, while as late as *Cymbeline* he differentiates between Guiderius and Arviragus, Cymbeline's two sons, making Guiderius, the future king, the quick and firm man of action; and Arviragus, the younger, the more imaginative and finer spoken. In *King John* as in *2 Henry VI* we have three pretenders to royalty; Arthur, John and the Bastard: and they all lack something. Arthur is the genuine heir, but he lacks years and probably character. When he tells Hubert

> So I were out of prison and kept sheep,
> I should be as merry as the day is long,[23]

he may well reveal himself to be of the kidney of Henry VI, who had the same wish. John is kingly only in appearance and in the possession of the crown: in mind he is hasty and unstable. The Bastard is illegitimate in birth but in other ways he is one of Shakespeare's great versions of the regal type.

Masefield, swayed by his hatred of Shakespeare's Henry V and observing several clear examples in Shakespeare of the unsuccessful idealist contrasted with the coarse but successful worldling, decries the Bastard, whom he considers a prototype of Henry V, and contrasts his worldly efficiency with the refined idealist nature of John.[24] This is to complicate John and to simplify the Bastard overmuch. John is a bad king, or only good when not himself. The Bastard is a fuller man than the Henry of *Henry V*, and probably just because Shakespeare was not yet critical enough of the efficient man of action and of his limitations to desire to set up an idealist by whom to measure or even reprove him. Shakespeare's first picture of the true king, slightly drawn, was to come a little later in Theseus.

Middleton Murry has written so well of the Bastard's character and of the new vein of creation that went to his making that I need treat of him only as embodying Shakespeare's political opinions.[25] In writing about the kingly characters of *2 Henry VI* I said that to the qualities of the lion and the fox that of another animal, the pelican, had to be added to make the character of the genuine king. The Bastard has all three qualities. His masterful strength is obvious, and it comes out most brilliantly in the speech quoted above over Arthur's body. Only a man of the firmest character could have made up his mind so quickly when beset by such terrible perplexities. It is no accident that in the next scene John is shown weakly handing over the crown of England to Pandulph. And thereafter John's resolution hardens or falters as the Bastard is present or absent. Joined to resolution is speed of action. His defence of Hubert against Salisbury is instantaneous. As Salisbury draws, he retorts:

> Your sword is bright, sir; put it up again.[26]

And when at the end of the play he believes the dauphin to be in pursuit of the king's forces, his counsel is:

> Straight let us seek, or straight we shall be sought.[27]

As the fox he is cunning in a bluffer way than a more strictly Machiavellian character like Bolingbroke, but as effectively. Breaking in on the dauphin and the English rebels at Bury St. Edmunds, he feigns for John a confident defiance which the plight of the English forces was far from bearing out.

> Now hear our English king;
> For thus his royalty doth speak in me.
> He is prepar'd, and reason too he should.
> This apish and unmannerly approach,
> This harness'd masque and unadvised revel,
> This unhair'd sauciness and boyish troops,
> The king doth smile at; and is well prepar'd
> To whip this dwarfish war, these pigmy arms,
> From out the circle of his territories.[28]

In his first soliloquy, at the end of the first act, he confesses himself "a mounting spirit," who will study the weaknesses of the age so that he may "strew" or make less slippery "the footsteps of my rising." Yet even here, where he is delibertately making himself out as self-seeking as possible, he admits that he will learn to humour the times not in order to practise duplicity but to avoid being tricked himself:

> Which, though I will not practise to deceive,
> Yet, to avoid deceit, I mean to learn.[29]

In his second soliloquy, on Commodity, at the end of the second act, he again professes himself as bad as possible: only free from the corruption of graft because never tempted.

> And why rail I on this Commodity,
> But for because he hath not woo'd me yet?
> Not that I have the power to clutch my hand,
> When his fair angels would salute my palm;
> But for my hand, as unattempted yet,
> Like a poor beggar, raileth on the rich.
> Well, whiles I am a beggar, I will rail
> And say there is no sin but to be rich;
> And being rich, my virtue then shall be
> To say there is no vice but Beggary.
> Since kings break faith upon commodity,
> Gain, be my lord, for I will worship thee.[30]

Actually the Bastard has the English fear of being too openly serious and righteous; and this declaration is no more a sign of his being really corrupt than his later interjection,

> If ever I remember to be holy

argues his lack of religion. In actual deed he has the fidelity and the self-abnegation, or at least the conscientiousness, of the pelican. There is no insincerity in his words over John's body:

> Art thou gone so? I do but stay behind
> To do the office for thee of revenge.
> And then my soul shall wait on thee to heaven
> As it on earth hath been thy servant still.[31]

This is the same spirit which in the actual king takes the form of a sense of obligation to his subjects; the spirit which Theseus possesses, when, showing how persistently interested in politics Shakespeare was even in the act of comic creation, he blames himself for being "over-full of self-affairs": words which are not only the justification of Theseus as king, but the condemnation of a Richard II.

Analysed under the above three headings, the character of the Bastard appears frigid enough. It is because Shakespeare conceived him so passionately and gifted him with so unbreakable an individuality that all these kingly qualities take on a life that is quite lacking in the character that should have been finer still: the Henry V of the play which goes under that title. In the character of the Bastard Shakespeare achieves an astonishing break-away from his official self, and through it he develops two weighty political themes which give the play its proper and effective value as part of a great historical series.

Constance has been recognised as the second great character of the play: partly perhaps because Mrs. Siddons played her with enthusiastic devotion. Mark Van Doren rightly sees her as the last of the long series of mourning women who figure in the last three plays of the early tetralogy.[32] But she is rather different. There is nothing ritual or symbolic about her complaints; and her grief is private not choric. Without astonishing as the Bastard does she yet marks an advance in Shakespeare's process of differentiating and individualising character. We must think of her as young, beautiful, and witty; her youthful vitality and charm tragically canalised into a torrent of excessive grief. Philip hints at her beauty when he speaks of "the fair multitude of those her hairs." Through her quickness of wit she overreaches her mother-in-law every time, as when she puns on the word *will* in their first encounter in France—

> *El.* Thou unadvised scold, I can produce
> A will that bars the title of thy son.
> *Con.* Ay, who doubts that? a will? a wicked will;
> A woman's will; a canker'd grandam's will—[33]

and when she mimicks the language of the nursery:

> *El.* Come to thy grandam, child.
> *Con.* Do, child, go to it grandam, child:
> Give grandam kingdom, and it grandam will
> Give it a plum, a cherry, and a fig.
> There's a good grandam. [34]

Even in the extremity of her grief she can be witty, as when she aims her invective at Austria, who had vowed so pompously to fight till Arthur was set on the English throne. Referring to Austria's lion-skin she says:

O Lymoges, O Austria, thou dost shame
That bloody spoil: thou slave, thou wretch, thou coward;
Thou little valiant, great in villainy;
Thou ever strong upon the stronger side.
Thou Fortune's champion, that dost never fight
But when her humorous ladyship is by
To teach thee safety, thou art perjur'd too
And sooth'st up greatness. What a fool art thou,
A ramping fool, to brag and stamp and swear
Upon my party. Thou cold-blooded slave,
Hast thou not sworn like thunder on my side,
Been sworn my soldier, bidding me depend
Upon thy stars thy fortune and thy strength,
And dost thou now fall over to my foes?
Thou wear a lion's hide! doff it for shame
And hang a calf's skin on those recreant limbs.[35]

And when her grief threatens to dement her, she speaks with a rapid imagination akin to the feminine brilliance that Shakespeare was later to embody in Beatrice and Rosalind.

Death, death, O amiable lovely death,
Thou odoriferous stench, sound rottenness,
Thou hate and terror to prosperity;
And I will kiss thy detestable bones
And put my eyeballs in thy vaulty brows
And ring these fingers with thy household worms
And stop this gap of breath with fulsome dust
And be a carrion monster like thyself.
Come, grin on me, and I will think thou smilest,
And buss thee as thy wife.[36]

Mark Van Doren has written brilliantly on the prevailing style of the play. He takes for his text the famous passage about painting the lily and finds the excess of statement shown there to be typical of the play. But the excess, though uneconomical, is not null. It is the mark of a new burst of vitality; just as the Bastard's criticism of the style of the play is a further burst, only in a contrary direction, surveying in high sophistication the journey just completed. Speaking of the proposed match between Lewis and Blanch, the Citizen of Angiers ends,

for at this match
With swifter spleen than powder can enforce
The mouth of passage shall we fling wide ope
And give you entrance: but without this match
The sea enraged is not half so deaf,
Lions more confident, mountains and rocks
More free from motion, no, not Death himself
In mortal fury half so peremptory,
As we to keep this city.

However excessive, it is rousing rhetoric, but the Bastard (who can be rhetorical enough at times) is viciously critical of it:

Here's a story
That shakes the rotten carcass of old Death
Out of his rags. Here's a large mouth indeed
That spits forth death and mountains, rocks and seas,
Talks as familiarly of roaring lions
As maids of thirteen do of puppy-dogs.[37]

Nor is such criticism confined to the Bastard. It is indeed but one part of a recurring proof that in this play Shakespeare faces (even if he does not solve) that problem of reconciling his private with his official self. Chatillon's account to King Philip early in Act Two of the English expedition is rhetorial enough, yet it provides its own self-criticism in the line describing the young English volunteers,

With ladies' faces and fierce dragons' spleens.[38]

Here we have a sudden flash of realism. Shakespeare is thinking of the bright young Elizabethan desperadoes who volunteered for voyages across the Atlantic or expeditions against the ports of Spain. This realism comes surprisingly in a description where Eleanor is called

An Ate, stirring him to blood and strife.[39]

Having taken so decided a turn towards the language of men it is not surprising that Shakespeare should have abandoned in *King John* the language of ritual. Though there is some rhetorical repetition, as in Constance's lines on death quoted above, there is no antiphonal writing. Its lack corresponds to the comparative lack of formal cosmic lore.

In construction the play lacks unity. The first three acts do indeed give a well controlled account of complex political action, of the shifting motives of self-seeking and ambitious men, enlivened by the critical comments of the two most intelligent of the participants, Constance and the Bastard. The second act, containing all the business before Angiers, is the most lively and varied and entertaining as well as the most massive of all Shakespeare's war scenes. For a political scene, not an actual scene of war, Pandulph's persuading the Dauphin to persist in his plan of invading England (III.4) is brilliant. The opening lines of the play, where John defies Chatillon, are equally brilliant in their swiftness of exposition and make a perfect prelude to the amplitude of the business before Angiers. But in the last two acts the political action loses its width or its intensity: either narrowing to a more personal treatment as in the scenes of Arthur threatened with blinding and of the Bastard in perplexity over Arthur's body; or weakened and scamped as in the scenes of John handing the crown to Pandulph and of his death in the abbey orchard. And, even granted the altered scale of the last two acts, the different scenes in them have no organic relations. In itself the business over Arthur's body is superb, but its energy and its new freedom of style are quite alien to Arthur pleading with Hubert for his sight. This pleading is usually praised as very pathetic or condemned as intolerably affected. It is indeed affected, but to an Elizabethan audience would not have been intolerable. They probably enjoyed it as an exhibition of rhetoric; and as such it is finely built up, an elegant exercise in word-play, like many other scenes in Shakespeare. It does not, however, square very well with the more vigorous excesses of language noted earlier in this chapter: in fact it does not fit naturally into the play at all. The theme of rebellion may be prominent in the last two acts and give some coherence of subject matter, yet it does not arise naturally out of the peculiar virtues of the first three acts; occurring rather as a personal problem than as the master motive affecting the passions and fates of thousands of men. Nor does it knit the two last acts with the great scenes early in the play: it is simply not in our minds as we watch the armies before Angiers.

Nor is there any Morality motive in the background to give a felt though indefinable unity. The Bastard's personification, Commodity, does indeed recall such a figure as

Cloaked Collusion in *Respublica*, but is no more than a detail. England or Respublica herself hardly figures. In his last speech over Arthur's body the Bastard likens her to a bone fought over by dogs and at the close of the play he pronouces the great doctrine of her inviolacy if she is united within herself. But the rest of the play does not greatly reinforce these sentiments. There is for instance very little display of the different grades of society, little to correspond to the humbler characters in *2 Henry VI*, who figure as part of a cross-section of England. Hubert's description of the common people hearing and spreading rumours of Arthur's death might seem to belie this:

> I saw a smith stand with his hammer, thus,
> The whilst his iron did on the anvil cool,
> With open mouth swallowing a tailor's news;
> Who, with his shears and measure in his hand,
> Standing on slippers, which his nimble haste
> Had falsely thrust upon contrary feet,
> Told of a many thousand warlike French
> That were embattailed and rank'd in Kent.
> Another lean unwash'd artificer
> Cuts off his tale and talks of Arthur's death.[40]

But this we read more for itself, for its sheer descriptive poetry, for the delight it gives in showing Shakespeare's true (and in this play new) vein than for any large political motive it sets forth. We do not think of the artificers as members of the body politic.

In sum, though the play is a wonderful affair full of promise and of new life, as a whole it is uncertain of itself. In his next efforts Shakespeare was both to fulfil the promise and achieve a new certainty.

NOTES

1. *Holinshed*, quotation from III, p. 196.
2. *Alexander*, in his *Shakespeare's Life and Art* (London, 1939), p. 85. *Dover Wilson*, in the preface to his edition of the play.
3. *Courthope, History of English Poetry* (London, 1916), Vol. IV, p. 466.

4. *1 Hen. VI*, III.ii.80-3.
5. Probably in 1594. I accept Dover Wilson's dating.
6. *John*, V.iv.33-5.
7. V.v.1.
8. II.i.574-82.
9. II.i.589-90.
10. V.vii.25-7.
11. II.i.177-82.
12. I.i.39-43.
13. II.i.273.
14. *Sir Thomas More*, II.iv.54-5.
15. *John*, III.i.23-4.
16. V.i.12.
17. V.iv.52-7.
18. *Dowden, Shakespeare: His Mind and Art* (9th Edition, London, 1889) p. 170.
19. *John*, I.i.24-26.
20. IV.iii.45-59.
21. V.iii.125-34.
22. V.iii.139-59.
23. IV.i.17-18.
24. *Masefield*, in his comments on the plays in question in his *William Shakespeare* (London, 1911).
25. *Middleton Murry*, in his *Shakespeare* (London, 1936), pp. 159-69.
26. *John*, IV.iii.79.
27. V.vii.79.
28. V.ii.128-36.
29. I.i.214-5
30. II.i.577-88.
31. V.vii.70-3.
32. *Mark Van Doren*, in his *Shakespeare* (New York, 1939). This book is a series of studies of the separate plays, and all my references can be found in the relevant studies.
33. John, II.i.191-4.
34. II.i.159-63.
35. III.i.114-29.
36. III.iv.25-35.
37. II.i.447-60.
38. II.i.68.
39. II.i.63.
40. IV.ii.193-202.

Caroline F. E. Spurgeon

From *Shakespeare's Imagery and What It Tells Us*

King John, from the point of view of imagery, stands quite apart from the series of York and Lancaster plays. The proportion of subjects of the images is markedly different, and they seem to me to play as a whole a much more dominating part in creating and sustaining atmosphere, than is the case in any other "history" play.

The images in themselves are in many ways remarkable, and noticeably vivid. The dominating symbol, which out-dominates all others in the play is the body and bodily action. It is so in an entirely different and infinitely more imaginative way than in *Coriolanus*, where certain functions or persons in the state are rather weariesomely and perfunctorily compared with various parts of the body. Here one feels, on the contrary, that the poet's imagination was intensely and brilliantly alive, dancing with fire and energy like Philip Faulconbridge himself, and a great part of the extraordinary vigour and vividness of the images is due to the fact that Shakespeare seems to have thought more continuously and definitely than usual of certain outstanding emotions and themes in the play in terms of a person with bodily characteristics and bodily movement. It is not possible, especially in a play like *King John*, where Shakespeare's mind is full of a bodily symbol, entirely to separate images of body and bodily action from those of personification, for quite a number might equally well be classified under either heading. In such cases I usually put the image under "Personification" when that seems the most striking aspect, and under "Body" when the special movement appears accentuated.

For the only time in a play of Shakespeare's, images of nature or animals do not head, or almost head, the list, but take definitely the second and third place; by far the greatest number in *King John* are these personifications, reinforced by the large group coming under body or bodily action, making seventy-one listed images in all under these two headings.

The two great protagonists, France and England, the fate that befalls them under the guises of fortune, war and death; the emotions and qualities called into play by the clash of their contending desires: grief, sorrow, melancholy, displeasure, amazement, commodity; the besieged city of Angiers; all these, and other entities or abstractions, are seen by Shakespeare—many of them repeatedly—as *persons*; angry, proud, contemptuous, saucy, indignant, smooth-faced, surly and wanton; sinning, suffering, repenting, kissing, winking, wrestling, resisting, whirling, hurrying, feasting, drinking, bragging, frowning, and grinning. If one looks at it from this angle, one sees that Shakespeare has painted, as a kind of illumination or decorative marginal gloss to the play, a series of tiny allegorical pictures, dancing with life and movement, which, far from lessening the vigour of reality, as allegory sometimes does, increase its vividness and poignancy tenfold.

He sees England, here as elsewhere (cf. *R. II*, III.iii.96 and II.iii.92), as a pale-faced woman, with Neptune's arms clipping her about (*K.J.* V.ii.33), or standing with her foot spurning back "the ocean's roaring tides" (II.i.23), the mother of sons who in war, are reluctantly forced to "march upon her gentle bosom" (V.ii.24) and "fright her pale-faced villages" (*R II*, II.iii.92).

France, on the other hand, in the eyes of Constance, is a "bawd to Fortune and King John" (*K.J.* III.i.60); fortune, who joined with nature to make Arthur great, is corrupted, changed and sins with John, and has taken France with her golden hand and led her on "to tread down fair respect and sovereignty." The besieged city, the centre of their tussle in the early scenes, is thought of throughout as a *person*—a woman—engirdled with a waist of stone, whose brows, ribs, eyes, cheeks, and bosom are referred to, and of whom the adjectives resisting, contemptuous, winking and saucy are used (II.i.38, 215, 225, 384, 410).

And war is dominant throughout, a wild and ruthless force, a mighty being with "grappling vigour and rough frown" (III.i.104). Little pictures like that of the dogs "bristling" and "snarling" for the "bare-pick'd bone of majesty" (IV.iii.145-50), of the "jolly troop of Huntsmen," "with purpled hands, dyed in the dying slaughter of their foes" (II.i.321-3), of the "storm of war" blown up by Pandulph's breath (V.i.17) or the fire of war rekindled by it (V.ii.83), of John being urged to go forth "and glister like the god of war" (V.i.54), not to hide in his palace, but to run

> To meet displeasure farther from the doors,
> And grapple with him ere he come so nigh,
> (V.i.59-61)

enhance the consciousness of the very present "savage spirit of wild war" (V.ii.74) which broods over all.

Beside war stalks death, a terrible and gruesome figure, as seen by Faulconbridge, his dead chaps lined with steel, the swords of soldiers for his fangs, feasting and "mousing the flesh of men" (II.i.352). Or he appears as the skilful and ever victorious enemy, as Prince Henry sees him, who "having prey'd upon the outward parts," directs his siege

> Against the mind, the which he pricks and wounds
> With many legions of strange fantasies.
> (V.vii.15-18)

To the distraught Constance he is a "carrion monster," the embodiment of all that is most abhorrent and repulsive; yet such is her agony that he is to be longed for and fondled and greeted as a lover, so that she is moved to cry,

> O amiable lovely death!
> Thou odoriferous stench! sound rottenness!
> Arise forth from the couch of lasting night,
> . . . . .
> Come, grin on me, and I will think thou smilest,
> And buss thee as thy wife.
> (III.iv.25-35)

It is worth noting that though fortune, war and death are thought of as persons, King John, who is England's greatest enemy, is always pictured as a portion of a body only, which seems in some strange way to create of him something specially sinister and horrible. Pandulph thinks of him as represented by the hand which clasps Philip's in seeming amity, and warns the French king that he may

hold a serpent by the tongue,
A chafed lion by the mortal paw,
A fasting tiger safer by the tooth,
Than keep in peace that hand which thou dost hold.
(III.i.258-261)

He sees that hand dipped in blood, and tells Lewis that when John hears of his approach, if Arthur be not already dead, the king will kill him, and then his people will revolt from him

And kiss the lips of unacquainted change,
And pick strong matter of revolt and wrath
Out of the bloody fingers' ends of John.
(III.iv.166-168)

John thinks of himself as a foot, which, wheresoe'er it treads, finds Arthur as a serpent in his way; and the most terrible and haunting image in the play, which indeed sums up its whole movement, is when his own followers revolt against him as Pandulph prophesied they would, and on the king's bidding them to his presence, Salisbury in their names angrily refuses to

attend the foot
That leaves the print of blood where'er it walks.
(IV.iii.25-26)

At the end too, when John gets his deserts, this same feeling of his being but a fragment—a mere counterfeit of humanity—is again emphasised, this time in his own bitter cry that his heart is cracked and burned, that all the shrouds wherewith his life should sail

Are tuned to one thread, *one little hair,*
(V.vii.54)

and that all his faithful servant and his son are now looking at

is but a clod
And module of confounded royalty.
(V.vii.57-58)

This presentation of King John is a good example of one of the varied ways in which Shakespeare—through imagery—often without our conscious recognition of his method, profoundly affects us.

Long before I noticed, in actual statistics, the unusual predominance in this play of images of personification and bodily action, I was generally aware—as all readers must be—of a marked feeling of vigour, life and energy radiating chiefly from Faulconbridge, and of an overpowering feeling of repulsion for John, hardly accounted for by the text. I now believe these two impressions to be partly due to the subtle effect of the curious but quite definite symbolism, which in a play crowded with pictures of dancing, wrestling, whirling human figures, lets us see the king as a portion of a body only, and that portion at times steeped in human blood.

Readers hardly need reminding how extraordinarily vivid are many of the personifications of emotions, such as Constance's two well-known descriptions of grief (*KJ* III.i.68 and III.iv.93), the later one carrying with it again the same contradictory attraction as in the case of death:

> Grief fills the room up of my absent child
> Lies in his bed, walks up and down with me,
> . . . . .
> Then have I reason to be fond of grief.

John's description of that "surly spirit, melancholy" and his action on the blood, and of "that idiot, laughter" when he is working Hubert to his purposes, is unusual and arresting, as is indeed the whole speech, with its five vivid personifications treading close on each other's heels in the space of sixteen lines (III.iii.31-46). So also Faulconbridge's account of the havoc and flurry wrought among John's few remaining followers when they hear he has yielded to the Pope is unsurpassed in terse pictorial quality:

> And wild amazement hurries up and down
> The little number of your doubtful friends.[1]
> (V.i.35–36)

John is very fond of personifications, but then so are many of the characters—Constance, Faulconbridge, Pandulph and Arthur—and this general tendency causes the strangest things to be visualised as persons—the cannon with their "bowels full of wrath" spitting forth "iron indignation"(II.i.210-12); the midnight bell, with "iron tongue and brazen mouth"(III.iii.37); even the insentient iron with which Hubert is to put out Arthur's eyes, and the fire which heats it, the "burning coal" which has not malice in it and is now cold, but which, if revived, will "glow with shame" for his proceedings (IV.i.106-14).

Like *King Lear*, where the symbol of a body torn and shattered is so vivid that it overflows into the ordinary language—the verbs and adjectives of the play—so here, the consciousness of the aspect of a living person, a face, an eye, a brow, a hand, a finger, with characteristic gestures and actions, is almost continous, and description takes naturally the form of which the following phrases, chosen at random, are a type. They might easily be multiplied two or threefold. "The *coward hand* of France" (II.i.158); "not a word of his But *buffets* better than a *fist* of France" (II.i.464-5); "peace and *fair-faced* league" (II.i.417); "the outward *eye* of fickle France" (II.i.583); "move the *murmuring* lips of discontent" (IV.ii.53); "the *gentle brow* Of true sincerity" (III.i.247); "O, that my *tongue* were in the thunder's mouth!" (III.iv.38); "outface the *brow* Of *bragging* horror"(V.i.49); "the *black brow* of night" (V.vi.17). It is not surprising therefore that we find nearly all the chief emotional themes or moving forces in the play summed up with unforgettable vividness in the little vignette of this type: the selfish motives of the two kings in the Bastard's sketch of

> That smooth-faced gentleman, tickling Commodity;
> (II.i.573)

the terrible position Blanch finds herself in with a newly-wed husband in one army and her uncle in the other, in her amazing and haunting picture of being torn asunder in opposite directions:

> Which is the side that I must go withal?
> I am with both: each army hath a hand;
> and in the rage, I having hold of both,
> They whirl asunder and dismember me;
> (III.i.327-30)

Constance's grief; Arthur's horror at the red-hot iron; the bewilderment and uncertainty of John's followers (V.i.35);

finger tips and footprint; and his mental and physical agony at the end, when forsaken, defeated and dying from a virulent poison which is burning him up internally, making a hell within him, he cries, in answer to his son's query, "How fares your majesty?"

> Poison'd,—ill fare—dead, forsook, cast off;
> And none of you will bid the winter come
> To thrust his icy fingers in my maw,
> . . . nor entreat the north
> To make his bleak winds kiss my parched lips
> And comfort me with cold.
> (V.vii.34-41)

In *Henry VIII*, so far removed in treatment and spirit from *King John*, the dominating image, curiously enough, is again the body and bodily action, but used in an entirely different way and at a different angle from that in the earlier play. The continuous picture or symbol in the poet's mind is not so much a person displaying certain emotions and characteristics, as a mere physical body in endlessly varied action. Thus I find only four "personifications" in the play, whereas in *King John* I count no less than forty.

In a play like *Henry VIII*, a large part of which it has been generally decided on good critical grounds is not written by Shakespeare, the question which immediately presents itself is whether there is any evidence or not in the imagery that one mind has functioned throughout. For our present purpose, however, I suggest we leave this question aside, and look at the way the running symbol works out as a whole.

There are three aspects of the picture of a body in the mind of the writer of the play: the whole body and its limbs; the various parts, tongue, mouth and so on; and—much the most constant—bodily action of almost every kind: walking, stepping, marching, running, and leaping; crawling, hobbling, falling, carrying, climbing, and perspiring; swimming, diving, flinging, and peeping; crushing, strangling, shaking, trembling, sleeping, stirring, and—especially and repeatedly—the picture of the body or back bent and weighed down under a heavy burden. Except for this last, I see no special symbolic reason for the lavish use of this image, other than the fact that it is a favourite one with Shakespeare, especially the aspect of bodily movement, and we find it in the imagery from various points of view in *King Lear*,

Hamlet, *Coriolanus*, *King John*, and in a lesser degree, in *Henry V* and *Troilus and Cressida*.

The opening scene—a vivid description of the tourney on the Field of the Cloth of Gold when Henry and Francis met—with its picture of bodily pomp and action, may possibly have started the image in the poets's mind, as it did in Buckingham's, when after listening to Norfolk's glowing words he asks,

> Who did guide,
> I mean, who set the body and the limbs
> Of this great sport together. . . ?
> (*H.VIII*, I.i.45–47)

Norfolk, trying to restrain Buckingham's anger with the cardinal, says,

> Stay, my lord
> . . . to climb steep hills
> Requires slow pace at first. . .
> . . . . .
> Be advised;
> . . . we may outrun,
> By violent swiftness, that which we run at,
> and lose by over-running;
> (I.i.129–43).

and the utter uselessness of the treaty which was the avowed object of the costly Cloth of Gold meeting is brought home by the amazingly vivid picture of a support or means of walking offered to the human body when no longer capable of any movement at all: the articles were ratified, says Buckingham, "to as much end as give a crutch to the dead" (I.i.171–72). At the end of the scene the original image returns, and the plot against the king is thought of as a body, so that when the nobles are arrested Buckingham exclaims,

> These are the limbs o' the plot: no more, I hope.
> (I.i.220)

We note as we read that many of the most vivid images in the play are those of movements of the body, such as Norfolk's description of Wolsey diving into the king's soul, and there scattering dangers and doubts (II.ii.27-28), Cranmer, crawling into the king's favour and strangling his language in tears (V.i.156-157), Anne's ejaculation about Katharine's deposition, and her divorce from the majesty and pomp of sovereignty, and Katharine's

> sufferance panging
> As soul and body severing.
> (V.iii.15–16)

Wolsey thinks constantly in terms of body movement: among his images are those of a soldier marching in step with a "file"(I.ii.42), a man scratched and torn by pressing through a thorny wood (I.ii.75–76), or set on by thieves, bound, robbed, and unloosed (II.iv.146–47); and in his last great speeches, which, in spite of falling rhythm, I incline to believe are Shakespeare's, he speaks of having *trod* the ways of glory, sees Cromwell *carrying* peace in his right hand (III.ii.435, 440, 445), urges him to *fling away* ambition, and pictures himself successively as a rash *swimmer* venturing far beyond his depth with the meretricious aid of a bladder (III.ii.358-61), a man *falling* headlong from a great height like a meteor or like Lucifer (III.ii.223, 371), and finally, standing bare and *naked* at the mercy of his enemies (III.ii.456).

The image of the back bent under the load recurs five times, and is obviously and suitably symbolic of Wolsey's state, as well as of the heavy taxation. Wolsey complains that the question of the divorce was "the weight that pulled him down"(III.ii.407), and after his dismissal, sees himself as a man with an unbearable burden suddenly lifted off him, assuring Cromwell that he thanks the king, who has cured him, "and from these shoulders" taken "a load would sink a navy,"

> a burden
> Too heavy for a man that hopes for heaven!
> (III.ii.380-85)

The idea of a man falling from a great height is constant in the case of both Wolsey and Cranmer; and the remonstrances made with their accusers are in each case exactly alike:

Press not a falling man too far; . . .
(III.ii.333)

. . . . .

'tis a cruelty
To load a falling man.
(V.iii.76–77)

The queen draws on the same range of bodily similes. She speaks of unmannerly language "which breaks the sides of loyalty," "bold mouths" and "tongues" spitting their duties out, and her description of the great cardinal, with the king's aid going swiftly and easily over the shallow steps until mounted at the top of the staircase of fame is extraordinarily vivid (II.iv.111–15).

The king also uses it with great force when relating his mental and emotional suffering and the self questioning that followed on hearing the French ambassador demand a "respite" [an adjournment] in order to determine whether the Princess Mary were legitimate, thus raising the whole question of the divorce.

He draws a picture of the word "respite" and its effect on him as of a rough and hasty intruder rushing noisily into a quiet and guarded place, shaking and splitting it, forcing a way in so ruthlessly that with him throng in also from outside many other unbidden beings, pressing and pushing, dazed and puzzled with the commotion and the place wherein they find themselves. "This respite," he declares,

shook
The bosom of my conscience, enter'd me,
Yea, with a splitting power, and made to tremble
The region of my breast; which forced such way
That many mazed considerings did throng
And press'd in with this caution.
(II.iv.181–86)

A little later, as he tells the court how he sought counsel from his prelates, he, like Wolsey, pictures himself as a man almost unbearably burdened, groaning and sweating under his load, when he turns to this bishop with the query,

my lord of Lincoln; you remember
How under my oppression I did reek,
When I first moved you.
(II.iv.207–09)

When we trace out in detail this series of images, we recognise that it is a good example of Shakespeare's peculiar habit of seeing emotional or mental situations throughout a play in a repeatedly recurring physical picture, in what might more correctly indeed be called a "moving picture"; because having once, as here, visualised the human body in action, he sees it continuously, like Wolsey's "strange postures" in every form of physical activity (III.ii.112-19).

I must not, however, here be led into the question of authorship, beyond stating that the imagery of *Henry VIII* distinctly goes to prove that in addition to the generally accepted Shakespearian scenes (I.i and ii, II.iii and iv, the early part of III.ii, and V.i), the whole of III.ii and of V.iii are also his, and that he at least gave some touches to II.ii.[2]

It will be seen that on the whole this running imagery in the histories fulfils a somewhat different function from what it does in either tragedy or comedy. It is, as I have said, simpler and more obvious in kind, and although, as in *Richard II*, it sometimes emphasises a leading idea, it does not, as in *Hamlet* or *Macbeth*, shed definite light on the central problem because, with the exception perhaps of Falstaff, there are in the histories no problems of character.

In two of the histories we note that the image symbolism quite definitely—in the method of the comedies—contributes atmosphere and quality to the play. Thus in *Henry V* the feeling of swift and soaring movement is markedly emphasised, and in *King John*, which in treatment stands out from all the other histories, the very marked and consistent "floating" image brings out the contrast between the surging vigorous life in most of the characters in the play, and the negation of life, which is evil, in the person of the cruel and craven king. It thus heightens immensely the imaginative and poetical effectiveness of the theme.

NOTES

1. This type of personification is of course to be found in other Elizabethan writers; but nothing more emphasises Shakespeare's supreme quality than to take things in him which are of the nature of commonplaces and to put them beside others. Compare here, for instance, Dekker's

   > Fantastic compliment stalks up and down,
   > Tricked in outlandish feathers.
   > (*Old Fortunatus*, II.ii)

2. For a fuller discussion of the authorship of *Henry VIII*, see my British Academy Shakespeare lecture for 1931, *Shakespeare's Iterative Imagery*, Oxford University Press, 1931, pp. 22, 23.

Adrien Bonjour

The Road to Swinstead Abbey: A Study of the Sense and Structure of *King John*

In view of the revival of interest in Shakespeare's Histories evinced by the recent publication of three important books of respectable scope entirely devoted to the historical plays, it may not be unseasonable to reexamine the whole question of unity in *King John*—even at the risk of crossing swords with great modern Shakespearean scholars.

Though opinions widely differed as to determining who was the hero, or whether there was one, the traditional verdict on the structure of the play has long been undisputed. Thus, to give a typical instance, the English Arden editor's assertion that the "want of a commanding central figure gives a certain regrettable looseness of structure to the play"[1] is echoed in America by Professor Neilson, who likewise thinks that the play was left without a leading motive or a truly central character."[2] Such critics as did not lavish the winter of their discontent on the structure of this unhappy play passed over the matter in ominous silence, whilst a few of them, like Mr. Middleton Murry, turned to the character of the Bastard Faulconbridge to find at least some radiance of a glorious summer.

This structural blemish must largely be held responsible for the fact, duly registered in the preface to the New Variorum *King John*, that the play "has never been one of the favorite or stock plays, such as *Henry IV* or *Richard III*."[3] To Professor Dover Wilson, moreover, our lack of interest in *King John* seems chiefly due to a certain lack of interest on the part of the author."[4]

Now, the traditional opinion on the structure of the play has indeed been confirmed, independently, by each one of the three great studies alluded to in such a way that the very juxtaposition of the words "unity" and *King John* should, by

Reprinted from *ELH: A Journal of English Literary History*, 18 (1951): 253–74 with the permission of the Johns Hopkins University Press.

now, practically amount to a contradiction in terms. Let us briefly cite the recent authorities.

Professor Tillyard, whom we shall first quote to follow the chronological order, is quite positive: "In construction the play lacks unity."[5] *King John* he holds to be "badly proportioned," even the *Troublesome Reign* is "better balanced" in construction,[6] and his final pronouncement is hardly less categorical: "in such, though the play is a wonderful affair, full of promise and of new life, as a whole it is uncertain of itself."[7]

The late John Palmer, whose *Political Characters of Shakespeare* appeared in the following year, is perhaps more emphatic even. "In 'Richard II' Shakespeare succeeded in merging both the political and the psychological implications of his theme in the human tragedy of a king deposed. He thus produced a play remarkable for its unity of design and temper. In 'King John' he failed to concentrate his material upon a central figure. The political issues were diverse and refractory; they refused to cohere. The play is accordingly little more than a succession of episodes, some of them brilliantly executed."[8]

Finally, in her study of *Shakespeare's "Histories"* published in 1947, Miss Campbell also devotes a chapter to *King John*: though she abstains, as a rule, from making any pronouncements on the artistic aspect of the drama, her theory implicitly carries with it a faulty structure of the play: "Many students, bothered by the unheroic hero, have, like Professor Wilson, tried to set up Faulconbridge as hero. . . . But *King John* with Faulconbridge as hero is a play without form and void, signifying nothing. He is outside the structure of the play as he is outside it historically."[9] However correct such an interpretation of Faulconbridge, as a mere "chorus," may appear if one takes the play to be a mirror of Elizabethan political problems, no doubt that dramatically at least, leaving what Miss Campbell herself admits to be "certainly the most heroic" character in *King John* "outside the structure of the play," spells sad failure indeed.

Nothing could be clearer on that score than Professor Prior's somewhat incisive reference, made in his admirable review of Miss Campbell's study, to "those who have tried, ineptly, to force some kind of unity into their interpretation of this diffuse play by insisting on Faulconbridge as the hero."[10] Indeed, the slight movement of impatience that lurks behind the tell-tale adverb is significant: one is made to feel that such an attempt at mending the loose and faulty structure of the play defeats its very purpose—

> As patches set upon a little breach
> Discredit more in hiding of the fault
> Than did the fault before it was so patched.

Considering the views which have thus been expressed, we may say that so striking a concensus has rarely been attained on a Shakespearean problem; and there is little doubt that authoritative critics would give short shrift to any attempt at vindicating the structure of *King John*. Yet we venture to suggest, and shall endeavour to show, that the question is not definitely settled, though the cumulative effect of the critics' censure proclaims such opinion heretic, and the following contention Quixotic.

If we now try to sum up the main reasons which, according to the critics, account for the defective structure of *King John*, we must single out in the first place the lack of a truly central character. This raises the crucial problem of the hero which needs must be at the very core of any serious discussion of the artistic aspect of the play. Secondly, the lack of a leading motive, or morality motive, which is in its implications closely connected with the preceding problem.

One shudders a little at reopening the question of the hero, that *panier de crabes* of Shakespearean criticism. Yet we have an inkling that the artistic approach to the problem, even if it should not allow us to get within sight of Shakespeare's actual dramatic purpose, may still prove capable of opening fresh vistas. And it is precisely on the question of the hero that a comparison between Shakespeare's *King John* and the *Troublesome Reign* offers the richest prospects.

Concerning the part which is assigned to John—to deal first with the character of the King—we are confronted with two diverging theories. Either King John is definitely not a hero, or he is something like an "unheroic hero." Upholders of the former opinion are numerous, and Furness condensed it in an expressive formula: "the titular hero is not the protagonist."[11] In the Arden editor's words, "John is at one and the same time the swift and resolute warrior leaping fearlessly upon his enemy, the champion of his country against Papal aggression, and the vacillating coward far worse than the murderer of Arthur, toadying to Pandulph and detracting from our sympathy with his awful death by the childishness of his unkingly lamentations. John is neither the hero nor the villain of the piece but an unpleasant mixture of both."[12] "Shakespeare's John is no hero," Professor Dover Wilson chimes in, "he is shifty and, after a show of considerable vigour in the first two acts, while his mother is alive to abet him, weak and cowardly."[13] It would be easy to heap further quotations to the same effect. As to the latter opinion, these are Miss Campbell's conclusions justifying King John as an unheroic hero: "The truth of the matter is that the history play was not often privileged to reflect a hero in its mirror, for that was not the mission of the history play. That Shakespeare was able to depict King John in his conflict with the church as speaking his eloquent defiance of the pope and the foreign priest without making him the great Christian warrior reflects the greatness of Shakespeare and of his understanding of the genre in which he was writing."[14]

Let us now examine what Shakespeare's modifications in his rehandling of the *Troublesome Reign* teach us concerning King John with a special concern for what Professor Prior calls "the dynamic relation between character and plot."[15]

At the very outset of the play we already meet with an apparently slight but significant departure regarding John's title to the throne. Quoting Elinor's confidential remark to her son's slogan:

> Your strong possession much more than your right,
> Or else it must go wrong with you and me:
> So much my conscience whispers in your ear,
> Which none but heaven, and you, and I shall hear.

Professor Dover Wilson, who was probably the first to call attention to it and reveal its importance, points out that "John is the hero of *The Troublesome Reign*, an Englishman, chosen by the barons of England in preference to the foreign Arthur, and fighting against foreigners and the Church of Rome. In *King John*, he is a usurper with no rights in the crown at all."[16] This is quite right, and the point is indirectly confirmed, long before Arthur's death, by a passage of the Bastard's Commodity speech. Faulconbridge vents his indignation at "this all-changing word" which, he cries out,

> Clapped on the outward eye of fickle France,
> Hath drawn him from his own determined aid,
> From a resolved and honourable war,
> To a most base and vile-concluded peace.
> (II.1.583–86)

Now the fact that Faulconbridge, whom we cannot possibly suspect of being partial to the French King, calls the latter's war against John in support of Arthur's claims an "honourable war," again shows on which side the rights are. Thus, if King John is considered as a usurper both by Elinor and Faulconbridge—the two characters who are closest to him in blood and the stoutest supporters of his cause—it is clear that Shakespeare wanted his audience to realize the fact. Yet what are the dramatic reasons that justify so important a shift in the moral situation of the king? Professor Dover Wilson immediately jumps to the conclusion that such a king would have forfeited the sympathy of the Elizabethan audience "from the outset. Shakespeare's John is no hero."[17] This conclusion seems, thus far, a little premature—but more on this later on. The main reason, we think, that accounts for the change is that it allows Shakespeare to make a dramatically much more effective use of Arthur's death. If John is a usurper "with no rights in the crown at all," it is obvious that Arthur, as the legitimate heir, is much more dangerous for him, and consequently, the temptation to do away with the boy—much stronger. And the motive of the crime is of paramount importance for an understanding of the whole drama.

It is no pure accident indeed if the second serious departure from the *Troublesome Reign* concerning John is directly linked with his position towards Arthur; so that to the shift in the moral situation of the King corresponds an equally important shift in his own character and actions. A comparison with the *Troublesome Reign* makes it evident that Shakespeare strongly emphasized and increased the King's guilt. On committing Arthur to the custody of Hubert in the *Troublesome Reign*, John merely expresses the following dilemma:

> keep him safe,
> For on his life doth hang thy Souveraignes Crowne.
> But in his death consists thy Souveraignes blisse.[18]

If this means a lethal wish it could not have been clothed in more ambiguous terms. This short passage is considerably expanded by Shakespeare into a subtle psychological study in which the King reveals his intentions to Hubert by degrees, after quite an elaborate approach to test how far he could trust him, and ultimately orders him to put the boy to death.[19] The contrast between the preparatory work—in which John first flatters Hubert at some length and, still veiling his purpose, mentions his platonic wish for being understood by mere transmission of thought, using conceit alone, puts then Hubert's loyalty to test—and the swiftness and brevity with which the order is finally expressed is admirable[20] and makes the scene one of the finest in the play. What is of particular interest for our point is not only that the scene is almost purely Shakespeare's creation but that John is thus clearly shown commanding Arthur to be murdered like "a very serpent in his way."[21] He has now become a criminal whose duplicity is all the more revolting that at the outset of this very scene, less than twenty lines before the dialogue with Hubert, John had told the boy:

> Cousin, look not sad.
> Thy grandam loves thee, and thy uncle will
> As dear be to thee as thy father was.
> (III.3.2–4)

This piece of irony emphasizes the blackness of John's design and makes his guilt total.[22]

Before we examine the dramatic consequences of this criminal deed—a turning point in the development of the play—let us dwell a while on its motivation. In his pertinent comments on the relation between character and action in Shakespeare's major tragedies, Professor Prior remarks that "we start out with certain premises about the character which have a bearing on the circumstances which open the play and which introduce the disproportion that initiates the action."[23] Now, though every allowance should be made for the fact that *King John* is no major tragedy, this point is general enough to hold good, within a restricted scope, in the case of John, too. The circumstances which open the play are evidently the fact that John is a usurper, Arthur the legitimate heir, and that the political situation arising out of it is further complicated by foreign intervention. As to the premises about the character which have a bearing on those circumstances, they are provided by the revelation—which Shakespeare took great care to make perfectly explicit—that John is a strong adherent of Commodity. And this introduces the disproportion that initiates the capital action, i.e., John's criminal order. Though the Bastard, in his Commodity speech, thrusts with peculiar vigour at King Philip, John is not forgotten either—"mad kings" indeed:

> John, to stop Arthur's title in the whole,
> Hath willingly departed with a part.
> (II.1.562–3)

And the conclusion of this eloquent and racy indictment makes no difference between both sovereigns: "Since *kings* break faith upon commodity." In the measure in which Shakespeare shows us John to be driven by Commodity, he subtly paves the way for the King's sinister action. This is made crystal-clear, retrospectively, by the Legate's words addressed "with a prophetic spirit" to the "green" Dauphin:

> John hath seized Arthur, and *it cannot be*
> That, while warm life plays in that infant's veins,
> The *misplaced John* should entertain an hour,
> One minute, nay, one quiet breath of rest.
> A sceptre snatched with an unruly hand
> Must be as boisterously maintained as gained;
> And he that stands upon a slippery place
> Makes nice of no vile hold to stay him up:
> That John may stand, then Arthur *needs* must fall,
> So be it, for *it cannot be* but so.
> (III.4.131–140)

This may be said to serve as some sort of justification—not moral, of course, but purely dramatic—for John's action. To Pandulph, that other and even greater master in the art of Commodity, such a course of action was inevitable: given the situation and the character of John (which the Legate rightly estimates according to his own standards), the King was bound to act in this way—and the fact that the audience already knows that he has just been acting so, simply adds to the scene the enhancing touch of dramatic irony. Character and action have thus been specifically connected, and the consequences of the deed, to which we must now revert, bring further confirmation of that "reciprocal relationship."

We hinted that John's criminal order was a turning-point in the development of the drama. As a matter of fact, the scene in which the "sly devil" of Commodity drives the King to the length of ordering the murder of Arthur—and, as was pointed out quite recently with reference to Leontes, Shakespeare makes the command to murder a child "the symbol for complete wickedness"[24]—is decisive for the evolution of his character.

Critics have often noted (and sometimes seem to have been puzzled by) the "show of kingly strength and dignity in which John is clothed"[25] in the first two acts, compared to his subsequent weak and cowardly behavior. That John is "the swift and resolute warrior leaping fearlessly upon his enemy, the champion of his country" must be conceded; that he is also "a vacillating coward . . . toadying to Pandulph" is obvious, but—and here we emphatically differ from the Arden editor—*not at the same time*! His "considerable show of vigour" enables him to master the course of events in the first part of the play, until he proves successful enough, in spite of foreign intervention, to beat his enemies and reduce his rival at his mercy. Thus far, though a usurper, he proved a competent ruler. But then he succumbs to the temptation of a criminal deed to ensure his position. And this marks for him the beginning of the end. Dramatically enough he is going to be gradually overwhelmed, in a terrible crescendo, by the rising tide of those events that his very crime broke loose. This is superb craftsmanship on Shakespeare's part.

The last picture we have of John, before the fatal dialogue with Hubert, is that of his triumph before Angiers. His next appearance after the criminal order is at the second coronation. We immediately notice a striking difference: the trend of the lords' expostulations and above all John's own attitude unmistakably show us a man who is no longer sure of himself. The motive for the second coronation is clear enough. When Pembroke thinks it is superfluous, considering that John's

> high royalty was ne'er plucked off;
> The faiths of men ne'er stained with revolt;
> Fresh expectation troubled not the land,
> With any longed–for change or better state
> (IV.2.5–8)

and when Salisbury later adds that it "makes sound opinion sick and truth suspected," they implicitly tell us that it was in order to prevent his "truth" from being suspected, and to forestall precisely such threatening events that John wanted to be crowned again. John himself, who has allowed them to vent their disapproval in almost forty lines, somewhat cryptically alludes to his own fears of Arthur: "And more, more strong [reasons] when lesser is my fear, / I shall indue you with," a hint which is taken over again by Pembroke: "Why then your fears, which as they say attend / The steps of wrong." The very choice of such an expedient gives us the measure of his fears. It is but a desperate effort to forestall the inevitable: thus the scene serves as an adequate prelude to the imminent succession of dreadful blows which are to strike the King and ultimately reduce him to a mere shadow of his former self.

The first of these is not long to come: just when the lords ask him to release Arthur, John is told by Hubert that his order has been carried out. The effect of the news on the lords is such that the King now realizes his terrible mistake:

> They burn in indignation. I repent:
> There is no sure foundation set on blood,
> No certain life achieved by others' death.
> (IV.2.103–05)

What a long remove from the triumphal scene before Angiers! Yet, however striking the contrast, the transition is not too abrupt and has been skilfully prepared, during what turns out to be John's longest absence from the stage, by Pandulph's "prophecy." So that John's repentance, after his first hard blow, vividly echoes the Legate's prophetic phrase:

> For he that steeps his safety in true blood
> Shall find but bloody safety and untrue.
> (III.4.147–48)[26]

The link between this first blow and John's criminal deed is thus perfectly obvious. Misfortunes never come single, and close upon this follows a twofold and even worse evil which, announced at that juncture, intimates that Destiny itself has now turned against the King. A huge army has been levied by the French, and the messenger adds,

The copy of your speed is learned by them;
For when you should be told they do prepare,
The tidings comes that they are all arrived.
(IV.2.113–15)

The turn of the tide is conspicuous if we compare the passage with John's address to the French ambassador at the outset of the play:

Be thou as lightning in the eyes of France;
Fore ere thou canst report I will be there,
The thunder of my cannon shall be heard.
(I.1.24–26)

Then he was the invader, now he is invaded. But this is not all; such swift and secret enemy action would, of course, have been excluded in Elinor's presence in France; yet, as the messenger reveals, "the first of April died / Your noble mother." This time John staggers under the unexpected blow: "What! mother dead! . . . Thou hast made me giddy / With these ill tidings."[27] He does not collapse yet and, after dispatching Peter of Pomfret, quickly sends the Bastard to win back the revolted lords.[28] But once alone, the weight on his heart is expressed in three words, pregnant and moving in their simplicity: "My mother dead!"

Thus, within a single scene, the King has been struck on three planes: in matters political ("my nobles leave me"), in matters military ("my state is braved, / Even at my gates") and in his affections ("my mother dead"); and so obvious is the link between his "bloody villainy" and those crushing events that John again repents his "murder" in strangely eloquent terms:

Nay, in the body of this fleshly land, (*strikes his breast*)
This kingdom, this confine of blood and breath,
Hostility and civil tumult reigns
Between my conscience and my cousin's death.
(IV.2.245–48)

Chaos in the state and chaos in his soul: this is the result of his criminal deed.[29] Therefore, when a critic like Professor Tillyard, who is anything but fresh and green in the old (and ever renewed) world of Shakespearean criticism, writes that "John's greatest crime, his inciting Hubert to kill Arthur, seems to contribute much less to his humiliations than does his own unstable character,"[30] we are tempted to assume that the dramatic significance of the scene has been curiously underestimated. And this all the more that the dramatic irony of the situation is particularly apposite. The time has now come when only Arthur alive would have saved John from the disastrous revolt of the nobles, from the threat of civil war just when a strong enemy power is at his gate, and thus it is the body of the dead child (whose death, though foreign to the King, had none the less been clearly ordered by him) which now deals him the heaviest blow! The nobles could have picked no stronger matter of revolt and wrath than out of Arthur's moving little corpse:

> *Salisbury.* Away with me, and all you whose souls abhor
> th'uncleanly savours of a slaughter-house,
> For I am stifled with this smell of sin.
> *Bigot.* Away toward Bury, to the Dauphin there!
> (IV.3.111–14)

The hour of civil war has struck: if ever criminal intent was "conscientiously connected" with its due punishment, it is in such a fateful irony.

It is only at this point that the King collapses: this is proved, of course, by his act of submission to the Legate. A parallel with the *Troublesome Reign* shows us that Shakespeare wanted to make John's yielding the crown to Pandulph an act of sheer weakness: the Machiavellian motivation of the *Troublesome Reign,* which was "but finely to dissemble with the Pope,"[31] has been completely abandoned. In the rest of the scene, the Bastard eloquently remonstrates with John on such "inglorious league" and tries to rouse his former pluck and spirit against his enemies in terms reminiscent of John's own vigorous speeches to the French, when in full possession of his energy. The King's decline could not have been more vividly represented. No wonder if John, now feeling in Faulconbridge his superior, entrusts him with the "ordering of this present time." John's moral abdication also means his moral end, so that his death through poison, the ultimate blow, destroys but the shadow of a king. Yet, he has expiated, and that is why Prince Henry's and the Bastard's beautiful words at his death in

Swinstead Orchard, far from being incongruous, are fittingly elevated and strangely moving, like a pardon giving lasting rest to a tormented soul. We shall see that this admirable and tragic conception of John's career is given full form and significance only in conjunction with that of the Bastard, to which we must now turn.

As was the case with John, we are also confronted here with two main theories. For a group of critics, Faulconbridge is considered as a mere provider of comic relief (at best a poor substitute for the lack of a central figure),[32] or as the personification of a chorus (and consequently outside the structure of the play). The latter conception, recently propounded by Miss Campbell, was partly anticipated by John Palmer. "Finding no focus for his play in the King, Shakespeare," the critic maintained, "contrives to give at least an appearance of unity by introducing a character whose function it is to provide a point of sanity or reasonable court of appeal in a world at sixes and sevens. The result is a group of political persons and a series of political situations objectively described for what they are worth and the reaction to these types and situations of a character who, while he takes an active part in the events of the play, is also in a sense its chorus."[33]

Another group of critics decidedly follow the New Variorum editor's opinion that "Faulconbridge carried all before him from his first scene . . . to the final words of the play," and tend to make of him the real hero of the drama.[34] Mr. Middleton Murry, for instance, sees in him, "the healthy substance of the corrupt shadow which is King John": to him "The Bastard is a true hero, and he is Shakespeare's first."[35] But it was left to Professor Dover Wilson to present more cogent arguments still in favour of Faulconbridge as a hero, and this not only within the restricted scope of character delineation, but also with regard to the theme of the play. The contrast between Faulconbridge and John was deliberate: the King's character "is evidently drawn as a foil to that of the real hero, the Bastard." Faulconbridge is no less than "an early Henry V, called by fate to prop the falling fortunes of a kingdom ruled by an earlier and meaner Macbeth."[36] Professor Dover Wilson, however, feels bound to admit that the "situation makes awkward stuff for drama."

That Shakespeare enhanced the character of Faulconbridge is obvious—a glance at the *Troublesome Reign* immediately proves it—and we can dispense with the demonstration. Let us however single out a few characteristic points which may help us to bring into focus Shakespeare's actual purpose. What strikes us as an outstanding general feature is a remarkable sense for gradation in the development of this character. The first scene in which the Bastard appears seems to corroborate the views of those critics who reduce him to a mere provider of the comic element in the play. On the face of it, he must be taken less in earnest than in jape, and the King himself gives in a nutshell the very impression of the audience: "Why, what a madcap hath heaven lent us here!"[37] And yet, a close observation with the corresponding scene in the *Troublesome Reign* soon shows how careful Shakespeare was to bring out more favourable shades in drawing the Bastard's character.

When Faulconbridge impudently claims that he is an illegitimate child before the King and his court, Shakespeare takes care that his mother should not be present and has her appear only when the Bastard is left alone.[38] The way in which the confession is wrung from his mother is significant. In the source play, on seeing that his entreaties are of no avail, Faulconbridge loses his temper and utters the most violent threats in order to terrify his mother:

> by heavens eternall lamps I sweare,
> As cursed Nero with his mother did,
> So I with you, if you resolve me not [39]

and, in spite of her tears, his anger still rising, he again repeats the menace. Shakespeare's Bastard, as we know, easily gets her confession by a mere display of wit, and never ceases to be in the best humorous vein. On the one side we had a violent and furious ranter, on the other a somewhat shameless but brilliant wit.

In the following scenes Shakespeare's treatment is no less characteristic: he entirely drops that part of the *Troublesome Reign* in which the Bastard was represented as a suitor to Blanch, whose hand he had been promised by the Queen; not only is it entirely to the Bastard's advantage not to play the part of a frustrated love, but Shakespeare did not want his animosity against the Dauphin to be grounded, even to a slight extent, on such a paltry motive.[40]

So far, we have remained in the periphery. With the end of the second act and the famous Commodity speech, however, a new and deeper aspect of the Bastard's character is disclosed which transcends by far anything we had in the source play: a certain complexity is revealed which was altogether lacking in his rougher prototype. When the Bastard rails at the way men are governed by Commodity, "the bias of the world," a perfect example of which he had just witnessed in the strange alliance of the rival kings, the revolt of his inherent honesty is but partly concealed under a veil of irony. As soon, however, as he realizes that he is about to make a spectacle of himself in his own eyes (just because it looks as if he had been prompted in his outburst by a virtuous indignation), he goes to the other extreme and accuses himself of being urged by sheer despite at not having been tempted as yet by Commodity. From now on he resolves not to care for anything but self–interest: "Gain, be my lord, for I will worship thee."[41] This "English fear of being too openly serious and righteous" (as Professor Tillyard pleasantly puts it), this reaction, which is but a mask for his own sensibility, is not devoid of a certain irony when we remember that Faulconbridge remains loyal, even in adversity, to the cause of the King.[42]

But of all Shakespeare's modifications, the most important for the moral portrait of the Bastard is the scene of the discovery of Arthur's body. Just as John's attitude towards Arthur actually proves to be what we might call the hinge of fate in the development of his career, the Bastard's attitude towards Arthur is likewise the real touchstone of his whole character. In the *Troublesome Reign* the Bastard is not present at the discovery; by having him witness the scene Shakespeare reaches a dramatic and psychologic effect of paramount importance. What comes out clearly is a confirmation of his absolute integrity contrasted to the King's perfidy. His first reaction proves his honesty; it is a revolt of his human sentiments against a criminal deed: "It is a damned and a bloody work, / The graceless action of a heavy hand." Then a silence due to the conflict in his soul between his loyalty to John and the horror inspired by what looks like a political murder; his inner struggle is revealed by the fact that he has no longer a single word to keep the lords from joining the French army, and his mental strain by the violence with which he vents his horror on Hubert, whom he suspects of having shared in the crime:

> Beyond the infinite and boundless reach
> Of mercy, if thou didst this deed of death,
> Art thou damn'd Hubert.
>
> (IV.3.117–19)[43]

He needs the outlet of another dozen lines, pitched to the same tune, before he allows Hubert to protest his innocence. Finally, convinced by Hubert's solemn denegations, he utters his complete perplexity—the time, indeed, is out of joint: "I am amazed, methinks, and lose my way / Among the thorns and dangers of this world." We almost have a glimpse of an early Hamlet. The Bastard here attains, on the spiritual and moral plane, the dignity of a great character. This point can scarcely be overestimated. The Bastard is now the man in whom centers the interest and sympathy of the audience: although we may approve the lords' indignation and side with them against John, the "ex post facto criminal," as soon as it leads them to join their country's enemies, they forfeit our sympathy; whereas the Bastard, who showed as great a disapproval of the deed, not only preserves our sympathy but wins more by keeping true to the King, because he realizes that John, "for all his crimes and his weakness, is the only possible rallying point in the hour of extreme national danger."[44] This moral test confers on the Bastard the depth, one might almost say the "high seriousness," worthy of a dramatic hero—and this precisely at the time when John definitely loses his grasp. The following scene is but the flaming confirmation of the fact. No longer able to cope with the difficulties which assail him and conscious of the Bastard's "dauntless spirit of resolution," the King unwittingly acknowledges a mind now greater than his own and entrusts him with the "ordering of this present time." This is a culminating point in the development of the Bastard's character who, if we may paraphrase one of his own words, has been as great in act as he has been in thought.

No wonder then if some critics, and not among the lesser, wanted to make of him *the* hero of the drama. This theory, however attractively propounded, does but scant justice to the fundamental structure of the play. Our main objection is that it would be difficult to an unprejudiced audience (or reader, for that matter) not to consider John as the hero in the first part of the play, at least up to the triumphal scene before Angiers. Shakespeare, it is true, makes us realize that he is a usurper, but the hint in itself is not sufficient to alienate the sympathy of the audience. John embodies English resistance to foreign enterprise; he disdainfully rejects the French ultimatum; he himself fights at the head of his troops in enemy territory, and exhibits a fair amount of energy and decision; skilled in military and diplomatic problems, he proves a genuine leader at a time when Faulconbridge is little more than a racy and attractive adventurer. The Elizabethan audience certainly approved of him as a resolute defender of his country and, thus far, had very little reason to consider him as unworthy of the crown. It is only from the moment in which his personal ambition drives him, in his fear of Arthur, to a criminal act that everything is rapidly transformed: this is the *primum mobile* of his degradation—and Faulconbridge it is who now rises to the status of a ruler or, more exactly, of *the* hero that the King himself had ceased to be.

In fact, we have to deal here with a deliberately contrasted evolution. John's career represents a falling curve, the Bastard's career a rising curve; and both curves, perfectly contrasted, are linked into a single pattern. The structure of the play is thus remarkably balanced; its pattern can be defined in very simple terms: decline of a hero—rise of a hero. Two characters and their interwoven destinies are gradually unfolded, together with the nation's destiny which they determine. John is at the height of his career at the beginning of the play, where England's destiny lies in his hands. The Bastard reaches his pinnacle at the end of the play, and he then shapes the destiny of the kingdom.

"Decline of a hero": John is at first true unto his mission; though a usurper, he proves a dignified and competent ruler, and his cause becomes one with the cause of the nation. Successful against a coalition of enemies, he reduced his rival at his mercy. But then his ambition urges him to do away with the obstacle embodied in the person of the boy Arthur, the rightful heir; he does not shrink from a criminal act, and thereby places his self–interest above the higher interest of the nation: he thus unconsciously betrays his mission. The penalty for his crime spells internal strife in the state, civil war at the hour of greatest national danger. Responsible for his vicissitudes, overcome by adversity, shaken by the conflict in his soul, he is left a weak, wavering and diminished man, a shadow of his former self. He is no longer a hero and practically hands over his power and authority to the man whose spirit now proves greater than his own, whose grasp on the political situation is much firmer, who, undaunted by adversity, alone proves equal to his task—in a word, to the hero that the Bastard has now grown into. And just because the Bastard never lost sight of the higher interest of the nation, while preserving his loyalty and personal integrity intact, he is now able to prevent a total collapse of the English forces, and succeeds, in restoring national unity: "rise of a hero."[45]

Rise and fall are thus determined by a dynamic evolution of two closely connected characters, and what is more, the course of this twofold evolution illustrates the very leading idea of the whole drama. Structurally, this is perhaps the highest achievement. The Coghillian notion of a governing idea has, of course, preoccupied critics. Some embodied it in Commodity, others in the doctrine of national unity. But they failed to clearly establish the unmistakable link between Commodity and the great lesson of national unity. The plea for national unity, in the Bastard's closing speech, is indeed the moral lesson of the play; but we must go further: what actually makes such unity possible? Now there is only one obvious answer: personal integrity in the man responsible for the destiny of the nation. Internal order, national strength and unity can only be maintained, in a period of crisis, by a ruler whose personal integrity is foremost and allows him to put the interest of the nation above his personal ambition or self-interest. Thus the problem of personal integrity gives the Commodity motive and the motive of national unity their ultimate significance. John fails to maintain national unity at the very moment in which it is most needed to because of the disintegrating effect of his criminal design, both on his people and in himself. To the split in the body politic corresponds a fission in the King's soul: in that sense the personal tragedy of John could be termed "les mains sales." The Bastard, on the other hand, spontaneously sets the interest of the nation above his self-interest; he remains unstained by Commodity and, having kept a total integrity in the most trying circumstances, finally proves to be himself the natural ruler that John had ceased to be. When everything seems to crumble about him in a crisis decisive for the future of the kingdom, he "alone upholds the day," prevents a complete disaster before the enemy and makes the reconciliation between lords and crown possible. Such is the reward of his unswerving loyalty. Nothing is clearer in that respect than his attitude towards Prince Henry, which critics have curiously passed over. When at the very apex of his career, when holding in his hands strength, authority and the future of the kingdom, he naturally, and as a matter of course, offers his oath of allegiance to the young Prince, by much his junior not only in years but in experience. Thus, at Swinstead Abbey, close upon the death of John, he presides over the transmission of power to Henry who, thanks to him, has now become the new King, "born to set a form upon that indigest" which John had "left so shapeless and so rude." This is the final illustration of the governing idea of the play.[46]

Aiming at a "unified understanding of the play as a whole," as was our purpose here, necessarily means leaving aside secondary aspects, such as the way in which minor characters were actively subordinated to the main issues, or the technique of dramatic irony. The latter aspect only would deserve a separate study. Yet, within the scope of the present paper, the few examples of dramatic irony which we have met with—and there are, of course many more—suffice to suggest that such a device has been used to give greater pitch and finish to the development of character and situation which ultimately convey the central idea of the play. Moreover, even minor examples of dramatic irony contribute to a greater cohesion in structure by the numerous connections they imply between different scenes and situations. Indeed, so firm and subtle is this technique in *King John* that it gives us an anticipatory hint of its brilliant use in *Hamlet*, which is probably Shakespeare's highest achievement in dramatic irony.

A few years ago a critic wrote of King John that "the world in which he moved was as chaotic as the man himself," and consequently "Shakespeare could make no dramatic sense of this distempered world. He just stands back and admires the fine confusion."[47] Nay, one might be tempted to remark, sometimes

> un beau desordre est un effet de l'art.

Yet, we suggest that Shakespeare's grasp was already firm enough to allow him to shape such chaos into a highly effective construction. Of course he could step back—even to the viewpoint of Sirius—but when it came to dramatic construction, he proved that he had learned the art of moulding his material into a unified whole.

In sum, far from failing in his dramatic purpose, Shakespeare attained a remarkably balanced structure by a dynamic representation of two closely connected characters whose evolution curves are, in their very contrast, almost perfectly symmetrical. Both leading characters, moreover, as complementary panels of a great diptych, illustrate in their general scheme the governing idea of the play. The organic unity thus achieved is finally enhanced by a series of cross-connections due, chiefly, to a very skilful use of dramatic irony.

In view of such a daring and profoundly original conception of the drama, it might perhaps be fit to revise the traditional theory which takes a faulty structure as granted, and thus reduces *King John* to the status of a *parent pauvre* in the promising family of Shakespeare's early plays.

NOTES

1. *Life and Death of King John,* ed. by Ivor B. John (London, 1939), p. xxxiii.
2. *The Complete Works of Shakespeare,* ed. by W. A. Neilson (Boston & New York, 1906), p. 478.
3. *King John, A New Variorum Edition,* ed. by H. H. Furness, (Philadelphia, 1919), p. x.
4. *King John,* ed. by John Dover Wilson (Cambridge, 1936), p. vii.
5. E. M. W. Tillyard, *Shakespeare's History Plays* (London, 1944), p. 232.
6. *Ibid.,* p. 218 and p. 215.
7. *Ibid.,* p. 233.
8. John Palmer, *Political Characters of Shakespeare* (London, 1945), p. 321.
9. Lily B. Campbell, *Shakespeare's "Histories," Mirrors of Elizabethan Policy,* (San Marino, Calif., 1947), p. 166.
10. Cf. *MP,* XLV (Nov. 1947), 137.
11. Furness, *ed. cit.,* p. x.
12. John, *ed. cit.,* p. xxxi.
13. Dover Wilson, *ed. cit.,* p. xliv and lix.
14. Campbell, *op. cit.,* 167.
15. Moody E. Prior, "Character in Relation to Action in Othello," *MP,* XLIV (May 1947), 237.
16. Dover Wilson, *ed. cit.,* p. xliv.
17. *Ibid.*
18. W. C. Hazlitt, *Shakespeare's Library,* V, 259.
19. *King John,* III, iii, 19–69.
20. *K. John.* Death. *Hub.* My Lord? *K. John.* A grave. *Hub.* He shall not live. (65–66).
21. III.iii.61.
22. The motive of a limited guilt, which we have in the *Troublesome Reign,* is adopted by Shakespeare in *Richard II*: the parallel between John and

Hubert, on the one side, Bolingbroke and Exton on the other, is not devoid of interest.

23. Prior, *op. cit.*, p. 226.
24. Paul N. Siegel, "Leontes a Jealous Tyrant," *Review of English Studies*, I, New Series, (Oct. 1950), p. 307.
25. E. Dowden, *Shakespeare: his Mind and Art* (London, 1889), p. 170.
26. It might be objected that Pandulph, being in a certain measure the villain of the piece, such phrases should not be taken at their face value. But the fact that the audience is aware of the truth of his former "prophecy" about King John confers an undeniable authority on the whole vision.
27. IV,ii,127, 131–2.
28. O, let me have no subject enemies,
 When adverse foreigners affright my towns
 With dreadful pomp of stout invasion!
 (IV.ii.170–72)
29. As in many other plays we have thus an instance of what Mr. Siegel calls the "theme of the tyrant's inner discord reverberating throughout his kingdom" (*op. cit.*, p. 307). Moreover, a fair deal of adversity was required to bring about John's moral collapse, and we very much doubt that Shakespeare ever conceived him as a king of shreds and patches. That John could not actually undergo the test of a criminal deed without some disintegration in his soul should not heighten the critics' contempt: conscience, indeed, does make cowards of us all. He is no thoroughbred villain either, out-gloucestering Gloucester to win the critics' plaudits.
30. Tillyard, *op. cit.*, p. 220.
31. *Troublesome Reign*, p. 291. It should be added that Shakespeare likewise omits the Legate's misgivings at John's submission.
32. Cf. John, *ed. cit.*, p. xxxiii; Palmer, *op. cit*, p. 323.
33. Palmer, *ibid.*
34. Furness, *ed. cit.*, pp. x-xi.
35. John Middleton Murry, *Shakespeare* (London, 1936), p. 161 and 168.
36. Dover Wilson, *ed. cit.*, pp. lx–lxi.
37. I.i.84.
38. The point is slight but well worth considering more closely. Shakespeare, indeed, is not content with removing the Bastard's mother from the scene in which her son claims his illegitimacy in presence of the court; he is careful, moreover, that her arrival should appear as a surprise for the Bastard:

 who comes in such haste in riding robes . . .
 O me! it is my mother; how now, good lady?
 What brings you here to court so hastily?
 (I.i.217, 220–1)

 It is not unlikely that, apart from the Philip Sparrow jest, James Gurney himself was introduced for the sake of pointing out the Bastard's delicacy of feeling, who insists on being left alone with his mother as soon as the conversation turns on the subject of his illegitimate birth.
39. *Troublesome Reign*, p. 238.
40. It may be worth noticing too, that the first altercation between the Bastard and Austria (II.i.134–49) is more to the advantage of the former in Shakespeare than in the *Troublesome Reign*, where the Bastard is more

violent but less witty in his sneer, and Limoges almost seems the sharper of the two.

41. II.i.598.
42. There is one point, however, where he might be regarded as true to his apparent purpose of worshipping but gain. When the King sends him to England to ransack the abbeys ("see thou shake the bags / Of hoarding abbots") he immediately answers: "Bell, book, and candle shall not drive me back, / When gold and silver becks me to come on" (III.iii.12–13). But we must remember that the real purpose of the measure was to make up for war expenses; and when we hear later on that the Bastard has duly performed his mission, there is not the slightest hint that he has made any personal profit in the bargain. Furthermore, we have again a slight touch of dramatic irony: the Bastard has just yielded with great gusto his rights, which should have brought him five hundred ducats a year, in favour of his brother against the dubious honour of Bastardy!
43. And the striking alliteration of the *d*'s gives singular stress to his words.
44. Dover Wilson, *ed. cit.*, p. lxi.
45. This is not the only instance of such a structure in Shakespeare. He used it again in *Henry IV* (as was pointed out to me by Professor Bonnard), if both parts are considered as a single drama, with Falstaff and Prince Hal. Our tentative solution of the problem of the hero has recently been published in French. See *Etudes de Lettres*, XXIII (Lausanne, 1950), pp. 3–15.
46. Far from being outside the structure of the play, the Bastard, we submit, represents an essential component—and so does John. Thus interpreted, the drama can (and perhaps ought to) be appreciated as a work of art, independently of Elizabethan policy. Our interpretation does not, of course, exclude the probability of the drama being a political mirror, as advocated by Miss Campbell. Yet we suggest that topical points have decidedly been subordinated to the requirements of dramatic art, and share Professor Prior's opinion that "historical studies cannot answer the ultimately important questions about the meaning of imaginative works." Cf. *MP*, XLV (Nov. 1947), 138.
47. Palmer, *op. cit.*, p. 323.

James L. Calderwood

Commodity and Honour in *King John*

Most critics of *King John*, even since the advent of the now no longer new criticism, have given their attention chiefly to the source problems of the play, especially to the relationship between *King John* and *The Troublesome Raigne*. As one result Shakespeare's play as a work of art in its own right has largely been ignored. The sporadic vigour of its verse and the vitality of the Bastard have often been remarked—the Bastard's Commodity speech is usually cited as a conspicuous example of both—but not so much for what they accomplish in the play as for what they tell us about Shakespeare's maturing dramatic powers, that is, for what light they cast before and after, but not on, the play in which they appear. Although the Commodity speech is indeed central to *King John*, it serves as more than an isolated instance of Shakespeare's progress from ceremonious rhetoric to a more lean and trenchant utterance: it not only underscores the principle of Commodity as one of the prevailing forces in men's lives, but by the extremity of its statement it also suggests the ethical imbalance which runs through the play. The view I am proposing is that *King John* represents a dramatic crucible in which Shakespeare explores and tests two antagonistic ethical principles, Commodity and Honour. The opposition between Commodity, or scheming self-interest, and Honour, loyalty in general but in its highest form loyalty to the good of England, comprises a basic theme to which almost every action and character of the play is vitally related. In its political implications the theme explores the qualities demanded of the kingly character; in its general pervasiveness and in its specific application to John and the Bastard, it imparts to the play a unity of structure generally denied it.[1]

Reprinted from *University of Toronto Quarterly*, XXIX (1960): 341–56 by permission of the author and University of Toronto Press.

Both elements of this theme are conspicuous early in Act I when the Bastard is offered a choice between personal gain—the land now declared legally his—and the honour of being acknowledged Coeur-de-lion's son. In accepting the latter, however, the Bastard does not choose nobly to sacrifice self-interest. Honour only apparently has much to do with his decision; he clearly associates it with Coeur-de-lion when he tells John that his supposed father, Faulconbridge, was "A soldier by the honour-giving hand / Of Coeur-de-lion knighted in the field."[2] But later, speaking to his now half-brother, he oversimplifies the alternatives when he says, "My father gave me honour, yours gave land." At the moment of choice he did not actually believe himself the son of Coeur-de-lion—later in the scene he solicits his mother for his real father's name. Instead, he had accepted honour as an investment in the future—"Brother, take you my land, I'll take my chance"—gambling on the "chance" that his continued association with John and Eleanor would produce dividends. His choice, then, has involved a public proclamation of honour, a private acceptance of self-interest. As we shall see later, this is the principal strategy by which Commodity makes its "smooth-faced" way in the world of *King John*. But, as we shall also see, the Bastard's motives in this scene undergo a change, or, more precisely, they pass through a series of changes that constitutes one of the first explorations which this play makes of the relationship between Commodity and Honour.

When he makes his choice, and immediately afterwards, the Bastard embraces self-interest while professing honour; but once he has achieved his immediate aim, the mocking and even flippant ironies of his speech assume a different cast. The opening lines of his first soliloquy are suggestive:

> Brother, adieu; good fortune come to thee!
> For thou wast got i' th' way of honesty.
> (*Exeunt all but Bastard.*)
> A foot of honour better than I was;
> But many a foot of land the worse.

The public graciousness is subjected, after the exit, to the diminution of private irony, the "way of honesty" to the measure of material gain. But the admission is also made, and privately, that the gain of new honour has been attended by the loss of old honour-legitimacy. The ambiguity of statement mirrors while it explores the ambivalence of the Bastard's moral self-consciousness. Yet it is only after he learns the truth of his parentage that he becomes genuinely involved with his new identity and graduates from the endorsement of honour as a pragmatic good to an avowal of it even against social scorn. The violence of his advocacy of his mother here is not, despite surface resemblance, the brash impetuosity of a Hotspur; it follows logically from, and reflexively illuminates, the fact that his soliloquy on "new-made honour" was self-satire as well as social satire. However, if in this first scene we are seeing the Bastard's growth of moral awareness, that growth is still embryonic. At the conclusion of the scene his conception of honour, though altered, remains unsophisticated; it is regarded less as the inherence of ethical values than as a transferable award which one can receive through inheritance or merit through physical exploit. The Bastard has not yet outgrown Hotspur. Nevertheless he has formed one resolution which we would do well to remember. Observing that flattery and deceit serve as "sweet poison for the age's tooth," he adds, "Which, though I will not practise to deceive / Yet, to avoid deceit, I mean to learn."

In Act II, lines 156–158, another choice is offered, not to the Bastard but to Arthur. The alternatives, however, are not the same as earlier. When John says,

> Arthur of Bretagne, yield thee to my hand,
> And out of my dear love I'll give thee more
> Than e'er the coward hand of France can win . . .

he not only characterizes the motives of France, and of himself, but also places Arthur in the position of having to choose between two kinds of Commodity and thus to announce by implication his self-interestedness. Arthur remains silent, refusing the terms of the choice not because he recognizes the phrasings of deceit but simply because he is utterly lacking in self-interest—"I am not worth this coil that's made for me." Constance, however, has no scruples about choosing for him, and she is willing to take what the "hand of France can win." Her self-interest is masked, not consciously perhaps, within the cliche of doting motherhood, and Eleanor is probably close to the truth when she says, "Out, insolent! thy bastard shall be king / That thou mayst be a queen, and check the world!"—which, incidentally, tells us as much about accuser as about accused. What Constance fails to realize, however, is the pervasiveness of Commodity. Perceiving it in John, she does not see that it is also the "bias of the world." It is perhaps because her own self-interest is not consciously masked that she fails to penetrate the conscious masks of others—of France in particular. Certainly a clearer awareness of the issues involved would have made her realize the irrelevance of exhorting Lewis to defy John on the basis of "thine honour, Lewis, thine honour!"

The position of Constance and Arthur is analogous to that of Blanche, who, like Arthur, achieves a genuine alliance with Honour only to find that Commodity, that "daily break-vow, he that wins of all," wins most from those who are innocently unaware of his nature. Only Blanche and the Bastard are untainted by the epidemic of deceit in which the marriage of expediency is conceived. Spurred by Eleanor to "Urge them while their souls / Are capable of this ambition," John delivers his proposal to France (Act II, scene 1, lines 484–86):

> If that the Dauphin there, thy princely son,
> Can in this book of beauty read, "I Love,"
> Her dowry shall weigh equal with a queen.

France hastily directs Lewis's attention to Blanche's face, and in that "book of beauty" Lewis finds, with remarkable decision, that he can indeed read *I love.* In fact, he reads it aloud and so grandiloquently that he draws the Bastard's immediate scorn for such patent dissemblance. Blanche informs Lewis in private that she is subservient to John's royal will; however, refusing to participate in the general deceit, she candidly adds, "Further I will not flatter you, my lord, / That all I see in you is worthy love." Despite her private misgivings, when John asks for her decision Blanche publicly pledges him her loyalty by saying, "That she is bound in honour still to do / What you in wisdom still vouchsafe to say." But in the world of *King John* this sort of honour, so innocent as to misconstrue Commodity as "wisdom," has little survival value. After her marriage and with the renewal of war, Blanche strives to expand her honour to encompass her obligations to both John and her husband Lewis. The result, as she says (Act III, scene 1, lines 328–30), is that

> I am with both; each army hath a hand,
> And in their rage, I having hold of both,
> They whirl asunder and dismember me.

Like Arthur, Blanch represents honour in a world of Commodity, and like Arthur, she is whirled by the forces of Commodity to her destruction.

Despite its dominant station in the hierarchy of men's motives, Commodity by no means receives the stamp of Shakespeare's dramatic approval. If it is the force against which Honour is tested, it is itself in turn tested by Honour. Whirled asunder by the two armies of Commodity, Blanche is not an object of derision but of sympathy. Yet the Honour she has embraced is found wanting—deficient because it is naive, because it is untempered by awareness, because it has survived no inner tests. Untested within, it succumbs inevitably to the test of Commodity from without. Blanche, like York in *Richard II*, yields to the will of her sovereign in the best accord with Tudor Doctrine; but her problem, like York's, is complicated by the presence of two sovereigns. If Shakespeare is glancing at Tudor Doctrine, then, as Lily Campbell feels he so often is,[3] it is not to extol that doctrine so much as to explore it, to test it dramatically, not in political but in human terms. The judgment of the drama is that the doctrine is simply too inflexible, too arbitrary, too unrealistic. Blanche's attempt to solve her insoluble dilemma leads to her destruction; York, reading the script of Tudor Doctrine with strict literalness, acts out his proper role and in doing so is deprived of essential humanity. Nevertheless, Shakespeare is no more deluded by the efficacy of Commodity than he is by the virtue of Honour; in the very process of discrediting Honour, commodity is itself discredited. That is, if there is any suspicion that Shakespeare is endorsing Commodity in *King John*, it should be dispelled by observing that Commodity is the means by which Shakespeare achieves satiric diminuation in the play. Austria, France, and Lewis, not to mention John, are all rendered ridiculous by the very fact that even among men so thoroughly Commodity-conscious, Commodity must be concealed behind a facade of Honour. The rents in the facade are the windows of dramatic deflation, as we can see, perhaps more clearly, with the English nobles.

Salisbury and Pembroke have been too often regarded as a momentarily dissonant but then beautifully harmonic chorus

Salisbury and Pembroke have been too often regarded as a momentarily dissonant but then beautifully harmonic chorus singing the praises of national unity for English audiences intensely patriotic following the defeat of the Spanish armada. If this is all that Shakespeare's audiences saw in the nobles—and there is no guarantee of that—then Shakespeare was giving his audiences a good deal more than they deserved. To begin with, the nobles' criticism of John's second coronation (Act IV, scene 2) is not, as it might seem, merely the constructive advice of loyal subjects. We should note the opening of the following scene:

> *Sal.* Lords, I will meet him at Saint Edmundsbury.
> It is our safety, and we must embrace
> This gentle offer of the perilous time.
> *Pem.* Who brought that letter from the Cardinal?
> *Sal.* The Count Melun, a noble lord of France;
> Whose private with me of the Dauphin's love
> Is much more general than these lines import.

The Bastard's greeting a moment later—"Once more to-day well met, distempered lords"—establishes the day of this exchange as still that of the previous scene. Either the nobles have been in communication with the Dauphin for some time then, or Melun's delivery of the letter to Salisbury represents Lewis' first overture. If the former is true, the nobles clearly were traitorous even before their criticism of John in scene 2, and if the latter is true, Lewis must have had some prior indication of their willingness to cooperate, else why send Melun to these particular nobles? In either event, suspicion is cast upon the nobles' high indignation at the announcement of Arthur's supposed death; and their protestations of dutiful subservience to John in the same scene (e.g., Salisbury's "Since all and every part of what we would / Doth make a stand at what your Highness will," Act IV, scene 2) acquire retrospectively an ironic, if not a hypocritical, cast. Moreover knowing that the nobles have already decided for their "safety" to embrace the "gentle offer of the perilous time," we can see that in their speeches over Arthur's body, Commodity, now motivating treason, has become for Shakespeare a most incisive means for subverting the lofty pretensions of offended Honour. Tillyard has rightly observed that "the levity of [the nobles'] reasoning" here is betrayed "by the extravagance of their sentiments";[4] however, the point is not so much that their reasoning is specious logically as that it is specious ethically. If their premise of Commodity is granted, their real reasoning is sound, if not terribly subtle: to take advantage of an ideally fortuitous opportunity for masking dishonourable action behind honourable indignation. Their roles are overacted, to be sure—especially Salisbury's, whose 25 lines of bombast are as devoid of genuine sorrow as the Bastard's single sentence is freighted with it. Pembroke, however, displays their real line of reasoning and demonstrates at the same time considerable genius for rationalization when he says that the heinousness of Arthur's murder "Shall give a holiness, a purity, / To the yet unbegotten sin of times"—for example, he would probably add, the not quite unbegotten sin of their own imminent treason.

When we see them next (Act V, scene 2), the nobles are still cloaking Commodity in the vestments of Honour. The business of signing to treason dispatched, Salisbury laments for 31 lines, all after the fact, that

> . . .such is the infection of the time,
> That, for the health and physic of our right,
> We cannot deal but with the very hand
> Of stern injustice and confused wrong.

He is perfectly accurate in everything, provided "right" be changed to read "profit"; and his conclusion, with its wish that "these two Christian armies might combine / The blood of malice in a vein of league," would be impressive indeed, if it did not remind us that the two nations already joined once in such a league—the very league that called forth the Bastard's speech on Commodity. Or again, when Salisbury's grief produces what Lewis calls "this honourable dew / That silverly doth progress on thy cheeks," it is a little difficult not to hear an echo of Salisbury's own comment when Hubert wept at the sight of Arthur's body: "Trust not those cunning waters of his eyes, / For villainy is not without such rheum." Although Lewis' answering speech is as fraught with noble sentiment as was Salisbury's, it is quite clear that both are speaking the language of ceremony on a stage of Honour. Even Lewis finally wearies of the extended hypocrisy and puts the matter in its real light by saying,

Come, come; for thou shalt thrust thy hand as deep
Into the purse of rich prosperity
As Lewis himself; so, nobles, shall you all . . .

Needless to say, this view of Salisbury and Pembroke implies that their final and seemingly glorious reversion to the English cause should be regarded with more than a little suspicion. Before dealing with that, however, let us return to the first half of the play again and examine John and the Bastard in the light of the theme we have been tracing. In the opening act we saw Shakespeare using the Bastard's changing attitudes towards Commodity and Honour as indices of his ethical development. Later, in Blanche, we saw internally untested Honour tested externally by and succumbing to the pressures of Commodity, and still later, in the English nobles, we saw Commodity used as satiric device to deflate pretensions of Honour. In all these instances Commodity and Honour were Shakespeare's principal means of characterization, and he also uses them to characterize John and the Bastard. We should not forget, however, that the process works reciprocally, that the persons in the drama are not only characterized by, but also characterize, the ethical principles. By her adherence to Honour in a world of Commodity, Blanche is characterized as honourable in what would seem to be an ideally pure manner. Yet she in turn, by proving too innocent to survive the pressures of Commodity, characterizes pure Honour as an impracticable moral guide. The nobles, on the other hand, have survived and even prospered so far largely because their Commodity was not unadulterated, because they were not unaware of at least the habiliments of Honour and of the manner in which these can be worn to further the ends of Commodity. Their successful application of Commodity, however, is such only within the illusion of life created by the drama; their successes within are simultaneously failures from without, from the perspective of audience or reader, and the inversion of effect is produced by satiric techniques. With the nobles we have seen Commodity thrust to the extreme of treason; with John we shall see it thrust to the extreme of murder.

During the first, and inferior, half of the play John represents for the most part "An English King," in Tillyard's phrase. Although his occupation of the throne is for self-interest, yet his interests coincide up to a point with those of England, for despite his virtues Arthur hardly qualifies as a desirable king. His youth, the domination of Constance, and the partisanship of the French all argue against the application of the rule of primogeniture. At any rate, when the play opens John not only is king but is kingly. He also has, significantly, the approval of Fortune.

As in *Richard III*, but less obtrusively, the supernatural invades the field of human action in *King John*. Events are determined by decision based upon either Commodity or Honour, but once the human decisions have been made, a supernatural judgment is pronounced upon them. Sometimes these judgments take the form of prophecy or of prophetic invocation—as with Constance, Pandulph, and Pomfret; at others they are to be inferred from the behavior of wind and sea; at still others they are identified as a quality of "the times." For example, early in Act II Fortune graces John's decision to invade France through the instrument of the unfavourable, to France, winds which delay Chatillon's return to warn King Philip. In Act IV, scene 2, when John receives tidings of the French invasion, Fortune has shifted sides. Early in Act III Constance confirms the fact that John still stands in grace when she tells Arthur that Fortune "adulterates hourly with this uncle John." It is at this point, however, that John's fortunes begin to change for the worse. He and Philip have just negotiated the betrothal of Blanche and Lewis, the bargain that elicited the Bastard's speech on Commodity. The indignant Constance delivers a prophetic invocation that "No bargains break that are not this day made. / This day, all things begun come to ill end." (Act III, scene 1, lines 93–94.) The bargain marriage league is indeed immediately broken, and John, who has begun to act upon Commodity, has made the first fatal step on the road to an "ill end."

Since John does win the ensuing battle with France, it would appear that he still remains in grace. But the victory and the capture of Arthur are at best a mixed blessing. Combining the agents of wind and sea in his metaphor, Philip (Act III, scene 4) implies that Fortune is still with John:

> So, by a roaring tempest on the flood,
> A whole armado of convicted sail
> Is scatterèd and disjoin'd from fellowship.

However, Pandulph immediately assures him that "all shall yet go well," and a little alter in this scene Pandulph says to Lewis:

No, no; when Fortune means to men most good,
She looks upon them with threat'ning eye.
Tis strange to think how much King John hath lost
In this which he accounts so clearly won.

Thus, although seeming to have remained the same, John's fortunes have actually altered in accordance with Constance's prophecy. But the Commodity marriage is not the sole or the most important reason for the decline of John's fortunes; it is only a prelude to the central scene of *King John* (Act III, scene 3) where the superb dramatic tension created by John's Iago-like probings of Hubert culminates in the terse agreement to murder Arthur:

K. John. Death.
Hub. My Lord?
K. John. A grave.
Hub. He shall not live.

This scene is central to *King John* both thematically and structurally. Having condemned to death the one person who utterly lacks a sense of self-interest, John serves both to damn and to be damned by Commodity. Prior to this scene the pace of play has been leisurely, the action deliberate, the scope of events wide. From this point on the scope narrows and the action becomes precipitous; scene now gives way to scene with abruptness and rapidity as the structure of the play mirrors while it helps display John's hurtle towards destruction. Fortune has clearly shifted, and as Pandulph says to the temporarily dispirited Lewis (Act III, scene 4, lines 146–48):

John lays you plots; the times conspire with you;
For he that steeps his safety in true blood
Shall find but bloody safety and untrue.

In the scene in which Hubert threatens to put out Arthur's eyes (Act IV, scene 1), the current of the action momentarily eddies. The scene has been much maligned for many good reasons, but the blatant sentimentality does serve a dramatic purpose. The principal function of the scene is to intensify John's guilt by a graphic dilation upon the cruelty of his intentions towards Arthur. This intensification of guilt is partly accomplished by contrasting John's orders with Hubert's attempts to carry them out, for if in John Commodity is now motivating cruelty and murder, in Hubert it is being sacrificed to Honour and mercy. Arthur is again the epitome of selflessness. Hubert has accepted John's commission partly from blind loyalty and partly from a desire for gain; however, when he finally relents, Hubert clearly renounces self-interest: "I will not touch thine eye / For all the treasure that thine uncle owes." His decision constitutes not only a renunciation but also an endangering of his self-interest—"Much danger do I undergo for thee." Hubert's later treatment at the hands of John and the English nobles illustrates once more that in *King John* Honour must be its own reward.

During the first half of the play the Bastard—"that mixture of greatness and levity," as Dr. Johnson saw him—is motivated by a spurious sense of Honour alloyed with some amount of self-interest. His levity rather than his greatness predominates. He is brash and reckless, quick both to perceive and to offer insult. His major interest is in acquiring prestige by avenging his father's death at the hands of Austria. However, his resolution in Act I to learn the ways of deceit, not to employ them but to recognize their employment by others, has not gone unobserved. In Act II not only is he a sardonic critic of hypocrisy and pseudochivalric bravado but he is also an ironic parodist of the absurd extremes to which Commodity inclines kings and armies. When the Citizen of Angiers (or Hubert, as the First Folio more logically has it) denies both armies entrance to the city, the Bastard with tongue in cheek exhorts John and Philip to join forces temporarily and, as John paraphrases him a moment later, "lay this Angiers even with the ground; / Then after fight who shall be king of it." Their acceptance of his ironic proposal reveals the folly to which men are led when a myopic preoccupation with schemes of self-interest blinds them to the fact that means may destroy ends. The *reduction ad absurdum* of Commodity has been reached.

However, the Bastard's ethics are by no means unquestionable. If he can recognize and deflate Commodity, yet he is willing to fight in one of its armies. Even his criticism of Commodity prior to the Commodity speech lacks the solidity of moral conviction, and when this criticism culminates in the Commodity speech it is not to renounce but to embrace Commodity. Both Tillyard and Bonjour contend that the final lines of the speech—"Since kings break faith upon Commodity, / Gain, be my lord, for I will worship thee"—are uttered merely in self-deprecation and that the Bastard never acts upon them. I agree that he is incapable of real villainy, and yet the commission John gives him to ransack the monasteries is obviously a reward for his rescue of Eleanor and his acquittal of himself in battle. To be sure, there is no mention of his having profited from the enterprise; however, the very nature of the commission would seem to imply tacitly that some of the liberated "angels" should be reincarcerated in the Bastard's pocket. At any rate, at the conclusion of Act III neither the Bastard nor John represents the lack of self-interest or the sense of responsibility to England demanded of the kingly character.

Act IV, scene 1, as mentioned earlier, serves to intensify John's guilt; and in scene 2 we find that the nobles have grown seditious. John's second coronation is a touchstone of his political insecurity. His situation worsens when Hubert falsely reports Arthur's death. Attempting to see John as a tragic hero, Bonjour finds him genuinely repenting of his decision to do away with Arthur. Certainly he regrets the decision once the supposed murder is announced, but it is difficult to believe that his regret is based on anything but the failure of the murder to serve his designs. When the nobles stalk out, John says, "They burn in indignation. I repent," and the juxtaposition of his political loss with his personal repentance is too obvious not to suggest a causal relation. Further on, when Hubert informs him that Arthur is not dead after all, John says, "Doth Arthur live? O, haste thee to the peers," and again the immediacy with which his thoughts flit from Arthur to his own political interests is revealing. Finally, since his desire for Arthur's death was rooted in Commodity, any genuine repentance on his part would involve a renunciation of Commodity. Instead, our next glimpse of him shows him in the act of capitulating to Pandulph (Act V, scene 1,), not of course for religious reasons but merely for Commodity. Receiving the crown back from Pandulph, he says:

> Now keep your holy word. Go meet the French,
> And from his Holiness use all your power
> to stop their marches 'fore we are inflam'd.

Clearly, the exchange of the crown carries the same stamp as the marriage league of Act II: it is merely a bargain entered into by John to prevent his deposition by the French.[5]

If John has sunk to contemptible depths of Commodity, even to the point of shaming An English King, the Bastard has steadily risen towards the genuine Honour befitting An English King. His words over the body of Arthur are the major indication of his spiritual growth; yet without some preparation this speech would mark an altogether too abrupt deepening of character—and Shakespeare provides the preparation. Returning from his forays upon the monasteries (Act IV, scene 2) the Bastard meets the irate departing nobles—"With eyes as red as new-enkindled fire," as he tells John. His first words to John are terse and restrained, suggesting a grave preoccupation. Disturbed by rumours and prophecies abroad, by news of the invading French and by the report of Arthur's death, he cannot help but suspect John. His remark that he has seen the nobles

> And others more, going to seek the grave
> Of Arthur, whom they say is kill'd to-night
> On your suggestion,

is most carefully phrased. He withholds comment on the nobles' accusation and in doing so tactfully offers John a chance to deny his guilt. It is in this scene that we see the Bastard beginning to make a distinction between An English King and the man John as king. His respect for the former prevents him from too hastily condemning the latter. Already he has come a good distance from the brash and impetuous young man of the first three acts. In the following scene 3 he again reveals his emotional growth by responding to Pembroke's "Sir, sir, impatience hath his privilege" with "'Tis true, to hurt his master, no man else"—a reply clearly demonstrating insight into his own earlier rashness.

All this prepares for the following scene when, over the body of Arthur, the Bastard makes the first of two major choices between Commodity and Honour. With England invaded, her forces divided and her king ineffectual, it is plainly to his advantage to follow the departed nobles. Yet when he says, "I am amaz'd, methinks, and lose my way / Among the thorns and dangers of this world," his words not only express his present bewilderment but also represent his sudden awareness of the superficiality of his previous ethics. The man of action becomes for an intense moment the man of thought. Shakespeare compresses within the remainder of the Bastard's speech his acceptance of Arthur's claim to the succession, his declaration against John as the man of self-interest, his recognition of England's loss of fortune, and his decision to ally himself, not with John, but with England. In short, the Bastard renounces with evident risk the principle of Commodity and commits himself to the highest form of Honour. By so doing, he becomes morally worthy of the crown.

It is no accident that immediately following the Bastard's speech we are shown (Act V, scene 1) John demonstrating his own moral weaknesses by capitulating to Pandulph and enduring unremarked such hypocritical sarcasm as Pandulph's "But since you are a gentle convertite, / My tongue shall hush again this storm of war." Indeed, far from feeling any sense of mortification, John is overjoyed, rejoicing that the prophecy of his deposition has come true differently than he had thought: "I did suppose it should be on constraint, / But, heaven be thank'd it is but voluntary." By such an act and such rejoicing, John forfeits all moral right to the crown. Not only by the juxtaposition of the two scenes, but also by the disparity of their attitudes within this second scene, the Bastard and John are thrown into dramatic contrast. John's attitude is obvious from, among other things, his choice of pronouns: "Would not *my* lords return to *me* again..."; "The legate of the Pope hath been with me, / And *I* have made a happy peace with him." The Bastard, on the other hand, speaks only of "us": "Shall *we*, upon the footing of *our* land..." (my italics). The absence of any ethical principles in John has resulted in the elevation of self-interest above the good of England. In the moment of crisis John has only himself to rely upon—and his self is a moral vacuum. Still trying to escape, or perhaps still unaware of, moral realities, he degenerates into feeble vacillations. The Bastard, despite his earlier suspicions, is clearly dumbfounded by John's total collapse. When he tries to stir him to action by defining the ideal reactions of a king (lines 43–61), the Bastard is defining himself. When he denounces as "inglorious" the league John has made with Pandulph, his convictions are those of An English King. Finally, when John says weakly, "Have thou the ordering of this present time," his words represent a symbolic relinquishment of the crown to the man who deserves it morally but not legally.

Yet if the Bastard has committed himself to Honour, it is no such ingenuous Honour as that which precipitated Blanche to destruction. It has at least once already withstood the severest inner tests of Commodity, and it has proven shrewdly adept at discerning Commodity in others. When (Act V, scene 2) he berates the French, the Bastard speaks not only as John's surrogate but as the symbol of An English King: "Now hear our English King, / For thus his royalty doth speak in me." The ambiguity of "royalty" is deliberate, for as the son of Richard I the Bastard has some claim to literal truth, and certainly his scornful defiance here by no means mirrors the John for whom he ostensibly speaks. However, the Bastard is not nearly so confident as he makes out; his "brave," as Lewis calls it, should remind us of his satiric deflations of chivalric bravado earlier in the play. What he is doing here, it seems apparent, is turning Commodity against itself, attempting to prevent the possible overthrow of England by deluding the superior French forces into arbitration. In short, he is using the techniques of Commodity in the service of Honour.

The following scene (Act V, scene 3) is particularly noteworthy. The shortest of the entire play, its very brevity calls attention to it as the culmination of a series of continuing contrasts between the Bastard and John. We have just seen the Bastard's shrewd attempt to delude the French with solitary defiance as he plays the symbolic role of An English King. Now we are shown John completely incapacitated—not by poison, for he has not yet gone to Swinstead Abbey where the poisoning occurs, but by a fever. The fever, which has troubled him for some time, is less physiological than psychological; it represents perhaps a form of divine punishment for Arthur's death as well as John's unconscious awareness that in moral reality he is not longer king. His symbolic relinquishment of the crown to the Bastard earlier is confirmed by the arrival of a Messenger with the words:

> My lord, your valiant kinsman, Faulconbridge,
> Desires your Majesty to leave the field
> And send him word by me which way you go.

This is not, one notes, the request of a subject, but the order and "desire," of one who is quite aware of his authority. Nor is John's prompt obedience to be taken lightly; feverish or not, the head of an army does not withdraw from the field without his withdrawal being interpreted as a signal of disaster. But John is only the titular head of England now and his withdrawal is not in the least damaging; the Bastard remains on the field, clearly in command, and, as Salisbury ruefully remarks, "In spite of spite, alone upholds the day." No sooner does the Bastard "desire" John to leave the field than Fortune turns against the French, for immediately after John acquiesces to the Bastard's order the Messenger adds:

> Be of good comfort; for the great supply
> That was expected by the Dauphin here,
> Are wreck'd three nights ago on Goodwin Sands.

The fact that the supply ships were wrecked "three nights ago" does not alter the fact that Shakespeare chooses to present the information dramatically at the precise point. Later (Act V, scene 5, the same information is reported to Lewis along with the news that "The Count Melun is slain; the English lords / By his persuasion are again fallen off." In short, the ill fortune that has dogged the English since John's decision to murder Arthur (Act III, scene 3) is reversed when the Bastard's symbolic private deposition of John is publicly confirmed by John's departure from the battlefield.

There are two obvious objections to this theory about the change of English fortunes: first, that the return of the English nobles seems more clearly to act as the symbolic cause; and, second, that the Bastard's later loss of his forces in the tides seems to belie the change. The return of the nobles, however, is a matter of simple expediency occasioned by Melun's warning that Lewis intended to execute them if he carried the day. No doubt the nobles have some trace of patriotic sentiment, or, if not that, they must at least realize from the narrowness of their escape that Commodity proves a most unreliable guide to action. However, the fact that before facing John they first ingratiate themselves with the young Prince Henry, who can serve as their intercessor with John, suggests that their interests are not entirely in the welfare of England.

The second objection—that the Bastard's loss of half his army in the Lincoln Washes argues against a change of English fortune—requires that we examine the Bastard's situation at this time. Through the second half of *King John* we have seen him steadily rising towards the station of An English King. In a symbolic sense he has deposed John and successfully led the English armies. With the news that John is dying, then, the opportunity has arisen for him to transform a symbolic kingship into an actual kingship; he has only to forswear Honour. This possibility is tentatively suggested by Hubert when he says (Act V, scene 4):

> I left [John] almost speechless, and broke out
> To acquaint you with this evil, that you might
> The better arm you to the sudden time
> Than if you had at leisure known of this.

Realizing that with the return of the traitorous nobles a power struggle may ensue, Hubert pledges his support to the Bastard. A few lines later, when the Bastard says, not so much to Hubert as to himself, "Withhold thine indignation, mighty heaven, / And tempt us not to bear above our power!" he is speaking not only with reference to the nobles but also with reference to himself, simultaneously acknowledging an impulse to kingship and admitting the dishonourableness of that impulse. As he said a little earlier to Hubert, "I come one way of the Plantagenets," and "one way" is not sufficient to justify an aspiration to the crown. Now, having phrased the alternatives of Honour and Commodity, he is reminded of something by his use of the word *power*. When he adds, "I'll tell thee, Hubert, half my power this night, / Passing these flats, are taken by the tide," he has realized that the loss of his army has personal as well as military implication, that this check of power also represents a form of divine injunction against any attempt to seize power for himself. As in the scene over Arthur's body, he again makes his decision quickly—"conduct me to the King"—and with this decision he again renounces Commodity and redeclares himself for the good of England, thus becoming most worthy of the crown at the moment of rejecting it. It is therefore, perfectly appropriate that the Bastard is given the concluding speech of the play, which is usually reserved for the king. He has confirmed his loyalty to England and to the soon-to-be King Henry III in this final scene. Yet this final speech of his, with its conspicuously qualifying "if"—"Naught shall make us rue, / If England to itself do rest but true"—is not just a set piece of perfunctory patriotism with which to conclude the play. The Bastard is too perspicacious and he has had too much experience with the renegade nobles not to be suspicious of their professions of Honour in this last scene. His closing speech is both a stirring proclamation of an ideal—but not, he realizes, untempered—national unity, and also his declaration to the nobles of the standard by which he has been governed and by which he expects them to be governed in the future. Thus, with what we might call "experienced" Honour dictating the terms to Commodity, *King John* concluded upon the same theme with which it began.

NOTES

1. Adrien Bonjour, in "The Road to Swinstead Abbey," *ELH*, XVIII (1951), offers the best, and indeed almost the only, defense of the structure of *King John*. All further references to Bonjour are to this article.
2. The text I am using is that of Neilson and Hill in *The Complete Plays and Poems of William Shakespeare* (Cambridge, 1942).
3. *Shakespeare's "Histories": Mirrors of Elizabethan Policy* (San Marino, 1947).
4. *Shakespeare's History Plays* (New York, 1946), 223.
5. Further evidence that John's exchange of the crown is rooted in Commodity can be found in his remark when he sends the Bastard after the nobles: "I have a way to win their loves again. / Bring them before me." (Act IV, scene 2, lines 169–70). Since John does not yet know that Arthur is alive, this cannot be his "way to win their loves again." Instead, it seems clear that he has already decided to use Pandulph as a means of stopping the French. His self-deposition is thus merely a tactic by which to insure his crown.

M. M. Reese

From *The Cease of Majesty*

Except that Mr. John Masefield has found it a "truly noble play," and Dr. Johnson applauded its "very pleasing interchange of characters and incidents," *King John* has received little favour from critics and has only occasionally appealed to audiences in the theatre. That there is no record of Elizabethan or Jacobean performance need not mean very much, as these records are scanty and haphazard, and the two re-issues of the quárto of the source-play, *The Troublesome Reign of King John*, argue a certain amount of public interest in the theme. It is not a play that it would have been prudent to offer at the court of Charles I's Catholic queen; nor, it seems, did anyone venture to revive it during the crisis of the Popish Plot. In fact there is no record of a performance until 1737; and a few years later, in 1745, with a Stuart rebellion brewing in Scotland, Colley Cibber produced a tendentious adaptation which he called *Papal Tyranny in the Reign of King John*. Unlike many of the botched versions of Shakespeare's work, this did not hold the stage for long, and subsequent productions in the eighteenth century, by Garrick, Thomas Sheridan, John Philip Kemble, and others, were tolerably respectful towards the folio text. It was a favourite piece in Kemble's repertoire, and Constance provided Mrs. Siddons with one of her most dramatic parts.

In the following century the play was chiefly valued for the opportunities it gave for spectacle and a pedantic antiquarianism. In 1823 Charles Kemble, with J. R. Planché as his designer, presented it "in the precise Habit of the Period, the whole of the Dresses and Decorations being executed from indisputable Authorities, such as Monumental Effigies, Seals, Illumined MSS, &c." Macready, who acted the play more than

Reprinted from *The Cease of Majesty*, published by Edward Arnold, London, and with permission of M. M. Reese.

once during the crisis of Catholic Emancipation, was almost equally intent upon pageantry and historical accuracy, and in 1852 Charles Kean, with Planché again the designer, aimed at "a total purification of Shakespeare, with every accompaniment that refined knowledge, diligent research and chronological accuracy could supply." Irving ignored the play, but in 1899 Beerbohm Tree put on a characteristically sumptuous production that included a lavish dumb-show of "The Granting of Magna Carta."

In the present century *King John* has never been very popular. It is not a satisfactory play, since it lacks a focal point. Shakespeare's customary insistence on the themes of patriotism, obedience and unity is here entangled in his stern exploration of Commodity. Faulconbridge, by far the most attractive and memorable of the characters, has a curiously equivocal function. Although closely drawn into the action, especially in the closing scenes, he is always in a sense standing apart, as commentator and symbol. Dramatically the central figure is, or should be, the King himself, and this is where the play's artistic weakness lies. For John is not an integrated character. At times he is a fumbling, uncertain, self-reproachful villain, a sort of meaner Macbeth; at times—because he is king—the great ocean towards whom all English loyalties should flow in tributary obedience; but never a man whose personal and political dilemmas insist upon being understood.

Unable to find in the play any central animating idea, Chambers dismissed it as "a bit of hack work,"[1] and possibly that is what it was. It may be that Shakespeare was bored: not, certainly, with the play's underlying issues, which still had enormous contemporary importance, but with the stale setting in which he was now obliged to examine them. Conceivably *King John* was a theatre chore demanded of him by his fellows because a rival company had had a success with a similar theme. This sort of thing was apt to happen in the Elizabethan theatre. The immense popularity of *Henry IV* prompted the Admiral's Men to their heavily-carpentered *Sir John Oldcastle*, and a few years later Shakespeare was himself called upon to write a romance with a woodland setting to match the success of the rivals' *Robin Hood*. He responded on that occasion with *As You Like It*, but the outcome might not always be so felicitous. If, then, it was the persuasions of his company that turned him to the story of King John, and they considerately put into his hands a copy of *The Troublesome Reign* (1591) to save him the labour of research and start his imagination working, he would at once have found that he had handled most of this stuff before. The virulent anti-Popery was new, but he found that uncongenial. All the rest—the pasteboard characterisation, the fighting in France, the treachery and vituperation, the meaningless iteration of defiance and lament—was wearisomely unsubtle and familiar: so familiar that he could not rouse himself to avoid the chronicle method to which *The Troublesome Reign* monotonously adhered. Certainly that is how it appears, and the unusual abundance of personifications and images of bodily action seems to betray a sense of conscious strain, as though Shakespeare realised his shortcomings and tried to flog the verse into an artificial energy.[2]

King John was probably written in 1596, after *Richard III*. Naturally this date is not favoured by critics who like to think that the sequence from *Richard II* to *Henry V* was composed as a deliberate tetralogy, a sort of dramatic epic, but the four plays of a tetralogy (if there was one) do not have to be written immediately one after the other, and Shakespeare's choice of theme was often dictated by the requirements of his company. *Much Ado About Nothing* certainly interrupted the Lancastrian sequence, which may explain its rather scornful title. The autumn of 1596 has been suggested as a date for *King John* on the ground that in Constance's grief over Arthur, Shakespeare was mourning the death of his own son Hamnet, who was buried at Stratford in August of that year. "For grief is proud and makes his owner stoop." Of course it could be so (and has anyone thought of dating *Hamlet* by the death of Shakespeare's father?", but this is not the way that artists usually work. Shakespeare was quite able to live a mother's sorrow without the sting of personal bereavement, and if he uttered his own feelings at all, it is likelier to have been through those characters who blamed Constance for lamenting overmuch. "Lady, you utter madness, and not sorrow."

Stylistically *Richard II* and *King John* are linked in several ways, notably in the marked absence of prose, but also there are striking differences. While nearly a fifth of *Richard II* is in rhyme, a natural characteristic of Shakespeare's sonneteering period, *King John* has very little rhyme outside the couplets that bring each scene to a conventional close, and the proportion of blank verse—2438 lines out of 2570—is the highest in the canon.

It is in many respects a transitional play. Shakespeare is discarding the self-consciously lyrical drama of Romeo and Richard for a more realistic treatment of history and comedy. *King John* is lyrical only in the outbursts of grief and in those passages where Shakespeare's imagination is stirred again to contemplate the horrors of invasion and civil war.[3] In other passages the play seems to have brought him to the threshold of the period in which prose would be his happiest medium, and this is especially evident when Faulconbridge is on the stage. Although there is not a single line of prose in the whole play, this is the medium that Faulconbridge instinctively needs for the expression of his quizzical, earthy personality. A play or two later he would have found it.

While the conceits of Constance have clear affinity with the language of Romeo, Richard II, and the *Sonnets*, her way of speaking is not allowed to dominate the play. Arthur, too, has his pretty pathos, and moves it in other people, but Faulconbridge is always a counterbalancing presence, infecting even courtly persons with his own laconic colloquialism, so that they come to mistrust the "wasteful and ridiculous excess" that likes

> To gild refined gold, to paint the lily,
> To throw a perfume on the violet,
> To smooth the ice, or add another hue
> Unto the rainbow, or with taper-light
> To seek the beauteous eye of heav'n to garnish.
> (IV.ii.11)

Of this excess the play itself is by no means innocent, but excess is at war with a more compressed and less declamatory way of saying things. As a whole the play is stylistically self-conscious and experimental. Shakespeare is less often disposed to linger upon a conceit and watch it grow, which had been the characteristic language of Richard II. Instead he often lets the imagery race ahead before an idea has been fully worked out, as in Salisbury's comment on John's second and unnecessary coronation:

> In this the antique and well-noted face
> Of plain old form is much disfigured;
> And, like a shifted wind unto a sail,

> It makes the course of thoughts to fetch about,
> Startles and frights consideration,
> Makes sound opinion sick and truth suspected,
> For putting on so new a fashion'd robe.
> (IV.ii.21)

King John also marks a transition in Shakespeare's political ideas. It is a bridge between his earlier histories and the maturer thought of the Lancastrian plays, and it announces his discovery of the true nature of political man.

Basically the play uses the same situation as *Richard II*, and not merely reaches the same conclusions but states them more emphatically. Richard was a bad king, but John is worse. Shakespeare declares him to be a usurper—which was doubtful—and gives him a greater responsibility for Arthur's death than his sources warranted; at the same time taking a few years off Arthur's age in order to underline the horror of the deed. John's flawed title, followed by his palpable wickedness, brings into question a subject's relationship with a man so evidently bad; and the answer, given in Faulconbridge's carefully weighted allegiance, says again that rebellion is the worst of evils. When he addresses Pandulph or the French, John is still, for all his faults, the voice of England, and this is the royalty that Faulconbridge momentarily inherits. The duty of obedience to a *de facto* king, however bad, could not be more explicitly stated; and because under the right leadership the English nobles return to that duty, the country is once again united. Faulconbridge makes the right decision, and he is the reason that majesty does not cease.

So far Shakespeare has only repeated himself. The new discovery that he makes in *King John* is that public and private morality do not always march together. England's saviour in the play is not a saint, nor even a particularly good man; but he is a man able to adapt himself to what his experience has shown him to be the necessities of political life.

A proper understanding of John himself was made impossible by his peculiar place in Elizabethan historiography. In the Middle Ages history was written by the clergy, whose enemies always came in for their unmitigated censure. John's bad reputation thus began early, long before constitutional historians discovered the importance of Magna Carta. He was branded as predatory and irreverent, scornful of the Church's teachings and covetous of its earthly treasures. As Holinshed put it, he was "little beholden to the writers of that time in which he lived," and for some generations he was regarded as one of the least satisfactory of kings. We saw in an earlier chapter how he was suddenly transformed in Bale's propagandist play into the brave and godly king who first threw down the gauntlet to Rome.[4]

So John, in whom the Victorians were to discover a resourceful opponent of English liberties, was reconstructed in Bale's reading of events as the earliest champion of our independence, frustrated in his high intent because his enemy was ubiquitous, implacable and strong and his own subjects unfortunately something less than heroic. Foxe the martyrologist also saw him as the baffled forerunner of mighty happenings, and Holinshed, who was usually content to accept whatever he read in the mediaeval chronicles, rejected their version of a king who, in his view, "had a princely heart in him and wanted but faithful subjects to have wroken himself of such wrongs as were done and offered to him." In official circles the beatification of John proceeded no farther than the express condemnation in the Homilies of the subjects who had revolted from him, but Shakespeare grew up in a generation that had come to think of him at least as the king who made the first brave stand against Roman tyranny. He was Moses to Henry VII, the saviour to come.

This was the John of *The Troublesome Reign*, which apart from Holished was probably the only source that Shakespeare used.[5] In the Induction to the printed text audiences who have taken pleasure in the triumphs of the Scythian Tamburlaine are now invited to do appropriate homage to a native champion of equal lustre.

> For Christ's true faith endur'd he many a storm
> And set himself against the Man of Rome,
> Until base treason (by a damned wight)
> Did all his former triumphs put to flight.
> (Ind. 6)

John is made to promise all that Henry VIII was later to accomplish. As a true servant of God he is "in arms against the Romish prince," and he swears to seize "the lazy abbey-lubbers' lands" and outlaw "the trental obsequies, mass, and month's-mind" that are the scenic apparatus of the Papal yoke. Clerical luxury and idleness are conventionally satirised, and "the Pope and his shavelings" come off ill in coarsely humorous episodes of "sport among the smooth-skin nuns" and "revel with fausen friars."

But John is not able to achieve all that he has promised. The unknown author cannot wholly escape the historical facts, and by the end of the play John is lamenting that

> I am not he shall build the Lord a house,
> Or root these locusts from the face of the earth.
> (Pt.II,sc.viii,106)

In this disappointment he finds consolation in his vision of the future:

> But if my dying heart deceive me not,
> From out these loins shall spring a kingly branch,
> Whose arms shall reach unto the gates of Rome,
> And with his feet tread down the strumpet's pride
> That sits upon the chair of Babylon.
> (108)

Up to a point his failure is easily explained. All, as Faulconbridge observes, "is the fruit of Popery." John's troubles began when, deserted by his nobles, he submitted to Pandulph to get help against the French.

> Since John did yield unto the Priest of Rome,
> Nor he nor his have prosp'rd on the earth:
> Curst are his blessings; and his curse is bliss.
> (100)

No doubt: but why was John deserted by his nobles? Even this can be blamed in part on clerical influence, for the machinations of the Pope are everywhere; but it is here that the author of *The Troublesome Reign* gets into difficulties and his picture of John as the warlike Christian hero begins to fall apart. No so disingenuous as Bale, who conveniently overlooked the whole episode, he has complicated his theme by introducing the story of Arthur, which occupies the central portion of the play. John struggles against the need to order Arthur's death, and in so far as the play concerns the personal tragedy of John, this is the crucial dilemma. Either way, alive or dead, Arthur was a danger to his crown: as Mary to Elizabeth's.

> For on his life doth hang thy sovereign's crown;
> But in his death consists thy sovereign's bliss.
> (Pt.I,sc.ix,32)

But his death does not bring the hoped-for security:

> Arthur is dead; ay, there the corsie grows:
> But while he liv'd, the danger was the more;
> His death hath freed me from a thousand fears,
> But it hath purchast me ten times ten thousand foes. . . .
> His life, a foe that levell'd at my crown;
> His death, a frame to pull my building down.
> My thoughts harpt still on quiet by his end,
> Who, living, aimed shrewdly at my room.
> (Pt.I,sc.xiii,234)

As John discusses it here, the problem is more political than moral, but later he accepts the moral responsibilities of his crime and recognises that it has rendered him unfit to lead his people into freedom.

> Thy sins are far too great to be the man
> T'abolish Pope and popery from thy realm:
> But in thy seat, if I may guess at all,
> A king shall reign that shall suppress them all.
> (Pt.II,sc.ii,169)

Through mere opportunism he submits to Pandulph in order to save his throne. The deterioration in his character is not concealed, and he ends the play devoid of virtue, a remorseful, self-confessing sinner, grasping only at the hope that where he has failed, a greater than he will succeed.

> Methinks I see a catalogue of sin
> Wrote by a fiend in marble characters,
> The least enough to lose my part in heaven.
> Methinks the devil whispers in mine ears,
> And tells me, 'tis in vain to hope for grace:
> I must be damn'd for Arthur's sudden death....
> How, what, when, and where, have I bestow'd a day

That tended not to some notorious ill?
My life, replete with rage and tyranny,
Craves little pity.

(Pt.II,sc.viii,71)

His hero having failed him—for this abject John is not really tragic even by the undemanding convention of "the fall of princes"—the author patches up the remainder of his play with a number of patriotic affirmations.[6] In date of composition *The Troublesome Reign* belonged to the anxious years of Mary's execution and the Spanish invasion. It was much safer to plead for national unity than to probe too closely into a sovereign's relationship with an inconvenient kinsman. So it was for Shakespeare too, even if he was writing seven or eight years later, and *King John* suffers from the same ambiguity in the treatment of the central character.

Read side by side, the two plays bring us very close to Shakespeare as he worked.[7] The language of *The Troublesome Reign* was not for him,[8] and it is fascinating to watch him give vigour and individuality to the speech of the Bastard, re-state the Papal claims for Pandulph, or lay a gloss of "wit" on the protracted grief of Constance. But he was broadly content to follow the general design of his original, preserving its chronological sequence and merely omitting, compressing or expanding to suit his own version of the story.[9]

A short comparison of the opening scenes will sufficiently illustrate his method. Both enact the episode in which Faulconbridge discovers his royal but sinister parentage. Shakespeare takes 276 lines over it, against *The Troublesome Reign*'s 431, and it is noticeable at once how he gets straight down to business, dispensing with the lifeless preliminaries of his source and opening dramatically with John's challenge to the ambassador of France, "Now, say, Chatillon, what would France with us?" In the fourth line Chatillon refers to John's "borrowed majesty" and already the play is in motion, with the audience early made aware that the King's title is in question. Where *The Troublesome Reign* takes 66 lines to get Chatillon off the stage, Shakespeare accomplishes this in 30 and then inserts a 14-line colloquy between John and his mother to develop the theme of usurpation and plant it firmly in the spectator's mind. This theme is something that Shakespeare has himself introduced into the plot. In *The Troublesome Reign* the opening speeches imply that John inherits in natural succession from his brother.

John's brief "Our abbeys and our priories shall pay This expedition's charge" (48–49) is shortened and transferred from lines 316–21 of the source, and the Faulconbridge family then appear, to be greeted in *The Troublesome Reign* with the fussy, ineffectual "Say, Shrieve, what are these men? What have they done? Or whereto tends the course of this appeal?"; and by Shakespeare with the crisp "What men are you?" The earlier play indelicately makes Lady Faulconbridge be witness to her humiliation, whereas Shakespeare does not bring her on until the claim is decided and the Bastard Philip has already been knighted as Plantagenet; and although in both plays she eventually admits her lapse from virtue, Shakespeare allows her only 57 lines, compared with 108, for the purpose. In *The Troublesome Reign* Philip roughly forces the confession from his mother, hammering away at her until she breaks down into involved and tedious utterance (400–21). Shakespeare resolves this into a brief, spontaneous admission:

> King Richard Cordelion was thy father.
> By long and vehement suit I was seduc'd
> To make room for him in my husband's bed:
> Heaven lay not my transgression to my charge!
> Thou art the issue of my dear offence,
> Which was so strongly urg'd past my defence.
> (*KJ* I.i.253)

Again, in the source Philip receives the confession without a thought for his mother's feelings, but Shakespeare closes the episode by finding him lines that will heal her wounds:

> Some sins do bear their privilege on earth,
> And so doth yours; your fault was not your folly. . . .
> With all my heart I thank thee for my father!
> Who lines and dares but say thou didst not well
> When I was got, I'll send his soul to hell.
> (*KJ* I.i.261)

To reduce the length of the scene Shakespeare cuts the altercation between the two brothers, his lines 134–62 compressing more than a hundred lines of the source, and he adopts a much more convincing means of resolving the question of Philip's parentage. *The Troublesome Reign* sends Philip into a trance (250–77) wherein, speaking in "a frantic madding vein" and vomiting gobbets of Latin, he senses "fumes of majesty" and discovers that he was royally fathered. Shakespeare does not care for these lunary intimations, and in his version the truth is learned when Queen Elinor reads "some tokens of my son in the large composition of this man." John and his mother have made up their minds before the wretched Robert has begun to argue. Philip himself comes to a similar conclusion when it occurs to him to wonder why he should be so unlike his brother; and it is revealing to see how Shakespeare develops and compresses an idea given by his source. This is *The Troublesome Reign*:

> Can Nature so dissemble in her frame,
> To make the one so like as like may be,
> And in the other, print no character
> To challenge any mark of true descent?
> My brother's mind is base, and too too dull
> To mount where Philip lodgeth his affects;
> And to his external graces that you view,
> Though I report it, counterpoise not mine:
> His constitution, plain debility,
> Requires the chair, and mine the seat of steel;
> Nay, what is he, or what am I to him,
> When anyone that knoweth how to carp,
> Will scarcely judge us one-country-born?
> (Pt.I,sc.i,365)

This is Shakespeare:

> Madam, an if my brother had my shape,
> And I had his, Sir Robert his, like him,
> And if my legs were two such riding-rods,
> My arms such eel-skins stuffed, my face so thin
> That in mine ear I durst not stick a rose
> Lest men should say "Look, where three-farthings goes!"
> And, to his shape, were heir to all this land,
> Would I might never stir from off this place,
> I'd give it, every foot, to have his face.
> (I.i.138)

Here is the characteristic Shakespearean concreteness; and here, as they do not in the generalised picture given in *The Troublesome Reign*, the unheroic lineaments of Sir Robert rise lifelike from the printed page.[10] In Shakespeare's text the laconic, bantering tones of the Bastard invigorate the whole scene, which in the source-play is insipid and protracted. His speech on "worshipful society", in which he delightedly contemplates the pitfalls and opportunities of his new-won state, is entirely Shakespeare's invention.

It is illuminating to pursue these comparisons throughout the play, but we must turn now to Shakespeare's handling of the religious and political ideas he discovered in the source. Except in a few short and inoffensive passages, he eliminates the crude anti-Catholic bias, and he deliberately refrains from presenting John as the Moses of the Reformation. He ignores the whitewashing process introduced by contemporary Protestant zeal. At the same time, when he does come to deal with the papal pretensions, his analysis is more lethal than anything the earlier author was capable of. He knew exactly where Pandulph's arguments would lead, and he felt too deeply about them to be able to make his answer in a spirit to cheap comedy and vulgar abuse. His way is to allow Pandulph to speak his own implicit condemnation, in the scene where he orders France to dissolve the recent compact with England. This episode is enlarged by Shakespeare (*KJ* iii.i.135–347) from a much shorter scene in *The Troublesome Reign* (Pt.I,sc.v,65–153). In the source, to establish a contrast with John's insolent defiance, the French King yields without protest to Pandulph's demands and rebukes John for his impiety. But Shakespeare gives him a long speech in which he accuses Pandulph of dissolving sacred vows and causing France and England to

> Unswear faith sworn, and on the marriage bed
> Of smiling peace to march a bloody host,
> And make a riot of the gentle brow
> Of true sincerity.
>
> (*KJ* III.i.245)

The Cardinal's reply is a grave statement of the prime allegiance owed by princes to the Church.

O, let thy vow,
First made to heaven, first be to heaven performed,
That is, to be the champion of our church.
(III.i.265)

But he then goes on to enmesh France in casuistries:

The better act of purposes mistook
Is to mistake again; though indirect,
Yet indirection thereby grows direct,
And falsehood falsehood cures, as fire cools fire
Within the scorched veins of one new-burned:
It is religion that doth make vows kept,
But thou hast sworn against religion,
By what thou swear'st against the thing thou swear'st,
And mak'st an oath the surety for thy truth
Against an oath: the truth thou art unsure
To swear, swears only not to be forsworn:
Else what a mockery it should be to swear.

Pandulph is allowed a full and dignified presentation of his case,[11] and damns himself with his own falsity. Shakespeare's method is far removed from the naive crudities of *The Troublesome Reign*. Here, in all its specious subtlety, men could recognise the Jesuit "double talk" that played "fast and loose with faith" and brought confusion to their daily pieties. To rally the people against the Catholic threat *The Troublesome Reign* could do no better than stir up the memory of vanished abuses. Shakespeare sees the present danger. France's surrender to Pandulph,[12] the more significant for his earlier defiance, warns Elizabethans of the subtler enemy now in their midst.

But the exposure of Roman sophistries—except that he was concerned with any threat to national unity—was not the purpose of Shakespeare's play. In *King John* he gives fresh emphasis to the problems he has lately examined in *Richard II*. Richard was an insufficient ruler but he was none the less the legitimate, anointed king. The issue was whether he should be deposed by a usurper who might govern better, and the play seemed to conclude that legitimacy was inviolate and indefeasible. In *King John* the ethics of rebellion are re-examined in circumstances much more favourable to the rebels. Richard was the legitimate king, and although he ruled badly, he was not a criminal; John was a usurper, and in plotting the death of Arthur he was guilty of a dreadful crime. Yet the fundamental questions remain. Is rebellion justified? Who is really responsible for the country's dissensions: the usurping King, or the subjects who falter in their obedience?

Shakespeare begins the play by insisting on John's unlawful title. Chatillon's "borrowed majesty," for which there is no authority in Holinshed or *The Troublesome Reign*, is followed by Elinor's sharp reply when her son boasts the "our strong possession and our right" will dispose of the French challenge:

> Your strong possession much more than your right,
> Or else it must go wrong with you and me.
> (I.i.40)

John is king *de facto*, and possession is his only "right." But this must suffice even when his actions put a heavier strain on his subjects' loyalty. In the opening scene he is shrewd and energetic, defying Chatillon with the spirit expected of an English king and meeting the Faulconbridge deputation with a generous readiness to acknowledge princely qualities in a subject. But thereafter, both as king and as a man, he deteriorates: partly through defects in himself that swiftly become apparent, and partly through the working of the Shakespearean mystique that decreed that usurpers would not prosper:

> A sceptre snatch'd with an unruly hand
> Must be as boisterously maintained as gain'd.[13]
> (III.iv.135)

The scene outside Angiers reveals his shifty opportunism, the conviction that every man has his price, the innate dissimulation imperfectly masked by declarations of patriotism and principle. The capture of Arthur then exposes him to grimmer temptations, and he proceeds with little hesitation to the crime which will make his people ready to "kiss the lips of unacquainted change." In his instructions to Hubert (III.iii), although he pretends, Macbeth-like, to wish for darkness in which to unfold his purposes, he is not stayed by the moral caution or expedient doubts which made John of *The*

Troublesome Reign speak in riddles. His orders are unambiguous: Arthur is to die.

In thinking, later, to see the King's colour come and go "between his purpose and his conscience," Salisbury is probably misreading the signs, for it is not until the nobles have left the stage in rebellious fury that John expresses any sort of penitence, and then it is apparently something of a surprise for him to discover that

> There is no sure foundation set on blood,
> No certain life achiev'd by other's death.
> (IV.ii.104)

With the resilience of the naturally amoral he has soon recovered and is telling Faulconbridge that he has "a way to win their loves again," His satisfaction at being able to lay the blame on Hubert finally restores his courage and assurance, and in words that recall Bolingbroke's repudiation of Exton he declares that

> It is the curse of kings to be attended
> By slaves that take their humours for a warrant
> To break within the bloody house of life,
> And on the winking of authority
> To understand a law, to know the meaning
> Of dangerous majesty, when, perchance, it frowns
> More upon humour than advis'd respect. . . .
> How oft the sight of means to do ill deeds
> Makes ill deeds done!
> (IV.ii.208)

It was Hubert's villainous aspect, he says, that turned his thoughts to murder, and he denies that he expressly commanded Arthur's death.

In one respect this is the critical episode of the play, since it decides John's stature. He lacks the insight of Macbeth, who cursed the juggling fiends but always knew in his heart that they did but direct him the way that he was going. Macbeth accepted moral responsibility, and John does not. John, concerned only with the political consequences of his crime, can still his self-questionings by verbal paltering. Up to this point *King John* could have developed into the personal tragedy of a monarch tempted to take the evil way; the play, in fact, that the author of

The Troublesome Reign might have written if he had been capable of it. But this was not the play that Shakespeare chose to write. He was not yet ready to bare a murderer's soul, and in keeping the play firmly on the level of politics he deprived John of grandeur.

After this decisive scene with Hubert, John has little further part in the story. Faced with rebellion at home and an invasion by the French, he craftily divides his enemies by submitting to the Pope. Shakespeare recognises no patriotic martyrdom in this. He is careful to insist that surrender was not forced on John by desperate necessity, as it is in *The Troublesome Reign*. It is a deliberate act of expedience; and the crown is scarcely back upon his head before he is urging Pandulph to keep Rome's side of the bargain:

> Now keep your holy word: go meet the French,
> To stop their marches 'fore we are inflamed;
> (V.i.5)

and, left alone, he congratulates himself that his submission has not been made "on constraint." "Heav'n be thanked, it is but voluntary." As such, it is more shameful in English eyes, and it is John's abdication as a king. His royal function passes to Faulconbridge, who makes a last vain attempt to rouse him to his duty:

> Be great in act, as you have been in thought;
> Let not the world see fear and sad distrust
> Govern in the motion of a kingly eye:
> Be stirring as the time; be fire with fire;
> Threaten the threatener, and outface the brow
> Of bragging horror: so shall inferior eyes,
> That borrow their behaviors from the great,
> Grow great by your example and put on
> The dauntless spirit of resolution.
> (V.i.45)

All the John can answer is, "Have thou the ordering of this present time."

Melun's reference to "the old, feeble, and day-wearied sun" describes the King as the "black, contagious breath" of night envelops him. In a fever John is carried to Swinstead Abbey, where we are suddenly and surprisingly told that he has been poisoned by a monk: surprisingly because Shakespeare has scarcely mentioned the actions that might have exposed him to monkish vengeance.[14] Brought out to die, he multiplies the images that tell of death's swift encroachment, comparing himself in a last fine flash of language with a body cramped for space, a parchment shrunken by the fire, a vessel torn by storms. But his thought, as always, is only for himself. He dies, "a clod and module of confounded royalty," impenitent because bereft of understanding.[15]

Shakespeare has pared away all that was heroic in the John bequeathed to him by *The Troublesome Reign* and sixteenth-century tradition. Significantly, the play contains less cosmic lore than any other of the histories, for it does not suit Shakespeare's purpose to remind us that John may be the eagle or the sun.[16] When Faulconbridge bids him play the lion, he responds with a smug reference to his treacherous league with Pandulph and simply gives up his functions. The only greatness allowed him is an occasional choric greatness, when he becomes a symbol to embrace recovered loyalties or to defy Chatillon and the Pope. Shakespeare's purpose is to present an extreme example of a situation in which, if ever, rebellion might be justified. Salisbury's argument that "The king hath dispossessed himself of us" is much more than specious: Salisbury is no Northumberland. This is the cue for Faulconbridge, who heals the country's wounds by pointing the way to a higher duty.

> Now hear our English king;
> For thus his royalty doth speak in me
> (V.ii.128)

His moment comes when Arthur's mutilated body is found at the foot of the castle walls. The "distemper'd lords" immediately conclude that this is Hubert's work, done on the orders of the King, and they abandon themselves to a quite excessive display of horror. "This is the very top." It is indeed. Salisbury forbids his soul obedience to the King who has decreed this murder, and Pembroke and Bigot are similarly unrestrained. Their protestations are plainly influenced by aristocratic dislike of the low-born Hubert—"Out, dunghill!" Bigot shouts at him: "Dar'st thou brave a nobleman?"—but the scene loses its effect if we do not believe that their horror is genuine.[17] Faulconbridge is no less appalled than they:

It is a damned and a bloody work:
The graceless action of a heavy hand.
(IV.iii.57)

But he is less hasty to decide the guilt, and he swiftly lowers the emotional temperature by a characteristic order to Salisbury to put up his sword,[18]

Or I'll so maul you and your toasting-iron,
That you shall think the devil is come from hell.
(IV.iii.99)

The nobles angrily depart, to join the French invaders, and it is the Bastard's decision now that will decide England's fate.

The deed is "graceless" and will put its perpetrator "beyond the infinite and boundless reach of mercy." The world is an even wickeder place than Commodity's anatomist had thought it. But his mood is that judgment shall be hereafter. If Hubert is guilty, a thread from a spider's web shall be strong enough to hang him on; meantime the pressing need is England's, where a vast confusion waits and a thousand businesses are brief in hand. He hurries to the King and takes his master's regality upon himself. Given the dreadful choice between rebellion and the service of a rule whom he suspects to be indirectly responsible for this crime, he decides against sedition. By giving further offence to God, rebellion would only add one sin to another and make the punishment more terrible.

By the time the disaffected lords have joined the French, the single-mindedness of their late resolves has somewhat evaporated. It is a means of conveying, in terms of drama, that the Bastard's leadership has already begun to turn the tide, and it prepares us for their subsequent repentance. Salisbury is already deploring that "the infection of the time" has made an earthquake of nobility.

I am not glad that such a sore of time
Should seek a plaster by contemn'd revolt,
And heal inveterate canker of one wound
By making many.
(V.ii.12)

Sedition is no longer that clear and unmixed duty that passion had so recently declared it, and in the presence of the French he grieves

> That, for the health and physic of our right,
> We cannot deal but with the very hand
> Of stern injustice and confused wrong.
> And is't not pity, O my grieved friends!
> That we, the sons and children of this isle,
> Were born to see so sad an hour as this?
> (V.ii.21)

Faulconbridge then enters to add definition to these uncertainties. The monarch is in arms, "like an eagle o'er his aery towers,"

> And you degenerate, you ingrate revolts,
> You bloody Neroes, ripping up the womb
> Of your dear mother England, blush for shame:
> For your own ladies and poor-visaged maids
> Like Amazons come tripping after drums,
> Their thimbles into armed gauntlets change,
> Their neelds to lances, and their gentle hearts
> To fierce and bloody inclination.
> (V.ii.151)

He defies France and defies Pandulph, excusing John's late compact with the Pope as executed "rather for sport than need," and speaking in the name of England he promises the destruction of all her enemies.

It is simple, stirring stuff that reduces all the complex issues of the reign to the single one of patriotic duty. In the heat of the ensuing battle Salisbury breaks off to confess, "I did not think the king so stored with friends." This unexpected resistance puts them in a mood in which they are already half-prepared for Melun's revelation of France's intended treachery, and it is a relief to them to see the path of duty clear again.

> I do love the favour and the form
> Of this most fair occasion, by the which
> We will untread the steps of damned flight,
> And like a bated and retired flood,
> Leaving our rankness and irregular course,

> Stoop lowly within those bounds we have o'erlook'd,
> And calmly run on in obedience,
> Even to our ocean, to our great King John.
> (V.iv.50)

The final promise of unification under the young Prince Henry marks God's forgiveness of the former acts of revolt; a forgiveness made possible only by Faulconbridge's decision not to be a rebel too. Henry is "the cygnet to this pale faint swan," born

> To set form upon that indigest
> Which he hath left so shapeless and so rude.
> (V.vii.26)

In this closing scene, with its sober patriotism and grave, incantatory rhythms, John is become an alien figure, an unwished reminder of a sickness that is passing. He dies recounting the agonies that torment his "unreprievable contemned blood," and with his death, the burden of his evil is lifted almost palpably from the scene while the Bastard talks of sweet, healthy things, of "the lineal state and glory of the land," of *submission, faithful services*, and *true subjection*, and ends the play with his final invocation of an England impregnable in unity.

The unity has been his achievement, and his character, although dramatically it is often anomalous, adds a new dimension to a play in which Shakespeare otherwise says little that he has not said before. Faulconbridge owes his success to the inspired authority and purpose lent him as the vessel of royalty. Like Gaunt, he comes to speak for England, and there is a vast difference between his earlier self and the symbolic figure whose importance consists in what he stands for. We shall be mainly interested in the lessons he learns in the course of his transformation.

Shakespeare developed the character from the brash and noisy boaster he found in *The Troublesome Reign*, and used him in the first half of the play as the bystander whose function was to comment upon the action. The morality writers often employed this choric figure, and his role covered the whole range between credulity and cynicism, between naive acceptance and a sort of railing complicity. At this second extreme stood Thersites, and let us admit that there is more than a touch of

Thersites in the early Faulconbridge. He may not have the acrid tongue or scabrous mind, but between him at Angiers and Thersites at Troy the difference is only one of degree.[19] A schoolboy relish for personal abuse and the *tu quoque* is coupled with an unerring eye for the moral and tactical weakness in everyone else's position. A soiled mind affects to wonder at the evil in the world but is all the time adding to it. Like Thersites, too, he is frequently rebuffed and snubbed by the other characters. His scheme for the reduction of Angiers—much the grubbiest proposal put forward in a scene remarkable for its unblushing *realpolitik*—is not in the end accepted; and after Angiers he is off the stage for a long time, except for a short moment when he has just slain Austria as an act of personal vengeance for his father. When he does reappear, we find that the King has not been employing him on any great business. He has merely "sped among the clergymen" to collect their enforced contributions to the war.

"I am I, howe'er I was begot." This glorying in his lack of kinship puts him in the company of the other stateless men, like Iago, Parolles, Falstaff, Richard III, or Coriolanus. It may account for the uneasiness that seems to affect all the characters in *King John* when they are in his presence; and on the personal level he continues to be strangely unsuccessful. Even when John has virtually abdicated and he has become the embodiment of England, it seems that, strictly as a military leader, he has achieved remarkably little (V.i.30, V.vi.39, V.vii.58–64).

In his morality role of Simplicity he is just a blunderer, and he succeeds only when he is identified with *Respublica*. Shakespeare has his own way of preparing the audience to accept this new identification. As a Plantagenet and the son of Lion-heart, a high destiny may be indicated for Faulconbridge in the opening scene, but we are not sure of it until the tang of his speech shows it unmistakably. He speaks of England before fate calls him to speak for England. His sturdy shoulders bear all that the play contains of comedy and pictures of Elizabethan life, and with an energy that overruns the plot and the solemn political theme, his inexhaustible eloquence packs the stage with eelskins, toothpicks in the mess, the absey-book, Good Friday fast, young maids of thirteen with their puppy-dogs or old men at their bowls, "Old Time the clock-setter, that bald sexton Time," citizens crowding the streets to hear the prophet's harsh-sounding rhymes, toasting-irons, dogs that tug and scamble for a bone, spiders, beardless boys and cockered silken wantons, buckets dipped in wells, men crouching in stables and lying hugged with swine, thimbles, needles, maidens tripping to battle behind the town-crier's drum, or the unhaired sauciness of boyish troops. His "mere Englishness" breathes in every syllable of his racy, trenchant speech, ultimately resolving the ambiguities of his character and marking him as the man who will rouse the sleeping majesty of England.

Thus Faulconbridge redeems and crowns the play, since the action is seldom as interesting or important as his independent vision of it. Shakespeare has sometimes used this sort of character before (Berowne and Mercutio are examples), but it is new to the histories. Although implicated in the action, Faulconbridge stands outside it and surveys it, not consistently but at least with enough detachment to be able to deepen its significance by his commentary. He condemns rebellion, but that is only one of the things he says about it. He also offers a self-sufficient explanation of the mainspring of political behavior.

King John is the most cynical and disillusioned of the histories. By comparison *Richard III* is just a cautionary tale about a wicked magician, and in the political jungle of *King John* Richard himself would early lose his way in its thorns and dangers. Among its characters we may make an exception of Constance, whose mother-love, although she carries it to excess, is a decent human instinct, and she revolts from the treacheries and impersonal opportunism of the politicians. We may also except Arthur, with the reservation that Shakespeare's boys are seldom among his more endearing creations; and Blanch is just an innocent pawn in the game of power politics. But no one else in the play is a person of integrity, not even Faulconbridge, who cheerfully admits that he is tarred with the same brush as the people he condemns. Of the lesser characters, Robert Faulconbridge is ready to defame his mother and brother for a parcel of land; his mother has betrayed her husband; Lymoges is a bloody-minded blusterer, Melun betrays his master's secrets, Philip of France veers with every wind, Queen Elinor contrives for her son without honour or scruple; the men of Angiers propose a cynically treacherous compact for the saving of their city; Salisbury and his fellows find that sedition is a losing game before they decide to abandon it. Those who play a larger part bear a larger guilt. John, already a usurper, is also a killer; Pandulph deploys moral forces in pursuit of worldly ends; the

Dauphin, once teased for being so green and fresh in this old world, learns his lesson well enough to be ready to betray his allies when he has used them; and even Hubert, on the whole a sympathetic character, accepts a wicked mission and decides to "fill these dogged spies with false reports" when he has been talked out of executing it.[20]

It is a dark picture. Issues of right and wrong are debated freely, and every time the wrong prevails. Force and expediency appear in all the distorting colours of conscience, honour, patriotism, domestic piety and religious duty. Never before has Shakespeare's world been so ubiquitously and subtly evil. The dark, gesticulating figures of the Roses plays are wicked in a way that is easily understood. Noisy, passionate, violent, treacherous, ambitious, they never pretend to be other than they are; and their vices are offset by the decent ordinariness of the men and women whom they entangle in their schemes. Even Richard of Gloucester, who callously exploits all kindly emotions for his own purposes, disarms rebuke by his relish of his own virtuosity. Can so exquisite an artist be wholly bad? In *Richard II*, a play maturer and more thoughtful than any of these, we begin to be conscious of an evil of a different sort, that hides itself as virtue and knows how to temporise. When ambition has learned to play a waiting game and ruthlessness is masked as patriotism, the world becomes a more complicated and dangerous place. Bolingbroke's fair words and cool assessment of the odds show a sophistication that makes intriguers like Buckingham and Warwick seem innocent. But *Richard II* stops far short of being an unpleasant play. Its lyricism keeps it sweet, Gaunt's patriotism is idealised and clean, and York may hope for the best because he honestly believes in it. The atmosphere of *King John* is very different, for the whole currency of emotion has been debased. Evil no longer speaks as itself, it speaks as wisdom, justice, honour, and religion. Commodity is the only wear.

Faulconbridge is the character through whom Shakespeare mirrors this sense of the baseness of political life. The difference between him and York, who also has a choric function, explains the different atmosphere of the two plays. York is a representative of the nobler and more optimistic tradition in which he was nurtured, but Faulconbridge has no roots—his illegitimacy is symbolic. As a creature of his time, he is naturally adept at delivering sweet poison for the age's tooth, and his strength is his power of rapid assimilation. His earlier simplicity is swiftly accommodated to the ways of the strange new world in which he finds himself. Armoured in his self-possession, an immense and irresistible adequacy, he learns by practice and example. Before he is thus acclimatised, the regular runners in the rat race find him boorish and naive, and more than once he falters, momentarily astonished at their enormity, before he proves himself as apt as they. His resilience and intuitive adaptability will always restore his personal mastery of the situation.

At first he thinks it is all going to be great fun, and the exuberant boyishness of his first soliloquy (I.i.182–219) shows how much the world has yet to teach him. Knighthood promises all sorts of harmless amusements, like pretending in a superior way to forget people's names, or pulling the legs of travel snobs, or practising the polite shams of social intercourse. These he supposes to be the delights of the "worshipful society" to which he now belongs. But once he has seen high politics in action, he never speaks in this mood again. Coming with the King and his forces to the conference before Angiers, he listens in silence to the angry parley: a silence that lasts for fifty lines before the insolence of Austria excites him to speech, youthful and intemperate speech that only sidetracks the discussions. A cracker, Austria calls him, uttering superflous breath; and France contemptuously bids the "women and fools" to leave off their wrangling. Except for another short skirmish with Austria, Faulconbridge is then silent for a further two hundred lines, and when he does speak again he has learned the first rule of diplomatic conferences, which is that they have no rules. It is absurd, he says, for the people of Angiers to quibble about surrendering their wretched little city to its lawful master. They have no power of arms, and so the obvious solution is for France and England to combine against the "peevish town" and resume their differences when it has been levelled with the ground.

The citizens trump this audacious trick by proposing "fair-faced league," namely the marriage of Blanch, niece of England, to the Dauphin. To this alliance they will open their gates forthwith. When this plan is accepted, Faulconbridge has at last taken the full measure of his opponents, and the famous "Commodity" speech expresses his new-won knowledge. Never again will he be "bethumped with words" that dress policy in the language of virtue. He has seen his master John surrender part of his inheritance in order that Arthur shall not have the whole of it; and France, "God's own soldier" whose armour conscience buckled on, deflected from an honourable purpose to "a most base and vile-concluded peace." The agent is Commodity, "purpose-changer" and "daily break-vow," ceaseless foe of impartiality and straightforward action. Why, he finally asks himself, does he complain of this "bias of the world?" Only because he has not learned the trick of it; and when he has,

> My virtue then shall be
> To say there is no vice but beggary:
> Since Kings break faith upon Commodity,
> Gain be my lord, for I will worship thee.
> (III.i.595)

In the following scene he will be pupil to a consummate exhibition by Pandulph that will establish the accuracy of his conclusions. But first we are shown a very different reaction to the marriage compact. Faulconbridge has called this a "mad composition," since he has always wanted to fight Angiers, but he has learned to admire the technique. Constance, Arthur's widowed mother, is more directly involved, and she reacts in the traditional way—in the way of one who still expects to find honour in public life—to the slippery evasiveness of her friends. She is the last, and significantly the last, of the long vociferous sequence of women who in the earlier histories have been the mouthpiece of conscience. In them, all the countless victims have found a voice, for they have always spoken for more than their personal suffering. Their own part in the action has seldom been guiltless, but when, bereft of husbands and sons, they cry out against the unnatural violence and treachery of war, they protest for all humanity. Shakespeare has preserved a moral balance by allowing them to testify to the common pieties which the politicians blasphemously ignore.

Constance, then is apt to her cue. Her personal outrage at Arthur's disinheritance assumes a larger and nobler indignation as she contemplates the wickedness that daily masquerades as statesmanship. In this finer mood she will instruct her sorrows to be proud, for it is not only of her own grief that she speaks. On the stage Constance is hard to endure; and even to read, despite the rich imagination which finds in each succeeding metaphor the stepping-stone to yet another, her utterances "only serve to shew," as Johnson sourly remarked, "how difficult it is to maintain the pathetic long." But the substance of her grief preserves a magnificent consistency. She acknowledges Commodity but will not come to terms with it, and her superb invective flays all its adherents impartially.

That is the difference between herself and Faulconbridge, and the gradual change, which this play unmistakably reveals, in Shakespeare's developing outlook on the political scene. Faulconbridge is the first character to embody without compromise the exclusively political morality in which all the remaining histories are conceived.

Eventually he brings the play to an orthodox and familiar conclusion. Contemporaries had to be reminded of the need for unity, and so it is as the saviour of society that he is finally presented to us. It would be foolish to pretend that this is not his main function. But this is also the man who came to accept the Angiers pact, the Dauphin's treachery and Pandulph's smooth equivocations as the norm of political action. He espoused Commodity as a man might woo a courtesan who had yet to cross his path: if others enjoyed her favours, who should not he? In its venial forms Commodity is just the barrow-boy's goddess or the instinct to scramble aboard the band wagon; but it can also, as Faulconbridge discovered, mean betrayal, deceit and murder. Once he has accepted this, there can be no reconciliation between himself and Constance. In her simpler morality, wrong is wrong and no political needs or calculation can make it right. In the later histories there is no Constance. She disappears as finally as the sort of language she and her kind have spoken, and there is an obvious relation between the two.

But this does not mean that Constance is wholly right and Faulconbridge wholly wrong. Right and wrong, in this context, are question-begging words, and the emphasis of *King John* is on the idea that virtue may have more than one aspect. Whatever Faulconbridge may say in praise of Commodity, his actions show him to be far removed from the out-and-out Machiavellianism of Commodity's other disciples. To him it means something more than self-interest and expediency. It is a means to effective action, the code of behavior that a wise man will use if in public life he wants to get results. In politics it is often necessary to fight evil with evil. This is a doctrine which in the moral sphere can only end disastrously, as Hamlet found, but the political world has its own principles and usages, frequently at variance with the ethics of ordinary life; and the ultimate paradox of this discovery is that political morality, which from the traditional

Christian standpoint is often no morality at all, may be a means to the highest good, the safety, strength and unity of society.

Because he realises this, Faulconbridge, who is in many ways a bumptious bounder and seems to make a hash of his personal undertakings, is the right man to crown the play as defender of the established order. That order has survived because he has set the country's safety before the punishment of a "graceless" act for which only God can exact the fitting penalty. Thus the "surety of the world" is mended faiths of the lords who have been momentarily blind to the fundamental issues. He greets them as stars now moving again in their proper spheres, asserting his morality against theirs and showing them that *right*, even if a little tainted by Commodity, means only one thing when a country's safety is at stake.

Faulconbridge is a link with the Prince Hal of the plays to come. Hal is a slightly different and a better man, or it would not have been necessary for these plays to be written. But the appearance here of this concept of the political man, suggested only vaguely, if at all, in the earlier histories, means that *King John* is not a play to be ignored. Indeed the subsequent histories, although they are much better plays, develop and explore this idea without making any discovery of comparable importance. In Faulconbridge, the political man is humanised by his robust wit and intense patriotism; and while the wit is not indispensable (as Henry V will demonstrate), the patriotism undoubtedly is. As well as dedication, a certain disinterestedness of aim was necessary to give this figure validity in its own limited sphere. Shakespeare's feeling is that the political man is not a wholly amoral conception, since his cynicism and ruthlessness acquire some sort of sanction when they are devoted to the country's interest. Without patriotism the character is nothing.

In *Henry V* the political man is idealised and, within his limitations, entirely successful; and thereafter Shakespeare is no longer interested in this kind of success.

NOTES

1. *Shakespeare: a Survey*, 100.
2. See C. F. E. Spurgeon, *Shakespeare's Imagery*, 245–52.
3. As at II.i.23–30, 66–75, V.vii.112–18.
4. See above, pp. 69–70.
5. This has lately been questioned, notably by E. A. J. Honigmann in the Arden edition of *King John*. Honigmann believes that *The Troublesome Reign* is a corrupted version of Shakespeare's play, which must therefore have been some little time before 1591, probably under the impact of Mary's execution and the Armada. This is not the place for a detailed discussion of this thesis, but it does not convince. Honigmann's theory that *King John* was earlier than *The Troublesome Reign* was considered and demolished in anticipation by J. Dover Wilson in his Cambridge edition (1936), and there have been more recent refutations by F. P. Wilson (*Marlowe and the Early Shakespeare*, 114–19) and J. Isaacs (*Shakespeare's Earliest Years in the Theatre*, the British Academy Shakespeare Lecture, 1953). Whatever debasement took place between *King John* and *The Troublesome Reign*—and it is suggested that there may have been an intervening play—it is surely surprising that the copy used only one line of the supposed original, the commonplace "For that my grandsire was an Englishman" (*KJ* V.iv.42). Nor was it the usual practice of actors who plundered someone else's play for their own use, usually in the provinces, to lengthen the text and enlarge the cast. Yet *The Troublesome Reign* is 300 lines longer than *King John* and has 40 speaking parts compared with 23.
6. See above, pp. 82–84.
7. In this particular instance. His treatment of his sources varied from play to play, and the comparison with *The Troublesome Reign* illuminates his methods in one case only, and one in which he may not have been very much interested. Usually he borrows much more freely from the actual language of his source.
8. He reduces the classicism and Latinity in which the source abounded, e.g. at Pt.I.sc.i.250–52, 348–49; sc.ii.8–9; sc.iii.3–5.
9. He retained also many of the glosses and inaccuracies of the source, his method, as in all the histories, being to reduce the facts to a pattern that served his dramatic purpose. Thus he gathers all John's difficulties—with Arthur, with the barons, with France, and with Rome—into a single theme, although John did not in fact have to face them all simultaneously; he makes Arthur a child, in place of Holinshed's young knight; because she would be more pathetic as a widow, he conveniently forgets that Constance's third husband, Guy of Tours, was still alive, and fails to note that she died before Arthur; and he brings into a single scene the death of Constance (1201), the death of Elinor (1204), John's second crowning (1202) and the French invasion (1216).

10. Shakespeare here owed something to the actor who almost certainly played the part, the grotesquely thin John Sincklo, the "mere anatomy" and "father of maypoles," see *SWW*, 257.
11. Of this case Johnson justly remarks, "The propositions, that the *voice of the church is the voice of heaven*, and that *the Pope utters the voice of the church*, neither of which Pandulph's auditors would deny, being once granted, the argument here used is irresistible; nor is it easy, notwithstanding the jingle, to enforce it with greater brevity or propriety."
12. The original audience would have seen in this surrender a reference to Henry IV's conclusion that "Paris is well worth a Mass."
13. John's usurpation is emphasised in several references throughout the play, e.g. by Philip of France at II.i.95; by John himself when he says before Angiers, "Doth not the crown of England prove the king?" (II.i.273); by Elinor at II.i.471, "thy now unsured assurance to the crown"; by John's own insistence on a second coronation, and Salisbury's misgivings about the wisdom of this, IV.ii.21–27; and by Faulconbridge in IV.iii, where he speaks of Arthur as "the life, the right and truth of all this realm" and foresees in the expected reprisals against John "the decay of wrested pomp."
14. The omission is due to Shakespeare's casual use of *The Troublesome Reign*. In removing the anti–Catholic buffooneries of the source, he forgot that he had failed to provide a motive for the priests' hostility to John.
15. Miss Caroline Spurgeon noted (*Shakespeare's Imagery*, 248–50) how Shakespeare has reduced John's stature by frequently picturing him as only a portion of a body. This symbolism "in a play crowded with pictures of dancing, wrestling, whirling human figures, lets us see the king as a portion of a body only, and that portion steeped at times in human blood."
16. He bears these qualities only when Faulconbridge is speaking in his name, as at V.ii.149.
17. E. M. W. Tillyard (*Shakespeare's History Plays*, 223–24) speaks of the ill considered "levity" of their actions, apparently because they explode in anger against the King without first checking their facts, but this hardly seems to be the appropriate word. If the lords have been actuated only by "levity," the very different behavior of Faulconbridge loses much of its gravity and significance. Shakespeare takes great pains to show that the rebels have a very serious case.
18. His "Your sword is bright, sir; put it up again" anticipates a famous line from *Othello*.
19. His liking for coarse insult is made evident in the source. e.g. Pt.I.sc.ii.145–49, where he calls Limoges "loathsome dunghill swad" *et al*.
20. Hubert is strangely unsatisfactory. The King orders him to put Arthur to death, although by the time he appears in the prison the commission has apparently been changed to blinding. The stage is thus set for a classic discussion of the conflict between duty and conscience. The issue was at least as old as Antigone, and it was generally agreed in the sixteenth century that for a Christian the duty of obedience to the king stopped short of the commission of a crime. The Executioner puts the point when he says, "I hope your warrant will bear out the deed," but Hubert surprisingly disposes of the objection as "uncleanly scruples." In the end Hubert neither

kills nor blinds, but conscience is not his reason. Shakespeare chooses instead to have him overwhelmed by a rhetorical set-piece, and Arthur saves himself from the hot irons simply by piling up verbal points against an opponent who begins by wiping away remorse ("foolish rheum" and "tender womanish tears") but ends, in his own quibbles about heating the iron and reviving it with his breath, by falling into the same rhetorical tricks. When he finally admits defeat, he has not yielded to pity or any other emotion; he has been confounded by Arthur's superior dexterity (*KJ* IV.i).

To achieve this result Shakespeare departed from his source. In the corresponding scene (*TRKJ* Pt.I.sc.xii) Hubert acknowledges the traditional dilemma. The deed is bad, but "a king commands, whose precepts neglected or omitted, threateneth for the default." Once again Arthur prevails, but he does it here by reminding Hubert that he is imperilling his immortal soul (xii. 65–80); and Hubert finally desists because the "great Commander counterchecks my charge." Shakespeare deliberately refused this issue, and it is hard to see why.

Robert L. Smallwood

Introduction to *The New Penguin Shakespeare: King John*

At the end of *King John* the Bastard Faulconbridge, stepping forward from the cluster of figures around the corpse of the King, and from the hesitant, untried prince whose reign is just beginning, addresses the audience in the lines of direct, confident patriotism. The speech lifts the play from the historical period with which it has been concerned, and must have seemed vividly relevant for the audiences who first listened to it under the threat of Spanish invasion. For, in spite of the defeat of the great Armada of 1588, England still faced the danger of an attack by a foreign Catholic power with support from Catholic dissidents within the kingdom, and the Bastard's lines allude to this fear:

> This England never did, nor never shall,
> Lie at the proud foot of a conqueror
> But when it first did help to wound itself.
> Now these her princes are come home again,
> Come the three corners of the world in arms
> And we shall shock them! Naught shall make us rue
> If England to itself do rest but true!
> (V.vii.112–18)

These are the play's most familiar lines. They are often quoted out of context, and have even been heard at the conferences of modern political parties. Their naked patriotism may not command the assent of some readers, and *King John* has probably been undervalued through being remembered by this epilogue alone. To redress the balance it is necessary first to see the play in its historical and political context, and then to examine the way in which these boldly affirmative lines emerge naturally from the developing patter, their simplicity and directness forming an acceptable conclusion to the subtle and serious exploration of political questions that has gone before.

In *King John* Shakespeare deals with a period of English history nearly four centuries remote from his own age. Apart from *Henry VIII*, an untypical, late and possibly collaborative work, it is the only one of his history plays that does not belong within a recognizably integrated cycle of plays. In the two Lancastrian tetralogies we have eight plays, each with its own dramatic independence, which can nevertheless legitimately be viewed as a cycle, a pageant of English history from the son of the Black Prince to the Tudors. But *King John* stands alone, distant, isolated. The reign to which its closing scene looks forward, the long, complex, rather uninspiring reign of Henry III, seems to have meant little to the Elizabethans—at least, with all their prolific energy in turning history into drama, this was one of the few reigns they left completely untouched. The story of King John, therefore, is told in a vacuum; the reign is caught from the past in a pinpoint of illumination, vividly but temporarily engaging our attention. At the close its implications must overleap the intervening years, or recede into the mists of history. In the same scene as that in which the Bastard looks forward to an England always free from "the proud foot of a conquerer," King John sees himself as a "scribbled from, drawn with a pen / Upon a parchment" (V.vii.32–33), shrinking before the fire. It is a frightening evocation of the withering of memory wrought by time. Both the long perspective of the historical past and the immediacy of its political implications coexist in *King John*. The long perspective of a period far remote from his own allows Shakespeare to mould his material with more freedom than in most of his history plays. Though these include many unhistorical characters, none more conspicuous than Falstaff in the two parts of *Henry IV*, their roles are usually conceived apart from the main historical action, as commentators or comic parodists. In *King John*, however, Shakespeare places the largely unhistorical figure of the Bastard boldly in the centre of the political action. He also lures the audience into forgetting that John was succeeded by Henry III, while the dramatic focus falls with increasing certainty on the Bastard. This flirting with the fictional is one of the unique characteristics of *King John*; its purpose becomes clear if the pattern of the play is examined.

Though John's reign was remote enough to allow Shakespeare some freedom in his handling of fact, its political implications were well known to Elizabethan audiences. We do not know when Shakespeare wrote *King John*. It did not appear in print until the Folio of 1623, and there is no record of performance during Shakespeare's lifetime. It was, however, mentioned in 1598 in Francis Mere's *Palladis Tamia*. Its source was almost certainly the anonymous play *The Troublesome Reign of John, King of England*, published in 1591. (The general connexions between the plays are discussed in the Appendix to this edition; points of detail are examined in the Commentary.) Between the limits of 1591 and 1598 any date of composition is possible. Signs of immaturity in comparison with the history plays of the second tetralogy—*King John* lacks the richness of characterization of the *Henry IV* plays and sustained lyricism of *Richard II*, though like the latter play it is entirely in verse—have caused it to be placed early rather than late within these limits. A date of 1593 or 1594, just before *Richard II*, seems likely. But at whatever date in the 1590s *King John* made its first appearance on the stage, the political struggles which it depicts would have struck a sympathetic chord with its first audiences. Although the monkish chronicler's hostile picture of John had its influence in the writings of the sixteenth century, particularly through the work of the Catholic historian Polydore Vergil, there came with the Reformation a new image of John as a Protestant martyr struggling against papal dominance. John Foxe sees him in this way in his *Acts and Monuments of these latter and perilous days, touching matters of the Church*, that great "Book of Martyrs" first published in 1563 and many times reprinted, which came second only to the Bible in the devotional reading of English Protestants. Foxe's contemporary, John Bale, treated the reign in similar terms in his vigorously Protestant play *King Johan*. Originally written about 1538–40 and later revised, the play sees John as a "faithful Moses" trying to lead England from the tyranny of Rome. He is prevented from doing so by the rebelliousness of his subject, so that they are condemned to remain in "the land of darkness" until the time of Henry VIII, "who clearly brought us into the land of milk and honey." *The Troublesome Reign* shares the strongly anti-Catholic mood of Bale, and also sees John as a forerunner of

Henry VIII. In its last scene, for example, the dying King prophesies:

> From out these loins shall spring a kingly branch
> Whose arms shall reach unto the gates of Rome,
> And with his feet tread down the strumpet's pride.
> (II.1084–86)

There is little possibility of Bale's play having directly influenced *The Troublesome Reign*, for *King Johan* remained unprinted until the nineteenth century; but the two plays are part of the same general tradition.

Behind the religious topicality of the reign of John lay its political implications. In his three great volumes of *Chronicles*, first published in 1577 and republished ten years later in the enlarged edition from which Shakespeare drew many of his history plays, Raphael Holinshed sees the reign as a demonstration of "the fruits of variance" and "the gain that riseth of dissension." "No greater nor safer fortification can betide a land," he adds, "than when the inhabitants are all alike minded." In the "Homily against Disobedience and Wilful Rebellion," which Elizabethans would have heard regularly in church, John's reign is again used to teach this lesson. The author of *The Troublesome Reign* reasserts it in the concluding lines of his play:

> If England's peers and people join in one,
> Nor Pope, nor France, nor Spain can do them wrong.
> (II.1195–96)

The sentiment is echoed, in more general terms, by the Bastard in *King John*.

The Bastard's concluding lines, then, belong in a firmly established tradition, and the play as a whole deals with issues of topical significance to its first audiences. Many critics have taken this a stage further and suggested that in the play Shakespeare presents an allegory of the political situation in late Elizabethan England. Arthur is said to represent the imprisoned rival for Elizabeth's throne, Mary Queen of Scots, the barons the Elizabethan Catholic nobility, Pandulph's sentence of excommunication the Papal Bull of 1570 deposing Elizabeth, and Hubert the Queen's secretary Davison, an important agent in Mary's execution. But though comparisons of the situation of

Mary Stuart with that of Arthur Plantagenet occur in the writings of sixteenth-century Catholic apologists, and though an awareness of the tradition and political climate in which Shakespeare worked is important, it would be a crippling limitation of the power of *King John* to tie it too closely to the situation of the 1590s. It was, certainly, written for English audiences at a time when there was widespread fear of Catholic threat within and without, but the plays' examination of the behaviour of men in political situations has universal validity. Even in its most topical speech, the Bastard's concluding lines, Shakespeare has generalized the very specific references of *The Troublesome Reign*: the Pope, France, and Spain have become "the three corners of the world." This universalizing process is at its most conspicuous in the presentation of the King.

Shakespeare's portrait of King John is much less partisan and dogmatic than that of *The Troublesome Reign*. Gone is the idea of the Protestant hero fighting the might of Rome, gone are the references to Henry VIII and the comic scenes depicting clerical corruption. Shakespeare sees John as a fallible, uncertain, imperfect monarch, successful at first, and with his moment of glory in the full Protestant tradition as he confronts Pandulph in Act III, scene 1, but increasingly subject to the corrupting power of political need, so that his final collapse is total. Both the hostility of the pre-Reformation chroniclers and the admiration of the Protestant historians seem to be taken into account. This is true also in Holinshed, to whose work Shakespeare turned to supplement *The Troublesome Reign*. Relying mainly on Catholic historical sources but writing in the Protestant tradition, Holinshed, finds, in a rather bewildering summing-up, both that John "had a princely heart in him and wanted nothing but faithful subjects" and at the same time that he was "not so hardy as doubtful in time of peril," that he "wanted discretion," and that he was "one not able to bridle his affections." What are only flat, contradictory statements in the chronicle, however, become in Shakespeare an honest, open-eyed examination of human behaviour under stress. It is a portrait drawn from an interest in men, not from a propagandist political impulse.

In approaching the history of King John, then, Shakespeare was working with historical material that had already revealed its adaptability to varied interpretation, and which would have given him the opportunity, had he wished it, of composing a play immediately connected with contemporary politics. He chose instead a less dogmatic approach, a more searching exploration of a complex situation. In order to do so he followed the drastic reorganization of history which *The Troublesome Reign* had already established. He compressed into one the three major, and quite separate, conflicts of John's reign—that with France over Arthur, that with the Pope, and that with the barons. An increased emphasis on Arthur is among the most notable results; he remains in the play until the end of Act IV, though the historical Arthur died after less than five years (about a quarter) of the reign. Throughout, events from different periods are linked to provide dramatic motivation and explanation, so that the actions form a coherent whole, and a pattern of cause and effect, crime and retribution, emerges. Political problems are thus presented in intensified form to allow the exploration of questions of regal responsibility, political loyalty, and personal integrity.

This intensity comes partly from the compression of the time-scheme. Historically, John's reign lasted seventeen years, from 1199 to 1216. In the play there are obviously short intervals between Chatillon's embassy (I.i) and John's arrival in France (II.i), and between John's victory in Act III, scene 3, and the consolidation of it described in the following scene. There is a fairly definite time-gap after the end of Act III, with the subsequent return to England and the attempted blinding of Arthur (IV.i), and possibly another short interval between the death of Arthur (IV.iii) and John's surrender to Pandulph (V.i). But even where some elements in the text suggest a slight interval between scenes, the events are all closely connected. The action of the play if one wishes to think in the concrete terms which the dramatization of history appropriately disguises, occupies perhaps seven days over a period which, even allowing for an interval between Acts III and IV, seems to be no more than a few months. The boy Arthur of the time of the betrothal of Blanche and the Dauphin in Act II (historically occurring in 1200) is still a boy as the barons in Act IV plan the rebellion which occurred in 1216. At times Shakespeare specifically points out the swift passage of time. At IV.iii.104 Hubert tells the barons that "'Tis not an hour" since he left Arthur (in Act IV, scene i) and from scene to scene in Act V there is a constant emphasis on the rapidity with which events follow on each other's heels.

This sense of the terrible speed with which actions produce their effect is quite foreign to the long-drawn-out complications of Holinshed's account of the period, and very different also from the loose, rambling structure of *The Troublesome Reign*. It is reflected in the imagery of *King John*. Throughout there runs a pattern of fire and heat imagery which captures the idea of the speed with which events occur, and of the violence and rage of the participants. The violent action of the battle is a "hot malicious day" (II.i.351); the Kings are addressed as "fiery-kindled spirits" (II.i.314); the blood of John and Philip of France is "set on fire" (II.i.351); John consolidates his positions after his victory with "So hot a speed" that the Dauphin is astonished (III.iv.11); Hubert comes to the barons "hot with haste" (IV.iii.74); the Bastard arrives at King John's death-bed "scalded" with his "violent motion" (V.vii.49). The idea of fiery swiftness is constant throughout the play, and the pattern of imagery connects with the climactic events of the attempted burning out of Arthur's eyes and the burning poison which kills John. The latter is foreshadowed with powerful irony in the enraged exchange between John and Philip as hostilities are reopened at the end of Act III, scene 1:

> King John
> France, I am burned up with inflaming wrath—
> A rage whose heat hath this condition,
> That nothing can allay, nothing but blood,
> The blood, and dearest-valued blood, of France.
> King Philip
> Thy rage shall burn thee up, and thou shalt turn
> To ashes, ere our blood shall quench that fire.
> (III.i.340–45)

Along with this sense of the irresistible speed with which events march, reflected in the imagery of fiery activity, go images of ill-boding fateful powers forcing the characters along allotted course. The Bastard observed during the battle that the day "grows wondrous hot," and adds that "Some airy devil" hovers in the sky, pouring down mischief (III.ii.1–3). John, terrified by the speed with which events are turning against him in Act IV, begs "Withhold thy speed, dreadful occasion" (IV.ii.125). And the Bastard, sensing the danger in which England lies after Arthur's death, feels the presence of "vast confusion" waiting "As doth a raven on a sick-fallen beast" (IV.iii.152–53). These fateful images are part of the play's general pattern of personification, from the poetic exuberance which sees Angiers in human terms, winking, frowning, sleeping, to the more serious comparisons between the human body and the body politic which culminate in John's lines of terrible realization as his power slips away (IV.ii.423–28). Personification enhances the savagery of Hubert's signal to his accomplices in the blinding of Arthur, his stamp "Upon the bosom of the ground" (IV.i.3), and makes felt the horror the barons' rebellion, "ripping up the womb" of England (V.ii.152). It brings home the violence of war, the "savage spirit of wild war" (V.ii.74), seen as dogs snarling over a bone (IV.iii.148–50), or as blood answering blood (I.i.19), or bringing death in its train, also personified, his steel-lined chaps "mousing the flesh of men" (II.i.354). Personification also makes vivid the disgusting familiarity of that "smooth-faced gentleman, tickling commodity" (II.i.573).

The immediacy and reverberative power of much of the play's imagery combine with Shakespeare's choice of a historical period whose political significance had both contemporary and general repercussions, with his selection, reordering, and patterning of events into an encompassable and coherent shape, and with his intensification of the action in a compressed time-scheme moving often at head-long speed, to create a play of frequently intense dramatic force. To analyse this intensity it is necessary to examine the structural pattern of the play in more detail.

In the first scene of *King John* Shakespeare not only establishes a precise historical moment—John, newly placed on the throne, facing a challenge from France—he also fills in, economically but tellingly, its background. There is much looking back to the reign of John's predecessor, Richard Coeur-de-lion, and every reference presents it as a time of honour for England. We hear of the "honour-giving hand" of Coeur-de-lion (I.i.53) and of

> Richard, that robbed the lion of his heart
> And fought the holy wars in Palestine.
>
> (II.i.3–4)

Lady Faulconbridge cannot be blamed for her surrender to the man

> Against whose fury and unmatched force
> The aweless lion could not wage the fight.
> (I.i.265–66)

The reign was one in which embassies were dispatched to the Holy Roman Emperor "To treat of high affairs" (I.i.101)—a contrast, indeed, with the sordid wrangling of international politics that opens John's reign. The present is carefully set against the past, and direct links between them provided by Shakespeare's sources are conspicuously omitted. Holinshed tells us plainly that on his death-bed King Richard "unto his brother John . . . assigned the crown of England, and all other his lands and dominions, causing the nobles there present to swear fealty unto him," and *The Troublesome Reign* begins with a formal little episode of twenty lines in which John is presented by his mother to the English nobles, as a "second hope" after Coeur-de-lion. Shakespeare removes all this. Richard I's will is mentioned later, but only during the unseemly quarrelling of Constance and Eleanor before Angiers (II.ii.191–94), a situation which robs it of all persuasiveness. John is presented as a king who, in his confrontation with Chatillon, shows a firm, even an inspiring, temper. But though he is succinct and unflinching before the bold impertinence of the embassy, we quickly learn of a "most lawful claim" to his throne by the son of his elder brother. Even in these first exchanges the word *usurp* is flung at John, and, as soon as Chatillon has departed, his mother, in a private exchange, adds her voice to the accusations, undercutting his expansive "Our strong possession and our right for us" with the withering

> Your strong possession much more than your right,
> Or else it must go wrong with you and me.
> (I.i.40–41)

This denial of the legality of John's rule is matched later in the play by the Bastard. In his soliloquy at the end of Act II he speaks of the King of France's withdrawal from "a resolved and honourable war" against John (II.i.585), and at the end of Act IV he refers to Arthur as "England" (IV.3.142)—that is, the King of England. John's two most loyal supporters, then, leave us in no doubt of their opinions of the legitimacy of his rule. These deliberate modifications to his source material are part of

Shakespeare's careful establishment of a complex and testing political situation.

Act I begins with Chatillon's proud claims for Arthur and Queen Eleanor's whispered endorsement of them. Act II presents Arthur to us in all his powerless right. Holinshed had depicted Arthur as a young man capable of leading armies in battle (historically he was seventeen in 1204, when he probably died), and so, on some early occasions, does *The Troublesome Reign* (though the anonymous author seems later to have decided to show Arthur as a child). Shakespeare consistently depicts Arthur as a small boy incapable of fending for himself. His mother's widowhood is also frequently asserted to increase our emotional sympathy with the cheated, powerless child. Arthur's rights are powerfully argued by the French King (II.i.99–109), and Shakespeare even goes so far as to have Constance describe him as Eleanor's "eldest son's son," an ambiguity which pursues the ideas of the legitimacy of Arthur's claims to a point where history is strained (see Commentary to II.i.177). Not only does Shakespeare stress the combination of powerlessness and right in Arthur's claims; he also asserts the likelihood of his proving most royal. Even Queen Eleanor refers to him as a "green boy" who promises "a mighty fruit" (II.i.472–73). With his constant courtesy, his persuasive power in the prison scene, and the courage of his attempted escape, we are left in no doubt of his potential regality.

Shakespeare departs from his sources, then, in emphasizing Arthur's powerless royalty, just as he has deliberately drawn attention to the "strong possession" of John's usurpation. But he also takes care to establish the context in which Arthur's effort to achieve his right must operate. The first act looked back to an image of the hero warrior-king in King Richard. The second act begins with the very clear, firmly stated identification of the Duke of Austria as the man through whom King Richard "came early to his grave" (II.i.5). And a few lines later we watch Arthur embracing the killer of the king whose inheritance is now in question. Our view of Arthur can scarcely ever recover from this first sight of him. Even the things that make him pathetic and touching disqualify him as a possible ruler: his childishness, his weakness, his anxiety to avoid trouble. Above all is the fact that his hopes for power depend entirely on foreign support: the removal of John will mean that England is ruled by the puppet of King Richard's principal enemies. Perhaps a usurper who acts with strength and speed when his country is threatened is preferable to this rightful ruler who brings the inevitability of foreign domination. Shakespeare presents us with the impossible choice between the man in possession and the claimant with legal right, between the vigorous man of action and the helpless child.

For the time being, however, there is no need to face the direct choice. Between the first mention of Arthur and the presentation of him with his allies, our attention has been diverted by the appearance of the bastard son of King Richard, providing a third variation on the theme of the Coeur-de-lion inheritance. In the political confrontation before Angiers, with both sides disguising simple greed in the pomposity of their claims, the Bastard voices the audience's increasing contempt for power politics. At the end of Act II he rightly convicts both sides of seeking only convenience, self-interest, profit—or, as he terms them collectively, "commodity." The Bastard's role in Act II stems directly from the circumstances of his introduction in Act I. The gaiety, wit, and colloquial impertinence of his language there, and the delightful precision of social observation in his first soliloquy, provide a splendid change from the grim politics that have gone before. Firmly identified as Coeur-de-lion's son, first by Queen Eleanor and later by his own mother, the Bastard immediately establishes a relationship of easy friendliness with the audience. The witty, often bawdy, remarks with which he undercuts the tedious earnestness of his half-brother seem rather to be asides to the audience than comments to anyone on stage. We are, as we sit back to enjoy his liveliness, slow to realize that a miniature parallel to the main action is being presented to us. Here is another disputed inheritance, a man in possession without the right and a powerless claimant opposing him. There is even a will in the background, over which the parties can wrangle. John finds for the man in possession, asserting the legal fiction of the Bastard's legitimacy in spite of the clear visual evidence he has already admitted. He could scarcely, in his position, do otherwise. When the Bastard decides to give up his "fair five hundred pound a year" (I.i.69) and allow right to take its course, his behaviour contrasts for the first, but not the last, time with that of his King. "Brother, take you my land. I'll take my chance" (I.i.151): it is a self-commitment to the present, a willingness to accept what fate brings, which is immediately attractive. It goes with his confident sense of his own identity—"I am I, howe'er I was begot" (I.i.175).

The relationship between the Bastard and the audience, beginning in the light-hearted amusement of Act I, will develop into one of the principal structural props of *King John*. While we watch, with increasing commitment, the growing dependability of his involvement in national affairs, that label "Bastard," so conspicuous in the speech prefixes of a printed text, will, in the theatre, tend to be forgotten. As the failure of the usurping John grows more obvious, and after the death of the powerless, French-dominated boy, Arthur, our attention in the struggle for King Richard's inheritance focuses more firmly on King Richard's son. Only at the end of the play are our developing hopes and involvement turned in a more legitimate direction.

The establishment of this relationship between the Bastard and the audience in the first act, our response to the magnetism of his personality and to the spontaneous honesty and amusement of his observation, qualify him for the role of commentator on the political pretensions of the disputants before Angiers. Power politics is here revealed as a sham. Two kings jockey for audience and recognition before a commoner; the mothers of a king and a would-be king abuse each other in terms worthy of brawling fishwives. Behind the facade of Arthur's rights, Philip inadvertently allows us an occasional glimpse of his own greed; amongst the pomposity of royal plurals John suddenly reveals his grasping selfishness in that urgent appeal to the citizens to "let *me* in" (II.i.269). The men of Angiers, through their smooth-tongued spokesman, claim "loyalty" to the King of England;

> he that proves the King,
> To him will we prove loyal.
>
> (II.i.270–71)

What kind of loyalty is this, which refuses to commit itself until superior might is revealed? With growing bewilderment and contempt we watch the charade, and turn gratefully to the Bastard and his series of deflating asides. In a world where political loyalty is impossible, where there can be no ultimate political right because the law is administered by a usurper, where even the traditional recourse to trial by combat results only in a draw, we find a natural refuge in cynicism. The Bastard provides it, and at the same time opposes one honest true emotion against the hypocrisy all around him: hatred for the man who killed his father. Words as a stalking-horse for self-interest are his particular target. He is savagely contemptuous of the fine verbal package in which the peace proposals are presented from Angiers (II.i.455–67), and the Dauphin's formal speech of wooing receives his bitter, richly deserved, mockery (II.i.504–09). At the end, having watched John give away the French possessions which he had gone to battle to protect and heard Philip himself admit that he has sold the cause of the defenceless mother and son in whose "right we came" (II.i.548), we are ready to listen to the Bastard's brilliant analysis of the political impulse which has dominated the scene.

It was a favourite study of the Elizabethans to draw morals and to teach lessons from the events of history, and with trenchant accuracy the Bastard draws his lesson from what he has been watching. In a world where might is right, where the man that holds the kingdom "holds the law" (III.i.188), where men withhold their allegiance until superior force reveals where allegiance may most advantageously be placed, he isolates "commodity" as the governing principle. The analytical precision of the Bastard's summing-up, the destructive wit of it, mark a definite milestone in the play's development. At the end of the soliloquy he find himself in danger of losing his detachment in the vigour of his "failing," and turns the tables on himself with that light-hearted self-awareness that we met in the first act:

> And why rail I on this commodity?
> But for because he hath not wooed me yet.
> (II.i.587–88)

His observation is saved from over-earnestness; the motives and actions we have been watching are really too contemptible to be worth getting angry about. And so the Bastard, fresh from his experience of politics in action, steps back from the brink of pomposity to observe himself, to decide that he may as well swim with the tide and continue to provide "sweet poison for the age's tooth":

> Since kings break faith upon commodity,
> Gain, be my lord—for I will worship thee!
> (II.i.597–98)

It is the verdict of an uncommitted man on what he has seen. Hitherto commenting only from the sidelines, the Bastard now faces the issues that his examination of politics has raised and finds nothing to be loyal to except the self-interest which he has seen so dominant. It is a stage in his development; more painful events will forge a new attitude.

The second act has examined, and identified, commodity at work in politics. We know by the end of it what it is and how it operates. But its manifestations so far have been only hypocritical grandiloquence and a treaty of convenience which has sold all the reasons for going to war. In the next act the effects of commodity will be shown biting home. As they do so a new kind of politician enters the play.

Pandulph is different from the politicians we have seen so far because he is loyal to an ideal which he keeps unswervingly, fanatically, before him. His belief in the absolute rightness of papal supremacy allows him to justify any means in seeking his ends. We turn from watching political principles dissolve before the temptations of commodity to the spectacle of uncompromising political and religious belief devouring commodity, and everything else that comes in its way, for the service of its own aims. Pandulph shows brilliant political acumen in his dealing with the English and French rulers, and, in a world where bargains are broken sooner than kept, his consistency is not without an element of surprise. At the end of the play for example, having secured John's surrender, he works loyally for him, and ironically enough, is partly responsible for bringing about the final solution.

Pandulph's most important scenes, however, are in the third act. His sudden intervention moves the play into a new realm. Philip and John, as the Bastard has so pointedly told us, have hitherto allowed the immediate convenience of the moment to make their decisions for them. The arrival of Pandulph forces these pliant, self-seeking monarchs into a reassessment of their positions. Shakespeare allows this jolt to shift John, for the only time in the play, into that stereotype Protestant hero presented by some of his sources. In the speeches of defiance between John and Pandulph the play has its most sustained parallels with *The Troublesome Reign*, including all the familiar phraseology of Protestant polemic: "Italian priest," "supreme head," "usurped authority," "juggling witchcraft" (III.i.147–60, 162–71). It is John's finest hour, a performance directed unhesitatingly to crude popular appeal.

The speed he showed in arriving at Angiers, his vehemence in the verbal wrangles, the whole image of him as "English John" (King Philip's phrase at II.i.10), culminate here, in this rant against papal tyranny. The mood is to sustain itself through the subsequent battle, where John's speed is again prominent, but the downhill course begins soon after that, and the bubble is quickly burst. But even in the height of the confrontation the hollowness of what John is saying reveals itself. The reference to "usurped authority" is at the centre of the sham. John's own authority, on the admission of his staunchest supporters, is usurped. When usurpers appeal to patriotism to accuse others of usurpation, we are in a situation without landmarks for loyalty. Pandulph brings to this situation the destructive fanaticism of his service to the Pope, but to the English audience for whom Shakespeare wrote the appeal to such an authority would be unacceptable. The effects of the void thus created are explored in Act IV. For the time being, however, the focus is on Pandulph.

Having forced John into his hasty and apparently unthinking declaration of a political stand which, from his behavior in the preceding scene, is unexpected, and which, given his position, is ultimately untenable, Pandulph turns to Philip, dismissing all order, all government, in his single-minded adherence to the papal cause:

> All form is formless, order orderless,
> Save what is opposite to England's love.
>
> (III.i.253–54)

On other lips, on the Earl of Northumberland's for example, vowing revenge for his son's death in the first scene of *2 Henry IV*, this is the cry of the arch-rebel, defiance of all authority. But Pandulph works for what he sees as a higher authority, "the church, our mother"; the stigma of rebellion does not attach to seeking her good. And so the fantastic verbal gymnastics in which he indulges to dissuade Philip from keeping his oath are, indeed, as Dr. Johnson observed, "irresistible—provided that one accepts the proposition that the voice of the church is the voice of heaven." There is nothing in the play to suggest that we should accept this, but faith, order, loyalty, even commodity, are all turned to its service. Philip, movingly expressing his dilemma, is allowed no easy way out; he has to bow to authority—whether "higher" or not depending on the view one takes of Pandulph's argument. It is, however, the only coherent political authority in the play, and it will ultimately claim John, here temporarily self-assertive and defiant, as surely as it claims Philip. Philip's choice is John's, in the end; the ruler clings to power.

King Philip's surrender to Pandulph marks his withdrawal from serious participation in the action of the play. The scene ends with war imminent. Its first victim is Blanche, in the previous act the pawn of the commodity-seeking politicians, and now, horribly, at the mercy of the warriors:

> each army hath a hand,
> And in their rage, I having hold of both,
> They whirl asunder and dismember me.
>
> (III.i.328–30)

The obedience and honour which she had shown in the negotiations before Angiers cannot survive in the harsh world into which the play is now moving. The more savage fates of madness and death await Constance and Arthur, the other suffering innocents in the political struggle. A harder, more deeply resilient, attitude will be necessary to deal with the brutal events made inevitable by Pandulph's arrival. The Bastard's increasingly successful search for a sense of purpose to balance Pandulph's fanatical dedication will be shown in the second half of the play.

The last scene of Act III is a summing up of what has occurred, and a prediction of what is to come. It follows John's overwhelming success in battle, the Bastard's settling his score with Austria and establishment of his military prowess in the rescue of Queen Eleanor, and John's reaching agreement with Hubert over the fate of Arthur. The tense excitement of John's edging stealthily towards the point in that conversation with Hubert, terrified of the self-commitment that putting his thoughts into words will mean, ingratiating himself with the man he hopes will serve him, leads up to the final whiplash of the monosyllables in which understanding is reached (III.iii.66). John, who only a few lines before was cutting an impressive figure as the representative of English Protestantism, here, fresh from his military triumph, orders the death of a child. The Bastard is absent while it happens; he will not return until the consequences of John's action are all-too-painfully clear. But Arthur himself is present, a silent and touching reminder of the pain and suffering brought by the corruption of power. In the following scene Pandulph urges the Dauphin to invade England, and predicts what we have just observed:

> O sir, when he shall hear of your approach,
> If that young Arthur be not gone already,
> Even at that news he dies.
>
> (III.iv.162–64)

The clarity of Pandulph's political insight is as impressive as the equanimity with which he contemplates the murder of a child. The death of Arthur will polarize political attitudes and loyalties, and Pandulph's cool acceptance of it helps to establish his relative position. Our knowledge that what he says about Arthur is already true warns us also of the probable accuracy of his predictions of the panic in England that will greet any "natural exhalation in the sky" or "distempered day" (III.iv.153–59); all these things will arrive in the second half of the play, throwing John's subjects into terror and rebellion. That the calculating eye of Pandulph has foreseen them, and their advantage to his cause, keeps them in perspective in the rapid, panicky atmosphere of Acts IV and V.

The third act closes with John committed to an action which, in the opinion of the play's most astute judge of political affairs, will lead to his downfall. Its final scene has gathered together the threads of John's period of success, summed up in the envious praise of King Philip and his son. It has shown, in the deftness with which Pandulph has provoked the Dauphin to invade England, how commodity and single-minded devotion to a political creed can work together as an all-but-irresistible force, taking advantage of any means, including a child's death. With the Bastard temporarily absent from the play, the unscrupulousness which he could wittingly characterize as commodity turns into something more ruthless and savage. He will return to find his previous detachment inadequate to the new situation; harsh choices, serious self-commitment, will be demanded. Producers often, and rightly, allow an interval in performance after Act III. There is a break in the time-scheme here of indeterminate but, for the only time in the play, possibly lengthy duration, and the action shifts from France back to England. Act IV begins with the horrible consequences of political self-seeking exposed: the eyes of an innocent child are to be burned out.

Arthur is the most important and the most touching of the victims of the struggles for power in the play. His cousin Blanche, as we have seen, is the first and perhaps the most pathetic. His mother Constance protests longest and most eloquently against the inevitable destruction of helpless right by powerful might, though her failure is already clear before the great scenes of Arthur's suffering. Her long display of rhetorical, histrionic grief in the third act was a great theatrical attraction in the eighteenth and nineteenth centuries, and such actresses as Mrs. Siddons and Helena Faucit played the part often. More recently critics have accused Constance of being long-winded and even ranting, and her speeches have been cut and sometimes even burlesqued in performance. There is, certainly, an exaggeration about her grief, an insistence and concentration that sort ill with the shiftiness around her. But it is real and intense nevertheless, and should be played for its full effect. She greets the news of the Angiers marriage-settlement with outrage; the Bastard had seen it with amused contempt. Both play their part in shaping our attitude to what we have observed in Act II. In a famous passage, Mrs. Siddons describes how, as Constance, she used to stand, at the end of Act II, holding Arthur's hand and listening to the march of the marriage procession "because the sickening sounds of that march would usually cause the bitter tears of rage, disappointment, betrayed confidence, baffled ambition, and, above all, the agonizing feelings of maternal affect to gush into my eyes." Constance is coldly, savagely betrayed; her suffering is one of the inevitable effects of other's pursuit of power, and we watch it immediately after its cause has been so searchingly analysed by the Bastard. But as we do so we should remember that behind it lies also Constance's disappointment in her own pursuit of power, her "baffled ambition" as Mrs. Siddons puts it; there is, indeed, some truth in Eleanor's taunt that Constance wants to "be a queen and check the world" (II.i.123), however strong Arthur's theoretical claims may be. Constance's vividly expressed sense of betrayal, and, after the capture of Arthur, her uncontrolled despair, are part of the examination of the political struggle. Eloquent in weakness, she is left with words as her only weapon; and when she has shown that wrong is indeed wrong, there is nothing further she can do. Her suffering in Act III, scene 4, helps to define our attitude to John, whom we have just seen order the murder of her child. She makes her protest, vain but superb, and dies, we later learn, "in a frenzy" (IV.ii.122). She has tried to outface the march of commodity. The verbal force of her hostility makes it conspicuous, but her defeat is no less inevitable than that of Blanche, who is "whirled asunder and dismembered" after her much briefer protest.

It is in the fate of Arthur that the savage destructiveness of the quest for power reaches its climax. Shakespeare's consistent presentation of him as a helpless child, with no personal role in the political struggle, increases the poignancy of his destruction. The prison scene (IV.i) is significantly altered from its equivalent in *The Troublesome Reign*, where Arthur and Hubert debate the nature of a subject's duty and whether Hubert is bound to carry out the command of his sovereign when it transgresses God's law. Shakespeare substitutes an emotional clash between brutal strength and helplessness; Arthur, from being a political theorist in *The Troublesome Reign*, becomes a terrified child pleading for his eyes. The dramatic economy of the play demands that Arthur report the kindnesses he has done Hubert, and this has led critics to accuse the boy of priggishness. But the memory of his kind acts is important to the situation, and there has been no time for us to see them. The desperate use of every possible argument in Arthur's frantic pleading is in any case in keeping with the mood of the scene. Political debate has gone because the preceding three acts have devalued politics, have left nothing to be loyal to. Arthur's appeal is to Hubert's pity and to his essential humanity. The break-through, when it comes, is sudden and absolute:

> pretty child, sleep doubtless and secure
> That Hubert, for the wealth of all the world
> Will not offend thee.
>
> (IV.i.129–31)

Hubert leaves commodity behind in these lines. The suffering and terror of Arthur force him into a searching examination of where his loyalties lie. He takes a firm stand, in a world where shiftiness has been the rule, and he takes it by personal decision after frightening hesitation. It is an example which the Bastard will follow.

Arthur, like his mother and like Blanche, has only words to protect his weakness from the brutal ambition and unyielding power around him. With Hubert, words for once succeed. But it is only a temporary success. Arthur is one of those destined by the march of history to be destroyed in the struggle for political dominance. The circumstances of his death are unknown to anyone in the play; his dying words detect his "uncle's spirit" (IV.iii.9) in the stones that kill him, but only the audience hears. He goes out of the play in the same minor key as we have heard from him throughout. The ambiguous manner of Arthur's death, with no straightforward responsibility assignable to anyone and the audience alone in possession of the truth, allows it to be used as a touchstone in the scenes that follow: in the reactions to it of the English lords, John, Hubert, and the Bastard, the problems of the play are crystallized.

From our position of superior awareness we watch the discovery of Arthur's body by the English lords. Their course is settled; they enter discussing their plans to join the Dauphin, while Arthur's corpse lies unobserved. This is a significant change from *The Troublesome Reign*, where the lords' discovery of the body is the motive for their invitation to the Dauphin, and the structure of Shakespeare's scene inevitably gives a hollow ring to the lords' speeches of grief. The death of the innocent Arthur is hideous and shocking; it cries out for protest from any man of honour. What is unsatisfactory about the reactions of Salisbury, Pembroke, and Bigot is the pat immediacy with which they let it appear to determine them in a course in fact already decided, and the haste with which they arrive at judgements of guilt which the audience knows to be false. The contrast of their verbosity with the simple firmness of the Bastard's judgement is telling:

> It is a damnèd and a bloody work,
> The graceless action of a heavy hand—
> If that it be the work of any hand.
>
> (IV.iii.57–59)

The truth of that last line produces in the audience a grateful response to the one man who seems to be groping towards the knowledge they possess. It intensifies the relationship between the Bastard and the audience that has been developing since the first act, and at the same time alienates us from the blind and arrogant confidence of the lords. The alienation continues with their brutal treatment of Hubert, whom we watched only two scenes before as he rose above the values of a world thrusting for power. When the lords depart and leave the scene to the Bastard and Hubert, a crucial stage of the play's development is reached.

Before examining it, some further exploration of the surrounding context is necessary.

The sources from which Shakespeare worked are, on the whole, unequivocally hostile to the baronial revolt against John. To Holinshed the lords' proceedings are "sinister" and their opinions "wilful"; *The Troublesome Reign* follows the "Homily against Disobedience" in emphasizing the lords' obedience to the Pope in rebelling against John as one of several ways of evoking our antipathy to them. Our attitude in *King John* is less straightforward. We are spared the spectacle (shown in full in *The Troublesome Reign*) of the nobles swearing allegiance to a foreign prince. Shakespeare substitutes Salisbury's long speech of grief at the necessity of rebellion (V.ii.8–39). The tone here is complex. Some critics have suggested that Salisbury is a hypocrite, hiding the self-interest of rebellion behind crocodile tears. But such a view means that the lines would have to be played entirely insincerely, as a calculated but obvious sham. The difficulty with this is that Shakespeare offers no hint of it in the speech itself. The lines are highly patterned and involved, of course, but in this they reflect the ambiguity of Salisbury's position as a rebel seeking justification. Taken at their face value they convey, with considerable dramatic force, a real sense of doubt and sorrow. On the other hand, the context gives them a fuller perspective. The lords' hasty and visibly wrong conclusions in Act IV, scene 3, bring them to this moment of grief and doubt and to the need for elaborate self-justification. Their contempt for Hubert's honest tears ("Trust not those cunning waters of his eyes," IV.iii.107) leads, ironically, to our suspicion of the "honourable dew" that "silverly doth progress" down Salisbury's own cheeks; their suspicion of John's motives is sardonically balanced in the antidote which the Dauphin offers for Salisbury's grief:

> Come, come; for thou shalt thrust thy hand as deep
> Into the purse of rich prosperity
> As Lewis himself.
>
> (V.ii.60–62)

And finally their treachery to John is answered in the Dauphin's treachery to them. In the turbulent situation created by commodity and the search for power, the lords set themselves up as judges and find only insecurity and humiliation. Their silence before the Bastard's onslaught in Act V, scene 2, contrasting with their confident self-assertion in Act IV, scene 3, is symptomatic of their failure. They prove inadequate to the stresses of a difficult situation; in some ways they are as much the victims of the power struggle as Constance and Arthur.

The failure of the lords to find a satisfactory way forward from the havoc created by the unscrupulous self-seeking epitomized in the death of Arthur is paralleled in the increasingly obvious failure of King John in the second half of the play. John returns from France in the full flush of success. In his only appearance in Act IV, flanked by the scenes of Arthur's suffering and death, command is slipping away from him. Apparently at the height of his power, during the pomp of a second coronation, he encounters the bitter opposition of his nobles. A rapid series of blows cuts deep into his position. The Dauphin's invasion, so sudden and unexpected, turns John's own earlier achievement against himself: "The copy of your speed is learned by them" (IV.ii.113). And the death of his mother, the strength of her support realized only when lost, shakes him almost to incoherence. In this first scene in which he appears without Queen Eleanor, John loses his grip. The news of the panic within England, the report of the five moons, the terror and despair of the people, precisely fulfil Pandulph's prophecies. Unlike the author of *The Troublesome Reign*, Shakespeare wisely leaves out the theatrical representation of the astronomical phenomenon; the audience is not asked to share John's stresses and fears, but to judge his response to their challenge. In this second scene of Act IV we watch him fail on every count. In a speech which brings together the play's recurrent imagery of the physical body and the body politic, he shows a new awareness that political and personal morality cannot be separated:

> My nobles leave me, and my state is braved,
> Even at my gates, with ranks of foreign powers;
> Nay, in the body of this fleshy land,
> This kingdom, this confine of blood and breath,
> Hostility and civil tumult reigns
> Between my conscience and my cousin's death.
> (IV.ii.243–48)

John's collapse in the last two acts is shown as stemming directly from his abuse of power in ordering Arthur's murder. The long interview with Hubert in Act IV, scene 2, recalls in detail the earlier interview between them as John made known his desire for Arthur's death. John's attempt to unsay what was there said is not only degrading; it also reminds us of his clear responsibility. When his panic leads him to abuse Hubert's person (IV.ii.220–24), he is contemptible. In one scene the "English John" of the first half of the play is destroyed.

It is in this scene that the Bastard reappears. He left the play before Arthur's death was planned and returns after it has been (falsely) announced. He is uncontaminated by what has occurred and seems almost menacing as he faces his king. He has met the lords "going to seek the grave / Of Arthur, whom they say is killed tonight / On *your* suggestion" (IV.ii.164–66); he has brought bad news but finds John in no condition to receive it:

> But if you be afeard to hear the worst,
> Then let the worst unheard fall on your head.
> (IV.ii.135–36)

As John collapses, the Bastard gains in stature and the pattern of the play's final movement is established. By the end of the scene, with John now seeking to revoke even his abuse of Hubert's appearance, he is a despicable, even an absurd figure. There is no surprise in our next finding him kneeling in surrender before the papal legate. Shakespeare leaves John abject and contemptible in Act IV, scene 2, and then shows us Arthur's death and the Bastard's reaction to it. He has a new hero to establish in the final scenes; the undisguised cowardice and humiliation of John's surrender to Pandulph lead appropriately to the formal passing of command to the Bastard: "Have thou the ordering of this present time" (V.i.77).

The steps by which the Bastard has arrived at the point where he can accept this challenge have in some ways been anticipated by Hubert. From the impersonal taciturnity with which he accepted John's terrible commission in Act III, scene 3, Hubert has come, in the prison scene, to reveal honour and truth beneath a stern exterior. Though his part is not large, Hubert is the first person in the play to learn that personal honesty and integrity are more important than commodity or even than political loyalty. In the following scene with John he maintains this new-found self-possession in the face of the King's collapse, and in the confrontation over Arthur's corpse it is Hubert, the commoner, treated with contempt by the nobles, who behaves with true honour. At the end of Act IV, scene 3, a commoner and a bastard are left to protect what remains of English honour, the rightful claimant to the throne dead, the nobility in revolt, and the King no longer in control of the situation.

The coming together of Hubert and the Bastard has an element of comedy in a scene of the deepest seriousness, as the sharpness of the Bastard's anger repeatedly prevents Hubert from pronouncing his excuses. The audience is ready to enjoy the delay, the slight relaxation of tension, confident that the truth will emerge: the Bastard's anger is justified; Hubert's innocence is certain. The crime is roundly condemned:

> Beyond the infinite and boundless reach
> Of mercy, if thou didst this deed of death,
> Art thou damned, Hubert.
> (IV.iii.117–19)

The denial of guilt, when it comes, is calm and straightforward and is wholly accepted; in the next scene the Bastard is prepared to stake his soul on Hubert's innocence (V.i.43). The alliance of Hubert and the Bastard is inevitable, for they are the only two characters in the play who respond with honesty to the political situation. Both move from selfishness, through crisis, to a realization of an essential honour, of the need to commit themselves to what, in spite of expediency or convenience, they are forced to recognize as right. Hubert's crisis is in the prison scene; the Bastard's comes with the discovery of Arthur's corpse. The scene marks a major turning point in the pattern of the play, and the Bastard's presence in it is Shakespeare's deliberate choice (he does not appear in the equivalent scene in *The Troublesome Reign*). There was a new sense of sternness about the Bastard as he confronted John's panic in the previous scene, but it is the sight of Arthur's corpse which hardens his resolution and reveals his quality. His instinct for truth, hitherto revealed only in comic and satirical assessments of the corrupt behavior he has observed, leads him, in spite of the overhasty declarations being made all round him, to an intuition of the situation that the audience knows full well: "If that it be the work of any hand" (IV.iii.59). And against the assembled strength of the English nobility he displays the respect for truth which is his most vivid demonstration of honour. His protection of Hubert is unhesitating. The emergency galvanizes him into an awareness of what he really believes in: "Your sword is bright, sir; put it up again" (IV.iii.79). The line reminds us of Othello's "Keep up your bright swords, for the dew will rust them" (I.ii.59), and the moment has the same impressive display of courage and authority. On the Bastard's command the peace is kept; the nobles run off to the Dauphin and the commoners take stock of the situation.

The Bastard's respect for truth, and his courage, have already been demonstrated. The passionate intensity with which he goes on to question Hubert's guilt, and the completeness with which he trusts the honesty of his denial, reveal his personal moral goodness. The cynicism and detachment behind which he has sheltered are hammered out of him by the sight of Arthur's corpse. Hubert, appropriately, is by to hear his examination of the situation as, with a new self-awareness, he seeks a way forward. He still accepts the rightness of Arthur's claim to the throne; the earlier reference to Philip's "honourable war" (II.i.585) leads into the unequivocal statement here: "How easy dost thou take all England up" (IV.iii.142). The young man previously so witty and clear-sighted, and so detached, is now embroiled and confused by events:

> I am amazed, methinks, and lose my way
> Among the thorns and dangers of this world.
> (IV.iii.140–41)

But having examined his own position he looks beyond it. Arthur is dead, he does not know how. With his death

> The life, the right and truth, of all this realm
> Is fled to heaven.
> (IV.iii.144–45)

But this total acceptance of Arthur's claim cannot be the end of the matter. Time goes on, and though "England" may be "taken up" in the person of Arthur, the larger "England" remains, in danger of losing life and right and truth in a more general sense than that implied by the death of a claimant to its throne. A foreign prince is advancing through the country, the nobility is in revolt, the king in panic, the people in terror. The movement from a particular loss to the general danger in those two contrasting uses of "England" in the fourth and seventh lines of the speech measures the rapidity with which the Bastard moves forward to an assessment of a proper course—one of unselfish action on behalf of his country, accepting and moving beyond immediate uncertainty and danger. Like Hubert earlier he achieves self-possession. There is no talk about "pure honour" such as we have just heard from the lords (IV.iii.25). The situation does not allow of judgements in such black and white terms. There is no one with an untarnished claim to loyalty, but a choice must be made: "vast confusion waits." The death of Arthur has become irrelevant because a new situation is created by it. When the decision comes—"I'll to the King" (IV.iii.157)—it is a compromise with the conscience expressed in the first half of the speech, but also a self-dedication to the best course in the circumstances. Without fuss or rant the Bastard chooses a course of loyalty to the King who represents the only hope for the nation. The choice is made without illusions but with common sense and courage, and is followed with unswerving commitment. The "tempest" will be resisted. The scene ends with the bustle of vigorous action. The crisis is past. Hubert and the Bastard, the only two characters to accept with personal integrity the implications of the play's political lessons, move forward to confront "A thousand businesses."

The following scene confirms what has here emerged. John gives up his crown to Pandulph and the Bastard's rapidly growing authority is formally recognized: "Have thou the ordering of this present time" (V.i.77). During the next few scenes he is in control of English affairs. His confrontation with the Dauphin in Act V, scene 2, is an impressive display of national pride in a scene whose incisive directness contrasts interestingly with those earlier prebattle posturings before Angiers. The "warlike John" to whom the Bastard refers (V.ii.176) has little connexion with the degenerate king we have just left; it is a forceful picture of the ideal English monarch whose "royalty doth speak" (V.ii.129) in the Bastard. His vigorously hurled challenge leads into a rapid series of battle scenes which firmly establish the Bastard's dominance. He "alone upholds the day" (V.iv.5) and even has John leave the field (V.iii.6). The Bastard's successful control of English affairs—with help from Melun's betrayal and from the storm which wrecks the Dauphin's supplies—leaves him, by the penultimate scene of the play, in undisputed authority. In this short, intense scene, for which there is no equivalent in the source, the atmosphere of taut anxiety built up during the battle scenes reaches a climax. Hubert and the Bastard, by now secure in the audience's trust, meet in the dark, with English fortunes in the balance, to face the news of John's approaching death. Hubert has come, immediately danger threatens, to the one man in whom there can be confidence:

> To acquaint you with this evil that you might
> The better arm you to the sudden time
> Than if you had at leisure known of this.
> (V.vi.25–27)

The play has mentioned no heir to John, and here is the Bastard, alone in authority, receiving news of the King's poisoning. The third of the heirs of Coeur-de-lion is left now with sole claim to our respect and trust. And yet, even in greeting Hubert in this scene, the Bastard has reminded us that he comes only "one way of the Plantagenets" (V.vi.11); he can never have a legitimate claim to the crown. In bringing us to this moment Shakespeare has caused our sense of dramatic excitement to overtake our more prosaic knowledge that John was succeeded by Henry: the existence of John's son is kept hidden until the news of the King's imminent death is brought to the man who has already taken over power from him. Then the fact is dropped casually:

> The lords are all come back,
> And brought Prince Henry in their company.
> (V.vi.33–34)

The Bastard falters a moment; his prayer is strangely enigmatic:

> Withhold thine indignation, mighty heaven,
> And tempt us not to bear above our power.
> (V.vi.37–38)

Though obscure, the words might be interpreted as a request for help in resisting the temptation to treat Henry's claims as John once treated Arthur's. But the moment quickly passes as the Bastard reaffirms the decision, made over Arthur's corpse, to get on with the task in hand, to dedicate himself to the duties he has taken on. The answer to the vast questions raised by the death of John is the same as that at the death of Arthur; there are still "A thousand businesses" to worry about, and the Bastard, with Hubert, presses on with the task of facing them.

The confusion of the political situation is not much alleviated by our first acquaintance with Prince Henry in the final scene. The intellectual concentration with which he explores the idea of death's capture of the mind is fascinating, but gives no indication of likely political aptitude. Nor does the strange, opaque beauty of the lines with which he follows it:

> I am the cygnet to this pale faint swan
> Who chants a doleful hymn to his own death,
> And from the organ-pipe of frailty sings
> His soul and body to their lasting rest.
> (V.vii.21–24)

The appearance of King John diverts our attention from the Prince, though we may questioningly remember the confidence of that "lasting rest" as we watch what Swinburne called the "sullen and slow death-pangs of Shakespeare's tyrant." John's death is disturbing and painful to witness. The imagery of heat and fever here reaches its climax as the inward burning of the poison rages:

> I am a scribbled form, drawn with a pen
> Upon a parchment, and against this fire
> Do I shrink up. . . .
> And none of you will bid the winter come
> To thrust his icy fingers in my maw,
> Nor let my kingdom's rivers take their course
> Through my burned bosom.
> (V.vii.32–39)

There is no looking forward here, none of the prophecies of Henry's VIII's coming to complete the struggle against Rome that the dying John is allowed in *The Troublesome Reign*: just the "one poor string" to keep his heart going until he receives the bitter news of the loss of the Bastard's troops. He dies, a "module of confounded royalty," the precise moment of his passing unmarked, while the seemingly hopeless situation is being described. Ironically we learn only a few lines later that the war is already virtually over. We wonder, as we watch him die, about that "lasting rest." John himself seems to be suffering a hell in life:

> Within me is a hell, and there the poison
> Is a fiend confined to tyrannize
> On unreprievable, condemned blood.
> (V.vii.46–48)

There is no sign of repentance, no indication of hope of salvation; only that unobserved, despairing death. Shakespeare leaves deliberately vague the theological question of John's immortal fate. But the dramatic impetus of the play is clear; the Prince's reference to "lasting rest" is picked up in the Bastard's desire to wait on the King "to heaven"(V.vii.24, 72). Ambiguous, usurping, erratic, "English John" seems finally to be given the benefit of the doubt, and the play emerges from the past and looks, at first a little hesitantly, forward.

That the Bastard can be trusted to use authority and power with honour and truth has become clear in the preceding scenes. The pattern of the play is completed when the son of Coeur-de-lion kneels before the boy-king. The Bastard commands the scene, treated with deference by the nobles, organizing the details of John's funeral, still anxious that proper precautions be taken against the enemy. How easily the man who once took "Gain" for his "lord" might here snatch ultimate power! But he reveals his worthiness to rule, nowhere better than in his self-dedication to service:

> on my knee,
> I do bequeath my faithful services
> And true subjection everlastingly.
> (V.vii.103–05)

And was there, after all, ever any other possibility? Was not the audience's hope of final power for the man whose career they have most intimately shared always a daydream? In his great moments of crisis in the play, beside Arthur's corpse, in the darkness after the battle, at John's death-bed, the role the Bastard chooses for himself is always that of loyal, and active, service. He even sees his soul serving John after death "As it on earth hath been thy servant still" (V.vii.73).

The Bastard's kneeling before Prince Henry ensures that government, and indeed history itself, will go on in orderly fashion. The Prince who must try to "set a form" on the work which John has left "so shapeless and so rude" (V.vii.26–27) will take up the reins. His success may be no greater; there is no particular sense of anticipation about the coming reign as we watch the boy king at the end of the play. The complexity of the political events through which we have passed is even reflected in the mixture of motives which will lead to the peace-making—the Bastard's military preparation, the French losses, Pandulph's diplomacy. There is no over-simplification, no unequivocal sense of triumph.

As the play draws to a close our suspension of disbelief relaxes and our sense of historical perspective returns. The events of John's reign which have so occupied our attention recede into the past: "O, let us pay the time but needful woe" (V.vii.110). Even the new King, about to take over, is really a figure from the past, long since dead:

> Even so must I run on, and even so stop.
> What surety of the world, what hope, what stay,
> When this was now a king, and now is clay?
> (V.vii.67–69)

The characters from history fade from our view. But not everything passes. And the one character from the play who has no historical reality, whose role has been almost entirely of the dramatists's invention, steps forward into the present to deliver the epilogue. The relationship the Bastard has enjoyed with the audience ensures our attention; the honesty and courage with which he has faced the treacherous complexity of the play's political issues must ensure also our respect. The particular truth of these final lines for the audience to whom they were first addressed is undeniable: that they are spoken by a character who has faced, with integrity and common sense, the perennial struggle for honour in a corrupt world gives them a more general significance.

In *King John* Shakespeare explores the motives and behavior of men in a conflict for power. His choice of a historical period remote and yet reasonably familiar allows him to do so both with a certain freedom and with the expectation of an immediate response from his audience. The concentration of events around the central question of the fate of Arthur clarifies the issues; the foreshortening of the time-scheme results in a dramatic intensification, reflected in the imagery, of the pressures affecting those involved in the conflict. The struggle exposes the hypocrisy of political grandiloquence; it leads to the destruction of innocent victims in Arthur and Constance and Blanche, and the humiliation of bewilderment of the lords who presume to adopt a course based on inadequate self-awareness and shallow judgement. The corrupting greed for power exposed in John is set against the frightening picture of ruthless fanaticism in Pandulph. But against all these the play reveals the gradual movement from cynicism and detachment to self-possession and integrity in Hubert and the Bastard. Because this is a history play dealing with public virtues and vices, their morality reveals itself in patriotic action; but the struggle and its solution are not unlike those which Shakespeare was to explore in different terms and with more tragically introspective heroes.

Part II
Henry VIII

From *The Boston Evening Transcript*, January 9, 1894

Tremont Theatre: *Henry VIII*

The second week of Mr. Henry Irving's engagement at the Tremont Theatre began last evening with Shakespeare's *Henry VIII*, the principle features of the cast being as follows:

King Henry VIII	Mr. William Terriss
Cardinal Wolsey	Mr. Irving
Cardinal Campeius	Mr. Lacy
Duke of Norfolk	Mr. Haviland
Earl of Surrey	Mr. Clarence Hague
Duke of Suffolk	Mr. Tyars
Duke of Buckingham	Mr. Frank Cooper
Queen Katharine	Miss Ellen Terry
Anne Bullen	Miss Coleridge

One might almost say that Mr. Irving was predestined to mount *Henry VIII* sooner or later. If it is perhaps not the play of Shakespeare's in which the greatest amount of pageantry and scenic show is possible, it is certainly the one in which the poet himself has taken the greatest pains to indicate a great deal of scenic display by actual stage direction. And Mr. Irving's fondness for and mastery in this sort of thing have well-nigh passed into a proverb.

No matter what feelings one may have about the texts of *Henry VIII*, it is hard to speak of the performance last evening without giving its scenic side the first place. As a piece of stage mounting, *Henry VIII* may well be called Mr. Irving's masterpiece, so far. For apposite beauty and historical correctness of scenery and costumes, for lavish gorgeousness of scenic effect, for artistic grouping of masses on the stage, and life-like vividness of concerted action, it outbids all that he has shown us hitherto. It is a wonderfully beautiful, impressive and magnificent feast for the eye, the receptive sensitiveness of the eye being still further stimulated by the almost constant appeal of excellent, dignified, and always appropriate music to the ear. As a piece of *mise en scene*—in the widest significance of the term—it is incomparably fine.

And yet this wonderful show, with all its beauty and grandeur, impressed us somehow quite as forcibly with the inexorable limitations of scenic display as a factor in a great drama, as it did with its glorious possibilities. We have felt much the same thing whenever we have seen a truly great dramatic work mounted with equal care and lavishness, whether by Mr. Irving here, or by whom you please at Paris, Berlin, or Bayreuth. The more splendid and the nearer to perfection the stage mounting was in detail and ensemble, the farther short it seemed to fall of completely satisfying us dramatically; the more convincingly did we feel that Wagner's dramatic theory—which is in the main Mr. Irving's too—of "complete and immediate presentation to the senses" was but founded on a half-truth, at best. And perhaps this half-truth may in the end be no truth at all. With all the scenic wonders we have seen on the stage, here and elsewhere, we cannot but feel that, in the drama, a thousand merely material appeals to the senses are not worth one appeal to the imagination: that the finest stage picture producible by the arts of scene painting, costuming, and stage lighting can never vie with that ideal picture magically called up before the mind's eye by the poet's verse or the musician's score. In the end, one may say that the scenic show, as a factor in the drama, only whets the appetite it is meant to satisfy, and this too in a ruinously increasing ration, the finer and more elaborate it is. It is like the rapid-transit problem—double your means of rapid transit, and you quadruple the population you have to deal with. The more carefully elaborate, the closer to nature and reality you make your scenic show, the more vividly do you suggest to the spectator all that you have left undone. He has an unconquerable desire to have it still more perfect; the yellow flame of your stage picture shows black against the bright sun-disk of the ideal picture his insatiable imagination craves.

Almost all theatre-goers, save the hopelessly frivolous and those who are the victims of special fads, have at least some sense of dramatic proportion; they feel, if only subconsciously, that, as the stage holds the mirror up to life, so must it also take cognizance of the Carlylean principle in life, that "clothes must hold men." Last evening we could not help feeling, while looking at that gorgeous procession that escorts the Lady Anne to her coronation—"Yes, that is all very splendid; now make every man in that procession a Henry Irving, and every woman an Ellen Terry, and the thing will be really worth while!" The clothes and trappings were most lordly and regal; but the people who wore them were for the most part too unmistakably mere supers and undergraduates. The dramatic illusion was not there. And what one most craves on the stage is just the dramatic illusion; all else is but of secondary moment. Merely stimulate the imagination and it has all the inexhaustible realms of fancy to draw upon; try to satisfy it by merely material means, and you find that you might as well try to quench fire with oil—the appetite grows with what it feeds on.

Our only excuse for here setting forth these, possibly rather transcendental, considerations is that they were really and unavoidably suggested to our mind by what we saw at the Tremont Theatre last evening. Nay, more than this, these were the most prominent and forcible suggestions we got from the performance. Of the leading impersonators of the characters in Shakespeare's play only one figure rose to commanding prominence, dramatically speaking, out of this general sea of scenic splendor; and this figure was Mr. Irving's Wolsey. Snap judgments are in general not worth much, but in this instance we are quite willing to let our enthusiasm of the moment speak out, unrestrained by critical timidity. We should call Cardinal Wolsey the most entirely great impersonation Mr. Irving has yet given us; he has actually eviscerated Shakespeare's character, turned him inside out on the stage. The all-subduing pride of the man, his "unbounded stomach," his native unscrupulousness refined by sacerdotal astucity, his penetrating intellectuality, and that ever sensible undercurrent of parvenu brutality which no worldy training could ever completely tame, are all blended together with the most consummate art, and placed before you with a vividness and completeness that leaves nothing to be desired. In Wolsey all those arts of facial expression and insinuating vocal inflexion that hit so wide of the true mark in Mr. Irving's Mephistopheles show themselves as unmistakably and convincingly true of aim. Add that personal force, that quality of being, which Mr. Irving shows in all his impersonations, and you have a Wolsey such as may fairly be said to seek his fellow on our stage. We cannot think of a moment in the part in which Mr. Irving was not admirable. It was a thoroughly great piece of acting—in spite of the actor's frequent and characteristic misreading of his lines.

Miss Terry's Queen Katharine has much that is charming; one can criticise little in her conception and performance of the part, save a constant nervous fidgetiness from which Miss Terry cannot free herself. What was lacking was personal force. The assumption was from beginning to end on all too small a scale. Mr. Terris's Henry VIII is decidedly better than his Henry II in "Beckett"; he now and then makes at least an attempt at flexibility. It seemed to us that he took the traditional "bluff" in King Hal's character rather dangerously *au pied de la lettre,* and often fell from "bluffness" into something uncomfortably resembling rowdyism. Still be it said to his great credit that he gives us a Henry with a good stiff back-bone, and not the merely whimpering voluptuary we have sometimes seen on the stage in Henry's shoes. You feel in him that Henry was a man, if not an entirely agreeable one. Mr. Cooper made a truly dignified Buckingham, showing both vivacity of temper and depth of feeling; in reading his lines he now and then falls into tricks which may have been caught from his principal. For instance, one would have gathered from what he said that he was "lord high constable of Buckingham," as well as duke of that name. Miss Coleridge was capital as Anne Bullen, acting and looking the part admirably. The rest did about as well as usual.

H. A. Clapp

From *The Advertiser*, January 9, 1894

Mr. Irving Opens the Week at the Tremont

The representation of *Henry VIII*, which was given at the Tremont Theatre last night, was in many respects memorable. It is more than doubtful if the recollections of any of the present race of Bostonians includes any performance of the play worthy to be compared in scenic beauty and completeness and perfection of detail with this which is now offered to us by Mr. Irving and his company. Praise in this kind may be as large and high as possible without insincerity or extravagance. But in respect of matters more weighty and significant than any and all forms, modes and shows spectacular, there is neither occasion nor possibility for any strain of very lofty adulation. The character of Wolsey has been repeatedly impersonated by great English and American actors, and the standard they have set is one to which Mr. Irving can now scarcely hope to attain; while Miss Charlotte Cushman's assumption of Queen Katharine remains and will remain, in the memory of all who witnessed it, unique in its native nobility, its tender humanness, its profound and spirit-searching pathos. Comparison direct may be no decenter than the lie direct, and is not to be indulged in. But the one word is to be used which shall with kind frankness simply say that there is a greater glory for interpretations than lies in the limbs and outward flourishes, and that the highest distinction of the theatre is in the truth and power of the actor's art.

The version of *Henry VIII* presented last evening was interesting and able. The cutting was of a large and fearless king, but was managed with cleverness and with a proper respect for the author,—or authors, if it be true, as it seems to be, that Mr. William Shakespeare and Mr. John Fletcher collaborated in the production of this historical drama. A feature of the fourth act which was novel to our playgoers was the coronation procession of Queen Anne Bullen and equally unwonted was the use of a fragment of the fifth act, the christening of Elizabeth being presented as a tableau vivant, supplemented by a portion of Cranmer's famous prophecy of the infant's greatness and a bit of King Henry's closing speech.

Wolsey's character, as it is drawn by Shakespeare, is marked by the fullness and splendor of the master-poet's skill as long as the "o'er great cardinal" is in power, and his "pride, ambition, duplicity and passion for intrigue" are in clear evidence. It is exceedingly difficult to believe in the identity of this Wolsey with that of the Wolsey who, after his downfall from power is humble, gentle, generous and spiritually minded. Without seeking farther, we may doubtless find the only possible explanation in the circumstance that Shakespeare followed straight in the tracks of George Cavendish, the lover and high-hearted biographer of the Cardinal, who both recognizes the arrogance and selfishness of Wolsey in prosperity, and depicts his repentance as genuine,—"a real renovation of the heart and rejuvenescence of the soul." That such a change might be is conceivable. Mr. Irving plays the part in his own peculiar way, not illuminating any of its obscurities, but displaying its traits with his own intellectual lucidity and penetration. He is justly careful not to exaggerate the outward harshness and rancor of Wolsey's pride and to accentuate his smoothness—his "full seeming with meekness and humility"—before king and court. Mr. Irving also adds quite definitely a quality of slyness, in furtive smile, tone and gesture, which has the effect of making a heavy addition to the burden of the cardinal's spiritual baseness. Everywhere, of course, Mr. Irving is picturesque. The difficult speeches of Wolsey—especially those which follow his downfall—are beyond Mr. Irving's power. He interprets them quietly, and at moments his voice has a rare suggestive sweetness, with a fine pathetic suggestion in it, but such long-sustained poetic sentences demand an elocutionary variety and vitality which Mr. Irving does not possess, and many of the noblest lines in the part failed of their true effect, and of any adequate effect.

Miss Terry's assumption of Queen Katherine was full of life, grace, and sensibility. It has moments of great beauty, especially when she addressed herself with wifely tenderness to the king, and the fire and vivacity of the declamation were often admirable. But it seemed to us that Miss Terry's effort did not indicate either directly or indirectly the extraordinary nobility and greatness of the nature of the Queen, or touch any chord of the listener's spirit into full vibration of sympathy with Katharine's deep-hearted grief. Her final scene was managed with the ability of a most competent actress, but the note of physical force was too strong considering the near approach of death and quite too strong for poignancy of pathos. At other performances Miss Terry will doubtless avoid—what was probably an accident or inadvertance last night—the dividing of her attention between the pillowing of her head and the utterance of her most exquisite lines:—

> Cause the musicians play me that sad note
> I named my knell, whilst I sit meditating
> On that celestial harmony I go to.

Mr. Terriss played King Henry with immense vivacity and spirit, and with a directness so agreeable that one might easily be careless to note his occasional missing of the best emphasis in the delivery of his text. A loud and decent competency marked the efforts of the other chief performers, Mr. Cooper leading easily with his Buckingham.

The setting was what we have declared it to be. The scenes were as beautiful as any ever beheld in the city, all the interiors being sumptuous and impressive and the landscapes and architectural pieces noble in the extreme of the scenic art. The view of the river and of the towers and houses of the city in Buckingham's final scene was memorable. The costumes in richness, elegance, and fitness surpassed and gave great continual pleasure. The complicated dance—a kind of minuet and country dance combined—performed by the King and his attendants and the ladies in Wolsey's palace, was perfect in its kind and a piquant delight to ears and eyes of the spectators.

William T. W. Ball

From *The Boston Traveller*, January 10, 1894

Irving's *King Henry VIII*
A Production Notable from Every Standpoint

As a Stage Pageant It Is in Advance of Anything Heretofore Presented—Irving's Wolsey a Wonderful Character—Miss Terry an Original Katharine—Not a Weak Spot in the Play.

Shakespeare's *King Henry VIII* is a work that is rarely played nowadays. This is by no means because it is lacking in dramatic interest, but rather from the fact that it is a somewhat difficult matter to find in one company, however well constituted, three players with the ability to sustain such diverse and exciting characters as Cardinal Wolsey, Queen Catharine [sic] and bluff King Harry.

The play has been made the subject of a special revival at Drury Lane Theatre by John Phillip Kemble, at Covent Garden under William Charles Macready, and later at the Princesses' Theatre in London when under the management of Charles John Kean.

But it is safe to say that no approach to it as a stage pageant, notorious for the minuteness of its research and the absolute correctness of its architecture and its costumes, was ever dreamed of, as this wondrous presentation which is now before us, in which it would seem that the resources of the modern stage have been carried to their very utmost extent. Architecturally, the London of the Tudors is brought home to our very doors: while in matters of costume and the exhibition of the manners and customs of the people, the play is throughout racy of the time in, and the soil on, which its scenes are laid.

The play was first produced by Mr. Irving at the Lyceum Theatre, London, on the night of Tuesday, the 5th of January, 1892, before an audience made up of "notabilities from all ranks of society, representatives of art, literature and science, and the learned professions," and perhaps a word or two with regard to its production may not be out of place, for the ordinary playgoer, who goes to a theatre for the purpose of being simply amused, gives no consideration to the thought or labor bestowed upon such a work.

The piece was in preparation a full twelvemonth, and for half that time, at least, was in active rehearsal. Some of the brightest minds in England were engaged in researches tending to absolute accuracy in matters of architecture, costumes and appointments. The processions, displays and ceremonies of the times were reproduced with fidelity and Hans Holbein's portraits were closely studied and copied, so that there should be complete accuracy in matters of make-up, and, that each of the mimic characters should, as near as was possible, be an exact reproduction of the original.

To accomplish all this not alone required great thought and labor, as will be seen at a glance, but it also called for a vast outlay of money, far larger than was ever previously expended on the foundation of a single drama, and before Mr. Irving had raised his curtain in the initial performance, the play had cost him £16,000, or $80,000 in our own currency. Now, this seems incredible, but the fact remains, and is capable of proof.

In the text of the play many incisions have been made, more so, perhaps, than in any other stage version, but in no wise is the story impaired, the harmony is in no sense broken, and indeed what may be looked upon as a complete acting play is the result.

To be paradoxical, in fact, though we are given in one sense less, in another we are given more, of Shakespeare, for we have thrown in the Coronation Procession of Anne Bullen, with all of its splendor and attendant street gamins, and a portion of the fifth act of the original, never before presented in this city, in which the christening of the infant Elizabeth is portrayed.

Then again, we had a full and complete cast. There were no doubles. There was no blending of the parts of Cromwell and Griffith, as in the past, but each one of the dramatis personae stood out a distinct individualization.

And, what is greatly to the point, every character was sustained by an actor or actress of intelligence. It was not that there was a good Wolsey, a fair Buckingham or a passable King, but parts which in the past have been slighted and intrusted to dramatic nonentities, such, for instance, as the Cardinal Campeius, Griffith, Capucius and the Lord Chamberlain were sustained by actors of acknowledged abilities.

Of the impersonations of character in the play, Mr. Irving unquestionably leads with his noble delineation of Wolsey. He must have made the many sided characteristics of the great cardinal a profound study, and these he depicts with masterly ability.

Wolsey was the greatest man of his age, and by many was considered the greatest diplomatist of any age: while in most minds his name is connected with all that is proud, unscrupulous, grasping and magnificent even to regality, still he never forgot his origin and the people from whom he sprung.

If he was indeed grasping, it was that he might be magnificent even to the workman and the beggar. If the King was the first pillar of the state, he assuredly was the second, and that he occasionally abused the license which was allowed him cannot for a moment be denied. He was a patron of learning, and he was ambitious beyond, perhaps, all ordinary bounds, and was, indeed, a "man of an unbounded stomach."

He was well versed in human nature, and was himself withal an accomplished man of the world, a point which Mr. Irving does not lose sight of. Throughout the play he sounds "all the depths and shoals of honor," and the performance as a whole is grandly conceived and well executed. He was dignified, noble and commanding in the imperiousness of a will which was hidden under the craft of the accomplished courtier that he was in the earlier portions of the play; while his latter scenes were dominated by a touching sweetness and resignation to his fate combined with a world of pathos which was above all commendation.

If in certain portions of the play, I have listened to grander elecutionary and declamatory bursts, I have yet to call to mind a more evenly sustained, consistent, or satisfying impersonation of the cardinal from beginning to end; no, not even by that transcendent actor, Macready.

That Mr. Irving's performance is not without certain blemishes no one will for a moment deny, and these were to be found in the declamatory passages, which we have had delivered with greater impressiveness and with more sonorous accents by other actors. But there was no striving for startling points at the risk of consistency, but rather a continuously harmonious and level treatment which was all the more welcome. His byplay with Cardinal Campeius was exquisite, and he made a tool of that prelate, winding him completely round his finger; and full of significance were the lines,

Learn this, brother,
We live not be grip'd by meaner persons.

Mr. Irving was at his best in his coloquial speeches, and was very happy in his final scene with Cromwell, where he uttered the noble lines of the master with rare discretion, and his final exit was a touching picture of pathos, humiliation and resignation. In makeup he was every inch the ecclesiastic, and his tall, commanding figure was an excellent foil to the bulky Henry.

People may cavil as much as they will at Mr. Irving's performance, but it will be many a long day, take it for all in all, before they will meet with its equal.

Some of Mr. Irving's speeches were notable. Take, for instance, this, in the trial scene:

I do profess
You speak not like yourself; who ever yet
Have stood to charity, and displayed th' effects
Of disposition gentle, and of wisdom
O'ertopping woman's power. Madam, you do me wrong:
I have no spleen against you; not injustice
For you or any; how far I have proceeded,
Or how far farther shall, in warranted
By a commission from the consistory—
Yea, the whole consistory of Rome. You charge me
That I have blown this coal. I do not deny it;
The King is present; if it be known to him
That I gainsay my deed, how may he wound,
And worthily, my falsehood! Yea, as much
As you have done my truth. If he know
That I am free of your report, he knows
I am not of your wrong. Therefore in him
It lies to cure me; and the cure is to
Remove these thoughts from you, the which before

His highness shall speak in, I do beseech
You, gracious madam, to unthink your speaking,
And to say so no more.

And in the brief burst to Surrey in the downfall scene, he replies with fire to the taunts of that nobleman, who charges him with being a traitor,

Proud lord, thou liest:
Within these forty hours Surrey durst better
Have burnt that tongue than said so.

And

How much me thinks I could despise this man,
But that I am bound in charity against it.

These sparkled with the true Promethean fire, and showed in themselves the great artist.

Mr. William Terris' King Henry, taken in its entirety, was beyond all odds the best I can call to mind in the remembrance of half a century. In dress and makeup it was a perfect study, and

I do assure you
The King cried Ha

throughout with good emphasis and discretion. His readings were, in the main, commendable, while his acting was bright and spirited, yet withal kingly and forcible. It was a thoughtful, careful and well digested piece of acting, and from beginning to end there was a directness of purpose in the assumption which was worthy of all praise.

It was a performance that will live long in the memory, and it was as creditable to the actor as it was agreeable and refreshing to the auditors.

Mr. Cooper was more than the average Buckingham, and he delivered his lines with meaning and sincerity. It may be that he was not quite venomous enough in speaking to the Duke of Norfolk and Lord Abergavenny, in the first scene of the first act in speaking of Wolsey as "our reverend cardinal," "this butcher's cur," "this Ipswich fellow," "this holy fox or wolf, or both" "our count cardinal," and so on. A little more sarcastic emphasis on these expressions would have given more effect to the speeches, and heightened the force of their delivery greatly. Yet Mr. Cooper's brief, but arduous, part was well conceived, and may be regarded as a dramatic treat.

Nothing but words of commendation can be had for all the other parts, and especially noticable was that sterling actor, Mr. Howe, for the tenderness and manly consideration with which he surrounded the part of Griffith. The few lines he had to deliver were spoken with a rare beauty and in tones of subdued tenderness, and with a discretion becoming the part of the trusted servitor which he was enacting.

We have had greater Queen Katharines than Ellen Terry, but never one that was sweeter, more graceful, more womanly, or more wifelike. It was a touching performance, and there were moments when it was one of great beauty. She looked every inch the queen, the daughter of a king, and in costume and makeup was admirable. Katharine died in her 51st year, and Miss Terry made up the queen to appear about 45, which was very judicious. In her acting she made much of her first scene with the King and Wolsey, where she was the woman and wife, and was most impressive in the trial scene, though not as intense or startling as Mrs. Warner or Miss Cushman. Her exit was finely managed, and she spoke the lines

> I do refuse you for my judge; and here
> Before you all, appeal unto the Pope
> To bring my whole cause 'fore his holiness,
> And to be judg'd by him,

And

> Now, the Lord help!
> They vex me past my patience! Pray you pass on:
> I will not tarry; no, nor ever more
> Upon this business my appearance make
> In any of their courts.

in a manner which won her hearty plaudits. In her scene with the two cardinals, likewise in the death scene, there was no striving for effect, but a general smoothness which was the result of resignation and decaying powers. The lines were well delivered, and with exact meaning, and the gradual passing away of the Queen was skilfully managed, and with all the finesse of an accomplished artist.

As said above, we have had stronger Katharines. Yet Miss Terry will be sure to broaden her reputation by her assumption of the part. One thing is certain, and greatly in her favor: She gives us an original idea of the character, and is the slave or copyist of no predecessor.

The other female characters were well done, the Anne Bullen being sprightly and captivating, and the Old Lady, her friend, was well conceived and acted.

In *Henry VIII* Mr. Irving has given us a wonderous dramatic treat. It is a mine of beauties and of grandeurs. It is a stage representation such as has never before been equalled, and as such is commended to every lover of the drama.

Muriel St. Clare Byrne

A Stratford Production: *Henry VIII*

I have selected the Stratford production of *Henry VIII* for a "descriptive analysis" for various reasons, chief among them being the producer's evident desire to remain faithful to the author's intentions, his treatment of the text, and his utilization of a kind of stage which permitted him to secure effects impossible in an ordinary picture-frame set.

When the audience entered the theatre, instead of seeing a curtain, they had before their eyes a lighted permanent set which remained unchanged and unhidden until the end. An excellent compromise between a platform and a picture-frame stage, it suggests a basic design which might well provide a happy and practicable solution to the problem of securing the effect of the Elizabethan stage within our modern theatres. Miss Tanya Moiseiwitsch is to be congratulated on the pleasing and dignified appearance as well as on the admirably functional qualities of this set, with its varied levels, its ample forestage, fifteen feet deep, and its well-thought-out modifications and rearrangements of the gallery and the inner-stage.

The text, though cut in places and abridged by one brief scene (V,ii), was so nearly the whole text in words, and so definitely the whole text in statement and intention, that it is probably the most complete and satisfactory version given in the commercial theatre since Shakespeare's time. In the average production *Henry VIII* is perhaps the most viciously and unintelligently cut play in the whole canon. The tradition is thoroughly bad, writing it off as no play at all, and treating it as a thing of pageantry with a few fine scenes and star opportunities.

The continuity was genuine, not fake. The average Shakespearian producer seems unable to realize that continuity is not the same thing as speed. Because he can manipulate his scenery or curtains in a matter of seconds instead of minutes it does not alter the fact that with his every black-out and every sliding, turning, dancing, flying or other ingenious scene-shift, continuity is destroyed. The flow of the Shakespearian action from scene to scene is a problem of bridge-and-break which must be done by words and movement. Tyrone Guthrie demonstrated this so successfully and used his property shifters with such tact that one was hardly aware how and when tables and stools had appeared or disappeared. The fluidity of movement and the power and pace thus given to the action were wholly admirable, and he caught the rapidly shifting emotional interest with a sureness we associate to-day with the films rather than with Shakespeare.

Yet another help to the continuity, in that it never called attention to itself, was the lighting, which had no colour and remained unaltered throughout, except when imperceptible light cues varied the emphasis. Set and lighting together gave a basic steadiness and reality which were a positive aid to concentration. One cannot avoid front-of-house lighting if a forestage is required, but there is no doubt that to the modern production-conscious audience its manipulation and its changes are a source of distraction. Everything here, however, combined to focus our whole attention on the actor, which is as it should be. Even the colour of the set helped, the woodwork being a natural light greyish oak in appearance, setting off the fine costumes admirably. It was a great pleasure to get rid of the usual theatrical reversal of colours, and to exchange century-darkened panelling and the wrong bright clothes for the genuine light background of the Tudor life and the dark sober magnificence of its costumes. These were beautiful and congruous, and little details, such as the embroidered stockings worn by Henry in the Masque, showed how much loving delight in the authentic had gone into the designs. The reds and purples and the white and gold of the clerics provided a handsome contrast to the blacks and greys, yellows, russets, etc., of the noble personages.

The angling of the Elizabethan stage so that gallery and study are brought nearer to the audience is an excellent idea for a modern theatre. If the Elizabethan layout is faithfully preserved, depth must be sacrificed for the sake of lines-of-sight, and the space for movement which is thus lost is not compensated for by the upper-stage facilities gained. The set had no proscenium doors, but there was an ample downstage entrance (right), a fine large door entry, set at an angle, just above the dais, a large passage entry immediately above the study on the left, and an entry to the gallery. The orchestra pit was used for entrances and exits, the steps coming up from stage right and emerging just left of stage centre. The only touches of permanent colour decoration were Henry's state, and in the background and along the proscenium arch the banners with the Tudor badges—the Union rose, the red dragon, the fleur-de-lis of France, the Beaufort portcullis, etc.

It was of great advantage to the play to let us take in the set before the action started. Because one could register, for example, the impression made by the single pillar, two-thirds upstage right, with the red dragon banner of the Tudors to its left and a shaft of light striking across it diagonally and falling on the steps leading up to it, one was the more ready and receptive for the use made of that particular area and its symbolical value. The possible pace of a play must relate to the response of the audience, and there seemed a greater alertness than usual in this response, just because familiarity with the background before the stage was peopled had made us all better aware how and where to look without diverting any conscious attention from the players.

The Prologue was spoken by the Old Lady, Anne Bullen's friend (Wynne Clark)—a sound device to associate its serious and pertinent comment with the theme of the Tudor succession which is responsible for the structure of the whole play. Miss Clark was a perfect Holbein portrait to look at, and she seized her twofold opportunity firmly: the quality of life in her, the persuasive zest of her way of speaking and the authenticity of her appearance, all struck the dominant note of the entire production. The emphasis laid on the "truth" of the play, "our chosen truth," came over with full force as she drew us straight into a novel intimacy, speaking from the extreme front of the forestage (left). When she adjured us

> think ye see
> The very persons of our noble story
> As they were living,

upstage, right, the Dukes of Norfolk and Suffolk with three other nobles were seen for a moment in converse—a moment of breath-taking reality upon which the mind dwells with delight, especially when looking back over the production as a whole and realizing how skilfully their sober-suited group, caught in the shaft of light by the solitary pillar, drew the attention unconsciously to this significant feature which was afterwards to be related at important moments to the vital matter of the play. Then, as she began to speak her last line, what had held us as the timeless instant dissolved; and the play itself swept into action with the entry, right, of the Duke of Buckingham (Leon Quartermaine). The vigorous attack in this opening scene was remarkable. Norfolk (Michael Gwynne) and Buckingham held the attention by their obvious delight in the rhetorical force of speeches which are generally cut down by the theatre to a mere thirty or forty lines, and used less for their own sake than as a build-up for Wolsey's entry.

Wolsey's procession entered from the orchestra pit so that as it advanced upstage and across from the left the Cardinal encountered Buckingham almost centre, and with his back to the audience as he passed him. If we were waiting for a repetition of Irving's great moment we were to be disappointed, for we did not see Wolsey's face as "the Cardinal in his passage fixeth his eye on Buckingham, and Buckingham on him both full of disdain": but it was perhaps judicious not to challenge this bright legend, and to let us see only Buckingham's expression, giving us instead, as the procession moved upstage, a magnificent and raised central position for Wolsey (Harry Andrews), where he could turn and face the audience and dominate the scene as he spoke the lines which prepare us for Buckingham's doom.

The only properties used throughout were long tables and joint stools, and the passage beneath the gallery, upstage of the study, was designed to give them easy and unobtrusive entry. The assembling of the furniture for the Council Chamber involved, consequently, no loss of time or continuity. A table and stools were set downstage centre for Wolsey and various officers and scriveners. As the King (Anthony Quayle) entered to take his seat on the dais it was clear that, although in costume and make-up this was recognizably the Henry of the Holbein portraits, the producer had taken his cue from historical fact rather than from theatre tradition and was presenting us not with the grossly corpulent figure of the later years of the reign but with the fine burly young man that was Henry in his prime. Queen Katharine (Diana Wynyard), though beautiful, was old in comparison with her hearty, ruddy, young husband.

This scene showed very clearly what magnificent opportunities for variety, grouping and dramatic movement the varied levels and unusual layout of this semi-Elizabethan stage offer to a producer who understands how to use them. Pictorially and dramatically the first grouping of the three principals was very striking—Henry in his chair of estate, four steps up, facing three-quarters left, dominating the whole scene: Katharine, upstage of him, but a step lower, perfectly yet naturally placed for her spirited attack on Wolsey's oppression of the common people, and Wolsey below them and to their right on the forestage—the group admirably balanced by the mass of the crowd opposite and upstage left. For the examination of Buckingham's Surveyor, Wolsey moved across to the far end of the table opposite the King: the Surveyor stood above the table and spoke first to Wolsey and only turned afterwards to the King. Finally, as the excitement of his revelations mounted up, Henry came pounding down from the dais, thrust a clerk sprawling from a stool at the end of the table, and sat down and pushed the examination to its vigorous conclusion.

It was a strong, dramatic and highly significant move this bearing down of the King from the edge of the conflict into its heart. When the play opens Wolsey is at the height of his power, with Henry relying on him for everything. The pretended threat both of his own life and to the Tudor succession is what brings him into the arena to deal with his own affairs. His move took him nearly half-way across the stage, and we shall remember it when at the end of the trial-scene he comes down again from his throne and goes the whole way across to stage left and stands at last free of the great Cardinal.

As the Surveyor-scene ends, the next is already beginning, with the entry of the Lord Chamberlain and Lord Sands discussing the latest Court scandals. Though obscure and topical, only two short passages of detail (II.5–13 and 26–32) have been cut, and the scene is played with such vivacity, and the characters, especially Sands, are so quickly individualized, that it holds the interest and covers the preparations for Wolsey's banquet till it merges into the actual banquet-scene. Sands is a lively, raffish old gentleman, slightly red of nose and lecherous inclination—a perfectly legitimate interpretation of the text. For the banquet two long tables are set more or less at right angles to the gallery, well over to stage left, while Wolsey's banners replace the King's. The display, however, is almost negligible: the banquet is successful as a scene because it is *acted*. The guests are lively, noisy and coarse; and, if their manners are perhaps more reminiscent of the city than the court, there is no infidelity to the text. Wolsey enters above in the gallery as the gaiety is at its height, immediately after Anne Bullen (Kathleen Michael) has been effectively established in a brisk passage with Lord Sands. This Anne Bullen looks very well and she is tremendously alive, outstanding even amongst this group of vigorous, assertive and attractive young women. The Masque is well done and the masquers in their Tudor green-and-white and their golden straw hats look as authentic as the spectators. What is more, the masquing costume gives us at precisely the right moment the best possible opportunity of realizing Henry as the *young* man in the prime of life: and if we take 1527 as the year which brought the declaration of his love for Anne Bullen, and this scene as its dramatization, then, by happy coincidence, the King and his impersonator are, in fact, precisely the same age. It is no derogation from Anthony Quayle's performance to allow that this has certainly contributed to its rightness.

The meeting between Anne and the King is excellent. She has jumped on a stool to see the masque over the heads of the crowd and suddenly Henry catches sight of her and stands transfixed—quite literally *caught*, vitality drawn to vitality, as she returns his gaze and meets its challenge. Miss Michael and Anthony Quayle play this moment for all it is worth: I have never seen it more strikingly and convincingly rendered, not the value of the King's love for Anne more effectively established, and as I believe, given precisely the stress which the author intended.

As the revel starts again and hurls itself off with the disappearing banquet tables, the walking-gentlemen scene, which precedes Buckingham's execution, begins. Here the producer has taken something of a liberty with the text by getting rid of the Second Gentleman and giving his part to Sands. As a device it seems reasonable: the cast is enormous, Sands' own part disappears at this juncture and it is theatrically a pity to lose a real character who has just registered effectively with the audience, while dramatically it aids both continuity and concentration to keep a known rather than to introduce a new minor personage. Of more interest, as a recurrent problem of Shakespearian production, is the treatment accorded to the scene. Not for the first time, Guthrie's theatrical inventiveness has drawn upon him some magisterial rebukes. It would be more to the purpose to recognize first his courage and correctness in keeping such scenes; an easy way out of the difficulty they present is to cut them altogether; or one can escape censure by letting them be as dull as most people find them. This is not Guthrie's way: he believes that the author has intention in what he writes and that it is our business to find out how to put a scene across to our own audience. In the present instance, having the right kind of stage at his command, he makes his walking-gentlemen *walk*—a genuine platform-stage device and therefore entirely legitimate. His next deduction is equally logical: they are walking through the streets of London to see the Duke going to execution, and he has no chorus to say to his audience "Work, work your thoughts" and *see* that walk; so instead he lets his actors mime the background of incident, of the *Gare l'eau* variety, which might reasonably be supposed to enliven their progress. It is novel and entertaining, and it makes the audience laugh. Is comic relief at this point destructive of the author's intention in the matter of the tragedy of Buckingham, or is it legitimate and Elizabethan? That Buckingham's beautifully spoken farewell was not spoilt for the audience by this little episode was made quite clear by rapt attention and two great bursts of applause. Of one thing we may be certain, walking-gentlemen scenes must have had more in them than we find to-day if they held the Elizabethan audience. Is this, Guthrie prompts us to ask, the kind of thing the Elizabethan actors did with them?

At this point there was some cutting, and the action was altered so that Henry in his study overheard the talk which heralds his divorce; but it was interesting—and highly indicative of the producer's attitude—to find the passage between Campeius and Wolsey on the subject of Pace's death retained. Its matter is obscure Tudor politics and completely uninteresting to the average auditor, but it has its function, both dramatic and theatrical, confirming Wolsey's personal ambition at this crucial moment.

As they went off, with the business of the divorce resolved on, Anne Bullen and the Old Lady entered upstage, and came down to the forestage left, where they sat and wound wool as they talked. The intimate forestage playing, here as elsewhere, gave great scope for facial expression and made one realize for the hundredth time how much subtlety we lose when the actors retire into the picture frame. One could *see* Anne experiencing the whole idea of what is to happen: it made her part much more vital and significant than it usually seems. The business of the Lord Chamberlain's message from the King was accompanied by the presentation of a small bouquet from which a pearl necklace dropped to the ground when Anne took the flowers, making an admirable silent moment for the three players and giving the Old Lady a delightful cough of comment. There is also a letter in the bouquet, and this Anne reads as she moves away from them, so that the Chamberlain's important comment on the succession theme (II.75–79) can be spoken to the Old Lady, which makes it more natural and effective than when it is taken as an aside.

In the Blackfriars Hall scene the bishops' procession, preceded by choristers, vergers and scribes, entered from the orchestra pit, their full canonicals and the banners of the Sees making a fine show. The procession of Wolsey and Campeius entered by the large doorway upstage right and advanced towards us, Campeius taking the seat at the right end of the table and Wolsey at the left. The gallery was crowded, Norfolk, Suffolk, Sands and the Old Lady being noticeable, and of course, the First Gentleman. The anticipative susurration of "The King," was a genuine crowd whisper, but Henry did not enter, as expected, with the Guard: he came hurriedly in alone, upstage right, and went straight to his chair with the ruffled expression of the man who has missed his cue. The effect of this was to enhance the dignity of Katharine's entry, upstage left, with Griffith, Patience and two gentlewomen. She came straight down left, and sat at the extreme side of the forestage—a position which then gave her a magnificent move across to the King's state at the direction, "she goes about the Court."

In her appeal it was to the King alone that Katharine addressed herself, rejecting the authority of the Court from the opening line:

> Sir, I desire *you* do me right and justice.

I do not think this was the word-stress implied by Tudor English, but it gave great poignancy, intimacy and naturalness to what can easily become a set piece of rhetoric. Miss Wynyard made one feel as if it were being spoken for the first time. Henry played to it very well, deeply embarrassed, and moved as he had no wish to be. Then the intervention of the two Cardinals carries the action away from the personal plane at once, and baffled and silenced by the impersonal, impervious, irresistible process in which circumstance and the King's will have entangled her, she allowed Campeius to lead her to the bar of the Court, from which she delivered her attack on Wolsey with fine force, leaving it immediately after and moving upstage. Wolsey followed her to protest his good intentions, and she was thus perfectly placed, just above him, upstage centre, for her final refusal of the jurisdiction of the Court. She curtsied to the King while Campeius protested, turned to depart, and was stopped by Griffith at the gallery stairs. Having dealt with him she then swept on up the stairs and delivered her "I will not tarry" from the gallery, in a magnificent and commanding position. Throughout, as in the Surveyor-scene, she spoke with a clear purity and naturalness that delighted the ear.

The interest of this scene was held after Katharine's departure by the unusual method of trusting the author and playing the whole of his text simply and sincerely. It was the real test of the producer's understanding of his matter, and of historical imagination, that he kept Henry's long speech (II.153-207) entire, save for some half-dozen lines. In most stage versions it is cut from I.170 to I.220; and this is the key passage in the play. Anthony Quayle rendered it with sincerity and conviction, beginning slowly as if thinking out this case of conscience, warming up as he went on to speak of the deaths of all his male heirs and of the danger to the Tudor succession and the realm, finally turning with vigorous appeal to the Bishop of Lincoln who stood downstage left and pulling him in as a witness, and then sweeping round the Court with eye and gesture and invoking the support of the Archbishop of Canterbury, standing upstage right by the pillar. It was a natural and yet vivid handling of a really difficult exposition.

It was a brilliant stroke of production to go all out for a naturalistic effect after Campeius had moved the adjournment of the Court; and to hold a total and overwhelming silence until the King chose to break it. The bishops went into a marvellous ecclesiastical huddle of copes and mitres, oozing consternation and disapproval, and Henry strode angrily across to the far left of the forestage, and spoke his aside directly to the audience. Then, at

> My learn'd and well beloved servant Cranmer,
> Prithee, return:

with a commanding gesture he summoned the Archbishop of Canterbury forth from the crowd, upstage right. Cranmer's consequent move, down the steps centre, and across to the King, was a joy to watch, and has won critical notice as well as popular acclaim. It stressed the significance of Wolsey's isolated position, and made a striking conclusion to the first part of the play, but in point of fact it is plain both from the wording and from the references in the next scene (III,ii,63–67, 402–04) that this apostrophe to the absent Cranmer is all part of Henry's aside. It is inconsistent to retain these later references and then amalgamate Cranmer and Canterbury for the trial; and to use Cranmer like this for its ending is to ignore the author's dramatic intentions. As he has planted Cranmer verbally at nine different points before he allows him to appear in person in Act V there is obvious intention behind this somewhat unusual procedure. Cranmer's dramatic function is to show the all-powerful and wise monarch in action and to prophesy the greatness of Elizabeth. It is *not* his function to replace Wolsey, and the point of the end of the trial-scene is to show that at last the lion knows his strength and that the King will stand alone. His strength when established, as it should be at this moment, is in his aloneness. Wolsey has failed him: the movement begun in the Surveyor-scene is now completed. It cries for visual realization. Cranmer's appearance at the trial and his magnificent move to the support of the King are, therefore, to me, functionally wrong—a sacrifice of the author's dramatic intention to theatrical effect.

For the scene of the Queen and the Cardinals, Katharine and her four maids seated themselves on joint stools and on the floor, downstage right. The queen looked older, but with a strange added loveliness—a calm in her expression which spoke of ravaging strife of mind and spiritual agony, endured and survived. There was royal self-command in every movement and gesture: it was to the hands that one had to look for the signs of emotional strain; though this groundling will swear to it that when the Cardinals were announced her face sharpened as she braced herself for this new ordeal.

In the opening passage both sides were sparring quietly and warily for advantage; and the first round when to Katharine, as the author meant, when the warm, rich response of the whole audience came on "Good my Lord, no Latin." Then the battle begins in earnest, with the Cardinals one each side of her, Wolsey to the right, Campeius on the left. She listens with impressive stillness of demeanour until Campeius expatiates upon Wolsey's "noble nature" and good intentions. This is too much: there is a little impatient tapping of the foot; she rises and walks away from them, gaining herself the necessary opening aside for her next speech: when the group re-forms Wolsey and Campeius are together on her left. Miss Wynyard's whole expression, and particularly the eyes, added greatly to the poignancy of "the last fit of my greatness"; and the touch of anger at "but little for my profit," and the tears in eyes and voice at "far hence, in my own country, lords," were all most affecting. Her stillness in these passages is especially noteworthy: the eyes alone move, until, with shrivelling scorn, she blazes momentarily into attack in the "cardinal sins" speech. After this outburst and the deep, bitter, natural pathos of the description of her utter ruin and friendlessness which follows, again under rigid control she sits immobile while they make their final attempt at persuasion, and there is a grave and touching dignity in her

> Pray forgive me
> If I have used myself unmannerly.

As they rise to go Wolsey offers her his ring to kiss, and she looks at him, dismissing the gesture only with her eyes, every inch the Queen and descendant of the proudest royal line in Europe as she precedes them from the chamber.

So to Wolsey's doom. As the Cardinals and her maids follow the Queen out, the nobles, Wolsey's enemies, enter to the attack. The opening of the scene is played for all it is worth, with steadily mounting force, Norfolk in particular establishing even more firmly his clear-cut and outstandingly Tudor portrait. The condescending huntin'-shootin'-fishin' intonation he gave to his approval of Cranmer, "a worthy fellah," was a pretty touch, and incidentally was not missed by the audience. A trifle, but indicative, as everything else, of the completeness and integrity of the producer's naturalistic conception.

This scene of the baiting of the great Cardinal is always effective, but on this fine spacious stage, with its varying levels, it was even more so than usual. The strength and significance which can be given to purposeful moves from upstage to downstage could not have been more excitingly demonstrated; and the mounting tension was fine as Henry came swooping down on his unsuspecting victim, with these power-greedy lords jackalling in after the lion. Norfolk delivered his last line with real Tudor insolence:

So fare you well, my little good Lord Cardinal.

Which brings us to the query—how good is this Wolsey? My own answer is, just as good as the author meant him to be. One must insist: this is not *The Downfall of Cardinal Wolsey*—that was another play belonging to the Henslowe repertoire, now lost. The author has not provided a hero, in the ordinary sense of the word, but a play for genuine teamwork, demanding a number of first rate players, not rival stars and still less one "bright particular star." It is a realistic historical play, as the author insisted in the Prologue, not an historical adaptation with a strict eye to the main theatrical chance. It is a play about the Tudor succession, by an Elizabethan. It was the test of Harry Andrew's conception, I thought, that the nearer he came to the audience the better I like his performance. I found him most real in his end, and just as the Queen's face seemed to sharpen with anxiety and distress in III,i, so here Wolsey's seemed to grow lined and stricken even as he was speaking.

As Wolsey made his exit by the orchestra pit, a silent scene was substituted for the coronation show. Anne herself came dancing on to the stage, and went proudly up the central steps and off as the bells began to ring out. It seemed to me a legitimate and imaginative touch, if we grant that Guthrie does well to cut the coronation procession which otherwise gives us our last glimpse of Anne Bullen. I was more moved by Miss Michael's brief moment, the gaiety and then the proud carriage of the slight figure and that thrown-back head, than I have ever been by the famous "show." It was more real, and therefore more congruous in this play, than the splendours of spectacle.

The coronation is given as seen through the eyes of the crowd, represented by the First Gentleman and Sands, who are joined at I.55 by the Lord Chamberlain instead of the anonymous Third Gentleman of the text. It is the First Gentleman's big opportunity and George Rose takes it with both hands. He has the most engaging toothy grin which he flashes on and off like a child with an electric torch: to the life he is the pushful, eager procession hunter who will always elbow his way to the front row for the wedding or the funeral. He knows all about everybody who is anybody; he was the man who noticed how the Duke of Buckingham, when his judgement was pronounced, "sweat extremely": it is he who can tell us that Cranmer has pronounced the sentence of divorce and that Katharine lies sick at Kimbolton. He has the little mannerisms which mark the excitable utterance of the brisk gossip-hound: his "Cin-*que* ports" and "HWhitehall" win appreciative chuckles, and he finally bounces his way into the affection of us groundlings when at the climax of his excitement he matches the rhythm of his ecstatic "and all the rest are Countesses" with four excited little leaps. The effect was greatly helped by the excellent crowd noises off; but the text was, after all, the author's, and more than even the earlier example Guthrie's handling of this scene made me question just how far the lack of producer's imagination has damped down the force and vigour of walking-gentlemen scenes in general. What Guthrie and his actor have realized, in this instance, is that the whole passage is the grandmother and grandfather of all running commentaries. To look for the answer to the walking-gentlemen problem in acting, character work and the facilities of the Shakespearian stage is a solution that deserves something better than jibes about tricks.

Before the commentators had finished a chair had been brought on and set well downstage left for the scene at Kimbolton. Katharine was helped in, old and ill, and already remote from the world. Miss Wynyard looked and acted the dying Queen supremely well—that is to say, as written, on the realistic note. She hardly moved her head, only her eyes, and the little movement of her nerveless hand, up and down, on the arm of her chair, at "nothing," in "as he is now, *nothing*," was an infinitely pathetic and eloquent comment on the theme of ruined greatness. When Griffith—most sympathetically played, as a Welshman, by Robert Hardy—spoke Wolsey's praise she turned her head slightly, painfully, and smiled at him. She dropped asleep, and then, opening her eyes, saw the vision in the vacant air above our heads, playing the whole thing straight at us. It was finely and convincingly done; and the last speech to Capucius was beautifully spoken, with that momentary return of strength which flickers up before death which the author so obviously demands by providing this extremely moving farewell—a most skilful avoidance of anticlimax, after the exaltation of the vision, to bring us back to the realistic plane without any jolt.

Before Katharine has been led off the next scene has begun with the entry, upstage center, of Gardiner, who appears to be as drunk as the King and Suffolk who come reeling in a moment later. The treatment of Gardiner, in this generally realistic production, runs true to the tradition of the theatre, where "the part of the bloodly-minded Gardiner has always been given to the first comic actor." The picture comes back into realistic focus, however, as Henry sobers well and quickly, and the way in which he deals with Cranmer, the innocent, unworldly churchman, is excellent, jollying him along with practical advice and gracious encouragement. Of genuine structural importance, however, is the way in which, in these four speeches, Henry manoeuvres himself into the centre of the play. The dramatist is using his anticlimactic breathing space to work around to the triumph of the King which is the assertion of the theme, and the scene ends with the announcement of the birth of Elizabeth. The next scene, where the King and Dr. Butts observe from above the Council's insolent treatment of Cranmer, was cut—the only instance here of the cutting of an entire scene. Most productions cut the entire episode (V,i–iii).

The council-chamber scene which follows showed once again the producer's mastery of movement. It was a pleasant little touch, hailed with delight by the audience, to let Cromwell, now risen in the world and Secretary to the Council, use his former master's slightly pompous trick of an admonitory or introductory "a'hem." That the audience was still alert to appreciate such niceties of production is eloquent testimony to the quality of life in the performance. But it was the amount and the interest of movement and the free use of so much of the stage that gave such life and such a lift to what in less skilled hands might have been a very static council-table scene. Henry had a fine entry upstage, which enabled him to bear down swiftly upon the table and take up a commanding position above it, centre. The councillors scattered right and left before his onslaught—a clever reversal, this, of the closing-in on Wolsey, in which four of the same gang had been concerned. As they circled nervously around, Henry sat and made Cranmer sit too, and then staged his carefully prepared scene of vigilant and active kingship which preludes the final assertion and triumph of the Tudor succession theme. It is the necessary dramatic complement to the Surveyor-scene and its implications. With a fine show of the famous Tudor rage he turns upon these other ministers who would also tyrannize and oppress, and rends them until the Lord Chancellor pours oily prelatical reasonableness upon the storm, and it subsides. With power thus vindicated by its defence of virtue Henry is ready enough to take the cue which the Chancellor so tactfully provides: in a moment he is bluff King Hal again, banging Cranmer on the back and jabbing him in the ribs over "You'll spare your spoons!" for now the matter in hand is reconciliation and the christening of Elizabeth, and the bells for the final scene have started before they are off the stage.

While the table and stools are being cleared away the porter and his man, in the orchestra pit, are repelling the crowds who are storming the doors. The porter staggers up, his face almost obliterated by a large dollop of whitewash—or was it genuine Tudor blanc-manger?—and while the crowd roars off-stage, he and his man sit on the step above the pit, drinking their ale and describing the tumult. Choristers in the procession enter from the pit, followed by the nobility and gentry, while from upstage right the bishops enter, all in white and gold, and Cranmer appears above in the gallery. The pageantry and pattern of the mingling of the various crowds and of the white and gold pennons carried by the Guard seemed neither so skilful nor so purposeful as in the other massed scenes: I felt it belonged to another convention and was assailed by memories of the pantomime finale. The original stage-direction here deserved more sympathetic consideration.

The nobles marched up into the gallery and the infant princess was brought on in their midst in the arms of the old Duchess of Norfolk under a white and gold canopy. Cranmer came down from the gallery and took up his position by the pillar, the King went up into the gallery and stood there holding his child, and then Cranmer spoke his prophetic vision of the glory of the Elizabethan age, or, if one so prefers to phrase it, the dramatist pronounced his gravely beautiful valediction over the age that bred him. It should be recorded that the interruption of the Duchess's sneeze, which roused critical protest, was removed after the first night. Unfortunately, the passage about James I was cut (II.40–56). To concentrate on Elizabeth gives immediate theatrical effect, but to delete James destroys dramatic intention. The essential and final explicit statement of the theme is the triumph of the Tudor succession, which turns to failure if we end on the prophecy of the death of the Virgin Queen.

I was much impressed by the way the production made the oration balance the Prologue. (The Epilogue is, God bless us, a thing of naught; though while Miss Clark was speaking it she persuaded me for the moment that it really did mean something.) But as the speaking and staging of the Prologue coaxed us at once into a belief in the immediate reality of what we were about to see, so Cranmer's oration, just because it looked forward to what, for us, had been realized nearly four centuries ago, made the play itself retreat from us again, back into "history." For me, at any rate, it brought the wheel full circle.

Muriel St. Clare Byrne

From "Dramatic Intention and Theatrical Realization"

"Judge by results," wrote Lascelles Abercrombie, "by any results that may come of living in the art of the play and attending to every thing it consists of."[1] Producer, actor, designer, critic, and audience are identified as recipients of the author's intention; but what the individual auditor receives is the experience of life which the author intends to impart, as transmitted through the refracting glass of this orchestrated and collective response of the executants, however close that interpretation may be and however little it is modified, as a happening, by a total audience response. Just as the sensitivity of an ear for great poetry is cultivated by continually submitting oneself to the experience, so all these recipients of drama, in their varying degrees of expertise and instinctive creativity, are conditioned in their response to the author's intention by standards and associative values derived from their accumulated theatre experience. Consciously or unconsciously, they refer scenes, situations, and characters to theatrical predecessors and cognates known to them. A scene for which there is no precedent, or where the effect achieved does not square with the expectation aroused by its label, inevitably attracts comparative evaluation, and the author's handling of it is instinctively referred, especially, but not exclusively, by professional intermediaries, to similar emotional and visual effects, whereas ideally it should lodge and germinate in the mind in its own particularity.

It was an experience of this kind with the trial scene in Shakespeare's *Henry VIII* which originally alerted me to the danger of "good" and "bad" evaluation-by-comparison, which results when cognates of class A set standards for specimen X.

Reprinted from "Dramatic Intention and Theatrical Realization" by Muriel St. Clare Byrne in *The Triple Bond: Audience, Actors & Renaissance Playwrights*, ed. Joseph Price. Pennsylvania State Univ. Press, University Park, Pa. (1975).

Examining Spedding's contention that it was a companion picture to Hermione's trial in *The Winter's Tale,* finding this supposed resemblance superficial and misleading, and then comparing the scene with the trials in *The Merchant of Venice* and *The White Devil,* I realized that whereas these three could reasonably be compared and classified as effect A, the *Henry VIII* trial had nothing in common with them and had to be taken as X, the unknown quantity.[2] Every theatrical effect legitimately obtained by these others was flatly contradicted by the effects of the Blackfriars trial, which was entirely unrelated to them in my own experience of the play in both the theatre and the study. However the scene is cut or staged, theatrically it "flops" when Queen Katharine, after her impassioned and moving appeal to Henry, leaves the court as magnificently as she entered it, so that the only character who speaks the language of emotion is removed at I.133, and the remaining 108 lines, if not savagely cut or even entirely omitted in performance, are devoted to an historical and academic statement of the King's case, in which the emotional temperature drops to zero. It flops, that is, *if,* as in the other three plays, we look for terrific personal conflict packed with theatrical excitement, the clash of opposed personalities, the scoring of points, suspense and its resolutions, surprises and all the devices of dramatic tension which constitute normal audience expectation.[3] But because the scene does not end on Katharine's exit, if we have any real belief in our author, whoever he may have been, we must credit him with that intention in what he does and must not say "This is bad," because we have been cheated of the popular fare for which we crave "the same again, but longer and louder." What we must ask is "*Why?*"

If we ask the right questions, we get the right answers. The remaining 108 lines set forth the author's theme explicitly. This is the play's intention—what the play is about—namely, the Tudor succession, realized by an Elizabethan, who had lived through the struggle and the last phases as "something understood": understood in terms of the price paid for it in blood and tears and what, by 1613, it had meant to a man born into the Elizabethan greatness, who had also lived through the disillusionment and the fears and scruples that had shaken his own generation in the last years of the great Queen's reign and the first years of her successor's, of which *Lear, Timon,* and *Troilus and Cressida* give us the measure. This achievement is the substance of Cranmer's prophetic vision at the conclusion, which in Tyrone Guthrie's 1949 Stratford production could be described as the writer's "gravely beautiful valediction over the age that had bred him," spoken in the spirit in which it was written.[4] Though even in this, the best production I have seen,[5] the completeness of the author's final intention was frustrated by the omission of the concluding tribute to James I.

Grasp the answer to this crucial question of theme and the treatment of the story and its several episodes becomes clear. This author is not writing another chronicle history; there is no distance of centuries or epochs between him and the story, nor is he in any doubt, having digested the whole of Holinshed's 180 double-columned pages, that he needs just four episodes to carry that theme. To suggest, as so many critics have done, that the play consists of "a number of unrelated scenes"[6] is to ignore the dramatist's intention. This is no haphazard dip into the Holinshed lucky-bag; it is the selectivity of a brilliant mind, in which genuine historical insight is balanced by an equally sure dramatic instinct and is theatrically "realized" in the arrangement of the episodes and the unity given to the whole by the sustained, consistent angle of vision from which they are all viewed, until we reach the last act and its triumphant conclusion. He has selected three main historical episodes and the semiapocryphal Cranmer—Gardiner scenes, all leading up to the birth of Elizabeth as the climax of the action and the theme it carries. The critical creative impulse to rewrite the author's play according to one's own ideas must be resisted.[7] Structurally his action-plot is simply the removal of obstacles, enabling the theme or idea-plot to be brought to a successful issue. Its three tragic episodes are the destruction of Buckingham, who threatens the Tudor succession, the divorce and the death of Katharine, who has failed to ensure it with a male heir, and the destruction of Wolsey, who threatens the Anne Boleyn marriage, culminating in the showpiece of the coronation scene which in theatrical realization must outdo the trial scene as spectacle and in its own day undoubtedly did so. The necessary anticlimactic movement between the coronation and the climax of the birth of Elizabeth is the Cranmer—Gardiner episode, which in the theatre suffers from a bad tradition and tends to be either cut or clowned, but has genuine thematic value if honestly handled, in spite of Spedding's assertion that these scenes "are utterly irrelevant to the business of the play" and have "poetically no value but the reverse." The real "business of the play" is the Tudor succession, and as Henry must now be more fully, personally, traditionally, and sympathetically established for the conclusion of the action, so that the affirmation of the theme includes the individual as well as the idea, he is shown in the familiar "bluff King Hal" guise in which, as one might say, contemporary playgoers knew him by heart. Gardiner, by his association with Wolsey, has been identified with the negation of the theme; Cranmer, by his support of the divorce, with its affirmation; and Henry now takes the center of the stage in true kingly style—a *deus ex machina,* commanding reconciliation and resolving the theme in a concord:

> As I have made ye one, lords, one remain,
> So I grow stronger, you more honour gain.
> (V.iii.181–82)

It is, once more, the old national moral emphasized by Shakespeare in the whole series of the history plays—in unity and concord at home lies true strength.[8] Theme and action unite as Henry stands forth at his most effective—the Tudor purpose, the national purpose, incarnate in the person of the Tudor monarch, at this moment fully, plainly, and explicitly symbolic of the force he represents.

Not only does the Cranmer episode resolve all discords on the symbolic plane, in preparation for the triumphant conclusion, thereby entirely justifying its position in the play, but its treatment also has a definite tonal value in the action plot. It introduces a romantic note to bridge the gap between the realistic level of the preceding scenes and the raised, emotional, visionary level of the conclusion. As action, it is an episode in the older and more theatrical manner, with the romantic touches of the monarch's talismanic ring and the rescue of the virtuous minister by the all-seeing, all-powerful, righteous and just rule, as which, for the only time in the play, Henry at last appears. He never speaks better, more royally, or to more purpose than in these four speeches. It is a simple yet subtle transition, effectively carrying us over by its vigor from Katharine's death to the final rejoicing, and thus fulfilling its proper anticlimactic function. I have never been able to understand how the theatre can bring itself to ignore so completely the natural movement of the play, as it does when it omits this episode in its entirety, and goes—as in Irving's and Tree's versions—straight from Katharine's death to Elizabeth's christening. If both are to be played for their true value, a pause, a breathing space between them, is essential.[9] The recoil after crisis and before climax is so written into all normal Elizabethan play structure, and is so essential for the full effect of the conclusion, that indecent haste of this kind argues an irresponsibility to the dramatic material and a lack of attention to what the author has to say, which destroy confidence in the dramatic integrity of the producer's approach. The idea that the scenes of *Henry VIII* are "unrelated" is in fact promoted when the theatre treats them in this fashion.

Recognizing that the theatrically popular trial scene of the time is here treated realistically and deliberately avoids the dramatic tension of conflict, we must accept intention. This author is discarding the theatrical convention for something nearer to life, for historical fact and for realism, not only in structure but also in style, which is something quite other than the percentages of "'ems" and "thems" and tricks of phrasing. He is vitally concerned with angle of vision and consistency of tone and purpose—a fusing of style and structure which make us realize that the writer's cast of mind is individual, unique. As he says in his Prologue, "All is true." On the stage you can launch one emotional force against another and the exhilaration of conflict with another human being carries you on; you can sweep aside lawyers with their Latin and legal jargon and the spirit does not submit to the inexorable processes of law and reason. In life, as the author of *Henry VIII* insists, it is not like that. Emotion and human feeling spend themselves in vain against the impersonality of the process that has trapped its human victims; and you cannot fight a personal duel, sustained on both sides by personal hate, when no one will meet you as such an opposer. Katharine appeals to her husband in eloquent and moving words—to meet only silence. Her appeal is personal, but Henry is no longer a person, and the law and the Church, speaking as one, deal briefly, courteously, firmly with her request for delay. As far as they are concerned, the human values for which she pleads do not exist. She is up against the process, the machine, the rocklike wall-face of law itself. Passion hurls itself unavailingly against the dispassionate, as in a

Galsworthy trial scene: "Is this relevant, Mr. Frome?" asks the judge.

> William Falder, you have been given fair trial . . . throughout the trial your counsel was in reality making an appeal for mercy. . . . And this plea of his, which in the end amounted to a passionate appeal, he based, in effect, on an indictment of the march of Justice. . . . *The Law is what it is*—a majestic edifice, sheltering all of us, each stone of which rests on another. I am concerned only in its administration.

It is the equivalent of a deliberately nonemotional statement of the reasons that must decide an issue against all the personal sympathies of the audience, as when the judge sums up against Falder in *Justice*, or when Shaw's Inquisitor puts the case against Joan of Arc. We do this kind of thing well today, perhaps better, and our prose medium is more suited to lengthy monologues which explain the precise reasons, intellectual or customary, laudable or reprehensible, sound or sophistical, that account for behavior and for the course of the action we are witnessing. The function of such speeches is to strike a balance between our emotional and intellectual responses to the writer's purpose and our understanding of it. The Elizabethan writer, I fancy, reckoned to deal with little beyond the emotional reactions; the Jacobean began to wrestle with the intellectual statement and the response to it, as in Ford's long exposition of honor in *The Broken Heart* (III.i). The exposition of Henry's scruples of conscience is skillfully handled, for its date, and it is likely to have held a contemporary audience, although it fails to hold a modern one, but there is no reason why it should have been less successful in its own day than our equivalent attempts.

This particular investigation of dramatic intention and theatrical effect, which I have summarized very briefly, had a further consequence that I did not anticipate. Being totally uncommitted over the divided authorship issue I had intended simply to give the pros and cons and leave the reader to make up his own mind;[10] and I am still as skeptical as I was then about the stylistic arguments used by literary critics to distribute portions of Elizabethan plays, even among known collaborators.[11] But the approach to the play itself, accepting the authors effects as intended, convinced me that *Henry VIII* was indubitably Shakespeare's, and further converted both Dr. A. W. Pollard and Professor Caroline Spurgeon to this view. I also found, six months later, that Professor Wilson Knight, in his own production of the play, had anticipated some of my arguments and come unequivocally to the same conclusion.[12] Since then, Professor R. A. Foakes, in his admirable introduction to the 1957 New Arden edition, has given us the most judicious and perceptive editorial account of the play, *considered as a play*, and of the authorship problem, that I know.[13] I think the basic resemblance between my 1935 essay and his appreciation, which is as balanced as it is brilliant, together with the fact that he ends it as I did mine, suggests that modern criticism has been steadily advancing along the right lines, even as modern productions since Guthrie's in 1949 have dealt with the play as a play, not simply as a vehicle for actors.

Professor Foakes concludes that perhaps the play should be thought of as "the last innovation of a mind forever exploring; and if the history of its supposed deficiencies can be forgotten, then the conception of the play may be allowed its full originality, as a felicitous new solution to problems posed by the nature of the material with which Shakespeare's last plays deal."[14] My conclusion in 1935, before the Guthrie production, was that the real play, which has been buried for too long beneath its own effective scenes and the authorship controversy, should prove, if properly produced, a rational entertainment for intelligent people. The mind that conceived this dramatic experiment was very evidently that of an experienced man of the theatre. You must know all about "theatre" before you can afford to reject it for the sake of the theatre. This 1613 experiment with fresh dramatic values reminds me of that daring and tremendous experiment which is the last twenty minutes of *A Doll's House*. Ibsen, in 1879, aged fifty, had behind him the experience of preparing the productions of 145 typical well-made plays of his day, and had himself written *the* model of all such, two years previously, in his *Pillars of Society*. When the tarantella ends, all the situations, tricks, and methods of the well-made play are hustled off the stage, and the real drama begins. Similarly, the mind that conceives *Henry VIII* decides that physical action, heroes, conflict, romantic poetry, and all the rest of Elizabethan stock-in-trade are to be hustled off his stage for the sake of a sober and truthful play, a great theme, and a closer touch with reality. The author does not successfully anticipate Ibsen's experiment, which made the discussion of ideas the dominant interest in modern European drama for nearly half a century. But the future toward which this 1613 experiment was reaching out is the future that was Ibsen, the great poet–dramatist of two and a half centuries later.

For our identification parade, therefore, we have found a mind. Is it recognizable or not? Are we in touch with the kind of mentality we may legitimately associate with the forty-nine-year-old Shakespeare?

The Shakespeare we all know and admire was an original genius. He refused to go on writing the same play over again. He had an extremely practical conception of the business of playwriting, but at the same time found scope in the writing of plays for the exercising of a very daring mind. It is perhaps a commonplace to say that he was always experimenting with dramatic methods—more particularly toward the end of his career. But it cannot too often be reaffirmed that this delight in experiment is always the characteristic of the great and original mind, and not of the merely popular writer. Sir Edmund Chambers finds "the reversion to the epic chronicle at the very end of Shakespeare's career is odd."[15] But surely there is nothing odd in the spectacle of an original mind discovering that there is still something new and exciting to be done with the old material, which it has used so often, although never before in this particular way. What I find odd is the idea that a popular writer like Fletcher, who has discovered the formula that everyone wants, who never otherwise touches this particular kind of play, and never employs methods comparable to those we have been analyzing, should, at the height of his success and popularity, revert to an outmoded type. Oddest of all is what can only be described as the basic improbability that there should be any failure of the full and accepted theatrical effect if Fletcher is concerned in the writing of a scene. It is axiomatic that his situations will hold, whereas the whole trouble with *Henry VIII* starts from the fact that the situations do not hold, in the old, easy, normal, accepted theatrical way, because something quite different from the normal theatrical effect is what the author intended.

If we seek to identify a mind, surely the mind which, around 1602, took a grimly realistic attitude to the romantic *Troilus and Cressida* story and to the heroic-epic treatment of war is a more likely guess than the mind which habitually exploited the tragicomedy formula and allowed the audience both to have its cake and eat it. Surely the mind which had already between 1600 and 1604 expressed its dissatisfaction with the romantic formulae that serve as plots for *All's Well* and *Measure for Measure* is more likely to turn toward realism in tone and attack than the specialist in the exploitation of emotionalism? Not for Fletcher the poetry that might be squeezed from the "pure crude fact" of the chronicle history; the melodrama and the excitement of the end of Bonduca and her daughters, yes; but not the sober quietude and poignancy of the death of Katharine;

> Remember me
> In all humility unto his highness:
> Say his long trouble now is passing
> Out of this world.
>
> (IV.ii.160-63)

Shakespeare was only fifty-two when he died. Had he lived on and continued to write plays it is possible that he would have made the one experiment which none of the Jacobean writers had the vitality to attempt. Having presumably said what he had to say about life, and seeing what was happening to blank verse, he could have turned his energies to the development of English prose for dramatic purposes. There is no doubt that the Shakespeare of the histories and the middle comedies, around 1600, was finding prose a more suitable medium for some of the material he was handling.[16] The tragedies had yet to be written, and for them he would create their own astounding blank verse; for dramatic purposes there has been no further development since that creation. But it is not a vain imagining that, had he eventually turned to the "realistic" manner, as the writer of *Henry VIII* does, he might have put his mind to the problem which occupied the mature Ibsen, who in 1883 criticized the "immense injury" done by verse to the art of the theatre; "I myself, for the last seven or eight years, have hardly written a single verse, but have cultivated exclusively the incomparably more difficult art of poetic creation in the plain unvarnished speech of reality."

As a true poet Ibsen had set himself the task of writing poetry without the aid of the high style, of which Shakespeare had proved himself a rare master. There is none of the high style in *Henry VIII,* though time and again we hear the authentic accents of poetry. To put it at its lowest, if we accept *Henry VII* as Shakespeare's, we are committing ourselves to no more than saying that it is an unexpected and daring experiment in a new kind and a new style, and a much better and more original experiment than was *Cymbeline.* It is not the work of "a tired mind," but the work of a great mind tired of the theatrical convention in which it has been working. "Shakespeare is not content with perfection of achievement at any stage of his career; he must always go on to a stage beyond."[17] The stage beyond is not necessarily the stage better, but it enlarges the boundaries, thrusts into unexplored territory, carries the dramatic adventure a step further, even if no one follows up the experiment for a couple of centuries. For those who feel that nothing of vital importance happened to drama between Shakespeare and Ibsen, *Henry VIII,* as his last play, may perhaps acquire a new significance.

How fully his own audience was always "with" him we know in general terms only. Just how far away the perception of succeeding centuries could drift we know from the adaptations and recorded mutilations of his text and the perversities of interpretation that still from time to time afflict us in performance; and we have had to wait for our own century to catch up with his intention, not only in *Henry VIII* but in *Troilus and Cressida, Measure for Measure, All's Well, Antony and Cleopatra,* and *Love's Labour's Lost. Henry VIII's* critical and theatrical history provides an outstanding example of the failure of literary criticism and stage production to give proper consideration to the facts of dramatic intention, as expressed in structure and style; but the succession theme was pinpointed in 1918, and the case for Shakespeare as sole author was supported by Marjorie Nicolson and Baldwin Maxwell in 1922 and 1923, by Peter Alexander in 1930, and by Professor Wilson Knight in 1936. With the New Arden edition, and finally with Professor Sprague's 1964 account of "the play in performance" in his happily timed quadricentenary studies of Shakespeare's *Histories,* I believe that this remarkable play, for so long, as he says, "badly treated on the stage and rather worse in the study,"[18] has been definitively rehabilitated by the investigation of "what the author meant." But concentration on intention is still erratic, and when at this moment of writing we are confronted with a naked Desdemona, in defiance of three explicit author's stage directions about her smock or shift for her nightly wearing, progress, perhaps, "seems here no painful inch to gain." Slow it has been, but "e pur si muove"; and all who know the work of the scholar to whom this volume pays tribute will recognize that the two sections of this essay are simply footnotes to the principles and practice which have, throughout, determined his own approach to drama, the theatre, and the play in performance, and have also done so much to inspire and guide students of the drama, and especially of Shakespeare, to listen to what the author says, to see straight and recognize and respect intention.

NOTES

1. Lascelles Abercrombie, *A Plea for the Liberty of Interpreting*, The British Academy Annual Shakespeare Lecture, London: Humphrey Milford, 1930, p. 29.
2. James Spedding, "Who Wrote Shakspere's *Henry VIII*," *Gentleman's Magazine*, n.s. 34 (1850): 115-24, 381-82.
3. Cf. also *The Atheist's Tragedy* (1611), *The Tragedy of Chabot* (c. 1613) with "the furious eloquence of my accuser" (act III), and *Appius and Virginia* (c. 1608), "I undertake a desperate combat." But here, theatrically, trial scene excitement is promised, no trial takes place, and "excitement" vanishes in Katherine.
4. Muriel St. Clare Byrne, "A Stratford Production: *Henry VIII*," *Shakespeare Survey*, (1950): 120-29.
5. As originally performed at Stratford-upon-Avon. It had fallen off by the time it was put on at the Old Vic.
6. For example, John M. Berdan and C. F. Tucker Brooke (eds.), *The Life of King Henry the Eighth*, New Haven: Yale University Press, 1925.
7. Even Spedding let himself go over this entrancing game and mapped out some alternative scenarios, including one which would take us on to the birth of Anne Boleyn's stillborn son and her own execution, which he considered would give us a great tragedy of retributive justice; and when forced back upon the play itself he could only conjecture that Shakespeare had originally projected a grand historical piece which must have culminated in the final separation of the English from the Romish Church, "which being the one great historical event of the reign would naturally be chosen as the focus of poetic interest." Cf. Spedding, "Who Wrote *Henry VIII*," pp. 117, 123.
8. To which, as to the succession theme, Sir J. A. R. Marriott draws attention in *English History in Shakespeare*, London: Chapman & Hall, 1918.
9. Charles Kean, in 1855, did his best to cut, without losing the whole value of the author's structural pause, by providing a brief composite scene, including some of Henry's interview with Cranmer and the Old Lady's

announcement of the birth. It was, however, omitted after the first night, when the performance ran from 8:30 to 12:00, and will be found only in the first edition, *Shakespeare's Historical Play of King Henry the Eighth . . .* First Performed on Wednesday, 16th May, 1855, London, John K. Chapman & Co., 1855, V.i.

10. For Shakespeare's authorship I was proposing to cite Marjorie Nicolson, "The Authorship of Henry the Eighth," *PMLA*, 37 (1922): 484-502; Baldwin Maxwell, "Fletcher and Henry VIII," *The Manly Anniversary Studies in Language and Literature,* Chicago: University of Chicago Press, 1923, pp. 104-12; and Peter Alexander, "Conjectural History, or Shakespeare's *Henry VIII,*" *Essays and Studies,* 16 (1930): 85-120.
11. Cf. my paper on "Bibliographical Clues in Collaborate Plays," The Library (June 1932): 21-48 and also Baldwin Maxwell's conclusion that "in a strict sense Spedding cannot be said to have made any test whatsoever," as he did not show that the characteristics of style upon which he based his argument were peculiar to Fletcher ("Fletcher and Henry VIII," p. 104).
12. G. Wilson Knight, *Principles of Shakespearian Production,* London: Faber and Faber, 1936, and "A Note on Henry VIII," *Criterion,* 15 (1936): 228-36.
13. King Henry VIII, *The Arden Shakespeare,* ed. R. A. Foakes, London: Methuen, 1957.
14. Ibid., p. lxii.
15. Edmund K. Chambers, *William Shakespeare: A Study of Facts and Problems,* Oxford: Clarendon Press, 1930, I:497.
16. Harley Granville-Barker, *Prefaces to Shakespeare: Hamlet,* London: Sidgwick and Jackson, 1936, p. 7.
17. Abercrombie, *Liberty of Interpreting,* p. 29.
18. Arthur Colby Sprague, *Shakespeare's Histories: Plays for the Stage,* London: The Society for Theatre Research, 1964, p. 159.

James Spedding

On the Several Shares of Shakespeare and Fletcher in the Play of *Henry VIII*

Mr. Collier observes that the principal question which arises with regard to the play of *Henry VIII* is when it was written. *By whom* it was written has not yet been made a question, so far as I know; at least not in print. And yet several of our most considerable critics have incidentally betrayed a consciousness that there is something peculiar either in the execution, or the structure, or the general design of it, which should naturally suggest a doubt on this point. Dr. Johnson observes that the genius of Shakspere comes in and goes out with Katharine, and that the rest of the play might be easily conceived and easily written—a fact, if it be a fact, so remarkable as to call for explanation. Coleridge, in one of his attempts to classify Shakspere's plays (1802), distinguished *Henry VIII* as *gelegenheitsgedicht*; in another (1819) as "a sort of historical masque of show-play"; thereby betraying a consciousness that there was something singular and exceptional about it. Ulrici, who has applied himself with a German ingenuity to discover in each of Shakspere's plays a profound moral purpose, is obliged to confess that he can make nothing of *Henry VIII*, and is driven to suppose that what we have was meant only for a first part, to be followed by a second in which the odds would have been made even. Mr Knight, whose faith is proof against such doubts, does indeed treat *Henry VIII* as the perfect crown and consummation of the series of historical plays, and succeeds in tracing through the first four acts a consistent and sufficient moral; but when he comes to the fifth, which should crown all, he is obliged to put us off with a reference to the historians; admitting that the catastrophe which history had provided as the crowning moral of the whole is not exhibited in the play, "but who (he asks) can forget it?"—an apology for the gravest of all defects which seems to me quite inadmissible. A peculiarity of another kind has also been detected, I forget by whom, namely, the unusual number of lines with a redundant syllable at the end, of which it is said there are twice as many in this as in any other play of Shakspere's—a circumstance well worthy of consideration, for so broad a difference was not likely to be accidental; and one which is the more remarkable when viewed in connection with another peculiarity of style pointed out by Mr. Knight, viz. the number of passages in which the lines are so run into each other that it is impossible to separate them in reading by the slightest pause at the end of each. Now the passage which he selects in illustration is one in which the proportion of lines with the redundant syllable is unusually *small*; and therefore it would appear that this play is remarkable for the prevalence of *two* peculiarities of different kinds, which are in some degree irreconcileable with each other.

I shall have something further to say on these points presently. I mention them here only to show that critical observers have been long conscious of certain singularities in this play which require to be accounted for. And, leaving the critics, I might probably appeal to the individual consciousness of each reader, and ask him whether he has not always felt that, in spite of some great scenes which have made actors and actresses famous, and many beautiful speeches which adorn our books of extracts (and which, by the way, lose little or nothing by separation from their context, a most rare thing in Shakspere), the effect of this play *as a whole* is weak and disappointing. The truth is that the interest, instead of rising towards the end, falls away utterly, and leaves us in the last act among persons whom we scarcely know, and events for which we do not care. The strongest sympathies which have been awakened in us run opposite to the course of the action. Our sympathy is for the grief and goodness of Queen Katharine, while the course of the action requires us to entertain as a theme of joy and compensatory satisfaction the coronation of Anne Bullen and the birth of her daughter; which are in fact a part of Katharine's injury, and amount to little less than the ultimate triumph of wrong. For throughout the play the king's cause is not only felt by us, but represented to us, as a bad one. We *hear*, indeed, of conscientious scruples as to the legality of his first marriage; but we are not made, nor indeed asked, to believe that they are sincere, or to recognize in his new marriage either the hand of Providence, or the consummation of any worthy object, or the victory of any of those more common frailties of humanity with which we can sympathize. The mere caprice of passion drives the king into the commission of what seems a great iniquity; our compassion for the victim of it is elaborately excited; no attempt is made to awaken any counter-sympathy for *him*: yet his passion has its way, and is crowned with all felicity, present and to come. The effect is much like that which would have been produced by the *Winter's Tale* if Hermione had died in the fourth act in consequence of the jealous tyranny of Leontes, and the play had ended with the coronation of a new queen and the christening of a new heir, no period of remorse intervening. It is as if Nathan's rebuke to David had ended, not with the doom of death to the child just born, but with a prophetic promise of the felicities of Solomon.

This main defect is sufficient of itself to mar the effect of the play as a whole. But there is another, which though less vital is not less unaccountable. The greater part of the fifth act, in which the interest ought to be gathering to a head, is occupied with matters in which we have not been prepared to take any interest by what went before, and on which no interest is reflected by what comes after. The scenes in the gallery and council-chamber, though full of life and vigour, and, in point of execution, not unworthy of Shakspere, are utterly irrelevant to the business of the play; for what have we to do with the quarrel between Gardiner and Cranmer? Nothing in the play is explained by it, nothing depends upon it. It is used only (so far as the argument is concerned) as a preface for introducing Cranmer as godfather to Queen Elizabeth, which might have been done as a matter of course without any preface at all. The scenes themselves are indeed both picturesque and characteristic and historical, and might probably have been introduced with excellent effect into a dramatised life of Henry VIII. But historically they do not belong to the place where they are introduced here, and poetically they have in this place no value, but the reverse.

With the fate of Wolsey, again, in whom our second interest centres, the business of this last act does not connect itself any more than with that of Queen Katharine. The fate of Wolsey would have made a noble subject for a tragedy in itself, and might very well have been combined with the tragedy of Katharine; but, as an introduction to the festive solemnity with which the play concludes, the one seems to me as inappropriate as the other.

Nor can the existence of these defects be accounted for by any inherent difficulty in the subject. It cannot be said that they were in any way forced upon the dramatist by the facts of the story. The incidents of the reign of Henry VIII could not, it is true, like those of an ancient tradition or an Italian novel, be altered at pleasure to suit the purposes of the artist; but they admitted of many different combinations, by which the effect of the play might have been modified to almost any extent either at the beginning or the end. By taking in a larger period and carrying the story on to the birth of Anne Bullen's still-born son and her own execution it would have yielded the argument of a great tragedy and tale of retributive justice. Or, on the other hand, by throwing the sorrows of Katharine more into the background, by bringing into prominence the real scruples which were in fact entertained by learned and religious men and prevalent among the people, by representing the question of the divorce as the battle-ground on which the question between Popery and Protestantism was tried out, by throwing a strong light upon the engaging personal qualities of Anne Bullen herself, and by connecting with the birth of Elizabeth the ultimate triumph of the Reformed religion, of which she was to become so distinguished a champion, our sympathies might have been turned that way, and so reconciled to the prosperous consummation. But it is evident that no attempt has been made to do this. The afflictions, the virtue, the patience of Katharine are elaborately exhibited. To these and to the pathetic penitence of Wolsey our attention is especially commended in the prologue, and with them it is entirely occupied to the end of the fourth act. Anne Bullen is kept almost out of sight. Such reason and religion as there were in Henry's scruples are scarcely touched upon, and hardly a word is introduced to remind us that the dispute with the Pope was the forerunner of the Reformation.

I know no other play in Shakspere which is chargeable with a fault like this, none in which the moral sympathy of the spectator is not carried along with the main current of action to the end. In all the historical tragedies a providence may be seen presiding over the development of events, as just and relentless as the fate in a Greek tragedy. Even in *Henry IV*, where the comic element predominates, we are never allowed to exult in the success of the wrong-doer, or to forget the penalties which are due to guilt. And if it be true that in the romantic comedies our moral sense does sometimes suffer a passing shock, it is never owing to an error in the general design, but always to some incongruous circumstance in the original story which has lain in the way and not been entirely got rid of, and which after all offends us rather as an incident improbably in itself than as one for which our sympathy is unjustly demanded. The singularity of *Henry VIII* is that, while four-fifths of the play are occupied in matters which are to make us incapable of mirth—

> Be sad, as we would make you: Think ye see
> The very persons of our history
> As they were living; think you see them great
> And followed with the general throng and sweat
> Of thousand friends: then in a moment see
> How soon this mightiness meets misery!
> And if you can be merry then, I'll say
> A man may weep upon his wedding day—

the remaining fifth is devoted to joy and triumph, and ends with universal festivity:

> This day let no man think
> He has business at his house; for all shall stay:
> this little one shall make it holiday.

Of this strange inconsistency, or at least of a certain poorness in the general effect which is amply accounted for by such inconsistency, I had for some time been vaguely conscious; and I had also heard it casually remarked by a man of first-rate judgment on such a point that many passages in *Henry VIII* were very much in the manner of *Fletcher*; when I happened to take up a book of extracts, and opened by chance on the following beautiful lines:

> Would I had never trod this English earth,
> Or felt the flatteries that grow upon it!
> Ye have angels' faces, but heaven knows your hearts.
> What will become of me now, wretched lady?
> I am the most unhappy woman living.
> Alas! poor wenches, where are now your fortunes?
> Shipwrecked upon a kingdom, where no pity,
> No friends, no hope; no kindred weep for me,

Almost no grave allowed me:—Like the lily,
That once was mistress of the field and flourish'd,
I'll hang my head and perish.

Was it possible to believe that these lines were written by Shakspere? I had often amused myself with attempting to trace the gradual change of his versification from the simple monotonous cadence of the *Two Gentlemen of Verona*, to the careless felicities of the *Winter's Tale* and *Cymbeline*, of which it seemed as impossible to analyse the law as not to feel the melody; but I could find no stage in that progress to which it seemed possible to refer these lines. I determined upon this to read the play through with an eye to this especial point, and see whether any solution of the mystery would present itself. The result of my examination was a clear conviction that at least two different hands had been employed in the composition of *Henry VIII*; if not three; and that they had worked, not together, but alternately upon distinct portions of it.

This is a conclusion which cannot of course be established by detached extracts, which in questions of style are doubtful evidence at best. The only satisfactory evidence upon which it can be determined whether a given scene was or was not by Shakspere, is to be found in the general effect produced on the mind, the ear, and the feelings by a free and broad perusal; and if any of your readers care to follow me in this inquiry, I would ask him to do as I did—that is, to read the whole play straight through, with an eye open to notice the larger differences of effect, but without staying to examine small points. The effect of my own experiment was as follows:—

The opening of the play—the conversation between Buckingham, Norfolk, and Abergavenny—seemed to have the full stamp of Shakspere, in his latest manner: the same close-packed expression; the same life, and reality, and freshness; the same rapid and abrupt turnings of thought, so quick that language can hardly follow fast enough; the same impatient activity of intellect and fancy, which having once disclosed an idea cannot wait to work it orderly out; the same daring confidence in the resources of language, which plunges headlong into a sentence without knowing how it is to come forth; the same careless metre which disdains to produce its harmonious effects by the ordinary devices, yet is evidently subject to a master of harmony; the same entire freedom from book-language and common-place; all the qualities, in short, which distinguish the magical hand which has never yet been successfully imitated.

In the scene in the council-chamber which follows (Act i, Sc. 2), where the characters of Katharine and Wolsey are brought out, I found the same characteristics equally strong.

But the instant I entered upon the third scene, in which the Lord Chamberlain, Lord Sands, and Lord Lovel converse, I was conscious of a total change. I felt as if I had passed suddenly out of the language of nature into the language of the stage, or of some conventional mode of conversation. The structure of the verse was quite different and full of mannerism. The expression became suddenly diffuse and languid. The wit wanted mirth and character. And all this was equally true of the supper scene which closes the first Act.

The second act brought me back to the tragic vein, but it was not the tragic vein of Shakspere. When I compared the eager, impetuous, and fiery language of Buckingham in the first Act with the languid and measured cadences of his farewell speech, I felt that the difference was too great to be accounted for by the mere change of situation, without supposing also a change of writers. The presence of death produces great changes in men, but no such change as we have here.

When in like manner I compared the Henry and Wolsey of the scene which follows (Act ii, Sc. 2) with the Henry and Wolsey of the council-chamber (Act i, Sc. 2), I perceived a difference scarcely less striking. The dialogue, through the whole scene, sounded still slow and artificial.

The next scene brought another sudden change. And, as in passing from the second to the third scene of the first Act, I had seemed to be passing all at once out of the language of nature into that of convention, so in passing from the second to the third scene of the second Act (in which Anne Bullen appears, I may say for the first time, for in the supper scene she was merely a conventional court lady without any character at all,) I seemed to pass not less suddenly from convention back again into nature. And when I considered that this short and otherwise insignificant passage contains all that we ever see of Anne (for it is necessary to forget her former appearance) and yet how clearly the character comes out, how very a woman she is, and yet how distinguishable from any other individual woman, I had not difficulty in acknowledging that the sketch came from the same hand which drew Perdita.

Next follows the famous trial-scene. And here I could as little doubt that I recognized the same hand to which we owe the trial of Hermione. When I compared the language of Henry and of Wolsey throughout this scene to the end of the Act, with their language in the council-chamber (Act i, Sc. 2), I found that it corresponded in all essential features: when I compared it with their language in the second scene of the second Act, I perceived that it was altogether different. Katharine also, as she appears in this scene, was exactly the same person as she was in the council-chamber; but when I went on to the first scene of the third Act, which represents her interview with Wolsey and Campeius, I found her as much changed as Buckingham was after his sentence, though without any alteration of circumstances to account for an alteration of temper. Indeed the whole of this scene seemed to have all the peculiarities of Fletcher, both in conception, language, and versification, without a single feature that reminded me of Shakspere; and, since in both passages the true narrative of Cavendish is followed minutely and carefully, and both are therefore copies from the same original and in the same style of art, it was the more easy to compare them with each other.

In the next scene (Act iii, sc. 2) I seemed again to get out of Fletcher into Shakspere; though probably not into Shakspere pure; a scene by another hand perhaps which Shakspere had only remodeled, or a scene by Shakspere which another hand had worked upon to make it fit a place. The speeches interchanged between Henry and Wolsey seemed to be entirely Shakspere's; but in the altercation between Wolsey and the lords which follows I could recognize little or nothing of his peculiar manner, while many passages were strongly marked with the favourite Fletcherian cadence;[1] and as for the famous "Farewell, a long farewell," &c., though associated by means of Enfield's Speaker with my earliest notions of Shakspere, it appeared (now that my mind was opened to entertain the doubt) to belong entirely and unquestionably to Fletcher.

Of the 4th Act I did not so well know what to think. For the most part it seemed to bear evidence of a more vigorous hand than Fletcher's, with less mannerism, especially in the description of the coronation, and the character of Wolsey; and yet it had not to my mind the freshness and originality of Shakspere. It was pathetic and graceful, but one could see how it was done. Katharine's last speeches, however, smacked strongly again of Fletcher. And altogether it seemed to me that if this Act had occurred in one of the plays written by Beaumont and Fletcher in conjunction it would probably have been thought that both of them had had a hand in it.

The first scene of the 5th Act, and the opening of the second, I should again have confidently ascribed to Shakspere, were it not that the whole passage seemed so strangely out of place. I could only suppose (what may indeed be supposed well enough if my conjecture with regard to the authorship of the several parts be correct), that the task of putting the whole together had been left to an inferior hand; in which case I should consider this to be a genuine piece of Shakspere's work, spoiled by being introduced where it has no business. In the execution of the christening scene, on the other hand (in spite again of the earliest and strongest associations), I could see no evidence of Shakspere's hand at all; while in point of *design* it seemed inconceivable that a judgment like his could have been content with a conclusion so little in harmony with the prevailing spirit and purpose of the piece.

Such was the general result of my examination of this play with reference to the internal evidence of style and treatment. With regard to external evidence, I can only say that I know of none which stands in the way of any of these conclusions. *Henry VIII* was first printed in the folio of 1623. It was printed no doubt as Shakspere's, without any hint that any one else had had a hand in it. But so were *Titus Andronicus* and all the three parts of *Henry VI*. The editors were not critics, and it was not then the fashion for authors to trouble the public with their jealousies. The play would naturally go by the name of Shakspere, having so much in it of his undoubted and best workmanship, and as such it would naturally take its place in the general collection. With regard to the date of its composition we have no conclusive evidence; but that which approaches nearest to that character goes to show that it was acted, and considered as a new play, on St. Peter's day, 1613, when the Globe Theatre was burnt down. The play then acted was certainly on the subject of *Henry VIII* and contained at least one incident which occurs in the present work—the discharge of chambers upon the arrival of the masquers in the supper-scene. It was called, indeed, *All is True*; but that title suits the present work perfectly well; and it may have been the original one, though the editors in including it among the histories preferred the historical title. There is evidence likewise that a play called *The*

Interlude of Henry VII was in existence in 1604, but none to show that it was by Shakspere, still less that it was the present play in its present state, which is to me, I confess, quite incredible. Altogether, therefore, I may say that if any one be inclined to think that *Henry VIII* was composed in 1612 or 1613, and that Beaumont and Fletcher were employed in the composition as well as Shakspere, there is nothing in the external evidence to forbid him.

Here, however, a new question will arise. Supposing the inequality of the workmanship in different parts of the play to be admitted, as by most people I think it will, may not this be sufficiently accounted for by supposing that it was written by Shakspere at different periods? May it not have been an early performance of his own, which in his later life he corrected, and in great part rewrote; as we know he did in some other cases?

I think not; for two reasons. First, because if he had set about the revisal of it on so large a scale in the maturity of his genius, he would have addressed himself to remove its principal defect, which is the incoherence of the general design. Secondly, because the style of those parts which upon this supposition would be referred to the earlier period does not at all resemble Shakspere's style at any stage of its development.

This is another conclusion which it is impossible to establish by extracts in any moderate quantity. But let any one who doubts it try it by the following test. Let him read an act in each of the following plays, taking them in succession:—*Two Gentleman of Verona; Richard II; Richard III; Romeo and Juliet; Henry IV* (part 2); *As You Like It; Twelfth Night; Measure for Measure; Lear; Antony and Cleopatra; Coriolanus; Winter's Tale*; and then let him say at what period of Shakspere's life he can be supposed to have written such lines as these—

All good people,
You that thus far have come to pity me,
Hear what I say, and then go home and lose me.
I have this day received a traitor's judgment,
And by that name must die: Yet heaven bear witness,
And if I have a conscience, let it sink me,
Even as the axe falls, if I be not faithful.
The law I bear no malice for my death,
It has done, upon the premises, but justice:
But those who sought it I could wish more Christians.
Be what they will, I heartily forgive them:

Yet let them look they glory not in mischief
Nor build their evils on the graves of great men;
For them my guiltless blood must cry against them.
For further life in this life I ne'er hope,
Nor will I sue, although the King have mercies,
More than I dare make faults. You few that loved me,
And dare be bold to weep for Buckingham.
His noble friends and fellows, whom to leave
Is only bitter to him, only dying,
Go with me like good angels to my end;
And as the long divorce of steel falls on me,
Make your prayers one sweet sacrifice,
And lift my soul to heaven!

If I am not much mistaken he will be convinced that Shakspere's style never passed, nor ever could have passed, through this phase. In his earlier plays, when his versification was regular and his language comparatively diffuse, there is none of the studied variety of cadence which we find here; and by the time his versification had acquired more variety, the current of his thought had become more gushing, rapid, and full of eddies; not to add that at no period whatever in the development of his style was the proportion of thought and fancy to words and images so small as it appears in this speech of Buckingham's. Perhaps there is no passage in Shakspere which so nearly resembles it as Richard II's farewell to his Queen; from which indeed it seems to have been imitated; but observe the difference—

Good sometime Queen, prepare thee hence for France:
Think I am dead: and that even here thou tak'st
As from my death-bed my last living leave.
In Winter's tedious nights, sit by the fire
With good old folks, and let them tell thee tales
Of woeful ages long ago betid:
And ere thou bid good night, to quit their grief,
Tell thou the lamentable tale of me,
And send the hearers weeping to their beds.
For why, the senseless brands will sympathize
The heavy accent of thy moving tongue,
And in compassion weep the fire out:
And some will mourn in ashes, some coal-black
For the deposing of a rightful King.

And if we compare the two entire scenes the difference will appear ten times greater, for Richard's passion makes a new subject of every passing incident and image, and has as many changes as an Æolian harp.

To a practised ear the test which I have proposed will, I think, be sufficient, and more conclusive perhaps than any other. Those who are less quick in perceiving the finer rhythmical effects may be more struck with the following consideration. It has been observed, as I said, that lines with a redundant syllable at the end occur in *Henry VIII* twice as often as in any of Shakspere's other plays. Now, it will be found on examination that this observation does not apply to all parts of the play alike, but only to those which I have noticed as, in their general character, un-Shaksperian. In those parts which have the stamp of Shakspere upon them in other respects, the proportion of lines with the redundant syllable is not greater than in other of his later plays—*Cymbeline,* for instance, and the *Winter's Tale*. In the opening scene of *Cymbeline*, an unimpassioned conversation, chiefly narrative, we find twenty-five such lines in sixty-seven; in the third scene of the third Act, which is in a higher strain of poetry but still calm, we find twenty-three in one hundred and seven; in the fourth scene, which is full of sudden turns of passion, fifty-three in one hundred and eighty-two. Taking one scene with another, therefore, the lines with the redundant syllable are in the proportion of about two to seven. In the *Winter's Tale* we may take the second and third scenes of the third Act as including a sufficient variety of style; and here we find seventy-one in two hundred and forty-eight; the same proportion as nearly as possible, though the scenes were selected at random.

Let us now see how it is in *Henry VIII*. Here is a table showing the proportion in each successive scene:

Act	Scene	Lines	Red. Syll.	Propn.	Author
I.	1.	225	63	1 to 3.5	[Shakspere.
	2.	215	74	–2.9	"
	3 & 4.	172	100	–1.7	Fletcher.
II.	1.	164	97	1.6	"
	2.	129	77	–1.6	"
	3.	107	41	–2.6	Shakspere.
	4.	230	72	–3.1	"

III.	1.	166	119	–1.3	Fletcher.
	2.	193	62	–3.	Shakspere.
	As far as the exit of King Henry.				
	3.	257	152	–1.6	Fletcher.
IV.	1.	116	57	–2.	"
	2.	80	51	–1.5	"
	3.	93	51	–1.8	"
V.	1.	176	68	–2.5	Shakspere (altered).
	2.	217	115	–1.8	Fletcher.
	3.	almost all prose			"
	4.	73	44	–1.6	"]

Here then we have, out of sixteen separate scenes, six in which the redundant syllable occurs (taking one with another), about as often as in *Cymbeline* and the *Winter's Tale*; the proportion being never higher than two in five, which is the same as in the opening scene of *Cymbeline*; never lower than two in seven, which is the same as in the trial scene in the *Winter's Tale*; and the average being about one in three; while in the remaining ten scenes the proportion of such lines is never less than one in two; in the greater number of them scarcely more than two in three. Nor is there anything in the subject or character of the several scenes by which such a difference can be accounted for. The light and loose conversation at the end of the first Act, the plaintive and laboured oration in the second, the querulous and passionate altercation in the third, the pathetic sorrows of Wolsey, the tragic death of Katharine, the high poetic prophecy of Cranmer, are equally distinguished by this peculiarity. A distinction so broad and so uniform, running through so large a portion of the same piece, cannot have been accidental; and the more closely it is examined the more clearly will it appear that the metre in these two sets of scenes is managed upon entirely different principles, and bears evidence of different workmen. To explain all the particular differences would be to analyze the structure first of Shakspere's metre, then of Fletcher's; a dry and tedious task. But the general difference may easily be made evident by placing any undoubted specimen of Shakspere's later workmanship by the side of the one, and of Fletcher's middle workmanship by the side of the other; the identity in both cases will be felt at once. The only difficulty is to find a serious play known to be the unassisted composition of Fletcher, and to have been written about the year 1612: for in those which he wrote before his partnership with Beaumont his distinctive mannerism is less marked; in those which he wrote after Beaumont's death it is more exaggerated. But read the last Act of the *Honest Man's Fortune,* which was first represented in 1613; the opening of the third Act of the *Captain,* which appeared towards the close of 1612; and the great scene extracted by Charles Lamb from the fourth act of *Thierry and Theodoret,*[3] which, though not produced I believe till 1621, is thought to have been written much earlier; and you will have sufficient samples of his middle style, in all its varieties, to make the comparison. In all these, besides the general structure of the language and rhythm, there are many particular verbal and rhythmical affectations which will at once catch any ear that is accustomed to Shakspere, whose style is entirely free from them; and every one of these will be found as frequent in the un-Shaksperian portions of *Henry VIII* as in the above-mentioned passages, which are undoubtedly Fletcher's.

Assuming then that *Henry VIII* was written partly by Shakspere, partly by Fletcher, with the assistance probably of some third hand,[4] it becomes a curious question, upon what plan their joint labours were conducted. It was not unusual in those days, when a play was wanted in a hurry, to set two or three or even four hands at work upon it; and the occasion of the Princess Elizabeth's marriage (February 1612-13) may very likely have suggested the production of a play representing the marriage of Henry VIII and Anne Bullen. Such an occasion would sufficiently account for the determination to treat the subject not tragically; the necessity for producing it immediately might lead to the employment of several hands; and thence would follow inequality of workmanship and imperfect adaptation of the several parts to each other. But this would not explain the incoherency and inconsistency of the main design. Had Shakspere been employed to make a design for a play which was to end with the happy marriage of Henry and Anne Bullen, we may be sure that he would not have occupied us through the four first Acts with a tragic and absorbing interest in the decline and death of Queen Katharine, and through half the fifth with a quarrel between Cranmer and Gardiner, in which we have no interest. On the other hand, since it is by Shakspere that all the principal matters and characters are *introduced,* it is not likely that the general design of the piece would be laid out by another. I should rather conjecture that he had conceived the idea of a great historical drama on the subject of Henry VIII which would have included the divorce of Katharine, the fall of Wolsey, the rise of Cranmer, the coronation of Anne Bullen, and the final separation of the English from the Romish Church, which, being the one great historical event of the reign, would naturally be chosen as the focus of poetic interest; that he had proceeded in the execution of this idea as far perhaps as the third Act, which might have included the establishment of Cranmer in the seat of highest ecclesiastical authority (the council-chamber scene in the fifth being designed as an introduction to that); when, finding that his fellows of the Globe were in distress for a new play to honour the marriage of the Lady Elizabeth with, he thought that his half-finished work might help them, and accordingly handed them his manuscript to make what they could of it; that they put it into the hands of Fletcher (already in high repute as a popular and expeditious playwright), who finding the original design not very suitable to the occasion and utterly beyond his capacity, expanded the three acts into five, by interspersing scenes of show and magnificence, and passages of description, and long poetical conversation, in which his strength lay; dropped all allusion to the great ecclesiastical revolution, which he could not manage and for which he had no materials supplied him; converted what should have been the middle into the end; and so turned out a splendid "historical masque, or shew-play," which was no doubt very popular then, as it has been ever since.

This is a bold conjecture, but it will account for all the phenomena. Read the portions which I have marked as Shakspere's by themselves, and suppose them to belong to the first half of the play, and they will not seem unworthy of him; though the touches of an inferior hand may perhaps be traced here and there, and the original connection is probably lost beyond recovery in the interpolations. Suppose again the *design* of the play as it stands to have been left to Fletcher, and the want of moral consistency and coherency needs no further explanation. The want of a just moral feeling is Fletcher's characteristic defect, and lies at the bottom of all that is most offensive in him, from his lowest mood to his highest. That it has not in this case betrayed him into such gross inconsistencies and indelicacies as usual may be explained by the fact that he was following the Chronicles and had little room for his own inventions. A comparison between this play and the *Two Noble Kinsmen*, the condition and supposed history of which is in many respects analogous,[5] would throw further light upon the question. But this would require too long a discussion.

NOTES

1. As for instance:—

   Now I feel
   Of what base metal ye are moulded,—Envy.
   How eagerly ye follow my disgraces
   As if it fed ye, and how sleek and wanton
   Ye appear in everything may bring my ruin!
   Follow your envious courses, men of malice:
   Ye have Christian warrant for them, &c.
2. Mr. Fleay does not admit any trace of Beaumont's hand in *Henry VIII*—F. J. F.
3. In this scene we have 154 lines with the redundant syllable out of 232; 2 in 3; exactly the same proportion which we find in so many scenes of *Henry VIII*; and no where else I think through the entire range of the Shaksperian theatre.
4. See note 1 above.
5. On this subject see an excellent article in the *Westminster Review*, vol. xlvii. p. 59; which is especially valuable for the discovery of some of Shakspere's very finest workmanship among the scenes of the underplot, which previous critics had set down as all alike worthless.

Marjorie H. Nicholson

The Authorship of *Henry the Eighth*

The problems connected with the authorship of *Henry the Eighth* are in some ways different from those usual in the doubtful plays. In the first place, the external evidence is singularly exact and definite and in no way contradictory. That a play dealing with the reign of Henry the Eighth and bearing either the title or the sub-title *All Is True* was being acted June 29, 1613 at the Globe Theatre is attested by at least three contemporary documents which tell of the fire which destroyed the theatre that day.[1] The publication of the play in the Folio of 1623 is, however, the only direct attribution to Shakespeare. According to one of the ballads written about the Globe fire, Heminge and Condell, the Folio editors, were both present at the time of the fire;[2] their later inclusion of the play in the Folio must, therefore, have been with full knowledge of its authorship. In the second place, the play is so evidently by two hands that, even as early as 1758, Roderick pointed out peculiarities of metre which did not seem to him Shakespearean.[3] A chance remark of Tennyson's that "many passages in *Henry the Eighth* were very much in the manner of Fletcher," combined with his own impressions, led Spedding to investigate the matter more fully, with the result that in 1850 he published his paper, "Who wrote Shakespeare's *Henry the Eighth?*"[4] As a result of this investigation and of the application of metrical tests, in the results of which his investigations were substantiated by those of Fleay, Furnivall, and others, he concluded that more than one half of the play had been written by Fletcher, and pronounced as Shakespearean only the following scenes: Act I, Scenes 1 and 2; Act II, Scenes 3 and 4; Act III, Scene 2 (to the exit of the king); Act III, Scene 2 (to the exit of the king); Act V, Scene 1—with alterations. With this decision, so far as the work of Fletcher is concerned, practically all later

Reprinted by permission of the Modern Language Association of America from *PMLA*, 37 (1922): 464–502.

critics have been in agreement. The problem, then, has long been one not of the sole authorship of Shakespeare, but of his part in the play.

The most striking and most important contribution to the discussion, since that of Spedding, is the paper which Robert Boyle in 1885 read before the New Shakespeare Society. In this he declared that Shakespeare had had no part in the writing of the play, but that it had been the joint work of Fletcher and Massinger.[5] Spedding and Boyle agreed, in the main, in regard to the Fletcherian scenes; both recognized, also, the lack of unity of conception and development and the feebleness and inconsistency of many of the characters. Boyle, however, based his contention in regard to Massinger on the grounds that at no time in his later period did Shakespeare collaborate with another dramatist and that no reason for such collaboration can be shown; that, even had collaboration been possible Shakespeare would hardly have allowed his work to be spoiled—as it certainly was—by an inferior dramatist; and that it was improbable that Fletcher, the lesser author, should have been given all the "big scenes" as he undoubtedly was. From this Boyle goes on to prove that the play which we now have, which was included in the Folio of 1623 "was not written by Fletcher and Shakespeare, but by Fletcher and Massinger, to supply the place of the lost Shakespeare play *All is True* destroyed in the Globe theatre fire in 1613."[6]

Boyle's theory is a clear and forceful one which leaves his reader with the impression that, if the hypothesis be granted, the conclusion must follow. Further consideration, however, makes one aware that it is an arbitrarily assumed hypothesis which not only does not solve all the former problems, but which raises others, equally difficult. For example, the fact that his metrical tests result in assigning to Massinger not only all the so-called Shakespearean scenes, but even some parts which other critics unanimously agree in assigning to Fletcher would lead one to wonder if the style of Massinger was similar not only to that of Shakespeare but also to that of Fletcher. And when Boyle acknowledges that "from the characteristics of metre alone it would be difficult to decide whether a particular passage or even play was written by Shakespeare or Massinger, so similar is the latter's style to Shakespeare's later dramas,"[7] we may justly inquire: why, then, attribute it to Massinger at all in the face of the evidence which gives it to Shakespeare? There are, at all events, three points which Boyle's theory cannot explain: There is, first of all, the inclusion of the play in the Folio, for, in spite of the fact that there are included plays which we now agree are "doubtful," we have no other example of the inclusion of a play which Heminge and Condell must have known to have been in no way the work of Shakespeare. There is, secondly, the reason for the writing of a second play. Even Boyle does not doubt that the *Henry the Eighth* which was being performed at the time of the Globe fire was Shakespeare's. His theory is that the present play was written to take the place of one destroyed at that time. This, however, is open to the serious objections that there is no more reason to suppose that the prompter's copy was lost than that it was saved, and that the play was already being acted, so that no new copy was necessary for the actors, while a new one could certainly have been made from their dictation if the prompter's copy had been lost, and, chief of all, that Shakespeare himself was alive at the time of the fire, so that there would hardly have been any need of calling on Massinger to rewrite his play! Thirdly, Boyle's theory does not in any way explain that very thing which caused Boyle's investigation—the lack of consistency in the play. He declares throughout that Massinger and Fletcher worked together on the play, yet pauses continually to show that Fletcher disregards hints which Massinger has given, that whole scenes are out of place, and that there is an utter lack of continuity in character development. Minor tests, moreover, such as Thorndike's "them-'em" test go to prove the impossibility of Massinger's collaboration; in the seven plays of Massinger which Thorndike examined, Massinger used the word "them" two hundred times and the contraction not at all, while in this one play alone, the scenes which Boyle would assign to Massinger contain seventeen cases of the contraction to eighteen of the full word—an incredible difference.

A study of sources of the play throws little real light upon the problem of authorship, but it does raise one point which may be significant. The chief source for the material used in the first four acts was the second edition of Holinshed's *Chronicle*, while practically all of the last act is founded upon Foxe's *Actes and Monuments of the Churche*. It is possible that Cavendish's *Life of Wolsey* may have been available since, although the book was not published until 1641, it was circulated in manuscript during Shakespeare's lifetime; it seems much more probable, however, that the authors did not consult this directly but used only such passages as Holinshed had included. Edward Hall's

Chronicle seems also to have been used occasionally. If we accept for the time being the division of scenes made by Spedding, we find that in the Shakespearean portions there are fourteen direct borrowings from Holinshed; three from Foxe; one from Hall; two which may be from Cavendish or Holinshed. Fletcher has ten from Holinshed, two from Hall, four from Foxe, four which may be from Cavendish or Holinshed. In all, there are approximately twenty in the Shakespearean scenes and the same number in the Fletcherian. The interesting thing is that in no other play of Shakespeare's are the borrowings more pronounced than in this, and in no play have the historical passages been so little revised. Both authors have simply versified long passages from the chronicles; even such a speech as the famous defence of Katherine is to be found almost verbatim in Holinshed. The historical material, moreover, has been handled with even more than Shakespeare's usual freedom. The play covers a period of twenty four years; the events are represented as happening on seven days. The chronological sequence has been violated frequently, and in some cases there is a compression of several great events into one scene. Four characters have been added to those of history, but they are all minor: the porter and Patience, who appear in the Fletcherian scenes; the Old Lady, and possibly Brandon, who appear in the Shakespearean. There is none of that prodigality of invention of minor characters to which we are accustomed in the earlier history plays of Shakespeare—nothing to suggest that band of rogues and drunkards and tattered soldiers who surrounded Falstaff; nothing to suggest those myriads of servants in the delineation of whom the dramatist delighted; there is, in the minor characters, but one suggestion of the Shakespeare we know—in the Old lady, who, lightly sketched though she is, has about her that canniness, that shrewd materialism which delights us in Juliet's nurse. There has been in this play no piling up of fictitious incidents, in addition to the historical events, such as we have seen in the earlier *Henry* plays; only two incidents here have not been taken directly from the chronicles: the meeting of Anne Bullen and Henry at the Cardinal's masque, and the Cardinal's fatal mistake in sending to the king a paper on which was a statement of his private wealth. The only conclusion, then, to which a study of sources leads us is that, if part of *Henry the Eighth* was written by Shakespeare, he showed himself less original than usual in his versifying of the chronicles, and even less careful than usual in his treatment of the historical chronology of events. Any theory of authorship which may be proposed must take that into account. It must also take into account the very serious consideration that, if this play is in any way Shakespeare's, it is the last that we have from his pen, and yet it must be evident to even a casual reader that it is, in every way, below the level of much of even his earliest work. In spite of all these things, however, I still venture to say that it *is* Shakespeare's in part, and that, properly understood, it is less an anticlimax than a fitting climax to his dramas.

First of all, is there any reason for Shakespeare's interest in such a subject at this time? It is hardly necessary to say that, if the original plan of the play was his, Shakespeare was not intending here a "history play" as history plays were understood before 1600. This was not by any means the first play upon a subject connected with the reign of Henry VIII. Shakespeare's company had already produced two plays dealing with Thomas Cromwell and with Sir Thomas More. In the Stationer's Register, under the date February 12, 1604-5 there is a memorandum relative to a play called *Enterlude of K. Henry 8th,* which has been identified with Rowley's *When You See Me You Know Me.* In 1605 there had appeared a spectacular production, exhibiting some of the events of Queen Elizabeth's early life and coronation, with a sequel celebrating the activity of London merchants and the foundation of the Royal Exchange—Thomas Heywood's *If You Know Not Me You Know Nobody.* Besides these, the Admiral's company had produced in 1601-2 two plays about Wolsey, the first called *Life,* the second, the *Rising of the Cardinal.* It does not seem to have been generally noticed that there was a pronounced revival of interest in these plays in the year 1613, possibly on account of the festivities attendant on the marriage of the Princess Elizabeth. *The History of Thomas Lord Cromwell* was reissued during that year, with the statement on its title page that it was "written by W.S."; *When You see Me, You Know Me* reappeared in 1613, as did also the first part of *If You Know Not Me You Know Nobody.* In addition to this, during the spring of that same year when the marriage of the Princess Elizabeth was celebrated there were produced no fewer than six Shakespearean plays. Whatever the cause of the revival of interest, we may see here an economic reason why the Globe Theatre should have desired a play on the subject of the reign of Henry and why Shakespeare should have been the one to write it. We have no reason to suppose that

Shakespeare's removal to Stratford would have caused him to lose that shrewd knowledge of the London theatre he had always had. It is, therefore, not difficult to believe that, either because the managers of the Globe asked it, or because he himself, with his usual business acumen, saw the possibilities, he turned during that spring to the chronicles dealing with the reign of Henry the Eight and drafted a play on the subject.

The question then is: what was that draft? What was it that Shakespeare had in mind when he set about the play which he never finished? Our own opinions of the play are so biased by the distorted version that we read that it is difficult for us to forget what Fletcher did to Wolsey and Katherine and Henry and Anne, yet that is exactly what must be done if we are to see what the play was to Shakespeare. If we accept the division of scenes made by Spedding and turn to the reading of the original play, we may, I think, by the simple device of reading the Shakespearean scenes apart from the others see what that idea was, and we will find that it was less a companion for such a play as *Henry the Fifth*—as has been suggested—than for a *Timon of Athens* or a *Lear*. In attempting any such reconstruction of the original play, it is essential to remember always that the act, as a unit, was apparently nothing to Shakespeare; that he wrote, except in the one or two cases in which he actually imitated the classical dramatists, not a five act play, but a succession of scenes; that his plays, as a rule, divide themselves into two parts, following the device of the popular drama before his time which was frequently concerned with the life and death or the rise and fall of a real or fictitious character. Sometimes, as we know, he himself marks for us the beginning of the second part, either by an actual figure such as that of Time in *The Winter's Tale* or by a device such as that of the witches in *Macbeth*. Usually the events of the second part balance those of the first part; always one will be seen to be a rising, the other a falling action. It is evident, also, that in any play which is Shakespeare's we may expect to find a striking use of his two favorite devices of repetition and contrast—repetition of the main idea in plots and sub-plots; repetitions of incidents and characters to bring out other incidents and other characters; sudden sharp contrasts of scenes and characters and situations. All of these devices I think we may find in even that part of the *Henry the Eighth* which he wrote; and when we have observed them, we shall perhaps see the reason why he did not conclude it, and why Fletcher, when he set to work on it, completed it as he did.

In reading Holinshed and the various other chroniclers, there was one thing about the period of Henry the Eighth which could not fail to impress Shakespeare, as it has impressed readers ever since his time: the tremendous reversals of fortune which characterized the individuals of that period. Buckingham, Wolsey, Katherine, Cranmer, Anne, Cromwell—where in one period would one find more characters who, through one man, the King, rose to greater heights or fell to more definite misery? Whether we look upon the Shakespeare of 1613 as the dramatist of human disillusionment, or merely as the dramatist who, more than any other, delighted in sharp contrasts, we can see why the reign of Henry should have seized upon his imagination. If, then, we omit entirely the Fletcherian scenes and consider only the story and the characters which Shakespeare actually introduces, we shall see what his plan was.

In that first abrupt scene, in the midst of a conversation between Buckingham and Norfolk in regard to that "sun of Glory," "that light of men," Henry the King, the splendor of whose meeting with the king of France is occupying all minds, reference is made almost at once, with great dramatic effect, to the man who is evidently the power behind the English throne—to the "right reverend" Cardinal Wolsey. At once Buckingham's anger flares up,

> The devil speed him! no man's pie is freed
> From his ambitious finger.

"His pride," another character says, "peeps through each part of him." Not pride and ambition alone, for we are told also of his malice and "potency"; that his nature is revengeful and his sword is sharp. At that moment there enters the Cardinal himself and sweeps across the stage, his eye fixed "with disdain" on Buckingham, who looks at him with equal disdain. From the beginning Shakespeare leaves us in no doubt in regard to Wolsey. The Cardinal threatens, even in this momentary appearance, that Buckingham shall lessen that big look and before even this short scene is over, we are given an opportunity of seeing how well the Cardinal keeps his promises. Buckingham's taunts that "the butcher's cur is venom mouthed," his names, "this fox," "this wolf," this "cunning cardinal" follow him. In vain does Norfolk counsel that "temperance" which Buckingham so evidently lacks. But that Buckingham's suspicions are well founded is shown by his almost instant arrest for high treason; thus he, who has shown himself loyal to his king is, with his friends, caught as he says "in the net" and goes to the Tower with the words,

> I am the shadow of poor Buckingham
> Whose figure even this instant cloud puts on
> By darkening my clear sun.

So ends the first scene. The second follows at once—a council chamber, Henry entering leaning on the shoulder of the Cardinal, clearly from his first speech under the influence of the Cardinal, turning from him only at the entrance of Katherine, who, kneeling, pleads to no avail for Buckingham. Wolsey has succeeded in deceiving the king, but he has not deceived Katherine. She charges him with being back of the trouble which stirs the country to revolt, she brings before the king his unjust taxation—a charge which he turns aside with his cunning subtlety and at once manages to make seem in his favor. Katherine's accusation has no effect other than to make Wolsey realize that in her he has a dangerous enemy. There follows the accusation of Buckingham, throughout which, it is to be noticed, Shakespeare shows Henry as persuaded by the Cardinal against his better judgment—Henry, in Shakespeare's hands is never bad; he is a weakling who is easily ruled by the keen intellect of the greater man. Most of all, however, the dramatist shows in Katherine a combination of those characteristics which we have learned to expect in the great women of Shakespeare: fearlessness, courage, steadfastness, keen judgment. The scene which follows, though presupposing others, is yet clear in itself—another of those swift reversals of fortune in which Shakespeare delighted. We have but seen Katherine at her height; we hear of her as one cast off by the king, and the news comes through the young lady-in-waiting who is to take her place, through Anne Bullen whom Shakespeare in this scene draws as a simple youthful attractive girl of the group of the youthful Portia and the youthful Juliet—the sort of character he delighted to portray. He shows her dwelling on the tragedy of the queen and showing that moderation of which the best Shakespearean characters are always exponents:

Verily,
I swear tis better to be lowly born
And range with humble livers in content
Than to be perk'd up in a glistering grief
And wear a golden sorrow

She has hardly had time to exclaim emphatically,

By my troth and maidenhead
I would not be a queen,

when there enters the Lord Chamberlain with the announcement that the king has created her Marchioness of Pembroke. The announcement, the derisive cacklings of the old lady, fail to move the girl in the least, for, like Katherine and Shakespeare's women in general, Anne has a level head. As Juliet in the midst of the emotion of the balcony scene could say,

But yet I have no joy of this contract tonight,
It is too rash, too sudden, too unadvised,

so Anne declares,

Would I had no being
If this salute my blood a jot; it faints me
To think what follows.

And at once, with a touch which is worthy of Shakespeare, she remembers her who has been a queen and is to be no longer,

The queen is comfortless and we forgetful
In our long absence; pray do not deliver
What here you've heard to her.

Another scene, and we are once more at a trial, but with a difference. She who was, by the king's own word, coequal with him at the trial of Buckingham, is now arraigned; she who knelt before the king to sue for Buckingham, now kneels to sue for herself. Close beside the king throughout is Wolsey. It is Katherine alone who dares to charge the Cardinal with being the instigator of the whole affair, who dares to say that he pretends to be humble but his heart is "crammed with arrogancy, spleen and pride." Shakespeare leaves us in no doubt as to the king's real feeling for Katherine, for as she leaves, he says:

> Go thy ways, Kate;
> The man in the world who shall report he has
> A better wife, let him in naught be trusted,
> For speaking false in that; thou art, alone,
> If thy rare qualities, sweet gentleness,
> They meekness saint-like, wife-like government,
> Obeying in commanding, and thy parts
> Sovereign and pious else, could speak thee out
> The queen of earthly queens.

Wolsey, perceiving the king's emotion, and fearful lest that lead him to interfere with his deep-laid plans, craftily calls upon the sovereign there in public to declare whether Katherine's charges are true. At this the king speaks, revealing to the audience the way in which, as in *Othello*, the crafty man of intellect has worked upon the man of emotion. No one can read the long defense of Henry and fail to notice the repetition of the word *conscience* which throughout the play comes in like a refrain—"the respite shook the bosom of my conscience," he says, and again, "thus hulling in the wild sea of my conscience," and finally, "I mean to rectify my conscience." It is easy to see the way in which Wolsey has been acting upon the king. It is another phase of this same weakness on the part of the king which, captivated by youthful Anne, led to his creation of the Marchioness of Pembroke, and which now, affected by Katherine, leads him to declare,

> Prove but our marriage lawful, by my life.
> And kingly dignity, we are content
> To wear our mortal state to come with her,
> Katherine our queen, before the primest creature
> That's paragoned i' the world.

And then, as the court is adjourned, the king utters a significant remark, mentioning a name which until this time has not been used:

> My learned and well-beloved servant, Cranmer,
> Prithee return; with thy approach I know
> My comfort comes along.

Packed into the next scene we find many things: the nobles warn that the fall of Wolsey is imminent; Katherine has already been set aside; Anne Bullen is the king's favorite, rumor says already his wife. Cranmer is mentioned again, this time as the coming man of the kingdom, the future archbishop; Wolsey, entering, shows us at once that his many lines have become entangled. He had thought that the divorce of Katherine would be the climax of his plots, but now he finds himself balked by the king's infatuation for Anne, by his evident intention of marrying her instead of the sister of the French king, as Wolsey had planned. At just this moment there appears the king who has found by chance the incriminating papers; like all weaklings who have been under the domination of stronger men, his intolerance and scorn are all the more bitter now that he has found out the crimes of his erstwhile favorite. He flings the incriminating paper at the Cardinal and sweeps out, leaving him alone. When Shakespeare had reached that point in the scene, he stopped; the rest of it—the famous charge of Wolsey to Cromwell (a very different Wolsey from Shakespeare's) is Fletcher's.

That, in the Shakespearean play, was doubtless to have been the end of the first part—the climax of the play. What was to constitute the second part has already been suggested in the continued references to Cranmer—it was to have shown the rise of Cranmer to the position of the chief counsellor of the king, the culmination of which, the turning of the King against Cranmer as he earlier turned against Wolsey, Shakespeare has shown in the one remaining scene which he wrote, in which he suggests that Cranmer has already risen to his height and is now about to fall. That scene, which Fletcher combined with the scene dealing with the birth of Anne's daughter, has always troubled critics who could find in the play which Fletcher made no use for the character of Cranmer except as the godfather of the infant Elizabeth, and who failed to see any reason for introducing the scene in which his possible treason is discussed. But we cannot read the scenes which Shakespeare wrote and fail to see that from the first Cranmer has been suggested as the coming important character, and that in the scene in which the nobles prophesy the fall of Wolsey, they prophesy with equal force the rise of Cranmer.

That is the original play. Did Fletcher add anything in the way of plot? I think not. He wrote the meeting of Anne and Henry, but that had already been suggested in the scenes which we have read; he wrote the farewell of Buckingham, the death of Katherine, the farewell of Wolsey—all of them completing scenes which had already been written,—the elevation of Cranmer, which was both anticipated and concluded by Shakespeare, the visit of the cardinals to Katherine, and the three scenes of pageantry—exactly the sort of scenes in which Fletcher always delighted. Shakespeare's work was introductory; he brought no scene to its conclusion. Fletcher's was entirely founded upon the parts already written; he began no new story in the play. Did the two authors, then, collaborate? Clearly they did not. Apart from the fact that we can find no case in which the later Shakespeare ever collaborated with anyone, the play itself solves that problem. Shakespeare wrote no one of the "big scenes." Moreover, in the case of each of the major characters, there is, in the final scene, an entire contradiction of the character as Shakespeare planned it. Thus Fletcher has sentimentalized the death of Buckingham; he has given us the dying dream of Katherine; Wolsey's complete change of character in his farewell to Cromwell, which in every sentence contradicts the character of Wolsey as Shakespeare painted it; he has even suggested the death of Wolsey which he could not show, telling us how, "an old man broken with the storm of years, he came to beg a little earth for charity." There is no one character in the play which we have today which can be said to be consistent. This could not possibly have occurred had the two authors been working together. What must have happened, clearly, is that Shakespeare, after he had blocked out the six scenes which we have today, gave up the idea of working on the play. But since, as has already been said, a play on the subject was an economic necessity, either Shakespeare himself, or the managers of the Globe theatre, with his consent, gave the rough draft to another author. Fletcher, since 1607, had been gradually coming to fill Shakespeare's place and would seem to have been the most popular dramatist with the public of the time; what more natural than that he should have been the one to complete the play? That the draft was given to him with Shakespeare's consent seems evident, since the play was to be presented within the year and Shakespeare would certainly be in a position to know that it was his play which was being used. It is possible that he outlined to Fletcher his original intention; on the other hand he may simply have given him the draft of the six scenes and referred him to the chronicles which he had used, which Fletcher evidently used throughout. At all events, it is clear that

Fletcher did not in any way carry out Shakespeare's original intention; Shakespeare must have known that he would not.

And now what, in the main, was that intention and why did Shakespeare himself not carry it out? The answer to one question is, I think, contained in the other; the answer to both is to be found in the play itself. The play was not to have been, as now, a collection of disorganized episodes; it was not, as has always been suggested, to culminate in the separation of the Anglican and Roman churches; that misunderstanding has arisen from various references in the Fletcherian scenes; in the parts which I have called Shakespearean, there are only three references of any sort to the Church, and those three are entirely subsidiary; the most serious of them is Wolsey's remark that Anne was a "spleeny Lutheran"; apart from that there is nothing to suggest that Shakespeare was interested, in the slightest degree, in the question of religion. The theme is given, I believe, in the sub-title, *All Is True*, by which the play was known at the time of the burning of the Globe. It occurs again in those lines which Fletcher included in the prologue—that prologue which suits the original play so much better than the play which we now have:

> think you see them great
> And followed with the general throng and sweat
> Of thousand friends; then in a moment see
> How soon that mightiness meets misery.

Those who hold to the theory of the "period of disillusion" will find here a suggestion that Shakespeare at this time understood thoroughly the meaning of those lines; whether we accept that idea or not, it must be clear that the original play was in no way distant from the other great plays of the last period. We have here the framework of a play which was to deal with the buffets and rewards of fortune—with that chance which at one time exalts a man and at another time casts him down—with characters who bear in themselves the seeds of their own misery—with the strange revolutions of fortune which now exalt one, now another. And in its succession of scenes of exaltation and misery, it does not fall below any of the great dramas, and is, indeed, reminiscent of many of them. Particularly in its rapid succession of rising and falling characters, in its suggestion of Nemesis, its balancing of parts and episodes in this latest of the history plays reminiscent of that early Richard III. Buckingham, headstrong, impetuous, refusing to listen to the counsel of "moderation," daring to do what he considers honorable—falling by those very characteristics which make him attractive—even in the one scene in which he appears has much of Hotspur; his death, in Shakespeare's hands would have been no long-drawn sentimental funeral scenes, but a brief moment in which the encomium, if one there was, would have been pronounced not by himself but by another Hal. Shakespeare's Katherine has in her much of the later Portia, more of Hermione, the simplicity and courageousness of all of Shakespeare's women; if Shakespeare ever attended a performance of the completed play, he must have smiled a little as the Katherine he knew went through the long-drawn dream and death scene which delighted Fletcher. Henry the King is, in Shakespeare's hands a popular idol, the "sun of men" and "glory of the world," but in reality weak and ineffectual, entirely under the domination of those around him; Shakespeare makes him weak not only in politics but in love; it is no villain who lays his plans skilfully to rid himself of Katherine, but a very human being who is one day attracted by a pretty face, and another day sincerely devoted to the wife whom conscience bids him cast away; that study of the conscience of a king, worked upon subtly by a keener intellect, would have been a tremendous thing in Shakespeare's hands. Most of all it is Wolsey we would have cared to see—Wolsey as Shakespeare saw him, for he is the supreme character of the play; a later Iago, he has all the cunning and the craft of Iago, but he has, more than that, big ends in view; he is the supreme power in England; in his hands there lie her destinies; far-sighted, shrewd, and intellect incarnate, he is the last of that great group of whom Don John was first—"determined to prove a villain" but a great villain. The first part of the play we may construct almost in its entirety, and there is no reason to believe that the second part would have fallen off, though we have little of it left. Buckingham at his height and realizing his doom; Katherine at her height as he falls, with Wolsey malevolently in the background plotting her downfall and his own rise; Anne rising to take the place of Katherine, and to complicate the situation for Wolsey, yet shuddering in the midst of her splendor to think what follows; Wolsey at his height, with Cranmer's name in the king's mouth; in the last part, the overthrow of Wolsey and the rise of Cranmer; possibly the fate of Anne—even perhaps the story of Cromwell which has been merely suggested, and through it all, through the fate which comes alike to good and evil, through the tale of Wolsey falling by his ambition, even as Macbeth, and Katherine falling in spite of all her virtue, as Juliet or Cordelia,—as the thread upon which all hangs, Henry himself, weak, easily led, perhaps pursued throughout by that conscience of which he speaks so frequently.

Why, then, did Shakespeare not finish the drama which, it must seem to us, might have been one of the most tremendous of all in its sharp contrast of light and shade, in the inevitability of its conclusions? Shakespeare and his people were very near in time to these people of whom they wrote, too near, perhaps, to criticise them with impunity. With fictitious characters it could have been done; with real characters, it is doubtful if the play-going Englishmen would have accepted it—as perhaps the play-going Englishmen of today would not accept a Bernard Shaw delineation of Victoria and her court! Whether they would have objected to the picture which Shakespeare drew or not, it is at all events certain that the taste of the play-goers of the time had changed; what they wanted now was not the "dry light" in which Shakespeare would have shown them the earlier court, but the haze of sentiment which Fletcher knew so well how to spread over his characters—which the play-going public of our own day seems more and more to crave. That this is true may be seen by what Fletcher did to the Shakespearean characters; in his scenes the bitterness and unequalness of fate is gone; with Fletcher, as with the popular dramatists of our own day, the bad are always punished, the good usually rewarded, or, if that is impossible, at least given death scenes which caused the eye to flow; and all, good and bad, are shown as regenerated at the last moment, and departing this life in the odor of sanctity and the pomp of oratory. Thus all the characters in *Henry the Eighth* are shown as truly great only when the external greatness is stripped from them; and since this could not be done with any consistency in the play as Shakespeare planned had it, Fletcher has covered up all the rough places with pageantry and visions and coronations and christenings, and has risen to heights which still hold enthralled the audience which loves oratory, and spectacles, and sentiment, and tears. For Fletcher was, to use Christopher Morley's apt term, the "Pollyananias" of his day—and his day, like our own, loved a Pollyananias. One would give much to have seen Shakespeare the day he attended the performance of *Henry the Eighth* or *All Is True.*

If there is anything at all to this supposition, it throws an interesting light not only upon Shakespeare's methods but also upon his point of view in those last years of which we know so little. We can see something of the workman here—we can watch him as he writes the pivotal scenes, the ones which are the crisis of each plot, leaving the others to be sketched in later; we can watch him stress those characteristics on which he is to dwell later; we can see that he took the chronicles, and with the passages before him, simply turned them into blank verse, intending later to polish them, as he did in earlier plays. The result is that even in the scenes we have we find that every important event has been mentioned, every character delineated, the whole story told us, either in prospect or in retrospect. And we can see, moreover, that, having blocked out the whole play as it was to have been, he definitely put it aside and gave it for completion to a man who would not complete it as it had been begun. Nothing could be more significant of the point of view of the dramatist of the time. His public no longer wanted the impersonality, the impassivity, the moderation of Shakespeare; they wanted the morals, the sentiment, the hazy mist of Fletcher; they liked Fletcher and they wanted Fletcher. They would not have liked the Wolsey Shakespeare knew.

Perhaps nothing more definite can be determined unless we come upon new evidence in records of the time, for the problems of *Henry the Eighth*, as was said at the beginning, are in many ways different from those of the other doubtful Shakespearean plays. So far as external evidence concerned, the problem is not so interesting nor so important as that in any other of the doubtful plays; so far as the dramatist himself is concerned, it seems to me much more important, for here we may perhaps find something of the craftsman, the dramatist and the poet.

NOTES

1. Wright, *Henry the Eighth* (Clarendon Press), p. vi; *The Annales*, or *Generall Chronicle of England, begun first by Mister John Stow continued*

until the ende of this presente yeere by Edmond Howes, 1615, p. 926; *Reliquiae Wottonianae* third edition, 1672, pp. 425, 426.

2. Stanzas on "the pittifull burning of the Globe playhouse in London" in *Gentlemen's Magazine*, 1816; reprinted in Halliwell-Phillipps, *Outlines* pp. 310-11.
3. Edwards, *Canons of Criticism*, 1758.
4. New Shakespeare Society's Transactions, 1874.
5. The same conclusion has been reached by H. Dugdale Sykes in a paper, "King Henry VIII," published in his *Sidelights on Shakespeare* (Shakespeare Head Press, Stratford-on-Avon 1919). He bases his conclusions entirely upon a comparative study of the diction of Massinger and the doubtful portions of the play.
6. *New Shakespeare Society's Transactions*, 1880-85, p.444
7. Ibid., p. 445.

William Hazlitt

From *Characters of Shakespeare's Plays*

This play contains little action or violence of passion, yet it has considerable interest of a more mild and thoughtful cast, and some of the most striking passages in the author's works. The character of Queen Katherine is the most perfect delineation of matronly dignity, sweetness, and resignation, that can be conceived. Her appeals to the protection of the king, her remonstrances to the cardinals, her conversations with her women, show a noble and generous spirit accompanied with the utmost gentleness of nature. What can be more affecting than her answer to Campeius and Wolsey, who come to visit her as pretended friends?

> Nay, forsooth, my friends,
> They that must weigh out my afflictions,
> They that my trust must grow to live not here;
> They are, as all my comforts are, far hence,
> In my own country, lords.

Dr. Johnson observes of this play, that "the meek sorrows and virtuous distresses of Katherine have furnished some scenes which may be justly numbered among the greatest efforts of tragedy. But the genius of Shakespeare comes in and goes out with Katherine. Every other part may be easily conceived and easily written." This is easily said; but with all due deference to so great a reputed authority as that of Johnson, it is not true. For instance, the scene of Buckingham led to execution is one of the most affecting and natural in Shakespeare, and one to which there is hardly an approach in any other author. Again, the character of Wolsey, the description of his pride and of his fall, are inimitable, and have, besides their gorgeousness of effect, a pathos, which only the genius of Shakespeare could lend to the distresses of a proud, bad man, like Wolsey. There is a sort of child-like simplicity in the very helplessness of his situation, arising from the recollection of his past overbearing ambition. After the cutting sarcasms of his enemies, on his disgrace, against which he bears up with a spirit conscious of his own superiority, he breaks out into that fine apostrophe—

> Farewell, a long farewell, to all my greatness!
> This is the state of man; to-day he puts forth
> The tender leaves of hope, to-morrow blossoms,
> And bears his blushing honors thick upon him;
> The third day comes a frost, a killing frost;
> And—when he thinks, good easy man, full surely
> His greatness is a ripening—nips his root,
> And then he falls, as I do. I have ventur'd,
> Like little wanton boys that swim on bladders,
> These many summers in a sea of glory;
> But far beyond my depth: my high-blown pride
> At length broke under me; and now has left me,
> Weary and old with service, to the mercy
> Of a rude stream, that must for ever hide me.
> Vain pomp and glory of the world, I hate ye!
> I feel my heart now open'd: O how wretched
> Is that poor man, that hangs on princes' favors!
> There is betwixt that smile we would aspire to,
> That sweet aspect of princes, and our ruin,
> More pangs and fears than war and women have;
> And when he falls, he falls like Lucifer,
> Never to hope again!

There is in this passage, as well as in the well-known dialogue with Cromwell which follows, something which stretches beyond common-place; nor is the account which Griffiths gives of Wolsey's death less Shakespearian; and the candor with which Queen Katherine listens to the praise of "him whom of all men while living she hated most" adds the last graceful finishing to her character. Among other images of great individual beauty might be mentioned the description of the effect of Ann Boleyn's presenting herself to the crowd at her coronation.

> While her grace sat down
> To rest awhile, some half an hour or so,
> In a rich chair of state, opposing freely
> The beauty of her person to the people.

Believe me, sir, she is the goodliest woman
That ever lay by man. Which when the people
Had the full view of, *such a noise arose*
As the shrouds make at sea in a stiff tempest,
As loud and to as many tunes.

The character of Henry VIII is drawn with great truth and spirit. It is like a very disagreeable portrait, sketched by the hand of a master. His gross appearance, his blustering demeanor, his vulgarity, his arrogance, his sensuality, his cruelty, his hypocrisy, his want of common decency and common humanity, are marked in strong lines. His traditional peculiarities of expression complete the reality of the picture. the authoritative expletive, "ha!" with which he intimates his indignation or surprise, has an effect like the first startling sound that breaks from a thunder-cloud. He is of all the monarchs in our history the most disgusting: for he unites in himself all the vices of barbarism and refinement, without their virtues. Other kings before him (such as Richard III) were tyrants and murderers out of ambition or necessity: they gained or established unjust power by violent means: they destroyed their enemies, or those who barred their access to the throne or made its tenure insecure. But Henry VIII's power is most fatal to those whom he loves: he is cruel and remorseless to pamper his luxurious appetites; bloody and voluptuous; an amorous murderer; an uxorious debauchee. His hardened insensibility to the feelings of others is strengthened by the most profligate self-indulgence. The religious hypocrisy, under which he masks his cruelty and his lust, is admirably displayed in the speech in which he describes the first misgivings of his conscience and its increasing throes and terrors, which have induced him to divorce his queen. The only thing in his favor in this play is his treatment of Cranmer: there is also another circumstance in his favor, which is his patronage of Hans Holbein. It has been said of Shakespeare—"No maid could live near such a man." It might with as good reason be said—"No king could live near such a man." His eye would have penetrated through the pomp of circumstances and veil of opinion. As it is, he has represented such a person to the life—his plays are in this respect the glass of history—he has done them the same justice as if he had been a privy councillor all his life, and in each successive reign. Kings ought never to be seen upon the stage. In the abstract, they are very disagreeable characters: it is only while living that they are "the best of kings."

It is their power, their splendor, it is the apprehension of the personal consequences of their favor or their hatred, that dazzles the imagination and suspends the judgment of their favorites or their vassals; but death cancels the bond of allegiance and of interest; and seen as they were, their power and their pretensions look monstrous and ridiculous. The charge brought against modern philosophy as inimical to loyalty is unjust, because it might as well be brought against other things. No reader of history can be a lover of kings. We have often wondered that Henry VIII, as he is drawn by Shakespeare, and as we have seen him represented in all the bloated deformity of mind and person, is not hooted from the English stage.

Anna Jameson

From *Characteristics of Women, Moral, Political, and Historical*

To have a just idea of the accuracy and beauty of this historical portrait, we ought to bring immediately before us those circumstances of Katherine's life and times, and those parts of her character, which belong to a period previous to the opening of the play. We shall then be better able to appreciate the skill with which Shakespeare has applied the materials before him.

Katherine of Arragon, the fourth and youngest daughter of Ferdinand, King of Arragon, and Isabella of Castile, was born at Alcala, whither her mother had retired to winter after one of the most terrible campaigns of the Moorish war—that of 1485.

Katherine had derived from nature no dazzling qualities of mind, and no striking advantages of person. She inherited a tincture of Queen Isabella's haughtiness and obstinacy of temper, but neither her beauty nor her splendid talents. Her education under the direction of that extraordinary mother, had implanted in her mind the most austere principles of virtue, the highest ideas of female decorum, the most narrow and bigoted attachment to the forms of religion, and that excessive pride of birth and rank, which distinguished so particularly her family and her nation. In other respects, her understanding was strong, and her judgment clear. The natural turn of her mind was simple, serious, and domestic, and all the impulses of her heart kindly and benevolent. Such was Katherine; such, at least, she appears on a reference to the chronicles of her times, and particularly from her own letters, and the papers written or dictated by herself which relate to her divorce; all of which are distinguished by the same artless simplicity of style, the same quiet good sense, the same resolute, yet gentle spirit and fervent piety.

When five years old, Katherine was solemnly affianced to Arthur, Prince of Wales, the eldest son of Henry VII; and in the year 1501, she landed in England, after narrowly escaping shipwreck on the southern coast, from which every adverse wind conspired to drive her. She was received in London with great honor, and immediately on her arrival united to the young prince. He was then fifteen and Katherine in her seventeenth year.

Arthur, as it is well known, survived his marriage only five months; and the reluctance of Henry VII to refund the splendid dowry of the Infanta, and forego the advantages of an alliance with the most powerful prince of Europe, suggested the idea of uniting Katherine to his second son Henry; after some hesitation, a dispensation was procured from the Pope, and she was betrothed to Henry in her eighteenth year. The prince, who was then only twelve years old, resisted as far as he was able to do so, and appears to have really felt a degree of horror at the idea of marrying his brother's widow. Nor was the mind of King Henry at rest; as his health declined, his conscience reproached him with the equivocal nature of the union into which he had forced his son; and the vile motives of avarice and expediency which had governed him on this occasion. A short time previous to his death, he dissolved the engagement, and even caused Henry to sign a paper in which he solemnly renounced all idea of a future union with the Infanta. It is observable, that Henry signed this paper with reluctance, and that Katherine, instead of being sent back to her own country, still remained in England. It appears than Henry, who was now about seventeen, had become interested for Katherine, who was gentle and amiable. The difference of years was rather a circumstance in her favor; for Henry was just at that age, when a youth is most likely to be captivated by a woman older than himself: and no sooner was he required to renounce her, than the interest she had gradually gained in his affections, became, by opposition, a strong passion. Immediately after his father's death, he declared his resolution to take for his wife the Lady Katherine of Spain, and none other; and when the matter was discussed in council, it was urged that, besides the many advantages of the match in a political point of view, she had given so "much proof of virtue, and sweetness of condition, as they knew not where to parallel her." About six weeks after his accession, June 3, 1509, the marriage was celebrated with truly royal splendor, Henry being then eighteen, and Katherine in her twenty-fourth year.

It has been said with truth, that if Henry had died while Katherine was yet his wife, and Wolsey his minister, he would have left behind him the character of a magnificent, popular, and accomplished prince, instead of that of the most hateful ruffian and tyrant who ever swayed these realms. Notwithstanding his occasional infidelities, and his impatience at her midnight vigils, her long prayers, and her religious austerities, Katherine and Henry lived in harmony together. He was fond of openly displaying his respect and love for her; and she exercised a strong and salutary influence over his turbulent and despotic spirit. When Henry set out on his expedition to France, in 1513, he left Katherine regent of the kingdom during his absence, with full powers to carry on the war against the Scots; and the Earl of Surrey at the head of the army, as her lieutenant-general. It is curious find Katherine—the pacific, domestic, and unpretending Katherine—describing herself as having "her heart set to war," and "horrible busy" with making "standards, banners, badges, scarfs, and the like."[1] Nor was this mere silken preparation—mere dalliance with the pomp and circumstance of war; for within a few weeks afterwards, her general defeated the Scots in the famous battle of Floddenfield, where James IV and most of his nobility were slain.[2]

Katherine's letter to Henry, announcing this event, so strikingly displays the piety and tenderness, the quiet simplicity, and real magnanimity of her character, that there cannot be a more apt and beautiful illustration of the exquisite truth and keeping of Shakespeare's portrait.

> Sir,
>
> My Lord Howard hath sent me a letter, open to your Grace, within one of mine, by the which ye shall see at length the great victory that our Lord hath sent your subjects in your absence: and for this cause, it is no need herein to trouble your Grace with long writing; but to my thinking this battle hath been to your Grace, and all your realm, the greatest honor that could be, and more than ye should win all the crown of France, thanked by God for it! And I am sure your Grace forgetteth not to do this, which shall be cause to send you many more such victories, as I trust he shall do. My husband, for haste, with Rougecross, I could not send your Grace the piece of the king of Scots' coat,

which John Glyn now bringeth. In this your Grace shall see how I can keep my promise, sending you for your banners a king's coat. I thought to send himself unto you, but our Englishmen's hearts would not suffer it. It should have been better for him to have been in peace than have this reward, but all that God sendeth is for the best. My Lord of Surrey, my Henry, would fain know your pleasure in the burying of the king of Scots' body, for he hath written to me so. With the next messenger, your Grace's pleasure may be herein known. And with this I make an end, praying to God to send you home shortly; for without this, no joy here can be accomplished—and for the same I pray. And now go to our Lady at Walsyngham, that I promised so long ago to see.

At Woburn, the 16th day of September, (1513.)
I send your Grace herein a bill, found in a Scottishman's purse, of such things as the French king sent to the said king of Scots, to make war against you, beseeching you to send Mathew hither as soon as this messenger cometh with tidings of your Grace.

Your humble wife and true servant,
Katherine.[3]

The legality of the king's marriage with Katherine remained undisputed till 1527. In the course of that year, Anna Bullen first appeared at court, and was appointed maid of honor to the queen; and then, and not till then, did Henry's union with his brother's wife "creep too near his conscience." In the following year, he sent special messengers to Rome, with secret instructions: they were required to discover (among other "hard questions") whether, if the queen entered a religious life, the king might have the Pope's dispensation to marry again; and whether if the king (for the better inducing the queen thereto) would enter himself into a religious life, the Pope would dispense with the king's vow, and leave her there?

Poor Katherine! we are not surprised to read that when she understood what was intended against her, "she labored with all those passions which jealousy of the king's affection, sense of her own honor, and the legitimation of her daughter, could produce, laying in conclusion the whole fault on the Cardinal." It is elsewhere said, that Wolsey bore the queen ill-will, in consequence of her reflecting with some severity on his haughty temper and very unclerical life.

The proceedings were pending for nearly six years, and one of the causes of this long delay, in spite of Henry's impatient and despotic character, is worth noting. The old Chronicle tells us, that though the men generally, and more particularly the priests and nobles, sided with Henry in this matter, yet all the ladies of England were against it. They justly felt that the honor and welfare of no woman was secure if, after twenty years of union, she might be thus deprived of all her rights as a wife; the clamor became so loud and general, that the king was obliged to yield to it for a time, to stop the proceedings, and to banish Anna Bullen from the court.

Cardinal Campeggio, called by Shakespeare Campeius, arrived in England in October, 1528. He at first endeavored to persuade Katherine to avoid the disgrace and danger of contesting her marriage, by entering a religious house; but she rejected his advice with strong expressions of disdain. "I am," said she, "the king's true wife, and to him married; and if all doctors were dead, or law or learning far out of men's minds at the time of our marriage, yet I cannot think that the court of Rome, and the whole church of England, would have consented to a thing unlawful and detestable as you call it. Still I say I am his wife, and for him will I pray."

About two years afterwards, Wolsey died, (in November, 1530)—the king and queen met for the last time on the 14th of July, 1531. Until that period, some outward show of respect and kindness had been maintained between them; but the king then ordered her to repair to a private residence, and no longer to consider herself as his lawful wife. "To which the virtuous and mourning queen replied no more than this, that to whatever place she removed, nothing could remove her from being the king's wife. And so they bid each other farewell; and from this time the king never saw her more."[4] He married Anna Bullen in 1532, while the decision relating to his former marriage was still pending. The sentence of divorce to which Katherine never would submit, was finally pronounced by Cranmer in 1533; and the unhappy queen, whose health had been gradually declining through these troubles of heart, died January 29, 1536, in the fiftieth year of her age.

Thus the action of the play of *Henry VIII* includes events which occurred from the impeachment of the Duke of Buckingham in 1521, to the death of Katherine in 1536. In making the death of Katherine precede the birth of Queen Elizabeth, Shakespeare has committed an anachronism, not only pardonable, but necessary. We must remember that the construction of the play required a happy termination; and that the birth of Elizabeth, before or after the death of Katherine, involved the question of her legitimacy. By this slight deviation from the real course of events, Shakespeare has not perverted historic facts, but merely sacrificed them to a higher principle; and in doing so has not only preserved dramatic propriety, and heightened the poetical interest, but has given a strong proof both of his delicacy and his judgment.

If we also call to mind that in this play Katherine is properly the heroine, and exhibited from first to last as the very "queen of earthly queens"; that the whole interest is thrown round her and Wolsey—the one the injured rival, the other the enemy of Anna Bullen—and that it was written in the reign and for the court of Elizabeth, we shall yet farther appreciate the moral greatness of the poet's mind, which disdained to sacrifice justice and the truth of nature to any time-serving expediency.

Schlegel observes somewhere, that in the literal accuracy and apparent artlessness with which Shakespeare has adapted some of the events and characters of history to his dramatic purposes, he has shown equally his genius and his wisdom. This, like most of Schlegel's remarks, is profound and true; and in this respect Katherine of Arragon may rank as the triumph of Shakespeare's genius and his wisdom. There is nothing in the whole range of poetical fiction in any respect resembling or approaching her; there is nothing comparable, I suppose, but Katherine's own portrait by Holbein, which, equally true to the life, is yet as far inferior as Katherine's person was inferior to her mind. Not only has Shakespeare given us here a delineation as faithful as it is beautiful, of a peculiar modification of character; but he has bequeathed us a precious moral lesson in this proof that virtue alone,—(by which I mean here the union of truth or conscience with benevolent affection—the one the highest law, the other the purest impulse of the soul,)—that such virtue is a sufficient source of the deepest pathos and power without any mixture of foreign or external ornament: for who but Shakespeare would have brought before us a queen and a heroine of tragedy, stripped her of all pomp of place and circumstance, dispensed with all the usual sources of poetical interest, as youth, beauty, grace, fancy, commanding intellect; and without any appeal to our imagination, without any violation of historical truth, or any sacrifices of the other dramatic personages for the sake of effect, could depend on the moral principle alone, to touch the very springs of feelings in our bosoms, and melt and elevate our hearts through the purest and holiest impulses of our nature!

The character, when analyzed, is, in the first place, distinguished by *truth*. I do not only mean its truth to nature, or its relative truth arising from its historical fidelity and dramatic consistency, but *truth* as a quality of the soul; this is the basis of the character. We often hear it remarked that those who are themselves perfectly true and artless, are in this world the more easily and frequently deceived—a common-place fallacy: for we shall ever find that truth is as undeceived as it is undeceiving, and that those who are true to themselves and others, may now and then be mistaken, or in particular instances duped by the intervention of some other affection or quality of the mind; but they are generally free from illusion, and they are seldom imposed upon in the long run by the shows of things and superfices of characters. It is by this integrity of heart and clearness of understanding, this light of truth within her own soul, and not through any acuteness of intellect, that Katherine detects and exposes the real character of Wolsey, though unable either to unravel his designs, or defeat them.

> My lord, my lord,
> I am a simple woman, much too weak
> T' oppose your cunning.

She rather intuitively feels than knows his duplicity, and in the dignity of her simplicity she towers above his arrogance as much as she scorns his crooked policy. With this essential truth are combined many other qualities, natural or acquired, all made out with the same uncompromising breadth of execution and fidelity of pencil, united with the utmost delicacy of feelings. For instance, the apparent contradiction arising from the contrast between Katherine's natural disposition and the situation in which she is placed; her lofty Castilian pride and her extreme simplicity of language and deportment; the inflexible resolution with which she asserts her right, and her soft resignation to unkindness and wrong; her warmth of temper breaking through the meekness of a spirit subdued by a deep sense of religion; and a degree of austerity tinging her real benevolence;—all these qualities, opposed yet harmonizing, has Shakespeare placed before us in a few admirable scenes.

Katherine is at first introduced as pleading before the king in behalf of the commonalty, who had been driven by the extortions of Wolsey into some illegal excesses. In this scene, which is true to history, we have her upright reasoning mind, her steadiness of purpose, her piety and benevolence, placed in a strong light. The unshrinking dignity with which she opposes without descending to brave the Cardinal, the stern rebuke addressed to the Duke of Buckingham's surveyor, are finely characteristic; and by thus exhibiting Katherine as invested with all her conjugal rights and influence, and royal state, the subsequent situations are rendered more impressive. She is placed in the first instance on such a height in our esteem and reverence, that in the midst of her abandonment and degradation, and the profound pity she afterwards inspires, the first effect remains unimpaired, and she never falls beneath it.

In the beginning of the second act we are prepared for the proceedings of the divorce, and our respect for Katherine heightened by the general sympathy for "the good queen," as she is expressively entitled, and by the following beautiful eulogium on her character uttered by the Duke of Norfolk:—

> He (Wolsey) counsels a divorce—a loss of her
> That like a jewel hath hung twenty years
> About his neck, yet never lost her lustre.
> Of her that loves him with that excellence
> That angels love good men with; even of her,
> That, when the greatest stroke of fortune falls,
> Will bless the King!

The scene in which Anna Bullen is introduced as expressing her grief and sympathy for her royal mistress, is exquisitely graceful.

> Here's the pang that pinches:
> His highness having liv'd so long with her, and she
> So good a lady, that no tongue could ever
> Pronounce dishonor of her,—by my life
> She never knew harm-doing. O now, after
> So many courses of the sun enthron'd,

Still growing in a majesty and pomp,—the which
To leave is a thousand-fold more bitter, than
'Tis sweet at first to acquire,—after this process,
To give her the avaunt! it is a pity
Would move a monster.

Old Lady

Hearts of most hard temper
Melt and lament for her.

Anne

O, God's will! much better
She ne'er had know pomp: though it be temporal,
Yet if that quarrel, fortune, do divorce
It from the bearer, 'tis a sufferance, panging
As soul and body's severing.

Old Lady

Alas, poor lady!
She's a stranger now again.

Anne

So much the more
Must pity drop upon her. Verily,
I swear 'tis better to be lowly born,
And range with humble livers in content,
Than to be perk'd up in a glistering grief,
And wear a golden sorrow.

How completely, in the few passages appropriated to Anna Bullen, is her character portrayed! with what a delicate and yet luxuriant grace is she sketched off, with her gayety and her beauty, her levity, her extreme mobility, her sweetness of disposition, her tenderness of heart, and, in short, all her *femalities*! How nobly has Shakespeare done justice to the two women, and heightened our interest in both, by placing the praises of Katherine in the mouth of Anna Bullen! and how characteristic of the latter, that she should first express unbounded pity for her mistress, insisting chiefly on her fall from her regal state and worldly pomp, thus betraying her own disposition:—

For she that had all the fair parts of woman,
Had, too, a woman's heart, which ever yet
Affected eminence, wealth, and sovereignty.

That she should call the loss of temporal pomp, once enjoyed, "a sufferance equal to soul and body's severing"; that she should immediately protest that she would not herself be a queen—"No, good troth! not for all the riches under heaven!"—and not long afterwards ascend without reluctance that throne and bed from which her royal mistress had been so cruelly divorced!—how natural! The portrait is not less true and masterly than that of Katherine; but the character is overborne by the superior moral firmness and intrinsic excellence of the latter. That we may be more fully sensible of this contrast, the beautiful scene just alluded to immediately precedes Katherine's trial at Blackfriars and the description of Anna Bullen's triumphant beauty at her coronation, is placed immediately before the dying scene of Katherine; yet with equal good taste and good feeling Shakespeare has constantly avoided all personal collision between the two characters; nor does Anna Bullen ever appear as queen except in the pageant of the procession, which in reading the play is scarcely noticed.

To return to Katherine. The whole of the trial scene is given nearly verbatim from the old chronicles and records; but the dryness and harshness of the law proceedings is tempered at once and elevated by the genius and the wisdom of the poet. It appears, on referring to the historical authorities, that when the affair was first agitated in council, Katherine replied to the long expositions and theological sophistries of her opponents with resolute simplicity and composure: "I am a woman, and lack wit and learning to answer these opinions; but I am sure that neither the king's father nor my father would have condescended to our marriage, if it had been judged unlawful. As to your saying that I should put the cause to eight persons of this realm, for quietness of the king's conscience, I pray Heaven to send his Grace and quiet conscience: and this shall be your answer, that I say I am his lawful wife, and to him lawfully married; though not worthy of it; and in this point I will abide, till the court of Rome, which was privy to the beginning, have made a final ending of it."[5]

Katherine's appearance in the court at Blackfriars, attended by a noble troop of ladies and prelates of her counsel, and her refusal to answer the citation, are historical.[6] Her speech to the king—

> Sir, I beseech you do me right and justice,
> And to bestow your pity on me, &c. &c.

is taken word for word (as nearly as the change from prose to blank verse would allow) from the old record in Hall. It would have been easy for Shakespeare to have exalted his own skill, by throwing a coloring of poetry and eloquence into this speech, without altering the sense or sentiment; but by adhering to the calm argumentative simplicity of manner and diction natural to the woman, he has preserved the truth of character without lessening the pathos of the situation. Her challenging Wolsey as a "foe to truth," and her very expressions, "I utterly refuse,—yea, from my soul *abhor* you for my judge," are taken from fact. The sudden burst of indignant passion towards the close of this scene,

> In one who ever yet
> Had stood to charity, and displayed the effects
> Of disposition gentle, and of wisdom
> O'ertopping woman's power;

is taken from nature, thought it occurred on a different occasion.[7]

Lastly, the circumstance of her being called back after she had appealed from the court, and angrily refusing to return, is from the life. Master Griffith, on whose arm she leaned, observed that she was called: "On, on," quoth she; "it maketh no matter, for it is no indifferent court for me, therefore I will not tarry. Go on your ways."[8]

King Henry's own assertion, "I dare to say, my lords, that for her womanhood, wisdom, nobility, and gentleness, never prince had such another wife, and therefore if I would willingly change her I were not wise," is thus beautifully paraphrased by Shakespeare:—

> That man i' the world, who shall report he has
> A better wife, let him in nought be trusted,
> For speaking false in that! Thou art, alone,
> If thy rare qualities, sweet gentleness,
> (Thy meekness saint-like, wife-like government,

Obeying in commanding; and thy parts,
Sovereign and pious else, could speak thee out,)
The queen of earthly queens. She is noble born,
And, like her true nobility, she has
Carried herself towards me.

The annotators on Shakespeare have all observed the close resemblance between this fine passage—

Sir,
I am about to weep; but, thinking that
We are a queen, or long have dreamed so, certain
The daughter of a king—my drops of tears
I'll turn to sparks of fire.

and the speech of Hermione—

I am not prone to weeping as our sex
Commonly are, the want of which vain dew
Perchance shall dry your pities: but I have
That honorable grief lodged here, which burns
Worse than tears drown.[9]

But these verbal gentlemen do not seem to have felt that the resemblance is merely on the surface, and that the two passages could not possibly change places, without a manifest violation of the truth of character. In Hermione it is pride of sex merely: in Katherine it is pride of place and pride of birth. Hermione, though so superbly majestic, is perfectly independent of her regal state: Katherine, though so meekly pious, will neither forget hers, nor allow it to be forgotten by others for a moment. Hermione, when deprived of that "crown and comfort of her life," her husband's love, regards all things else with despair and indifference except her feminine honor: Katherine, divorced and abandoned, still with true Spanish pride stands upon respect, and will not bate one atom of her accustomed state

Though unqueened, yet like a queen
And daughter to a king, inter me!

The passage—

> A fellow of the royal bed, that owns
> A moiety of the throne—a great king's daughter
> . . . . . here standing
> To prate and talk for life and honor 'fore
> Who please to come to hear

would apply nearly to both queens, yet a single sentiment—nay, a single sentence—could not possibly be transferred from one character to the other. The magnanimity, the noble simplicity, the purity of heart, the resignation in each—how perfectly equal in degree! how diametrically opposite in kind![10]

Once more to return to Katherine.

We are told by Cavendish, that when Wolsey and Campeggio visited the queen by the king's order she was found at work among her women, and came forth to meet the cardinals with a skein of white thread hanging about her neck; that when Wolsey addressed her in Latin, she interrupted him, saying, "Nay, good my lord, speak to me in English, I beseech you; although I understand Latin." "Forsooth then," quoth my lord, "madam, if it please your grace, we come both to know your mind, how ye be disposed to do in this matter between the king and you, and also to declare secretly our opinions and our counsel unto you, which we have intended of very zeal and obedience that we bear to your grace." "My lords, I thank you then," quoth she, "of your good wills; but to make answer to your request I cannot so suddenly, for I was set among my maidens at work, thinking full little of any such matter; wherein there needeth a longer deliberation, and a better head than mine to make answer to so noble wise men as ye be. I had need of good counsel in this case, which toucheth me so near; and for any counsel or friendship that I can find in England, they are nothing to my purpose or profit. Think you, I pray you, my lords, will any Englishmen counsel, or be friendly unto me, against the king's pleasure, they being his subjects? Nay, forsooth, my lords! and for my counsel, in whom I do intend to put my trust, they be not here; they be in Spain, in my native country.[11] Alas! my lords, I am a poor woman lacking both wit and understanding sufficiently to answer such approved wise men as ye be both, in so weighty a matter. I pray you to extend your good and indifferent minds in your authority unto me, for I am a simple woman, destitute and barren of friendship and counsel, here in a foreign region; and as for your counsel, I will not refuse, but be glad to hear."

It appears, also, that when the Archbishop of York and Bishop Tunstall waited on her at her house near Huntingdon, with the sentence of the divorce, signed by Henry, and confirmed by act of parliament, she refused to admit its validity, she being Henry's wife, and not his subject. The bishop describes her conduct in his letter: "She being therewith in great choler and agony, and always interrupting our words, declared that she would never leave the name of queen, but would persist in accounting herself the king's wife till death." When the official letter containing minutes of their conference, was shown to her, she seized a pen, and dashed it angrily across every sentence in which she was styled *Princess-dowager.*

If now we turn to that inimitable scene between Katherine and the two cardinals (act iii, scene 1), we shall observe how finely Shakespeare has condensed these incidents, and unfolded to us all the workings of Katherine's proud yet feminine nature. She is discovered at work with some of her women—she calls for music "to soothe her soul grown sad with troubles"—then follows the little song, of which the sentiment is so well adapted to the occasion, while its quaint yet classic elegance breathes the very spirit of those times, when Surrey loved and sung.

SONG

Orpheus with his lute-made trees,
And the mountain-tops that freeze,
  Bow themselves when he did sing
To his music, plants and flowers
Ever sprung, as sun and showers
  There had made a lasting spring.

Every thing that heard him play,
Even the billows of the sea,
  Hung their heads and then lay by
In sweet music is such art,
Killing care, and grief of heart,
  Fall asleep, on hearing, die.

They are interrupted by the arrival of the two cardinals. Katherine's perception of their subtlety—her suspicion of their purpose—her sense of her own weakness and inability to content with them, and her mild subdued dignity, are beautifully represented; as also the guarded self-command with which she eludes giving a definite answer; but when they counsel her to that which she, who knows Henry, feels must end in her ruin, then the native temper is roused at once, or, to use Tunstall's expression, "the choler and the agony," burst forth in words.

> Is this your christian counsel? Out upon ye!
> Heaven is above all yet; there sits a Judge
> That no king can corrupt.

Wolsey

> Your rage mistakes us.

Queen Katherine

> The more shame for ye! Holy men I thought ye,
> Upon my soul, two reverend cardinal virtues;
> But cardinal sins, and hollow hearts, I fear ye:
> Mend them, for shame, my lords: is this your comfort,
> The cordial that ye bring a wretched lady?

With the same force of language, and impetuous yet dignified feelings, she asserts her own conjugal truth and merit, and insists upon her rights.

> Have I liv'd thus long, (let me speak myself,
> Since virtue finds no friends,) a wife, a true one,
> A woman, (I dare say, without vain-glory,)
> never yet branded with suspicion?
> Have I, with all my full affections,
> Still met the king—lov'd him next heaven, obey'd him!
> Been out of fondness superstitious to him—
> Almost forgot my prayers to content him,
> And am I thus rewarded? 'tis not well, lords, &c.

> My lord, I dare not make myself so guilty,
> To give up willingly that noble title
> Your master wed me to: nothing but death
> Shall e'er divorce my dignities.

And this burst of unwonted passion is immediately followed by the natural reaction; it subsides into tears, dejection, and a mournful self-compassion.

> Would I had never trod this English ground,
> Or felt the flatteries that grown up it.
> What will become of me now, wretched lady?
> I am the most unhappy woman living.
> Alas! poor wenches! where are now your fortunes?
> [*To her women*]
> Shipwrecked upon a kingdom, where no pity,
> No friends, no hope, no kindred weep for me!
> Almost no grave allowed me! Like the lily that once
> Was mistress of the field, and flourish'd,
> I'll hang my head and perish.

Dr. Johnson observes on this scene, that all Katherine's distresses could not save her from a quibble on the word *cardinal*.

> Holy men I thought ye,
> Upon my soul, two reverend cardinal virtues;
> But cardinal sins, and hollow hearts, I fear ye!

When we read this passage in connection with the situation and sentiment, the scornful play upon words is not only appropriate and natural, it seems inevitable. Katherine, assuredly, is neither an imaginative nor a witty personage; but we all acknowledge the truism, that anger inspires wit, and whenever there is passion there is poetry. In the instance just alluded to, the sarcasm springs naturally out from the bitter indignation of the moment. In her grand rebuke of Wolsey, in the trial scene, how just and beautiful is the gradual elevation of her language, till it rises into that magnificent image—

> You have by fortune and his highness' favors,
> Gone slightly o'er low steps, and now are mounted
> Where powers are your retainers, &c.

In the depth of her affliction, the pathos as naturally clothes itself in poetry.

> Like the lily,
> That was mistress of the field, and flourish'd,
> I'll hang my head and perish.

But these, I believe, are the only instances of imagery throughout; for, in general, her language is plain and energetic. It has the strength and simplicity of her character, with very little metaphor and less wit.

In approaching the last scene of Katherine's life, I feel as if about to tread within a sanctuary, where nothing befits us but silence and tears; veneration so strives with compassion, tenderness with awe.[12]

We must suppose a long interval to have elapsed since Katherine's interview with the two cardinals. Wolsey was disgraced, and poor Anna Bullen at the height of her short-lived prosperity. It was Wolsey's fate to be detested by both queens. In the pursuance of his own selfish and ambitious designs, he had treated both with perfidy; and one was the remote, the other the immediate, cause of his ruin.[13]

The ruffian king, of whom one hates to think, was bent on forcing Katherine to concede her rights, and illegitimize her daughter, in favor of the offspring of Anna Bullen: she steadily refused, was declared contumacious, and the sentence of divorce pronounced in 1533. Such of her attendants as persisted in paying her the honors due to a queen were driven from her household; those who consented to serve her as princess-dowager, she refused to admit into her presence; so that she remained unattended, except by a few women, and her gentleman usher, Griffith. During the last eighteen months of her life, she resided at Kimbolton. Her nephew, Charles V, had offered her an asylum and princely treatment; but Katherine, broken in heart, and declining in health, was unwilling to drag the spectacle of her misery and degradation into a strange country: she pined in her loneliness, deprived of her daughter, receiving no consolation from the pope, and no redress from the emperor. Wounded pride, wronged affection, and a cankering jealousy of the woman preferred to her, (which though it never broke out into unseemly words, is enumerated as one of the causes of her death,) at length wore out a feeble frame. "Thus," says the chronicle, "Queen Katherine fell into her last sickness; and though the king sent to comfort her through Chapuys, the emperor's ambassador, she grew worse and worse; and finding death now coming, she caused a maid attending on her to write to the king to this effect:—

> My most dear Lord, King, and Husband;
> The hour of my death now approaching, I cannot choose but, out of the love I bear you, advise you of your soul's health, which you ought to prefer before all considerations of the world or flesh whatsoever; for which yet you have cast me into many calamities, and yourself into many troubles: but I forgive you all, and pray God to do so likewise; for the rest, I commend unto you Mary our daughter, beseeching you to be a good father to her, as I have heretofore desired. I must intreat you also to respect my maids, and give them in marriage, which is not much, they being but three, and all my other servants a year's pay besides their due, lest otherwise they be unprovided for: lastly, I make this vow, that mine eyes desire you above all things.—Farewell![14]

She also wrote another letter to the ambassador, desiring that he would remind the king of her dying request, and urge him to do her this last right.

What the historian relates, Shakespeare realizes. On the wonderful beauty of Katherine's closing scene we need not dwell; for that requires no illustration. In transferring the sentiments of her letter to her lips, Shakespeare has given them added grace, and pathos, and tenderness, without injuring their truth and simplicity: the feelings, and almost the manner of expression, are Katherine's own. The severe justice with which she draws the character of Wolsey is extremely characteristic! the benign candor with which she listens to the praise of him "whom living she most hated," is not less so. How beautiful her religious enthusiasm!—the slumber which visits her pillow, as she listens to that sad music she called her knell; her awakening from the vision of celestial joy to find herself still on earth—

> Spirits of peace! where are ye? are ye gone,
> And leave me here in wretchedness behind ye?

how unspeakably beautiful! And to consummate all in one final touch of truth and nature, we see that consciousness of her own worth and integrity which had sustained her through all her trials of heart, and that pride of station for which she had contended through long years—which had become more dear by opposition, and by the perseverance with which she had asserted it—remaining the last strong feelings upon her mind, to the very last hour of existence.

> When I am dead, good wench
> let me be used with honor: strew me over
> With maiden flowers, that all the world may know
> I was a chaste wife to my grave; embalm me,
> Then lay me forth: although unqueen'd, yet like
> A queen, and daughter to a king, inter me.
> I can no more.—

In the epilogue to this play, it is recommended—

> To the merciful construction of good women,
> For *such a one* we show'd them:

alluding to the character of Queen Katherine. Shakespeare has, in fact, placed before us a queen and a heroine, who in the first place, and above all, is a *good* woman; and I repeat, that in doing so, and in trusting for all his effect to truth and virtue, he has given a sublime proof of his genius and his wisdom;—for which, among many other obligations, we women remain his debtors.

NOTES

1. See her letters in Ellis's Collection.
2. Under similar circumstances, one of Katherine's predecessors, Philippa of Hainault, had gained in her husband's absence the battle of Neville Cross, in which David Bruce was taken prisoner.
3. Ellis's Collection. We must keep in mind that Katherine was a foreigner, and till after she was seventeen, never spoke or wrote a word of English.
4. Hall's Chronicle.
5. Hall's Chronicle, p. 781
6. The court at Blackfriars sat on the 28th of May, 1529. "The queen being called, accompanied by the four bishops and others of her counsel, and a

great company of ladies and gentlewomen following her; and after her obeisance, sadly and with great gravity, she appealed from them to the court of Rome."—See *Hall and Cavendish's Life of Wolse.*

The account which Hume gives of this scene is very elegant; but after the affecting naivete of the old chroniclers, it is very cold and unsatisfactory.

7. "The queen answered the Duke of Suffolk very highly and obstinately, with many high words: and suddenly, in a fury, she departed from him into her privy chamber."—*Vide Hall's Chronicle.*
8. *Vide* Cavendish's Life of Wolsey.
9. Winter's Tale, act iii. scene 2.
10. I have constantly abstained from considering any of these characters with a reference to the theatre; yet I cannot help remarking, that if Mrs. Siddons, who excelled equally in Hermione and Katherine, and threw such majesty of demeanor, such power, such picturesque effect, in both, could likewise feel and convey the infinite contrast between the ideal grace, the classical repose and imaginative charm thrown round Hermione, and the matter-of-fact, artless, prosaic nature of Katherine; between the poetic grandeur of the former, and moral dignity of the latter,—then she certainly exceeded all that I could have imagined possible, even to *her* wonderful powers.
11. This affecting passage is thus rendered by Shakespeare:—

> Nay, forsooth, my friends,
> They that must weigh out my afflictions—
> They that my trust must grow to, live not here—
> They are, as all my other comforts, far hence,
> In mine own country, lords.
>
> (*Henry VIII*, act iii, sc. 1)

12. Dr. Johnson is of opinion, that this scene "is above any other part of Shakespeare's tragedies, and perhaps above any scene of any other poet, tender and pathetic; without gods, or furies, or poisons, or precipices; without the help of romantic circumstances; without improbable sallies of poetical lamentation, and without any throes of tumultuous misery."

I have already observed, that in judging of Shakespeare's characters as of persons we meet in real life, we are swayed unconsciously by our own habits and feelings, and our preference governed, more or less, by our individual prejudices or sympathies. Thus, Dr. Johnson, who has not a word to bestow on Imogen, and who has treated poor Juliet as if she had been in truth "the very beadle to an amorous sigh," does full justice to the character of Katherine, because the logical turn of his mind, his vigorous intellect, and his austere integrity, enabled him to appreciate its peculiar beauties: and, accordingly, we find that he gives it, not only unqualified, but almost exclusive admiration: he goes so far as to assert, that in this play the genius of Shakespeare comes in and goes out with Katherine.

13. It will be remembered, that in early youth Anna Bullen was betrothed to Lord Henry Percy, who was passionately in love with her. Wolsey, to serve the king's purposes, broke off this match, and forced Percy into an unwilling marriage with Lady Mary Talbot. "The stout Earl of Northumberland," who arrested Wolsey at York, was this very Percy: he was chosen for his mission by the interference of Anna Bullen—a piece of vengeance truly feminine in its mixture of sentiment and spitefulness; and every way characteristic of the individual woman.
14. The king is said to have wept on reading this letter, and her body being interred at Peterbro', in the monastery, for honor of her memory it was preserved at the dissolution, and erected into a bishop's see.—*Herbert's Life of Henry VIII.*

Lee Bliss

The Wheel of Fortune and the Maiden Phoenix of Shakespeare's *King Henry the Eighth*

It is no longer necessary, I hope, to preface any discussion of *Henry VIII* with a tidy survey of the authorship controversy and a final defiant (or apologetic) resolution to set such questions aside in favor of other, literary and critical, interests. Since 1934, when Peter Alexander defended Shakespeare's sole authorship against the Fletcher partisans, criticism has tended increasingly to favor reinstating *Henry VIII* in the Shakespeare canon; even while arguing for a limited Fletcherian contribution, Cyrus Hoy for instance maintains that *Henry VIII* "has its place—and it remains secure when the disintegrators of Shakespeare have done their worst—in a greater canon than the Beaumont and Fletcher one."[1] Recent critical studies of *Henry VIII* have accepted the arguments for Shakespeare's sole authorship marshalled by R. A. Foakes in his Arden edition of the play and have devoted their attention to the play's importance in Shakespeare's *oeuvre*—as the last great history play, as a final dramatic experiment combining the fruits of his efforts in history, tragedy, and romance, or as another solution to structural problems encountered, but unresolved, in the late plays.

Unfortunately, the disintegrators' charges of chaotic structure, inconsistent characterization, and unShakespearean sentiment encouraged a militant reaction from the play's defenders, and proponents have made extravagant claims for the structural unity of *Henry VIII* as well as for its significance as the culmination of Shakespeare's career. Analysis which emphasizes Cranmer's prophecy—and the late romances—can produce a visionary myth of devil-Wolsey's defeat and the deliverance of England from "secular misrule and spiritual bondage" into the hands of "God's deputies, Henry and Cranmer."[2] Interpretation of *Henry VIII* in the light of Shakespeare's earlier history plays and their concern with the

Reprinted from *ELH: A Journal of English Literary History*, 42 (1975): 1–25, by permission of The Johns Hopkins University Press.

nature of good governance focuses the play as a final study in "the evolution of the ideal ruler";[3] a different unity is now evident, for "the action of the play shows us a King who reigns becoming a King who rules, and the principal episodes are made to serve this development."[4]

Both interpretations, that *Henry VIII* is history transformed into an expression of Christian myth and that it is history finally redeemed by myth, insist on Henry's gradual maturation, his emergence from this episodic "education of a prince" as a just and good king—even one partially identified with God. I do not share this heroic view of King Henry as either the champion of the Church of England or as a misled youth, akin to Shakespeare's tragic heroes in his "idealistic and overprompt emotional reaction,"[5] who finally attains self-knowledge and with it all the virtues of the ideal monarch. Such a simplification of the central figure implies a more uncomplicated unity of action than in fact exists. Those readings which relate the first four acts of *Henry VIII* to the concerns of the history plays do, however, give valuable attention to the political and moral complexities which the play devastatingly explores, "the world of intrigue and ambition portrayed so well in the earlier histories."[6] In this very paradoxical characterization lies one of H. M. Richmond's arguments for Shakespearean authorship, for he sees as eminently Shakespearean the play's "calculated oscillation of values, and the frequent reversals of our formal judgments and expectations of the principal characters."[7]

Confusing perspectives on character and action are more pervasive than has been allowed, and the result is an essential ambiguity in the play's "truths." The last act is not devoted to vindicating Henry; and the reconciliations and restoration through suffering are different in kind from those of the late romances, not an "attempt to create a similar total effect within the ordinary terms of causality and succession."[8] To read the play fairly, it is necessary both to avoid interpreting it backward, from the vantage point of the final romantic prophecy, and to resist the temptation to approach *Henry VIII* as a culmination which *must* draw on and resolve the problems and interests of an entire career. Thus while it would be unwise to isolate *Henry VIII* from the preceding plays, it is well to keep in mind that distinctively Shakespearean predilection for experiment rather than repetition and conspicuous eagerness to bend and transform conventions. With such caveats in mind, I shall focus my attention both on the moral complexity of the "historical" political world created in *Henry VIII* and on the problematic king himself, for the shadowy Henry is both the center of court power within the play and the focal point for a dramatic structure distinguished by constant and alarming shifts in its perspective on character and action. With a clear view of the way in which the play builds its disturbing effects, perhaps the final prophesy will seem less a retreat into fantasy (or obsequious flattery) than a significant, dramatically appropriate discontinuity.

Even before the appearance of the king, the first scene sets up a world in which establishing the "truth" in any given situation is exceedingly complicated; prior certainty repeatedly dissolves in the face of later revelations. As the play progresses, its probable subtitle "All is True" and the references to "truth" in the Prologue become increasingly perplexing and ironic.[9] If the facts of history remain constant, those treaties, taxes, deaths and births, rises and falls, become subject to many, even contradictory, interpretations. Any artistic work of course "interprets" through necessary selectivity and compression, but Shakespeare has dramatized the essential limitations in our knowledge of "truth" or human motivation through a proliferation of explanations within the play itself.

We are introduced to this pattern of contradiction—as well as to a predilection for personally biased reportage of events—through Norfolk's relation to Buckingham of the events of the Field of the Cloth of Gold. Norfolk maintains that he has been "ever since a fresh admirer / Of what I saw there," and goes on to describe this "view of earthly glory" in lavish terms which suggest that even ugliness was temporarily transformed by the magnificence of the occasion (I.i.3–4, 18–26).[10] Eighty lines later, however, we are told that the whole grandiose display was a hollow sham; the gilded pomp and pageantry in which Norfolk expressed his vision of earthly harmony merely draped a temporary political maneuver. In the beginning all had seemed true to Norfolk and, in his report, to us; only in retrospect can we see how false, how truly unstable and "earthly" that appearance was. Events throughout the play modify our reactions to what has already been seen as well as to subsequent incidents. Even in this first scene, we now realize that "admire" did not signify wonder in the sense of approbations, but rather an ironic sense of amazement at the disparity between a dream of transcendent and transforming harmony and the disconcertingly mutable political realities of an impoverished nobility and a broken treaty. Later events also illuminate the ominous suggestion that at Andren "no discerner / Durst wag his tongue in censure" (I.i.32–33).

The splendid scene of pomp witnessed by Norfolk was so fabulous "that Bevis was believed," yet it proved hollow. As a paradigm for the pattern and concerns of the play, this scene offers only empty pomp and friendship, but also a characteristic questioning of the truths established by individuals; personal bias in this play generally determines a character's interpretation of events. Although Buckingham at first seems to concur in Norfolk's rapt response to the golden pageant, as soon as he hears that his enemy Wolsey was responsible for this "great sport," he changes his tone. Now the festivities are "fierce vanities" (I.i.54). The violence of this hatred alarms Norfolk, and he warns Buckingham that it should be concealed, for Wolsey has the power to destroy those he dislikes. Norfolk advises deceit, dissembling one's malice, as the most "wholesome" policy; a darker implication of his friendly advice is the possibility that the most apparently healthy figures in this world are merely the best politicians. This whole complex scene of withheld information, shifting perspectives, and uncertain "truths" influences our expectations; caught once in easy acceptance of what we thought was a conventional report speech, we are now less ready to accept either the grand appearance of the moment or any single person's assertion. This attitude is certainly not discouraged by subsequent events.

The truth of Buckingham's guilt or Wolsey's responsibility for his fall is never clear. Buckingham accuses Wolsey of being "corrupt and treasonous" (I.i.156), yet Buckingham himself is arrested almost immediately on a charge of treason. He blames Wolsey for having taken a bribe to break the lately established peace with France, yet Norfolk has not heard of this; though Buckingham says it shall "appear in proof," because of his arrest this proof is never given. Buckingham says he will perish "under device and practice" (I.i.204); but is this true? Although he cries out "My surveyor is false: the o'er-great cardinal / Hath show'd him gold" (I.i.222–23), we never know whether he fears that Wolsey's gold has merely induced the surveyor to reveal harmful truths about his employer or whether he knows that his surveyor is corruptible and will fabricate lies if bribed. Buckingham's hearing before his king leaves us no wiser. Katherine impugns the surveyor's testimony, but Henry ignores her comment. Although the king commits Buckingham to trial by his peers, he has already judged Buckingham a traitor and refused him the royal mercy. Buckingham himself is ambiguous on the matter, and our doubts are encouraged rather than resolved. On the one hand, the charges of Wolsey's responsibility for innocent Buckingham's fate may be true, even though the nobles obviously also hated Wolsey because, despite his detested social status, he keeps them from power; we have heard Katherine's reflections on the surveyor and on Wolsey's lack of charity (I.ii.143). Is her "God mend all" after Henry has made his rather hasty decision a bitter comment on the corruption of earthly justice (I.ii.201)? On the other hand, the surveyor is never proved false and, whether we believe it or not, he boldly states "On my soul, I'll speak but truth" (I.ii.177). Testimony of Buckingham's wild ambitions—and credulity—is also not inconsistent with the intemperance we have seen, and his peers do find him guilty.

The confrontation scene leaves us wondering whether the appearance of treason (or innocence) here is as specious as the initial indications of peace; the apparently impartial description of the trial by the walking gentleman in II.i is tantalizingly non-committal. When asked what happened at the trial, the first gentleman answers "You may guess quickly what" (II.i.7); yet we are not sure whether they know that Buckingham is guilty (i.e., that it is common knowledge), or whether it is obvious that once he is condemned by the king the peers will not dare find him innocent. This report of the trial captures the court observers' sense—and acceptance—of the impossibility of certain knowledge of truth in this mutable, politic world. Despite the assumption of Buckingham's guilt—for Buckingham "alleg'd / Many sharp reasons to defeat the law," yet the many witnesses "accus'd him strongly, which he fain / Would have flung from him; but indeed he could not" (II.i.13–14, 24–25)—they also blame Wolsey's "tricks of state" for Buckingham's plight and England's sickness. To further confuse us, when one gentleman overflows with pity for the departed duke, the second gentleman cautions him: "*If* the duke be guiltless, / 'Tis full of woe" (II.i.139–40, italics mine).

Instead of offering us the balanced opinion or unbiased "fact" which we expect of the conventionally uninvolved commentator (such as the officers in *Coriolanus*, II.i), the court gentlemen merely restate the possible reasons for the objective, necessarily accepted fact of conviction for treason. Their dialogue pointedly fails to resolve the kinds of questions—truth or deception, guilt or innocence—which the play repeatedly raises. As disinterested observers, the gentlemen thus offer a significant response to the pattern of rises and falls, trials and judgments, which demand the court's attention. Absolute guilt and innocence cannot be established in this world, for both earthly glory and earthly justice seem to express no permanent, immutable values; indeed, Shakespeare capitalizes on the inconsistencies of the chronicles and with them enhances his use of multiple sympathetic perspectives. No one is presented as wholly innocent, or without self-interested motives (except perhaps Katherine, and she is guilty of not having borne Elizabeth and hence must fall); and so, despite the fact that the play is studded with trial scenes, establishment of the truth or guilt or innocence is not the play's prime consideration. The trials themselves and the quality of justice they reflect are important, as their number would suggest, but so too are both the continual process of rise and fall they reveal and the opportunity for self-awareness they offer.

While we experience the impossibility of knowing any definite political or moral "truth" about Buckingham, we also discover an inability—in the characters as well as in ourselves—to distinguish public and private matters in the tangled fortunes of Anne, Katherine, Wolsey, and Henry. The king's introduction to Anne at Wolsey's banquet is both unhistorical and inauspicious. The short preceding scene condemns Frenchified Englishmen and their trivial, dissolute manners; this otherwise puzzling scene is neatly juxtaposed with Henry's arrival as a foreign masquer to whom French must be spoken. The atmosphere is one of opulent gaiety and frank physical pleasure. Anne willingly kisses Lord Sands and trades ribald comments with him. Wolsey indelicately twits Henry about his obvious infatuation, and the king accepts the truth of Wolsey's joke:

> Wol. Your grace,
> I fear, with dancing is a little heated.
> King. I fear too much.
> (I.iv.99–101)

In II.i, after Buckingham has departed for his execution, the walking gentlemen turn to state gossip. 2 Gent. mentions the common talk of an impending separation between

Katherine and Henry. 1 Gent. says that he has heard the gossip but

> . . . it held not;
> For when the king once heard it, out of anger
> He sent command to the lord mayor straight
> To stop the rumour, and allay those tongues
> That durst disperse it.
>
> 2 Gent. But that slander, sir
> Is found a truth now; for it grows again
> Fresher than e'er it was, and held for certain
> The king will venture at it.
>
> (II.i.149-56)

Slander, that notoriously false and malicious variety of rumor, has grown into truth. Moreover, although the courtiers blame Wolsey, it is obvious that Henry does not want truths about himself to be known and discussed. The scene ends with an admission that it is dangerous for private men to discuss state affairs: "We are too open here to argue this; / Let's think in private more" (II.i.168-69). The following conversation adroitly pursues the subject of Henry's relation to Anne and Katherine while shifting its focus to the disgruntled nobility. Henry is said to be full of sad thoughts, and the Lord Chamberlain comments:

> It seems the marriage with his brother's wife
> has crept too near his conscience.
> *Suf.* [Aside] No, his conscience
> Has crept too near another lady.
> *Nor.* 'Tis so.
>
> (II.ii.16-19).

Norfolk's "'Tis so" ostensibly answers the Lord Chamberlain's comment, but for us it has reference to both remarks. In this world in which everything seems equally true (or equally questionable) we must accept both reasons as possible, and even as equally true.

Since Henry's motivation in the matter of the divorce is a constant topic within the play, it is worth noting that in compressing historical time Shakespeare has also artfully multiplied our doubts about Henry's religious scruples. Katherine's trial actually occurred four years before Henry's secret marriage to Anne Boleyn. Thus Henry's obvious impatience to be rid of Katherine is given additional significance by the compressed time scheme: Henry has secretly married Anne—apparently just after Katherine's inconclusive trial—while the question of the divorce is still "unhandled" (III.ii.58). Moreover, Suffolk's aside here and the Lord Chamberlain's later pun (II.iii.74-75) suggest at least a possibility that Anne is pregnant even before Katherine's trial. Since this dramatic situation results from conscious changes in historical chronology, its implications can hardly be fortuitous. Henry's impatience, and the disparity between his public speeches and his private actions and asides, render his motivation ambivalent; we feel that justice, though often mentioned, is really peripheral to the matter in hand.

Remarks within the play and Shakespeare's use of his historical material suggest Henry is more complicated than he would perhaps like to appear. After Suffolk's aside in II.ii, Henry dismisses the nobles in order to discuss with Wolsey and Campeius their "impartial judging" of the legality of Henry's marriage to Katherine. Henry's final public comment reflects his ambivalent posture:

> O my lord,
> Would it not grieve an able man to leave
> So sweet a bedfellow? But conscience, conscience;
> O 'tis a tender place, and I must leave her.
> (II.ii.140-44)

Henry here assumes the verdict which he wishes the judges to confer and, in the "must," offers them a veiled order to comply with his wishes. Perhaps more striking is Shakespeare's juxtaposition of Henry's plea of "conscience" with Anne's comment in the first line of the next scene. As if continuing a previous conversation with the Old Lady, Anne caps Henry's statement with "Not for that neither" (II.iii.1). Since we do not know the referent for her remark, we take the line both as a chatty introduction to Anne's own speech and as an evaluation of Henry's remorse of conscience. Henry's stated reasons are questionable, at least as any complete explanation of his behavior; the exact extent of his hypocrisy, however, is left open.

Although Anne here appears to be shy, modest beyond belief, and very concerned about Katherine's fate, we have seen her in a wanton light at Wolsey's banquet and the Lord

Chamberlain reminds us that she may be pregnant. The Old Lady's half of the dialogue is both cynical and bawdy; she accuses Anne of hypocrisy and taunts her about the splendors which "the capacity / Of your soft cheveril conscience would receive, / If you might please to stretch it" (II.iii.31-33). The malleability of one's "cheveril conscience" is certainly not a startling idea at this point in the play. The Old Lady's accusation reflects on Anne and, since Henry has so recently stressed the word, on the king as well. In addition, the pun on queen/quean calls Henry's character in question and degrades Anne, especially when we learn of her reward (in the form of a title and funds) "for pure respect," as the Old Lady sarcastically terms it (II.iii.95). If the Lord Chamberlain sees honor and beauty which will produce "a gem / To lighten all this isle," to the Old Lady Anne is simply "fresh fish" capitalizing on her physical attraction and Henry's lust (II.iii.78-79,86).

At her trial, Katherine, who in I.ii had pleaded for justice for both Buckingham and for the people, now asks it for herself. She accuses Wolsey of being her "foe, and . . . not / At all a friend to truth" (II.iv.81-82); Wolsey denies her accusation. It is impossible to remain completely neutral, and we tend to believe Katherine, especially since the two walking gentlemen have also blamed Wolsey for Katherine's present situation. After Katherine has left, however, Henry completely (and surprisingly) exonerates Wolsey and accuses Wolsey's enemies of having incensed the queen. (Both Henry and Wolsey handily skirt the issue of whether or not Katherine might be upset by the injustice, rather than the instigator, of the trial.) Whom do we believe? After Henry's peremptory opening comment, his veiled injunction to the cardinals, and his denial of Wolsey's influence—to say nothing of his aside at the end of the trial—we may justly wonder whether he is really dominated by Wolsey or whether he merely uses Wolsey for his own ends.

At the trial Henry offers a touching history of his prick of conscience, carefully marked off as the official version by "Then mark th' inducement: thus it came; give heed to't" (II.iv.167); he stresses his concern for religious rectititude and the national effects of his lack of a male heir. Such a state reason might be readily acceptable, although Shakespeare certainly saw—and exploited, in Katherine's references to her daughter and in the Old Lady's comic equivocations in V.i—the additional irony in the sex of Anne's gift to the English monarchy. Yet Henry proceeds to cast doubt on his sincerity by insisting that if they but find the marriage lawful he will gladly spend the rest of his life with Katherine. Henry has remained silent during the trial itself; his "Go thy ways Kate" speech of praise occurs only after Katherine has swept indignantly out of the court—that is, when no one remains to contradict him. In view of his relations with Anne and the fact that, barring the judges, everyone seems to see Katherine's dismissal as inevitable (because Henry has hinted that it is his "pleasure"?), Henry's protest rings a bit hollow. Within ten lines, Henry indicates in an aside that his private plans contradict those purveyed for public consumption:

> *King.* [Aside] I may perceive
> These cardinals trifle with me: I abhor
> The dilatory sloth and tricks of Rome.
> My learn'd and well-beloved servant Cranmer
> Prithee return; with thy approach, I know
> My comfort comes along. Break up the court;
> I say set on.
> (II.iv.233-39)

Henry is impatient, frustrated by his failure to receive immediately the verdict he obviously plans to obtain by any means. Most critics gloss over this speech because they wish to see Henry as a good man and, at least potentially, a model ruler. They place the blame for the obvious injustice done to Katherine squarely on Wolsey's shoulders and thereby salvage Henry's moral character: the most Henry can be accused of is "honest simplicity."[11] Yet Shakespeare has chosen to complicate Henry's position—and any easy political or historical interpretation of the play—with a jarring personal statement which closes an important scene. Moreover, Henry's speech is not a glaring inconsistency, best ignored or noted only as support for the dubious view that *Henry VIII* focuses on the defeat of Catholicism and the rise of Protestantism. Rather, it is consistent not only with what we have seen of Henry's shifting (and shifty) character and with what Katherine soon says to the cardinals, but also with the whole world of conflicting perspectives and ambiguous motives evident from the first scene.

Untouched by the ambiguity surrounding virtually every character, Katherine adheres to a system of absolute values and finds herself isolated from a world giving only lip service to those values. When she says of the cardinals "They should be good men, their affairs as righteous: / But all hoods make not monks" (III.i.22-23), the common proverb assumes resonance for the entire play: in this court it is almost impossible to determine the "real" man beneath his verbal facade. Declaring that "truth loves open dealing" (III.i.39), she defies both Henry, who tried to suppress rumors of the divorce, and the citizens and courtiers who were afraid to be seen discussing state matters. Her open truth destroys the cardinals' hypocritical assurance of the king's love and the infinity of her "hopes and friends":

> can you think lords,
> That any Englishman dare give me counsel?
> Or be a known friend 'gainst his highness' pleasure
> (Though he be grown so desperate to be honest)
> And live a subject?
>
> (III.i.83-87)

This is a rather bleak picture of an England where double-dealing seems the norm rather than the exception, where the king's "pleasure" may be derived from appetite but is understood as law, and where men hardly dare discuss—much less act upon—matters of national concern. Katherine may be a biased witness—as is everyone in the play except, perhaps the two gentlemen; yet because of her unquestioned goodness, her insistence on absolute values and her earlier disinterested love of justice, we trust her judgment more than, say Wolsey's. Her analysis sums up our glimpse of the darker side of this gilded world: Buckingham's plight when the king condemned him before his trial; the "view of earthly glory" where "no discerner / Durst wag his tongue in censure." It will have additional reverberations in Cranmer's trial. Katherine no longer blames Wolsey for her fate; on the contrary, Henry's ultimate responsibility is now assumed: "Heaven is above all yet; there sits a judge / That no king can corrupt" (III.i.100-01).

When Campeius suggests that Katherine commit her cause to the "king's protection," her answer strikes at the sincerity of Henry's professions of love as well as his concern with justice:

> Would you have me
> (If you have any justice, any pity,
> if ye be anything but churchmen's habits)
> Put my sick cause into his hands that hates me?

> Alas, 'has banish'd me his bed already,
> His love, too long ago
>
> (III.i.115-20)

Wolsey tells Katherine that she wanders "from the good we aim at," as indeed she does. Her idea of "good" is based on immutable values while the "good" aimed at in this world is governed by terrestrial expediency. She accuses them of duplicity and associates their personal hypocrisy with the more extensive—and insidious—moral corruption which pervades England: "Would I had never trod this English earth, / Or felt the flatteries that grown upon it: / Ye have angels' faces, but heaven knows your hearts" (III.i.143-45). Yet while Katherine may defy this world and refuse to accept its rules, she cannot change its nature; the other characters (at least until they fall) accept it, just as the two gentlemen accept Buckingham's fate, the divorce from Katherine, Henry's "conscience," and Anne's rise. Shakespeare vividly presents the personal cost—in pride and affection as well as in life itself—of history's march, but he refuses to simplify for the sake of plot either the public and political arena, with its untidy tangle of private and national issues, or the essential mystery in the human hearts which initiated those momentous historical events.

Wolsey's fall from power and the long-sought triumph of the discontented nobility shift our focus but deepen rather than resolve our questions about Henry and his court. We are told that Wolsey's intercepted letter to the Pope has incensed the king, though Wolsey's estimation of his sovereign's position is clearly quite accurate: "My king is tangled in affection to / A creature of the queen's, Lady Anne Bullen" (III.ii.35-36). While Henry's ire at Wolsey's interference and presumption of authority is perhaps justified by the threat Wolsey presents to England and its autonomy, this is not the first instance of Henry's reluctance to have the truth about himself known. Matters become even more confused when, five lines after we hear of the king's displeasure, we learn that Henry is already married to Anne. Almost immediately, Henry himself admits his tarnished moral position when he jocularly taunts Wolsey just before revealing his full anger: he chides Wolsey for being a bad manager of his earthly affairs and adds "sure in that / I deem you an ill husband, and am glad / To have you therein my companion" (III.ii.141-43). Wolsey claims that he has endeavored to match his performance to his professions, and the king replies: "'tis a king of good deed to say well, / And yet words are no deeds" (III.ii.153-54). We may justly wonder at the extent of conscious irony in Henry's righteous maxim, for Henry himself certainly offers occasions to doubt his credibility. Katherine condemned the English court for just such a divorce between word and deed, appearance and intent.

We are more certain of Wolsey's guilt than that of others accused, for he confesses the truth of some of the charges (II.ii.130ff.; III.ii.210ff); yet he too refuses publicly to acknowledge what he will in private admit. With the nobles he continues to maintain his innocence—and to sound remarkably like Buckingham, Katherine, Cranmer, and Henry himself: "So much fairer / And spotless shall mine innocence arise, / When the king knows my truth" (III.ii.300-02). Such is the shifting political world which most characters accept and to which they adapt with varying degrees of proficiency.

When Wolsey's private posture of righteousness drops he, like Katherine, discovers new truths in his fall from power. His "Vain pomp and glory of this world" speech reflects his recognition of different, transcendent values. This rejection of false worldly pomp and power as both physically and morally dangerous both echoes Anne's explicit fears in II.iii and recalls the more insidious revelation in I.i of the hollowness of the verbal and material flitter at Andren. Both the length and centrality of this scene indicate the importance of Wolsey's moral regeneration and movement toward Katherine's final calm transcendence of the political world. As a prologue to Anne's coronation, Wolsey's final speeches must affect our view of at least the procession itself. Then too, immediately following Anne's pageant Shakespeare offers us Katherine's private meditation and vision. The play begins to move on two levels: the public glory, now presented rather than reported, is surrounded by powerful scenes of private disillusionment and rejection. Temporal authority and pomp are insistently, visually, set before us, but Wolsey's and Katherine's adherence to higher, contradictory values frames and challenges the absolute worth of that tangible attraction.

Within the pageant scene, the conversation between the gentlemen presenter-figures bridges the emotional as well as political gap between the private and public spheres, the falling and rising stars. They too frame this scene of splendor with reminders of the harsh political realities upon which that worldly success so precariously rests. They immediately mention the contrast in national feeling on the present occasion and that on which they last met, Buckingham's journey from his trial to execution; they briefly remind us of Katherine's fate and the nobles' accession to positions of state power. The political whirligig is heavily emphasized, for when we see Anne and the new favorites march past the gentlemen repeat their observation.[12] 2 Gent. accepts, albeit somewhat cynically, the king's motive in casting off Katherine for Anne—"I cannot blame his conscience" (IV.i.47); Henry is excused as a man not a king, on the basis of Anne's angelic physical beauty, not on grounds of justice. It is perhaps the second gentleman's recognition of the fact that justice does not generally prevail in this world which prompts his answer to 1 Gent.'s wonder at the splendor and high social position of those in the procession:

> *1 Gent.* . . . and all the rest are countesses
> *2 Gent.* Their coronets say so. These are stars indeed—
> And sometimes falling ones.
> *1 Gent.* No more of that.
> (IV.i.53-55)[13]

The play on "falling" emphasizes the ambiguities and dangers inherent in political maneuverings, even in a time of "general joy." The procession passes, and the viewers immediately mention a potential breach in this apparent harmony, the enmity between Gardiner and Cranmer. Moreover, Anne's fate just three years after her coronation was too well-known not to lend an additional irony to her moment of triumph. These facts, together with the ominous *double entendre* and the framing reminders of Katherine's and Wolsey's fates (IV.i.24ff.,95), allow us to savor Anne's royal success and at the same time recognize the inevitable brevity of such glory.

Again, Shakespeare has made this "double view" possible by compressing the time lapse between actual events. Historically, Buckingham may have been executed nine years before Wolsey's death and Wolsey's death may have occurred three years before Anne's coronation, but within the play the individual rise and fall cycles are so rapid that the bystanders have a hard time keeping track—witness 3 Gent.'s difficulty in remembering that York-place is called Whitehall (IV.i.95ff.).

The pattern of falls seems broken with Cranmer's trial, usually seen as Henry's first independent royal act: an intervention in his role as Mercy to ensure true justice which "exemplifies the virtuous exercise of royal authority and dramatizes the final commitment of the King."[14] Can we make such clear distinctions when we see this episode within the structure of the entire play? It is preceded by four acts exposing ambiguity of motive, glaring disparity between public statements and private confessions, and a good deal of confusion, not just in our sympathies, but in our very ability to determine exactly that "truth" by which we are to form those sympathies. Although Cranmer is pardoned where others have been condemned, the form of "justice" he receives bears a strong resemblance to the political manipulation we have observed elsewhere in the play.

Act V opens with Gardiner's heated complaints about Cranmer to Lovell and the discovery of Cranmer's forthcoming trial. Lovell, less excitable and more politically observant, warns Gardiner that "Th' archbishop / Is the king's hand and tongue, and who dare speak / One syllable against him?" (V.i.37–39). Nothing has changed; the advice recalls Norfolk's to Buckingham in I.i., and we know the folly of questioning the king's "pleasure." What was implicit in Buckingham's trial, and made explicit by Katherine about her own, seems to be a constant in the politic court world. The verdict Henry gives may be different in Cranmer's case, but the principle, recognized by all, remains the same.

Henry himself says that in order to obtain justice for all concerned Cranmer must be committed to the Tower, "else no witness / Would come against you" (V.i.107–08). Yet, Henry, convinced by Cranmer's tears, gives Cranmer the royal ring which invalidates the court's power to commit him. Henry then castigates the judges and commands amity between both parties. In order to enforce his will Henry has Cranmer sit by him and then taunts the court: "now let me see the proudest / He, that dares most, but wag his finger at thee" (V.ii.164–65). Even granting Gardiner's spite, Henry's action stifles any legitimate grievance against Cranmer. Through the application of varying degrees of political pressure, Henry violates justice in each of the three trials.

I do not wish to strain a point beyond the bounds of credibility. Certainly we are made to feel that the impetus behind the complaints against Cranmer is personal antipathy and, moreover, that the lords' boorish treatment of Cranmer justifies Henry's reprimand. Yet we are also aware of a certain consistency in Henry's methods of administering justice. Henry tells Cranmer that he need not fear because "Thy truth and thy integrity is rooted / In us thy friend" (V.i.114–15). We can only agree: favored by Henry, you need fear neither your accusers not the courts; when the king is displeased, "truth and integrity," as Katherine discovered, are of no avail.

Cranmer, echoing Katherine's own attitude, protests that "The good I stand on is my truth and honesty. . . . I fear nothing / What can be said against me" (V.i.122, 125–26). Henry corrects Cranmer's naivete. As master of the political maneuvering on which his world is based, Henry understands that power, not integrity, governs life and death. (Consider the fear of even the frown of the powerful which constantly recurs in the play.) He warns Cranmer that his enemies are great men and that

> their practices
> Must bear the same proportion, and not ever
> The justice and the truth o' th' question carries
> The due o' th' verdict with it: at what ease
> Might corrupt minds procure knaves as corrupt
> To swear against you? such things have been done.
> (V.i.128–33)

Indeed. If Henry's advice recalls Buckingham's trial, it also reminds us of Katherine's recent charges against Henry himself. If men will lie and swear 'tis truth, neither certain knowledge nor earthly justice is possible. Henry himself pointedly draws the religious implications of the noble's animosity; far from being an ideal world, this is one in which "truth and integrity" have always been persecuted:

> Ween you of better luck,
> I mean in perjur'd witness, than your master,
> Whose minister you are, whiles here he liv'd
> Upon this naughty earth.
> (V.i.135–38)

Henry understands this "naughty earth" and is himself master of its methods. Such mastery may be the result of study, but to view *Henry VIII* as the education of a model king is perversely to ignore the king's character and his acceptance, and exploitation, of fallen men's vices and passions.[15] My analysis has offered a corrective, and therefore one-sided, view of Henry's characterization; I have stressed that side which seems to reflect the political statesman *par excellence* who is the rightful king of this world. If this view of Henry is not the only provided, it is certainly an important one and can be ignored only at great cost to a complete interpretation of the play. I wish not to deny that favorable views are given of Henry, but only to point out that those views are not allowed to stand unchallenged within the play. Certainly, Henry is repeatedly blessed, even by those he has helped to run, and there are some grounds for believing Henry to be naively lacking in self-knowledge and subject to Wolsey's control during the first half of the play. Thus despite the ambiguity surrounding his motives, Henry's actions are associated more than once with the will of heaven: for instance, when he is arrested with Buckingham, Abergavenny says "The will of Heaven be done, and the king's pleasure / By me obey'd" (I.i.215-16). It is unclear, however, whether Henry's "pleasure" is seen as a direct expression of heaven's will or whether any earthly occurrence is, in a broad sense, "the will of Heaven"; perhaps, as is more explicit in the cases of Katherine and Wolsey, the repentance and self-knowledge which accompany worldly ruin are always heaven's goal, irrespective of the moral nature of the temporal act which produces them.

The disturbing characterization of Henry and the political world he dominates may also be contradicted—or resolved—by the paradisal future predicted in the concluding scene. Heavily biblical in language and reference, Cranmer's inspired prophecy applies a visionary description of a golden age to the world of England under Elizabeth and James I. To accept Cranmer's vision of an earthly paradise as Shakespeare's praise of Elizabeth and James is also to accept its implicit progressive view of history, where a benevolent god provides the instrument (Elizabeth) for accomplishing the perfection of human existence. Yet even within the dramatic fiction of the play, the prophecy appears disjunctive rather than as the climactic revelation of a providential pattern in the events we have witnessed. The preceding play seems predicated on the assumption that merely superficial changes thinly mask repetitive life-cycles which are created and perpetuated by what in any Christian scheme would be understood as the nature of fallen man.

This cyclic emphasis, while most obvious in the rise of one person in and through the fall of another, is a pervasive element throughout *Henry VIII*. Seasonal and horticultural imagery, implying a natural and immutable pattern of growth and decay, spans the play: from the prophesied breach of the peace with France which, dormant earlier, is now "budded out" (I.i.94), through Katherine's comparison of herself with the dying lily of the field (III.i.151-53) and Wolsey's grand soliloquy on the state of man (III.ii.352ff.), to Gardiner's images of the unnatural termination of organic growth (V.i.20-23, 52-53). We have already noticed other references to this sense of repetition in human affairs in Anne's coronation procession and in the two gentlemen's comments on it. In addition, Buckingham feels caught in a pattern established with his father's betrayal by a trusted servant (II.i.105ff.), and the sense of impersonal but immutable recurrence is also projected forward through the audience's knowledge of the fate awaiting Cranmer, Anne, Cromwell, and the briefly mentioned Thomas More. Such suggestions of the cyclic nature of man's life are consonant with what we are shown of this very terrestrial political world; as 3 Gent. remarks when Gardiner's hatred for the "virtuous Cranmer" is mentioned. "However, *yet* there is no great breach; *when* it comes. . . ." (IV.i.106, italics mine). In this world such antagonism—and its consequence—seems inevitable.

Shakespeare was obviously well aware that the political world bears little resemblance to the promised land, and *Henry VIII* repeatedly emphasizes this distinction. All the principal characters come to realize that these worlds are not in practice compatible, that one must give up the "vain pomp and glory" to gain "the still and quiet conscience" (III.ii.365, 380). Justice in this world is provisional and expedient, a fact for which Henry is not blamed but of which he is well aware (V.i.128-38). Truth and equity are of incidental importance to the mechanisms of statecraft, and Buckingham, Wolsey, and Katherine all meet the fate which historically awaits Cranmer, Anne, and Cromwell. Wolsey advises Cromwell to lead a virtuous life, for "Corruption wins not more than honesty" (III.ii.444); yet it is fairer to say that it wins neither more nor less, for, whatever disparity may exist in their heavenly rewards, Katherine and Wolsey meet the same temporal fate. One's only hope for mercy (that quality which Buckingham erroneously thought he might receive from the king's hand) or justice (anticipated in Katherine's vision but denied her by Henry's court) lies in heaven. Self-discoveries, too, can be attained only by turning one's back on the fallible, impersonal operation of courtly reward and punishment. The one "truth" the play unequivocally teaches is that one cannot trust to the props of this world—not servants, friends, lovers, or monarchs; everyone except Henry, unchallenged master of the political world, must one day say with Wolsey: "Farewell / The hopes of court, my hopes in heaven do dwell" (III.ii.458-59).

In this sublunar world sickness prevails from the very beginning, where the physical illness which kept Buckingham away from the vale of Andren becomes a metaphor for the sickness of his temporal hopes. Disease imagery recurs in the discussion of French fashions and, more importantly, in the accusations which precede the "falls." To some extent, such imagery qualifies the visual splendor of courtly dance and pageantry; it reaches its most explicit expression in Wolsey's final meditations. The sickness which permeates the court is in fact the moral corruption produced by worldly ambition; Wolsey thanks the destroyer of those proud expectations for his unintentional "cure":

> The king has cur'd me,
> I humbly thank his grace; and from these shoulders,
> These ruin'd pillars, out of pity taken
> A load would sink a navy, too much honour.
> O 'tis a burden Cromwell, 'tis a burden
> Too heavy for a man that hopes for heaven.
> (III.ii.380–85)

Wolsey has gained self-knowledge and peace, and it is for this discovery of spiritual riches in the midst of temporal disaster that Wolsey actually blesses the king a few lines later.

Wolsey's words to Cromwell also integrate two common image clusters to suggest a new and more somber significance for the opulence which adorns the court. The splendid costumes and titles which mark the favored have been repeatedly described as burdens proudly borne: the "madams" at the Field of the Cloth of Gold "did almost sweat to bear / The pride upon them" (I.i.24–25); the Old Lady taunts Anne about becoming a duchess, "Have you limbs / to bear that load of title?" (II.iii.38–39); and Anne is described as laden with "all the royal makings of a queen" at her coronation (IV.i.87-90). Wolsey's imagery draws together these ideas and links the metaphoric burden of honor and pomp with the "sickness" which has barred his soul from heaven; in returning all his earthly goods, he gives the physical as well as the metaphoric weight back to Henry and hopes that be keeping only "My robe, / And my integrity to heaven" he can successfully free his thoughts for that higher world. Although Wolsey is cured of his spiritual disease, both he and Katherine mysteriously sicken and die. This illness is not moral, but rather a disinclination to be burdened with existence itself in a world which no longer holds meaning for the unambitious. As Katherine tells Griffith, she is "sick to death" and her "legs like loaden branches bow to th' earth, / Willing to leave their burthen" (IV.ii.1–3).

Given the disillusionment with the political world which accompanies the access of self-knowledge and remorse, re-integration of the transformed individual into society appears impossible. While a number of critics grant that in the first four acts *Henry VIII* continues the earlier histories' exploration of the nature of governance and justice, they wish to view both the conversions of the main figures and Cranmer's vision of a perfected sublunar world as restorations closely tied to those of the late romances. That concern with reconciliation and regeneration, they argue, Shakespeare now develops into a final transcendence of the Machiavellian world of history—either unsuccessfully, by superimposing an essentially escapist Christian myth of providential design on the recalcitrant facts of Henry's reign,[16] or triumphantly, by compelling belief both in the acquisition of "fortitude of soul" in the court and in the emergence of Henry as a Prospero-figure who "intervene[s] in events involving others . . . as high-priest, beneficent controller" and "representative of benevolent powers acting upon others."[17] Yet the conversions and reconciliations in *Henry VIII* are different in kind from those which characterize the late romances. Society cannot be renewed when the necessary spiritual conversions remain external to it. In *Henry VIII* the redeemed individuals die, executed at society's command or as outcasts rejecting a world incompatible with their spiritual health; in either case, they are replaced (with the possible exception of Cranmer) by ambitious worldlings unaffected by those private discoveries.

Among defenders of *Henry VIII* Clifford Leech alone refrains from attempting to create an encompassing unity which offers mythic resolution of all discordant elements. In a brilliant analysis of the effect of dramatic structure on the experience of time in the late plays, Leech discusses Shakespeare's efforts to fuse impressions of the cyclic ebb and flow of Fortune's domain, history, and the cause and effect sequence of unique conflict whose conclusion appears unalterable and hence aesthetically satisfying, resolved at some point outside fortune's power.[18] The conclusion of *The Tempest* balances a sense of resolution and triumph against the suggestion that in returning to Milan Prospero re-enters the world of flux to become Fortune's subject again; *Henry VIII* tips the scales toward that sense of uncompleted events beyond the scope of the play's dramatization. Despite the fact that the play ends with Elizabeth's christening and Cranmer's apocalyptic prophecy, for Leech the dominant impression is one of cyclic process: "Nothing is finally decided here, the pattern of future events being foreshadowed as essentially a repetition of what is here presented."[19]

Certainly Shakespeare's analysis of the political world's muddled truths, intrigue, and dubiety, and of the human nature which accepts that world, remains too essentially realistic and compelling to be negated by one final version of earthly harmony. When Cranmer foresees that "all the virtues that attend the good, / Shall still be doubled on her [Elizabeth]," we cannot but recall the fate of Katherine's goodness; when Cranmer says that "Truth shall nurse her," we cannot forget our experience of a world in which it is almost impossible to determine the "truth" of even simple, purportedly factual, statements. Rather than dismiss the final scene as escapist fantasy, egregious flattery, or a botched attempt to resolve the private and public tensions which generate the play's historical events, I prefer to view the conclusion a another experiment in providing a suggestion of resolution and finality to counterpoint the sense of fruitless repetition. Instead of attempting with Cranmer's visionary resolution to eclipse and supplant the expectations and mood of the preceding play, Shakespeare emphasizes the total dissimilarity between the England we have seen and the "future" England described. Cranmer prophesies a world which pointedly corrects every moral fault which we have seen exemplified in Henry and the court he dominates; our attention is shifted from the contingent, ambiguous world we inhabit to an idealized one in which truth can be known and justice meted out. This conscious shift in planes of perception contributes to a larger resolution, didactic as well as aesthetic.

Shakespeare offers, in the form of an ideal, a solution to the political world's sickness and corruption and an escape from the endless repetitions of history. His paean to Elizabeth and James I cannot be confined to literally "true" predictions of their actual reigns (already belied by the sublunar world of the original audience), or designed merely to feed nostalgic memories of

Elizabeth and satisfy the reigning monarch's taste for flattery. Rather, this praise fulfills the didactic function of panegyric in the Renaissance: idealized portraits which heighten the subject's exemplary traits in order to incite emulation.[20] In "Of Praise" Bacon states that "Some praises come of good wishes and respects, which is a form due in civility to kings and great persons, *laudando praecipere*, when by telling men what they are, they represent to them what they should be";[21] and Erasmus and Guazzo also "make it clear that praise can be counsel, not flattery, and is fitting for an address to great persons."[22]

Such a consciously didactic use of theatrical compliment is most closely associated with Ben Jonson's development of the court masque; indeed, in self-defense Jonson explicitly states his theory of praise:

> Though I confesse (as every Muse hath err'd,
> And mine not least) I have too oft preferr'd
> Men past their termes, and prais'd some names too much
> But 'twas with purpose to have made them such.[23]

The magical metamorphosis originated in the monarch-spectator's view of himself "transfigured by the virtues he ought to possess, the justice he ought to exercise, the magnanimity that should ennoble the "realm"; and this "mirror for magistrates" aspect for the performance was equally important for the rest of the audience, since their own wonder and admiration created a "frame of mind uniquely favorable to the absorption of all the virtues appropriate to them as loyal subjects."[24]

That *Henry VIII* is neither a masque nor a specific royal commission may be granted. Yet if R.A. Foakes is correct in thinking it inspired by the Princess Elizabeth's marriage and perhaps originally intended for court performance, both the superficial flattery and its larger didactic purpose would have been appropriate.[25] With the conventional disclaimer that he speaks truth not flattery, Cranmer specifically states that the Elizabeth he describes is "A pattern to all princes living with her (V.iv.22), and he proceeds to endow her—and her successor—with all the approved royal virtues.[26] The creation of an idealized royal mirror cannot be confined to masques alone, though the circumstances of royal commission and, occasionally, royal actors may make it most suitable to that form. Eugene Waith postulates a corresponding interest in exemplary images of heroic politics in the similarly static and formal heroic drama, such as *El Cid* and Dryden's *The Conquest of Granada*.[27] While direct address to the monarch may not be essential to the desired identification of royal spectator with idealized ruler, *Henry VIII* nearly duplicates the effect of the masque's direct address by, as it were, stopping the action while everyone, on stage and off, is held spellbound by the "wonders" of Cranmer's verbal portrait.

The masque-like elements, and their suggestion of a "golden world," offered by the play's dances and pageants have been noted by many critics. For me, the formal ceremonies and wondrous narrations in the first part of the play provide embodiments of an ideal society more tantalizing than real: the dance at Wolsey's banquet carries the seeds of Katherine's ruin; the glorious processions mark falls as well as rises. Our hopes for paradisal harmony are repeatedly dashed when the stately celebrations prove external shows merely gilding untransformed human hearts; by supplying the transformation so conspicuously absent in the play, Cranmer's prophecy gains the power to move us with wonder and admiration. The "golden world" of Cranmer's vision exists *in potentia* only. As an apocalyptic realization of all men's desires under the aegis of a good and wise monarch, it remains a goal, outside the historical world which must radically alter before it can grasp the transcendental values expressed in the vision. Precisely because it is metaphorically as well as literally "visionary," we can accept and believe the prophecy's perfection of men and language; the words which have echoed irritatingly throughout the play—"virtue," "truth," "honor"—seem no longer ironic but suddenly restored to full dignity by the image of a world in which they would be simple statements of fact.

In a brilliant triumph over chronological limitations, Cranmer, inspired with a glimpse of a future perfection, eulogizes the actual reigning monarch and figures forth the virtues which distinguish his subjects. The hopes of the fictional world of 1533 face the realities of 1613, with the result that Cranmer's prediction is endowed with an effect of prayer rather than statement. The biblical language which supports this effect and successfully distances the vision from the play's political world, also defines it as the consummation of the private, religious aspect of the play—Wolsey's final dedication to God and truth and Katherine's dream of a supra-mundane reward for virtue. The division between the temporal, physical world of expedience and history and the a-temporal realm of immutable values and spiritual fulfillment is thus finally transcended. If the physical embodiment of heaven on earth in Katherine's dream only emphasized the utter incompatibility of those realms, Cranmer's "dream" bodies forth in words a hope, a prayer, for real union, the final metamorphosis of one into a fleshly reflection of the other. At the same time, the sense in which Cranmer describes things hoped for, and prays for what he "sees," allows his words to bridge the division between prediction and history's fulfillment of that prediction without compromise or falsification.

Firmly rooted in the language of earlier, private, self-discoveries, Cranmer's prophecy offers an aesthetic rather than a logical sense of resolution and finality. By limning in the ideal king (and his realm) a shining example to the man endowed proleptically, it is hoped, with his virtues, it aspires to transform the public world in its image. The fact that this resolution is an ideal and not a dramatized reality demonstrates Shakespeare's lack of senile optimism; here the cost of the brave new world—even the mundane Protestant and political one—is greater than in any late romance, even *The Winter's Tale*. Though rapt before the ideal, we remember the "contemporary" political world's claustrophobia, its refusal of either pastoral alternative or temporary retreat from the insistent demand for submission. The "wonders" of *Henry VIII* are limited to a glimpse of what a transformed England, under an inspired monarch, might be. The vision is hortatory and must explode the play's framework to create a world where humanity's endless, profitless cycle of rise and fall can be translated into the more miraculous image of the death and rebirth of "the maiden phoenix."

NOTES

1. Cyrus Hoy, "The Shares of Fletcher and his Collaborators in the Beaumont and Fletcher Canon (VII)," SB, 15 (1962), 76. Thomas Clayton, in a review of Schoenbaum's *Internal Evidence and Elizabethan Dramatic Authorship*, ably questions the conclusive nature of Hoy's evidence for retaining even a limited portion of the play as Fletcher's. I believe that *Henry VIII* is in all important respects (e.g., the final "falls," Cranmer's prophecy) Shakespeare's, but if I may present Clayton's rhetorical question to Hoy as a statement, I am willing to let the matter rest here: "*Henry VIII* is a play by Shakespeare in which Fletcher possibly had a collaborator's hand of uncertain extent and touch" (*ShakS*, 4 [1968], 359).

2. This view of *Henry VIII* as "a Christian history play" is Howard Felperin's in "Shakespeare's *Henry VIII*: History as Myth," SEL, 6 (1966), 242.
3. H. M. Richmond rightly finds exciting the possibility that *Henry VIII* bridges the gap between "the English and Roman history plays and the worlds of the last romances." I am less sure that "it alone seems to illustrate in plausible historical terms the application of the spirit in which *The Tempest* was written to the actual events of the English sixteenth century," or that Henry emerges as a wise, mature monarch. All quotations taken from "Shakespeare's Henry VIII: Romance Redeemed by History," *ShakS*, 4 (1968), 336.
4. Paul Bertram, *Shakespeare and the Two Noble Kinsmen*, New Brunswick, N.J., 1965, p. 163.
5. Richmond, p. 342. Richmond goes on to liken Henry to "those potentially good but frequently misguided Shakespearean figures like Angelo, Othello, Lear and Anthony."
6. Ronald Berman, "*King Henry the Eighth*: History and Romance," *ES*, 48 (1967), 114.
7. Richmond, p. 338.
8. R. A. Foakes, "Introduction" to the Arden edition of *King Henry VIII* (1957, with corrections in 1964; rpt. London, 1968), p. xlvii. All quotations from the play are taken from this edition.
9. According to Thomas Lorkin's letter to Sir Thomas Puckering, on June 29, 1613, the Globe Theatre burned to the ground while "Bou^r^bege his companie were acting at ye Globe the play of Hen: 8." In a letter on the same catastrophe from Sir Henry Wotton to his nephew, the reference is to the King's Players' "new Play called *All is True*." This evidence, together with the repetitions of "true" in the Prologue and the likelihood of such a subtitle in reference to Rowley's recently revived play on the reign of Henry VIII, *When You See Me You Know Me*, indicates that *Henry VIII* might indeed have had the alternate title *All is True*. Foakes prints these letters (and additional evidence) in "Appendix I" of his Arden edition, pp. 179-80.
10. Felperin sees Norfolk's speech as mere "specious artifice" in which "precious diction" and "hyperbolic figures" mark the violation of a religious ideal (p. 234).
11. G. Wilson Knight, *The Crown of Life*, 1947; rpt. New York, 1966, p. 310; see also Foakes' introduction, pp. xlix-l, and Richmond, p. 345.
12. An interpretation of the play's splendor as an expression of perfection, a kind of translation of Cranmer's final prophecy into visual terms, negates the "double view" I try to demonstrate. For example, Ronald Berman finds the walking gentlemen's emphasis on the changes within the political hierarchy irrelevant to the golden world portrayed in the masque: "It is of course ceremonial, but more than that, it suggests a kind of massive allegory. The persons involved are for the moment liberated from their individuality. They are not human protagonists at all, but part of a vision of the beauty of form and artifice" (p. 113).
13. I here assign the speeches in accordance with F3, as do most modern editors, rather than with the Arden edition which follows W.S. Walker

(*A Critical Examination of the Text of Shakespeare,* 3 vols., 1860). I find 2 Gent. generally more politically aware—and cynical—than his interlocutors, and hence I think the first half of line 55 more appropriate for him.

14. Bertram, p.173. See also Foakes, pp. liii-liv; Richmond, pp. 346-47; Felperin, p. 242; and Frank Kermode, "What is Shakespeare's *Henry VIII* About?" in *DUJ*, 40 (1948), 53.
15. To hold, with G. Wilson Knight, that Henry's "dubious sincerity" is to be taken with "an amused tolerance" and that his "rough integrity [is] paradoxically the more convincing for his ill-concealed insincerity" (p. 309), is to explain away rather than integrate a prominent feature of this monarch. Mr. Knight's phraseology is perhaps without parallel, but essentially the same point is made by almost every other critic of the play.
16. Felperin concludes that *Henry VIII* "winds up as an escape from the realm of fact into another realm of myth, with a loss of imaginative intensity in the process" and that this final embrace of "traditional answers" cannot successfully whitewash an age "too littered with corpses and haunted by ghosts for it to have been anything but brazen" (p. 245).
17. Foakes, p. lxiii. Richmond, too, sees *Henry VIII* as transposing "the high dignity and mercifulness" of the late romances into an overtly historical cycle" which both illustrates an evolution historical and moral and "mitigate[s] the sour dichotomy between moral and political distinction" which lent such an ominous tone to Shakespeare's earlier histories (p. 348). More sensitive to the distinctions between moral levels in the play, Ronald Berman discusses the constant switching between the historical world of will and passion and the idealized golden court of the masque; he concludes that the mythical content of the masque finally redeems historical reality because the dance, rather than the individual expendable dancers, is made the symbolic center of the play's meaning (pp. 115-18).
18. Clifford Leech, "The Structure of the Last Plays," ShS, 11 (1958), 19-30.
19. Ibid., p. 29.
20. O. B. Hardison, Jr., *The Enduring Monument: A Study of the Idea of Praise in Renaissance Literary Theory and Practice,* Chapel Hill, 1962, esp. pp. 30-57. Hardison's discussions of Renaissance theories of elegy, of poems of praise such as Jonson's "To Penshurst," and of exemplary biographies such as the *Cyropaedia,* are all relevant to Shakespeare's idealization of his living and dead monarchs.
21. Francis Bacon, "Of Praise," *The Essays of Francis Bacon,* ed. Mary Augusta Scott, New York, 1908, p. 242.
22. E. W. Talbert, from a discussion of the tradition of public spectacles behind Jonson's masques in "The Interpretation of Jonson's Courtly Spectacles," PMLA, 61 (1946), 458. In *Ben Jonson and the Language of Prose Comedy,* Jonas Barish felicitously describes the function of masque as "a kind of mimetic magic on a sophisticated level, the attempt to secure social health and tranquility for the realm by miming it in front of its chief figure. The frequency of prayer as a rhetorical mode in the masques is hence not accidental," 1960; rpt. New York, 1970, p.244. See also Allan H.

Gilbert, "The Function of the Masques in *Cynthia's Revels*,' *PQ*, 22 (1943), 213-14.

23. An Epistle to Master Ion Selden," ll. 19-22, in *Ben Jonson*, ed. C. H. Herford, Percy and Evelyn Simpson, Oxford, 1947, VIII, 159. See also Jonson's preface to *Hymenaei* (1606), ibid., VII, 209.
24. Barish, p. 244. See also Dolora Cunningham, "The Jonsonian Masque as a Literary Form," *ELH*, 22 (1955), 108–24, and Stephen Orgel, *The Jonsonian Masque*, Cambridge, Mass., 1965.
25. Foakes' arguments appear on pp. xxx-xxxv of his introduction.
26. It is worth noting that Queen Elizabeth, presented with a similarly flattering portrait at Warwick in 1572, graciously acknowledged her acceptance of its intent: "I now thank you for putting me in mynd of my duety, and that should be in me" (from *The Progresses and Public Processions of Queen Elizabeth*, ed. J. Nichols; quoted in Talbert's article, p. 457).
27. Eugene M. Waith, in "Spectacles of State" (*SEL*, 13 [1973], 317-30), states that the accomplishment of this kind of entertainment is "to facilitate movement into and out of the fictional world, in the hope that its ideals may stick, so to speak, on the real persons" (p. 323). Waith's remark about Dryden's complimentary dedications is also pertinent to Shakespeare's use of the concluding eulogy in *Henry VIII*: a compliment to the work's putative inspiration is more than just a way to patronage; it serves as "the promulgation of a fiction which draws the dedicatee into the heroic world of the play" (p. 328).

F. W. Brownlow

From *Two Shakespearian Sequences:* Henry VI *to* Richard II *and* Pericles *to* Timon of Athens[1]

Henry VIII and *The Tempest* are both spectacular plays, but in other respects they are opposites. The Tempest is brief, spare, classically constructed; *Henry VIII* is a long, dramatic pageant, treating successive incidents in the style of a chronicle play. The plot of *The Tempest* is Shakespeare's own invention, a pure poetic fiction; *Henry VIII*'s plot is taken directly from historical materials which Shakespeare follows very closely. The plays' heroes are opposites, too.

Prospero, judged by really worldly standards, is a failure. He is like one of those gamblers who work out infallible systems of wagering or investing. In their imaginations everything works perfectly, but at the moment of action nerve fails or some hidden flaw is revealed, and dreams of fortune fade. The flaw in Prospero's scheme is that his "rough magic" cannot coerce nature beyond a certain point. It can bring Antonio, Sebastian and Alonso to the island, but it cannot change Antonio's heart against his will, nor can it make Prospero into a man of action. Whatever he had imagined himself doing to his enemies, his failure to do it puts him in the company of Richard II, Brutus and Hamlet, each of whom by a moment's yielding to sympathy sealed his own doom. Prospero's future in Milan is a very dubious one.

Henry VIII on the other hand is one of history's successes. Any politician who changes the ownership of more than half his country's land, and gets away with it, is a success. Henry's revolution, carried through with ruthless violence, still marks the English landscape, its evidences never more interesting than when his new order stands closely juxtaposed to the old which it displaced. At Fountains, the ruined monastery lies a few hundred yards downstream from the lay proprietor's house,

Reprinted from *Two Shakespearian Sequences:* Henry VI *to* Richard II *and* Pericles *to* Timon of Athens, by F. W. Brownlow, by permission of Macmillan, London and Basingstoke (1977).

built in 1611 in hayseed Renaissance style, and the two buildings make a contrast that Shakespeare, the poet and dramatist of contrasts, would have relished.

Just such an implicit contrast lies between the heroes of *The Tempest* and *Henry VIII.* Henry's world is a poetic version of the Milan to which Prospero returns, his England the poet's counterstatement to Prospero's island. Prospero rules a little world of his own making, a world of foregone conclusions, complete in itself, out of the normal currents of time and change, enjoying no future. Henry, however, rules and shapes an inherited England in a time of sudden portentous change, and his play is laden with a feeling of future events. *Henry VIII*, then, is a poetic as well as a chronological sequel to *The Tempest*.

The idea that the two plays are related by the very contrast between their forms, themes, subjects and characters is only surprising because somehow the tradition of criticism has taught us that in his later years Shakespeare ceased to surprise. The deeply entrenched notion that *The Tempest* is his last and consciously testamentary play has so bedevilled criticism of *Henry VIII* that despite its continual success in the theatre the play has been for most of its critics something to be explained away. *Henry VIII*'s actuality, its cool truthfulness—in a word, its worldliness—have always been incompatible with the Romantic version of Shakespeare's last years as a time of retired, semi-religious contemplation.

To explain the worldliness of Henry VIII, the Romantic critics brought in the hypothesis of mixed authorship. If, after stylistic analysis, it should prove that the objectionable parts of the play were by someone other than Shakespeare, then the appearance of the Romantics' idol was saved. The most popular candidate has been John Fletcher, a dramatist long considered the Noel Coward of the Jacobean theatre; and this attribution is related to another debunking hypothesis, which is that the real explanation of Shakespeare's career, when we get down to brass tacks, is the series of theatres he wrote for and the audiences who attended them. Thus one recent historian gives a lively, though not very charming, picture of Shakespeare sitting down with his business associates at the time they leased the Blackfriars Theatre to discuss what kind of play would best "go" in the new house. This, we are told, was the real cause of the later plays coming out as they did—a theory that would be more convincing had the partners arrived in limousines and swapped cigars.[2]

Neither the theory of mixed authorship nor that of a calculated appeal to public taste affects the real questions about *Henry VIII*. Collaboration does not itself affect the integrity of a work, nor does an artist's wish to please an audience. Just because Shakespeare, like most artists, had a practical grasp of business affairs, there is no reason to talk about him as if he were a huckster. The answer to such theories is in the basic fact that makes them possible, which is that Shakespeare's career spans with such marvellous neatness the vicissitudes of theatres and companies. Like J.S. Bach, he used the opportunities that came to him. It was part of his genius to be able to do so, and it puts the cart before the horse to say that instead of using, he was used.

More recently several critics have defended the play's integrity, both of authorship and design, against the older view that it is at best a commonplace, at worst an offensive popular "show," a kind of Jacobean *Cavalcade*. The older view takes the play much as it stands, as a medley of events, requiring of its audience no finer emotion than sentimental nationalism, no subtler political thought than the government is always right. The defenders' case turns upon the demonstration that *Henry VIII* is a dramatic and poetic whole, and the proof, generally speaking, takes two forms. First, the play's form is compared to the tragi-comedies', with which it has much in common. Beginning darkly, it ends with the prophecy of a glorious future, the play's whole action showing the gradual emergence of Henry as true King of a new, united England. Second, this action is shown to embody the teachings of contemporary political doctrine. According to one interpreter, for instance, the play is like a political morality, in which the King finally acts the part of Mercy when he saves Cranmer.[3]

This school of interpretation is a welcome development, a sign of a return to the text as we have it from the First Folio. Unfortunately, it has the effect of defending Shakespeare's aesthetic values in a way that does little credit to his moral or political sense. Hardin Craig, for instance, explains the play's rambling form by saying that a history play need have no clear form because only God's Providence can shape history.[4] Translated into practical English and applied to *Henry VIII*, however, this means that Shakespeare was a totalitarian. After all, the actual cause of Buckingham's, Katherine's and Wolsey's falls, as of Cranmer's rise, is the King. One might wish to say that in some sense eluding either his or our knowledge, Henry is an agency of Providence; but good taste, not to mention stronger considerations, should rule out an identification of Henry and Providence. Nonetheless:

> If God alone is stable, he has a kind of high-priest on earth, in the person of Henry. . . . When he administers the law himself, justice as of heaven operates. . . . Once the power of Rome is quelled in England, the King assumes his rightful dominance, and Cranmer symbolically kneeling to Henry, demonstrates the true idea of a protestant kingdom.[5]

There were undoubtedly some Tudor subjects prepared to say as much as this. There were also others who carried their refusal to say anything of the kind as far as the block and the gallows. Did the author of *King John* and *Richard II* really end up as a kind of Jacobean Eisenstein, glorying in the megalomania of the new regime and the helplessness of its victims? If *Henry VIII* is really the play its scholarly defenders say it is, then at the end of his career Shakespeare turned his intelligence and his humanity over to the state; the poet who questioned the moral basis of existence had no questions to put to the King:

> If his treatment of Katherine leaves a feeling of uneasiness in the modern mind, it is largely Henry's character, as fixed by history, rather than by the play to which this is due . . . there is no question of a morally false equation between her downfall and Wolsey's. He is abandoned by God, she suffers only the loss of a husband.[6]

These are high regions where the loss of a husband is as nothing to the loss of God. Besides, if Henry is God's high-priest on earth, then Katherine loses God as well as her husband and there is indeed an equation, morally false or not, between the two falls, and the dramatist, not "history," is responsible. But the critic's eye is not on the object before him. Just as *Henry VIII* has nothing to say about quelling Rome's power or about the true idea of a Protestant kingdom, so it says nothing about God's abandoning Wolsey. One the contrary, both the dramatist and his source see in Wolsey's fall an act of divine grace that saves his soul:

His overthrow heap'd happiness upon him;
For then, and not till then, he felt himself
And found the blessedness of being little;
And, to add greater honours to his age
Than man could give him, he died fearing God.
(IV.ii.64-68)

The average reader, given the choice, would no doubt rather read *Henry VIII* as a prototype of *Cavalcade* than of *Ivan the Terrible.* Aesthetic unity is not so important an artistic virtue that ordinary decency as well as the play's text have to be sacrificed to it. There is however a third way out, offering an escape from an unpleasant choice. Neither the play's attackers nor its defenders have much to say about the irony which provides a continual, running commentary on its action and which, once perceived, alters its whole aspect. Nor is there anything hidden or esoteric about it. Like all irony it works on the assumption that we will take certain implicit contrasts, such as that between *The Tempest* and *Henry VIII*, for granted and that, duly prepared, we will take a hint.

Henry VIII brings us closer than any other play to Shakespeare's sense of his own times. It does not make covert allusions by analogy and figure or settle great questions with a myth. Shakespeare is here writing about the England his parents and grandparents knew, about the events that decided the quality of his own times, that may even have influenced his own life. He is writing moreover with the expertise of a lifetime's work as poet and dramatist. He is the master of subtleties of construction and tone that no other writer can approach. He will need all his skill, too, for as the subtitle announces, he has set himself an extraordinarily difficult task. *All is True*: what kind of title is that for a poet's invention? Sidney defended poets against the charge of lying by saying that since the essence of poetry lay in the art of making fictions, no poet pretended to tell the truth; the truth of poetry lay in its imitative relationship to real life and character. Shakespeare's tragi-comedies, perhaps consciously and intentionally, exemplify Sidney's doctrine. His earlier histories seem to belong to a genre outside Sidney's scope, but even in them Shakespeare found a way of so mingling history and fiction that, whatever conclusions his audience might reach, he was himself left largely uncommitted.

All is True, however, is a challenge and a boast. While it would certainly draw in the customers, it would also make Shakespeare liable, in the minds of thoughtful spectators, not just for his facts (always allowing for the compression enforced by dramatisation), but for his interpretation of them. At the same time, it challenges the spectators because the sentence "All is true" inevitably suggests that although "all" may be true, it will also be incredible; and, as always, the moral challenge of the incredible is whether one should be amazed or appalled. The object of this boast or challenge was, in addition, the difficult subject of recent English history.

The problem of Shakespeare's subject was ideological because its real theme was the schism with Rome and, with it, a schism in national life between past and present, between Protestant and Roman Catholic, between, in concrete terms, man and man, between descendants and ancestors. Tudor government, persistent nationalism, skilful propaganda and the crude foreign policies of Spain and the Vatican had prevented the English schism from turning into civil war, and had also kept repression to comparatively mild levels. But the threat of a real national division was always present, and no Tudor government could tolerate criticism or even disinterested enquiry, whether in the press, the pulpit or the theatre.

A play like *Henry VIII*, subtitled *All is True*, would not have been allowed in Elizabethan England, but by the time of its production (1613) the earlier anxieties were over and after ten years of James I's rule the atmosphere was a little freer. There was a pro-Spanish peace party at court and in the Church; the persecution of Roman Catholics had quietened down, and the most violent Protestants were (for the time being) under control. Flurries of anxiety could awaken persecution, and the mob could always express dislike of its masters by accusing them of Popery; but on the whole, and especially within range of the court's political and religious atmosphere, there was more toleration. One interesting sign of this, already mentioned,[7] and close to Shakespeare's interests, was the tendency to rehabilitate Richard III. Another was *Henry VIII* itself, with its sympathy towards the government's victims and its persistent irony towards both the government and those who let themselves be drawn within the field of its influence.

Perhaps our times have taught us lessons in political realities that our immediate predecessors, born into a fundamentally civilised and decent world, lacked; yet one does not have to be especially sensitive to political nuance to see the ironies of *Henry VIII*, both the open ones and those more slyly implied. The open irony sets a standard of interpretation, putting a control upon the way we take words, and it begins in the first scene. Buckingham, with one sharp sentence, challenges Norfolk's account of the Field of Cloth of Gold as well as Cardinal Wolsey's part in it:

> What had he
> To do in these fierce vanities?
>
> (I.i.53–54)

His open contempt, as we learn from Norfolk's advice to him, is dangerous; but it has the effect of immediately setting forth a case, not just against the Cardinal, but also against the state he serves. It later appears that Norfolk shares Buckingham's opinion, his enthusiasm for the splendours of the two kings' meeting not affecting his assessment of its political result which "not values the cost that did conclude it" (l. 88). But he is a cautious man, and his reply to Buckingham's downright attack on Wolsey (whom he calls a "keech," i.e., a lump of suet) is a smooth sarcasm, the first explicit piece of irony in the play:

> Surely, Sir,
> There's in him stuff that puts him to these ends;
> For, being not propp'd by ancestry, whose grace
> Chalks successors their way, nor call'd upon
> For high feats done to th' crown; neither allied
> To eminent assistants; but spider-like
> Out of his self-drawing web, he gives us note
> The force of his own merit makes his way—
> A gift that heaven gives for him, which buys
> A place next to the King.
>
> (I.i. 57–66)

This cunning, intense rhetoric hints at much unspoken fear as well as contempt, and it is characteristic of *Henry VIII*'s irony in that it grows to a climax of open sarcasm in the last lines, implying that Wolsey has corrupted heaven as well as the commonwealth. In this play Shakespeare often makes an irony explicit by means of such a sting in the tail.

Norfolk's cautious speech also introduces a more covert form of irony, depending upon euphemism or intentional vagueness for its effect. He warns Buckingham that his quarrel with Wolsey has been noticed by "the state," a word which may signify a body like the Privy Council, but which in the context more probably refers to Henry himself. Norfolk then tells Buckingham that Wolsey's hatred "wants not a minister in his power," and this also, upon reflection, can only mean Henry. The first hint suggests that the King, acting independently, has observed the quarrel; the second suggests that the Cardinal has Henry in his pocket, and this equivocation raises the most important question in the play's first part: does the Cardinal rule Henry or not?

This first scene's atmosphere of ironic suggestion demands the closest attention of the audience, whose participation as a kind of mute chorus to the play is as necessary to the success of *Henry VIII* as to that of *The Winter's Tale* or *Cymbeline*. The scene prepares the audience, or rehearses it, for its understanding role in the play to come; its irony is expressed with a lightness that shows us how much Shakespeare came to rely upon his audience's responsiveness, knowing that on the day they would be there following him.[8]

The court scene that follows shows political lies in the making. In its first part Wolsey, forced by Queen Katherine's appeal to the King to remit an unjust taxation, instructs his secretary to announce that the remission came through his intercession. In the second part the false witness of the Duke of Buckingham's surveyor begins his master's end. The formal arrangement is important. In both parts Henry and Wolsey act as a pair, with the emphasis on Wolsey in the first part, on the King in the second. In both parts Queen Katherine advocates the truth. This balancing of roles shows that the notion of Henry's early dependence upon Wolsey exists more in the critics' imaginations than in the play, where Henry is his own man from the start. At first he operates through his ministers. At the play's end, in the vacuum left by Wolsey's fall, when the Council begins to show too much independence, he puts out his own authority undisguised when he protects Cranmer.

The scene also makes it clear that Divine Providence and royal justice are not the same thing. If anyone speaks for truth it is Katherine, who checks Wolsey—"My learn'd Lord Cardinal, / Deliver all with charity" (I.ii.142-43)—and tries to discredit the false witness. At the scene's end, when Wolsey and Henry are intent upon Buckingham's destruction, her cry "God mend all!"

is more than a sentimental interjection. Henry's final speech exposes his injustice plainly enough:

> If he may
> Find mercy in the law, 'tis his; if none,
> Let him not seek't of us. By day and night,
> He's traitor to the height.
> (ll. 211-14)

This is a grim, cruel joke because mercy, which is part of the King's prerogative, is not to be found in the law. One can go further and say that to anyone with a normal sensitivity to hypocrisy Henry's reply to Katherine's complaint about taxation carries no conviction:

> Taxation!
> Wherein? and what taxation? My Lord Cardinal
> You that are blam'd for it alike with us,
> Know you of this taxation?
> (ll. 37-40)

Wolsey's extremely tactful reply says that others are responsible besides himself, but also implies through its vagueness that he only did what he was told to do:

> Please you, sir,
> I know but of a single part in aught
> Pertains to th' state; and front but in that file
> Where others tell steps with me.
> (ll. 40-43)

There is an element of suppressed comedy in the smooth performance of King and Cardinal as each of them shifts the blame of an unpopular act and angles for the credit of revoking it. Wolsey's order that Katherine's intervention be kept secret typifies the fate of truth at this court.

Buckingham's downfall exposes completely the league between King and Cardinal as well as Katherine's isolation. Here lies the connecting link between the opening scenes and the divorce scenes. In proceeding directly from Buckingham's death to the royal divorce, Shakespeare passes over more than a decade and makes a connection, implicitly causal, explicitly moral, between the two misfortunes. Katherine's outspokenness somehow leads to her downfall and that in turn causes Wolsey's fall in which he, and we, discover plainly the King's service is not God's.

We first hear of an impending divorce between Henry and Katherine when two gentlemen, in the scene of Buckingham's death, speak of it as a machination of the Cardinal's "out of malice to the good Queen" (II.i.157). This is repeated in the next scene when Norfolk says that Wolsey, wishing to hit at the Emperor Charles, has dived into the King's soul and wrung his conscience over his marriage to his deceased brother's wife (II.ii.24-37). At the trial, however, when Katherine accuses the Cardinal of having "blown this coal," Henry relieves Wolsey of all responsibility. His story (II.iv.167-206) is that his "conscience first receiv'd a tenderness" during a conference with the Bishop of Bayonne.

There are, then, two theories current explaining the origin of the divorce. Either the King's conscience grew tender all by itself or else Wolsey irritated it; or, to take a third way out, agreeable to the Cardinal's and the King's habit of appearing to act in concert, they both had the same idea simultaneously, if for different reasons. There is no mystery about Wolsey's part in the divorce, since Shakespeare has shown the Queen's antagonism to him. The King's motive is the problem, both as a matter of historical fact and of practical dramaturgy, and Shakespeare's treatment of it is continuously and subtly ironic. First, he employs a mute irony of inference. For instance, he shows Henry flirting with Anne Boleyn before there is any mention of divorce (I.iv); and his constant hinting at Henry's independence bears fruit in the divorce scene where the King's exculpation of Wolsey (II.iv.155-209), which at first seems like a royal favour, proves in the end to be the first stage in Henry's dismissal of Wolsey. Second, Shakespeare uses explicit verbal irony to put the King's talk of conscience in doubt.

Shakespeare's irony in fact centres on "conscience," beginning with a comment aside by the Duke of Suffolk upon the official story of the King's motive:

Chamberlain. It seems the marriage with his brother's wife
Has crept too near his conscience.
Suffolk. [Aside] No, his conscience
Has crept too near another lady.
(II.ii.17-19)

There are the makings here of an obscene *double entendre* on the word, but before it appears in its full force there is a most significant little scene when Henry, professing to be about his "private meditations" (II.ii.66), rebukes the nobles for interrupting him but immediately welcomes the two Cardinals, Wolsey in particular, as "the quiet of my wounded conscience." There is a bitter irony here because the nobles, who do not altogether understand what is going on, have a more Christian care of the King than do the Cardinals. They stand by, watching, as Henry, having welcomed Campeggio, says to Wolsey:

> My good Lord, have great care
> I be not found a talker.

Many think that this instruction means only that Wolsey is to see that the visitor is well entertained. But since the whole point of the scene is that the Cardinals have arrived to put through the divorce, it is more likely to mean that Henry is giving more important instructions: "Now that I have come so far, you must see this thing through." This explains Wolsey's reply:

> Sir, you cannot.
> I would your grace would give us but an hour
> Of private conference.

It is however characteristic of this political play that a statement can be so completely ambiguous. The talk that follows, about "the voice of Christendom," "this just and learned priest," and so forth (ll. 86-98) is pure state fiction; and in case anyone should miss the point Shakespeare includes a conversation between the Cardinals about Wolsey's treatment of one Doctor Pace who, it seems, had shown more independence than prudence. "He was a fool," says Wolsey, "for he would needs be virtuous":

> Learn this, brother,
> We live not to be grip'd by meaner persons.

"Brother" is beautifully placed there. But the real bite follows, one of those stings in the tail of a speech or scene already mentioned, when Shakespeare, having disposed of the Cardinals' Christianity, similarly disposes of the King's conscience:

O, my lord,
Would it not grieve an able man to leave
So sweet a bedfellow? But, conscience, conscience!
O, 'tis a tender place; and I must leave her.

This has the true canting ring to it, since "able" also means sexually able, and "conscience," described as a "tender place," begins to sound like obscene slang.

In the next scene (II.iii) Anne Boleyn and an old lady discuss the Queen's misfortune. "By my troth and maidenhead," says Anne, "I would not be a queen." To this the old woman, reminiscent of Emilia in *Othello*, replies, "I would, / And venture maidenhead for't; and so would you":

. . . which gifts,
Saving your mincing, the capacity
Of your soft cheveril conscience would receive
If you might please to stretch it.
(II.iii.30-33)

After this, it would be too obvious to have anyone mention the "prick of conscience," yet in the next scene the phrase appears, suitably muted and cushioned from sounding too coarse an irony:

My conscience first receiv'd a tenderness,
Scruple, and prick . . .
(II.iv.170-71)

If one compares this line with its original in Holinshed, "a certain scrupulosity that pricked my conscience,"[9] one sees the mischievousness of Shakespeare's alteration. He has turned the innocuous verb "pricked" into a suggestion noun, placing it third of a series so that it takes most emphasis; and he has neutralised the perfectly respectable "scruple" by putting it between the dubious pair "tenderness" and "prick."

Meanwhile the scene between Anne and the old lady also has a sting in its tail which deflates Anne's protestations:

Anne. It faints me,
To think what follows.
The Queen is comfortless, and we forgetful
In our long absence. *Pray, do not deliver*
What here you've heard to her.
Old Lady. *What do you think me?*

Wolsey's motive is power, and he over-reaches himself, for in ridding the court of Katherine he brings into it, along with Anne Boleyn, Cranmer and his Protestants. Henry's motive is partly, if not fundamentally, sexual; and he also over-reaches himself because, as everyone who watched the play knew, Anne Boleyn turned out more sexual than he bargained for. As the play moves towards its specifically pre-Elizabethan material, its ironies are not so explicit. But there is one climactic moment of ironic revelation that throws its dubious light retrospectively and prospectively over the play's story when Henry finally abandons all pretence of legality and piety and decides to govern his own kingdom in his own way:

King. (Aside) I may perceive
These Cardinals trifle with me; I abhor
This dilatory sloth and tricks of Rome.
My learn'd and well-beloved servant, Cranmer,
Prithee, return.
(II.iv.235-40)

Naturally, the speech is spoken aside, since history does not preserve such moments for us; we can only infer them from the record.

This moment of revelation is also the moment of Protestantism's inception in England. There have always been Clotens in the audience who miss the point, and cheer the name of Cranmer and hiss the name of Rome; but Shakespeare is saying, as plainly as he could in 1613, that his England came into being because of Henry VIII's unmastered passion for a young woman.

As the reward for honesty and plain-speaking Buckingham and Katherine receive, one a beheading, the other divorce and abandonment. The fortitude and patience of their deaths shows the courage of their lives. Considered as dramatic characters, they undergo no last-minute discovery, no sudden reversal of belief or understanding. They are open to criticism therefore on the ground that since the essence of drama is conflict, the final scenes of their lives are undramatic. The drama, though, is in the counterpointing of their fall with others' rise. The opposition of Queen Katherine's "crowning" by the Spirits of Peace just before her death to the great show of Queen Anne's state crowning is bound to make one reflect upon the "fierce vanity" of the latter. It makes visible the distinction made from the play's opening scene onward between divine justice and state justice. The same is true of Wolsey's fall, opposed as it is to Cranmer's rise.

In misfortune Wolsey shows courage and dignity, as when he replies to the nobles (III.ii.203-372). They, when it is safe to do so, turn on him just as they abandon Katherine (III.ii.41-71). Although Wolsey's repentance in misfortune follows a familiar pattern, Shakespeare was following his sources in treating it as he did. The Cardinal's most famous words, explicitly separating the service due God and the King, are almost a direct quotation from Cavendish's *Life of Wolsey*:

> Had I but serv'd my God with half the zeal
> I serv'd my King, He would not in mine age
> Have left me naked to mine enemies.
> (III.ii.455-57)

An old tradition gives to a man's last words the credit of truth, and in Wolsey's speeches after his fall even the word "conscience" is rehabilitated. It occurs in a passage praising Thomas More; the lines are almost a prayer and, in the circumstances, rather chilling:

> May he continue
> Long in his Highness' favour, and do justice
> For truth's sake and his conscience, that his bones,
> When he has run his course and sleeps in blessings,
> May have a tomb of orphans' tears wept on 'em!
> (III.ii.395-99)

("Run his course" is a liturgical phrase, still to be found in the *Book of Common Prayer* at the last Collect of the service for consecrating a bishop: "that, faithfully fulfilling his course, at the latter day he may receive the crown of righteousness.") Wolsey's advice to Cromwell, that he should serve the King's faithfully, without ambition, is also portentous; not only did Cromwell come to the block, but he neglected his master's advice against ambition, thoughts that come to mind when we hear of his great advancement (IV.i.109, V.i.33). Unless Shakespeare intended to remind the audience of further deaths beyond the scope of *Henry VIII*, there would be no purpose in these references. There is also a foreboding of Anne's Boleyn's death (V.i.22).

Most important, Katherine, hearing of Wolsey's death, forgives him. At the beginning of this scene (IV.ii), the most finely written in the play, Katherine is still tangled in the loyalties of life and the world. Although she forgives Wolsey and sympathises with his suffering, she cannot forget the evils of his life:

> i' th' presence
> He would say untruths; and be ever double
> Both in his words and meaning. He was never,
> But where he meant to ruin, pitiful.
> (IV.ii.37-40)

Wolsey's doubleness is a quality of the world itself which Shakespeare has imitated in the characteristic irony of this play, and even Katherine is touched by it since her forgiveness is mingled with censure. Complete forgiveness of Wolsey immediately follows when Katherine's servant Griffith undertakes "to speak his good":

> This Cardinal,
> Though from an humble stock, undoubtedly
> Was fashion'd to much honour from his cradle.
> He was a scholar, and a ripe and good one;
> Exceeding wise, fair-spoken, and persuading;
> Lofty and sour to them that lov'd him not,
> But to those men that sought him, sweet as summer.
> And though he were unsatisfied in getting,
> Which was a sin, yet in bestowing, madam,
> He was most princely: ever witness for him
> Those twins of learning that he rais'd in you,
> Ipswich and Oxford! one of which fell with him,
> Unwilling to outlive the good that did it;
> The other, though unfinish'd, yet so famous,
> So excellent in art, and still so rising,
> That Christendom shall ever speak his virtue.

This disinterested speech, plain and declarative, gives like Prospero's epilogue, an effect of literal actuality. Katherine calls it "religious truth and modesty," and it leads her to meditate upon "celestial harmony." There follows the vision of the Spirits of Peace. Their white robes symbolise purity and salvation, their garlands of bays symbolise lasting honour on earth, and their garlands of palm symbolise eternal triumph and honour. In saluting Katherine they recognize her to be one of themselves. As she tells Griffith, their dance invites her "to a banquet," and the garland they hold over her promises "eternal happiness." In comparison with the vision music is "harsh and heavy."

Not much is said about this vision. One could I suppose take it as an example of the tribute vice so readily pays to defeated virtue, interpreting it as a pretty, generous and effective way of dismissing Katherine and her failure from the stage in order to prepare for a splendid welcome to the future. The trouble is that this quite gratuitous vision introduces an order of reality different from anything else in this very secular play. It says unequivocally that Katherine is to die blessed, and that the vision of blessedness turns secular affairs into unreality. Does the suppressed—or repressed—meaning underlying the play's irony condense here into literal statement? Are the defeats triumphs, the triumphs defeats?

In their deaths Cardinal and Queen draw together, and charity supersedes judgement in an order not of this world, where ambiguity rules to the end. The King's vindication of Cranmer (V.iii.130–47) recalls his earlier vindication of Wolsey. His reception of the news that he is the father of a girl is decidedly ambiguous (V.ii.158–70). Every technique, certainly, is employed to make the play's end as boisterous, as popular, as glorious as possible, but even here there is irony. Shakespeare, having required the subtlest participation of his audience, now casts them (V.iv) as a rowdy, good-natured London mob come to the christening procession as to any wonderful show:

> Is this Moorfields to muster in? Or have we some
> strange Indian with the great tool come to court, the
> women so besiege us?
>
> (V.iv.33–35)

The inference to be drawn is that crowds at a procession understand the real nature of things no better than groundlings at a theatre, capable of nothing but inexplicable dumb shows and noise. Thus Shakespeare provides both the popular joy and a more intelligent reflection upon it. In the popular mind there is a causal connection between the whole long story of Henry's reign and the birth of the great princess Elizabeth; but in the play, there is no such connection. Like Perdita in *The Winter's Tale,* the infant Elizabeth is a new-found future, wholly herself, the pure gift of Providence. Her England is as little connected with the play's England, or indeed with any England of the historical present, as Perdita's return to Sicily is due to any merit of Leontes'. Elizabeth's birth is sheer grace, akin to forgiveness.

Henry VIII is a remarkable play, a fascinating imitation in dramatic terms of the Gospel precept, "Render unto Caesar the things that are Caesar's, and unto God the things that are God's." Its method is objective, contrapuntal, and ironic. One can, if one wishes, simply take it as a fine show, revelling like London crowds then and now in the ceremonies of state; that pleasure, as far as it goes, is proper and well-justified. But if one takes the play's irony, then somehow one's unreflective pleasure needs to accommodate the knowledge that between the ceremony of the state and the ceremony of the soul there is no simple or necessary correspondence.

Indeed, the real critical question to be finally answered is whether the action of *Henry VIII* reconciles the state and the soul or not. Conventional criticism tells us that this play was meant to make its audience happy, to congratulate them upon being Englishmen; but the play's prologue tells each spectator that he must make up his own mind:

Those that can pity, here
May (if they think it well) let fall a tear;
The subject will deserve it. Such as give
Their money out of hope they may believe
May here find truth too. Those that come to see
Only a show or two, and so agree
The play may pass, if they be still and willing,
I'll undertake may see away their shilling
Richly in two short hours. Only they
That come to hear a merry bawdy play,
A noise of targets, or to see a fellow
In a long motley coat guarded with yellow
Will be deceiv'd. . . .
Therefore, for goodness' sake, and as you are known

The first and happiest hearers of the town,
Be sad, as we would make ye.

As a prologue to a play about Henry VIII, this is surprisingly detached. Some pointedly Shakespearean words (pity, belief, hope, truth) are so used as to tell certain spectators what kind of reception the author would like his play to have. But apart from dissociating his play from such vulgarities as Rowley's Henry VIII play, *When You See Me, You Know Me,* and defining the general tone as "sad," i.e., solemn, the author is cautious and tolerant. He gives his verbs "pity" and "believe" no objects, and puts nearly all his other verbs in the subjunctive. It is for the individual spectator to decide whether he weeps, pities, believes, finds truth or not. Like several scenes in the play, however, the prologue has a sting at the end:

And, if you can be merry then, I'll say
A man may weep upon his wedding-day.

This seems to dismiss a rather solemn prologue with a joke, but the mood is still subjunctive, and the joke is on the spectators, many of whom did of course take the play cheerfully. That being so, the implied response follows: a man *therefore* may (might as well?) weep at his wedding. True enough, if people were more reflective they would weep more at weddings, especially if they knew what led up to them and where they in turn would lead; but if they were really reflective, there would be no weeping at all because the initial mistake would not have been made, of taking things like *Henry VIII* cheerfully. "People," says the tramp in *Waiting for Godot*, "are bloody ignorant apes," and a similar thought, if less astringently put, could have been in Shakespeare's mind as he finished the prologue to *Henry VIII.*

Play and prologue alike exemplify a markedly Shakespearean attitude to words. The speculative tendency that leads him to pun and quibble endlessly with meanings is here extended by means of irony to the subject of an entire play. The irony of *Henry VIII*, indeed, works very like a quibble. In his verbal punning, especially of the obscene kind, Shakespeare often gives meanings that are not alternate but contrary:

Many a good hanging prevents a bad marriage.
(*Twelfth Night*, I.v.20)

Both meanings of Feste's joke are funny, in fact there are two jokes, and in the end one has to decide which joke one is going to laugh at. So with *Henry VIII*'s irony. One's first impression is of a cool ambivalence that offers, non-committally, alternate readings of history; but the ambivalence, like punning wit, is protective, and there is nothing ambivalent about the ambivalence itself.

NOTES

1. The subtitle [for the chapter: All Is True] is from Sir Henry Wotton's letter of 2 July, 1613 describing the performance of *Henry VIII* which burnt down the Globe Theatre. Quoted in Neilson and Hill, *op. cit.*, p. 903.
2. G. E. Bentley, "Shakespeare and the Blackfriars Theatre," *Shakespeare Survey*, 1 (1948), p. 42: "We can be perfectly sure, then, that from the day of the first proposal that the King's men take over the Blackfriars they had talked among themselves about what they would do with it and had discussed what kinds of plays they would have to have written to exploit it."
3. Frank Kermode, "What is Shakespeare's Henry VIII about?," *Durham University Journal*, n.s. 9 (1948), rptd in W. A. Armstrong (ed.), *Shakespeare's Histories*, Penguin Shakespeare Library, 1972.
4. Hardin Craig, *An Interpretation of Shakespeare*, New York, 1948, p. 357.
5. R. A. Foakes (ed.), *Henry VIII*, London, 1957, pp. lix–x. In his Shakespeare: *The Dark Comedies to the Last Plays*, Charlottesville, Va., 1971, pp. 173–83, Mr. Foakes has toned down the exaggerations of his *New Arden* introduction: "Rule is necessary, but kings, as Henry is an example, have to operate within the limited perspectives of all men" (ibid., p. 180); but he still maintains that the "emergency of Henry as ruler is part of the 'religious truth' of the play, overriding the contradictions, injustices and suffering that recur" (p. 182). Henry's emergency, however, is part of the political, not the religious, truth of the play.
6. Foakes, *Henry VIII*, p. lx.
7. See above, pp. 17–18.
8. Shakespeare's casting of the audience as the crowd in the christening scene (v.iv) is a sign of his confidence that the theatre would be filled to capacity.
9. Holinshed, *Chronicles* (ed. 1587), III, p. 907.

Kristian Smidt

From *Unconformities in Shakespeare's History Plays*

Probably a majority of critics have seen *Henry VIII* as a play separated not only in time but in kind from the early histories. It is certainly different, but not because of the amount of pageantry it contains, as is often asserted, nor because of its use of mythic elements, Christian or pagan, nor because of its alleged looseness of plot.[1] *Henry VIII* is unlike Shakespeare's English history plays of the 1590s because of its new approach to the treatment of character.

The pageantry is there, and the prologue apparently draws attention to it:

> Those that come to see
> Only a show or two, and so agree
> The play may pass, if they be still and willing,
> I'll undertake may see away their shilling,
> Richly in two short hours.

The citizens, we are told in the beginning of Act IV, "have shown at full their royal minds" by celebrating the coronation of Anne "with shows, / pageants and sights of honour." There is contemporary testimony, too, as to the magnificence with which the play was presented, thanks paradoxically to the fire which destroyed the Globe on that fateful midsummer afternoon in 1613. Sir Henry Wotton, describing the fire in a letter to Sir Edmund Bacon, has this to say of the spectacle he saw before it broke out:

> The Kings Players had a new Play called *All is True*, representing some principal pieces of the Reign of Henry 8. which was set forth with many extraordinary circumstances of Pomp and Majesty,

> even to the matting of the stage; the Knights of the Order, with their Georges and Garter, the Guards with their embroidered Coasts, and the like: sufficient in truth within a while to make greatness very familiar, if not ridiculous.

We must distinguish between dramatic and theatrical features, however. Sir Henry's sarcasm in that last sentence is levelled at the production of the play and does not implicate its essential nature. The ceremonial processions and arrangements that we witness have no structural importance and little thematic significance. They provide no action or information which does not sufficiently emerge from the dialogue, and are in fact spectacular additions to the basic dramatic scenes. Those who went to gape at shows could no doubt see away their shillings and feel richly rewarded without paying too much attention to more sophisticated matters. In an age when court masques had become popular it must have been tempting to transfer some of their attractions to the public theatre, and it was a simple matter to copy a few itemised descriptions of stately processions from Holinshed and use them for stage directions. There are perhaps more great ceremonies in *Henry VIII* than in the early plays, what with the trial of one queen, the coronation of another, and the christening of a princess, plus a formal meeting of the privy council. But there are funerals, coronations, and parliaments in the early plays as well, and Shakespeare, had he been so inclined, could as easily have inserted directions for additional pageantry in them as he did in *Henry VIII*. Indeed, for all we know, a number of dumb shows may have been included in the staging of the early history plays which do not appear in the printed texts, and we have no certain knowledge that Shakespeare himself included the directions for these spectacles in *Henry VIII*. The play is not dependent on them, and the characters are even occasionally impatient of ceremony. King Henry dispenses with the reading of the cardinals' commission from Rome at the beginning of Katherine's trial, and the queen refuses to submit to the impersonal forms of the tribunal. In the light of Katherine's personal dignity we might even be tempted to read a certain irony into Anne's submission to ceremony. It is hard to understand how Irving Ribner can characterise *Henry VIII* as "a patriotic pageant."[2] If we pay any attention to Queen Katherine's complaints of being friendless among enemies, or indeed to the actual state of a country where such men as Buckingham, Norfolk, Suffolk, Surrey, and Sands represent the ruling class, we can hardly find much occasion for patriotic complacency.[3] The patriotism is seriously qualified within the play and the pageantry is extraneous to its main concerns.

Nor are the mythic elements at all conspicuous. They are in fact concentrated in Cranmer's final prophecy of a golden age under Elizabeth and James I, which is briefly anticipated earlier in the play in Suffolk's praise of Anne Bullen (III.ii.50–52). Howard Felperin finds a double pattern of myth, "Tudor and Christian," in *Henry VIII*. The Tudor, or historical, myth is "that of a Tudor golden age emerging under the watchful eye of God from a long ordeal of tyranny and dissension."[4] But that ordeal is not dramatised or even referred to in *Henry VIII*, which has very few links backward to the Plantagenet tetralogies. The ordeals it dramatises are those of individuals, except for Wolsey's rapacious taxation scheme, which is quickly quashed by Henry's intervention. Theological dissensions are kept strictly in the background, and when an individual, Cranmer, is accused of heresy, Henry again personally intervenes to vindicate him. Prophecies of an age of peace and prosperity, it should be remembered, occur at the end of *Richard III* and *Henry V* as well, albeit not as oracularly uttered as in *Henry VIII*. There is little sense of "an overriding philosophy of history, that God directs all" in Shakespeare's last play, in spite of sympathetic interpretations which find it there.[5] As for "the providentially governed patter of worldly fall and Christian conversion," this is not turned into a myth in the sense that it directs the movements of the play. It is true that Wolsey and to some extent Buckingham suffer a "fortunate fall,"[6] but Katherine is in no need of conversion, and Henry needs only to have his eyes opened. Nor does the conversion of the most villainous character of the play, Wolsey, have any consequences for the subsequent action or for any of the other characters except perhaps Cromwell, since Wolsey's pernicious manipulations are continued by Gardiner. As Frederick O. Waage has remarked, "In *Henry VIII* those personal qualities in the principals which would allow them to insure the tranquil continuity of their state emerge only when death is denying them the power to insure that continuity." Waage thinks the play is characterised by "Shakespeare's *inability* to mythologize history," an inability which was caused, as Waage sees it, by the disappointment of millennial expectations on the death of Prince Henry in 1612.[7]

Ronald Berman has suggested the presence of a pagan fertility myth enacted by Henry and Anne, with "Anne and her daughter [. . .] envisaged as Ceres and Proserpina."[8] He might have extended his interpretations to include Katherine and Wolsey, for there is a *death* of nature as well as a rebirth if one is looking for mythic archetypes. But this is a typically modern explication which adds no significance to Shakespeare's treatment of historical persons and events. And in any case it would still have to be mainly based on the last act, with very little support from the central parts of this domestic and political drama.

The looseness of plot has been frequently alleged, and the New Penguin editor, A.R. Humphreys, takes an extreme position: "the play lacks integrated character . . . it is made up of notable episodes laid in sequence rather than generated dynamically one from another."[9] This question of structure used to be commonly seen as an aspect of the problem of authorship, and the more sentimental scenes, like those depicting the good ends of bad or worldly men, were attributed to Fletcher. But as in the case of *1 Henry VI*, an influential body of opinion seems now to have swung in favour of Shakespeare's sole authorship, though it is generally conceded that Fletcher may have contributed a few lines and passages.[10] I am content to leave the arbitrament to others and to take my stand, for the present purpose, with the upholders of Shakespeare's authorial integrity. Which means that if we find divided intentions it does not necessarily indicate divided responsibility. And should it ever be established that *Henry VIII* is the result of composite authorship it will at least not affect our analysis of the play itself.

With this in mind let us consider the complaints that have been made and can be made of the loose plot structure. Irving Ribner reviews the "poorly-connected series of episodes" which, in his opinion, constitute the play:

> It begins with the fall of Buckingham, who is promptly forgotten. Then follow the king's sudden infatuation with Anne Boleyn at a ball given by Wolsey, the trial of Queen Catherine, the sudden fall of Wolsey and the parallel rise of Cranmer. The coronation of Anne Boleyn is presented in great detail. There follows the plot of Gardiner against Cranmer and the Archbishop's absolution by the king, and the play ends with the report of Elizabeth's birth and an elaborate display

> of her christening, at which Archbishop Cranmer officiates as godfather and ends the play with an elaborate prediction of the great age of peace and prosperity which she is one day to bring to England.[11]

R.A. Law gives his support to Ribner, makes a similar enumeration of scenes, and asks rhetorically, "Are not such incidents . . . presented to us primarily because Holinshed also records these events during his long account of King Henry's reign?"[12] It is particularly the last act, and within it the last scene, that of Cranmer's prophecy, which have been found inconsequential, or even incompatible with the rest of the play. In 1850 James Spedding declared that the play "falls away utterly, and leaves us in the last act among persons we scarcely know, and events for which we do not care." Law contends that "This last act destroys all vestige of unity in the drama as a whole," while Waage calls the last scene "an artificial appendage tacked on the end to redeem the somber vision of the play as a whole."[13] Another main structure is "that the characters are inconsistent, that Buckingham, Wolsey, and Katherine become weak at their falls."[14] This may also be seen as an aspect of plot structure, but we will leave it aside for the moment.

It may be easily agreed that the structure is episodic and that the play focuses in turn on such divergent concerns as the destruction of Buckingham, the royal divorce, the unmasking of Wolsey, the vindication of Cranmer, and the birth of Elizabeth. In all these actions different characters successively take the centre of the stage and it is hard to decide where to place the centre of interest. If Henry's divorce and remarriage are the main issue one has to wonder what Buckingham is doing in the first two acts, and there is a major unconformity in his disappearance. If, on the other hand, the machinations and disgrace of Wolsey are mainly in question this would make sense of Buckingham but not of Cranmer. In other words the beginning and ending seem not to belong to the same play. It is certainly true that the last act brings a whole new set of people into prominence.

King Henry, of course, is there all along, but what does he *do* in the play? We do not see him courting Anne except by the briefest of glimpses, or indeed rejecting Katherine except by his silence when she pleads. Nor do we see him facing up to Wolsey openly. In fact we never actually see him overcoming anyone by force or persuasion. He is acted upon but he acts through others, both in toppling Buckingham, securing his divorce, and exposing the cardinal. Only when he steps in to save Cranmer in the fifth act does he become an agent in terms of plot and staging. We do get some information as to his activities by means of narrative and by implication. But even so the impression of his role tends at times to be blurred. And the same is true of Wolsey. Thus in the trial of Katherine there comes a point at the end of Act II when the king exclaims against Wolsey and Campeius for trifling with him: "I abhor / This dilatory sloth and tricks of Rome." Up to that point the cardinals have obviously been more zealous than the king in pursuing the divorce and it is not made at all clear why the roles seem to be suddenly reversed. To add to the uncertainty they are not actually reversed in the sequel to the abortive trial until after the prelates' private interview with the queen, when we learn (in III.ii) that Wolsey has asked the pope to halt the divorce proceedings on account of the king's being "tangled in affection" to Anne Bullen. Another blurring of roles takes place when the lords gather for their final onslaught on the cardinal and find that all they need to do is push home King Henry's attack. They are at once the king's instruments and his substitutes, and their ambiguous status is emphasised by their not having a written commission from the king. Not unnaturally Wolsey accuses them of envy and malice. The hunt is now theirs.

This blurring is an aspect of what is probably the major plot weakness of the play: the lack of adequately dramatic aims and motivation for the behaviour of the principals. It is shown in the ambiguity of the king's reasons for wanting a divorce, but it is mainly noticeable in the behaviour of Wolsey, the chief fomenter of trouble. At the beginning of the play Wolsey is already as powerful as he can ever hope to become in England. His plans to climb to the papacy do not really affect the plot, nor are they revealed till the moment of his disgrace (III.ii.210–13). His action against Buckingham lacks maturation and his action against Katherine is not really directed against her but against her nephew the emperor (II.i.162). Neither Buckingham's fall nor Katherine's serves to advance him. So apart from satisfying his spite it is hard to see what he is after.

The plot, then, is undoubtedly loose in many ways. But strangely enough, and whatever adverse critics may think, it has no remarkable faults or inconsistencies.[15] When expectations are specifically raised and then disappointed they concern relatively unimportant matters, or there are fairly plausible explanations for their not being fulfilled. Thus Buckingham in I.i promises to denounce the cardinal to the king and expose his treason, but since Buckingham is arrested and himself accused of treason before he can reach the king's ear we must assume that he never has a chance to counter-attack. In IV.i. the Third Gentleman expresses confidence that Cranmer "will find a friend will not shrink from him" in Thomas Cromwell if matters come to a head between the archbishop and the Bishop of Winchester, and if we remember these words we are likely to be surprised at the feeble support that Cromwell ventures for his friend at the critical moment in the privy council, actually voting with the others for his arrest. But it has to be left to King Henry, of course, to come to Cranmer's aid. I have mentioned King Henry's impatience with the "dilatory sloth" of the cardinals, whom we find immediately after his petulant outburst busily serving his cause with the queen. Other unfulfilled expectations I doubt if there are. It is worth observing that there is no open conflict between Katherine and Anne and we are nowhere led to expect one. Katherine does not even mention Anne at any time. Shakespeare could obviously have written a play in which such a conflict was featured, but he chose to keep the two women apart and the divorce distinct and separate from the marriage except for a very brief verbal hint (II.ii.17–18), and a vague suggestion through the ordering of scenes, that the king has a double motive for divorce. Katherine and Anne relate to the king and Wolsey, not to each other. Anne on the whole is kept in the background (unless we wish to stress her prominence in the coronation show), but by reasons of state she is closely woven into the causal fabric of the play and by her personal history she is firmly linked in the sequence of events.

Modern audiences no doubt have stock responses to Anne Bullen, and our sentimental romantic interest in her character could hardly have been foreseen by Shakespeare. He wrote a play principally about the fall of Katherine and Wolsey, into which the king's romance with Anne was woven more or less incidentally. Anne has speaking parts in two scenes, both of which represent Shakespeare's additions to the scanty material about her in Holinshed, and she appears as a mute in the coronation procession. But apart from these manifestations she is only the subject of talk and rumour, particularly in the long central scene in which King Henry's secret marriage to her is revealed. This is when Wolsey exclaims:

> There was the weight that pull'd me down, O Cromwell,
> The king has gone beyond me: all my glories
> In that one woman I have lost forever.

Henry VIII is a play of a peculiar nature, and it is possible that the dramatist to some extent thought of Anne as a symbolic figure whose importance would be adequately demonstrated in the magnificence of the coronation scene and indirectly in that of the christening of her daughter Elizabeth (where she is absent). She still seems to have an importance in excess of her part in the play, however, and this impression is largely based on the one relatively long scene entirely of Shakespeare's invention where she is really allowed to speak her mind. In the course of a conversation with a fruity Old Lady she assets that she would not be a queen "for all the riches under heaven." Everything points to her sincerity, but we are never given an opportunity to see it practised or to share in her thoughts and emotions again.

The only difficulty caused by the divided treatment of the two queens is that the lords are made both to grieve at Katherine's misfortune and to rejoice at the happy prospects of her supplanter. There is a contradiction here if one brings their utterances together, but it is a functional contradiction in that it serves to keep our sympathies uncomplicated.

In architectural elevation there may not be anything very imposing in *Henry VIII*. It is no towering edifice, based and buttressed, one substructure resting upon another. But everything is meshed, consequential, and more subtly interrelated than one may suspect at first. The lords' attack on Wolsey merges inextricably, as we have seen, with that of the king. The trial of Buckingham is not merely a display of power on the part of Wolsey but provides a perspective for the king's fears as to what may happen should he die without legitimate issue,[16] and also a point of reference for his warning to Cranmer near the end of the play that justice may be overborne by corruption.[17] The vision of Katherine's heavenly coronation follows upon Anne's earthly coronation. And so one might go on.

The last example is one of those mentioned by Foakes in illustration of the pattern of contrasts and oppositions which governs the play.[18] G. Wilson Knight, to whom Foakes is largely indebted, sees this pattern as a juxtaposition of sombre and light-hearted scenes with thematic overtones of far-reaching import:

> We have accordingly a series of warmly conceived humanistic scenes countering our three falling movements. Those were moralistic, on the pattern of medieval stories of the falls of princes; these are eminently Elizabethan. Effects are deliberately got by juxtaposition, as when Buckingham's execution follows Wolsey's feast and the death of Katherine the coronation of Anne. We attend diversely two views of human existence; the tragic and religious as opposed by the warm, sex-impelled, blood; the eternities of death as against the glow and thrill of incarnate life, of creation. These two themes meet in the person of the King.[19]

Foakes particularly emphasises the trials of Buckingham, Katherine, and Cranmer as keystones in the structure of the play, and includes that of Wolsey to make four:

> The character of these trials which form the groundwork of the plot is at once public, as they affect the state, and personal, as they affect the protagonists. The conflict they present between the public interest and private joy and suffering is indeed at the heart of the play, and all the contrasts already discussed between the neighbouring scenes relate to it.[20]

Both the pageantry and "the numerous scenes of walking lords or gentlemen, who discuss what has happened or is to happen . . . play a vital part in establishing this general conflict," according to Foakes.

All this is no doubt close to the truth. There is a pattern, almost a rhythm, of reversals and contrasts, to some extent dependent on an alternation of sad and humorous scenes. There is an insistence on ceremony and some use of the language of ritual. And there is a general conflict between public and private interests. But Knight is carried away by his own poetic imagination and patriotic eloquence far beyond the facts and qualities of the play itself when he finds everything not only in *Henry VIII* but in all of Shakespeare's work coming to a great climax in Cranmer's prophecy.[21] And Foakes, more sober, yet allows himself to be moved to praise of the wrong things when at the end of his structural analysis, turning from form to theme, he declares:

> This careful organization goes to shape a play radically different from Shakespeare's earlier histories in dealing with peace, and in having for its general theme the promise of a golden future, after trials and sufferings terminating in the attainment of self-knowledge, forgiveness, and reconciliation.[22]

One would like to think the prologue and epilogue as well as the rest of the play were written by Shakespeare. But even if they were by Fletcher or someone else, that someone could hardly have misunderstood the tenor and subject of the play so completely as to speak of woe and pity in the prologue and emphasise the role of Katherine in the epilogue if the general theme was "the promise of a golden future." What Knight and Foakes see as the promise of a golden future are rather, as Lee Bliss has it in one the most lucid and perceptive essays on *Henry VIII* I have come across, an attempt on Shakespeare's part to present an ideal contrast to the England of Henry VIII as Shakespeare actually described it.[23] The praise of Elizabeth and James I "fulfills the didactic function of panegyric in the Renaissance: idealized portraits which heighten the subject's exemplary traits in order to incite emulation."[24]

Knight and Foakes claim too much for this play and too little: too much for the patriotic ritual, too little for the psychology. This is probably because they misinterpret the significance of the pattern. Its interest is not in epic breadth but in moral insight. Where they come closest to recognising this fact is in what they have to say about the spiritual and political development of the king. Some critics seem to think that King Henry starts in almost abject dependence on Wolsey and grows in sense and authority till he is in complete command both of himself and his kingdom. This would make *Henry VIII* a play about the education of a monarch and King Hal another Prince Hal. Wilson Knight, however, whose portrait of Henry is a small masterpiece whatever one may think of his opinion, realized that even at first Henry "is not all under the influence of Wolsey,"[25] and Foakes sees him "as a strong, regal figure, the embodiment of authority," though "initially this authority is subdued under the sway of Wolsey."[26]

Henry develops not from weakness to strength but from being deceived and deluded to becoming clearsighted, and this development is one of the main strands of the action. A good deal of suspense is made to hang on the question: how long will the king continue to be taken in by the cardinal and how will he react when he is undeceived? There is a parallel development on the external, political level from his having a papist counsellor, queen, and heir[27] to his having a quasi-protestant counselor, queen, and heir. This movement in the play points naturally enough onward to Cranmer's vision of the reigns of Elizabeth and James. But to emphasise it too strongly would mean to see Katherine as an undesirable encumbrance at best and an evil influence at worst, one whom the king happily gets rid of along with Wolsey, whereas in fact she is depicted as a very saintly Catholic.

There is a vision and perspective nevertheless, provided we are not put off by the strangeness of the good king and the good queen appearing on opposites of a conflict. The double standard that this division implies is actually the key to the central mystery of Henry VIII. For Shakespeare in his last play staked his all on the knowledge that he had fitfully acquired and taught throughout his career as a dramatist, that which had gone into the making of a Bolingbroke, a Shylock, a Macbeth, a Cleopatra, a Lear, a Leontes, even a Caliban: the knowledge that goodness and badness in most human beings are relative to the point of view and that it is humanity which rises and falls and rises again with its individuals.[28] So Henry is a good man when judged by his own standards and a good king when judged by his subjects but an ungrateful and cruel husband when judged by his wife and queen.[29] He is independent enough in exercising authority but not, at first, in knowing how and when to delegate it. In this respect he is the opposite of the Henry VI of the *Contention* plays, who is clearsighted enough but incapable of exerting his authority. His flirtation with Anne while still married to Katherine is not allowed to damage his character in the opinion of his subjects, but it adds a touch of ambivalence to his moral standing in the totality of the play.

Wolsey, the consummate hypocrite, the Tartuffe of Renaissance politics, has few redeeming qualities. But it is this most unlikely person who is selected for the explicit demonstration of Shakespeare's moral theme. In the conversation between Katherine, herself about to die, and her gentleman usher, Griffith, in IV.ii, Wolsey's epitaph is spoken in two contrary and juxtaposed character sketches first by Katherine, summing up all the bad qualities we have seen in evidence, then by Griffith, not denying his faults but reminding Katherine and us that

> From his cradle
> He was a scholar, and a ripe and good one,
> Exceeding wise, fair-spoken and persuading:
> Lofty and sour to them that lov'd him not,
> But to those men that sought him, sweet as summer.
> And though he were unsatisfied in getting
> (Which was a sin) yet in bestowing, madam,
> He was most princely:
> (IV.ii.50–57)

Griffith calls to witness the colleges founded by Wolsey at Ipswich and Oxford and concludes by speaking of the cardinal's good end:

> His overthrow heap'd happiness upon him,
> For then, and not till then, he felt himself,
> And found the blessedness of being little;
> And to add greater honours to his age
> Than man could give him, he died fearing God.
> (ll.64–68)

This speech has the effect of making Katherine wish for an equally unbiased obituary for herself by "such an honest chronicler as Griffith." The conversation is also designed to show that for all her loyalty and patience, Katherine is not free from baser feelings of bitterness and hatred. Even in death, we see shortly afterwards, she has human failings. Her pride, which has been so admirable, flares up in a last moment of anger with the messenger who hurries in unceremoniously to announce the presence of Capuchius.

Shakespeare's historical characters were not given to sudden conversions in the early plays. In the case of Wolsey there was Holinshed's authority for his conversion, and Shakespeare in his late maturity was obviously disposed to give prominence to openings for grace. But in the early histories, too, men and women at the point of death were often made to speak with an insight and sometimes with a charity they did not possess before. Thus both Hastings and Buckingham in *Richard*

III blame only themselves for their misfortune and recognise the justice of God in the punishment which overtakes them, and the Yorkist butchers Edward and Clarence are both allowed to die in a spirit of religious humility. There is nothing quite so extraordinary, then, in the pious deaths of Buckingham and Wolsey as some critics maintain, nor are any of the characters inconsistently drawn merely because they are seen from different angles.

There *is* a case for inconsistency, as I have demonstrated in detail in my introductory chapter, in the portrayal of Buckingham during his last journey from Westminster to the Tower (II.i.55–136). He first declares to Sir Thomas Lovell that he forgives everybody, but immediately afterwards, speaking to Sir Nicholas Vaux, utters a curse against his "base accusers, / That never knew what truth meant." Since it is hard to see what Shakespeare could have intended by making the duke so contradict himself, I am inclined to think, not that Shakespeare nodded but that one of the speeches was an afterthought and that the other should have been deleted if the author had been firm enough or his editors observant enough. It seems likely, too, that the first speech, that addressed to Lovell, was the original one, being closest to Holinshed, and that it should have been replaced by the second speech, the one addressed to Vaux. This would mean that Buckingham is less humble and forgiving in his last moments than some would like to think. What cannot be denied if nothing is omitted in the scene as we have it, is that Buckingham's last sentiments are bitterly misanthropical.[30] Perhaps Shakespeare, as he finished the play, came to feel that the pious deaths of his two main opponents, Wolsey and Katherine, were enough, and that three would be too many. He precisely did not want too much abstract patterning. So insight and fortitude Buckingham may have gained, but not reconcilement with his enemies. It is possible to say that he makes a good end, but in observing the good ends made by various characters in *Henry VIII* we must not blind ourselves to the weaknesses they all also display, Buckingham in particular.

Shakespeare's mature experience of life itself must have had a lot to do with the balanced and mellow vision of humanity which we find in his later plays. But his early immersion in the chronicles of England gathered by Holinshed and Hall and his return to them during the composition of *Henry VIII* must have played an important part in shaping the psychological relativism which went along with his charitable treatment of both repentant and unrepentant sinners (Gardiner is let off very lightly in *Henry VIII*), especially when he portrayed men and women who once had real life. Holinshed and Hall themselves drew on different sources for their information and judgments and frequently present divergent or contradictory views of individual characters. Or they disagree between them about people and events.[31] Shakespeare may at times have been led into contradictory presentations more or less unwittingly by simply following his sources, and certainly his pictures of men like Richard II and Bolingbroke to some extent reflect the shifting attitudes of the chronicles. But he could hardly avoid being consciously struck by many of the contradictions and reflecting on their causes. He would have leant to look all round a person before trusting any one account. As early as the two Richard plays he had begun to probe inside his characters and to debate the question of identity. *Hamlet* represents his supreme moment of relativism in this internal exploration of the psyche. It is a further step, philosophically, and perhaps psychologically, to the existential view that we are what we seem to be, and that we may seem different beings to ourselves and others at different times and in different circumstances. This is a typically modern view, but it is anticipated by Shakespeare, and it is this kind of realisation which is dramatised in *Henry VIII*, where contradiction and ambiguity in the character portrayal are turned into a creative principle, one is tempted to say a principle of structure, so that the characters appear now in one line of vision, now in another. That is why it seems likely enough that the subtitle, or alternative title, of the play was indeed *All is True*, the name by which Sir Henry Wotton referred to it in his letter to his nephew. I take this to mean not primarily that everything is "historically authentic"[32] but that seemingly contradictory points of view are equally true. In fact the relativism extends beyond the interpretation of character to the understanding of manners, actions, and events. As Lee Bliss puts it:

> Even before the appearance of the king, the first scene sets up a world in which establishing the "truth" in any given situation is exceedingly complicated: prior certainty repeatedly dissolves in the face of later revelations. As the play progresses, its probable subtitle "All is True" and the references

> to "truth" in the Prologue become increasingly perplexing and ironic. If the facts of history remain constant, those treaties, taxes, deaths and births, rises and falls, become subject to many, even contradictory, interpretations. Any artistic work of course "interprets" through necessary selectivity and compression, but Shakespeare has dramatized the essential limitations in our knowledge of "truth" or human motivation through a proliferation of explanations within the play itself.[33]

Henry VIII is remarkable not chiefly for the depth of its probing and its subtlety of penetration, those qualities which we find so strikingly manifested in the great tragedies, but for its wisdom of understanding. Shakespeare may have sensed some of this wisdom in Holinshed, but he brought it out and fleshed it. And to demonstrate his ultimate answer to the riddle of identity he had to use characters who were also true in the sense of being historical. He, too, is the honest chronicler.

We should not be misled, then, by the looseness of the action. *Henry VIII* is a play of character rather than of plot and intrigue. And the action is chiefly organised to give prominence to the changing points of view with regard to characters, so much so that we are constantly assailed by conflicting impressions of them. It is by and by made perfectly clear that Buckingham is innocent of treason and the victim of injustice, but we cannot entirely doubt his surveyor's testimony against him. Wolsey is several times revealed as a machiavellian conspirator, but we cannot entirely doubt his professions of disinterested service. Henry's political sincerity seems unquestionable, but we cannot deny his concupiscence. Anne is both flirtatious and modest. Only Katherine and Cranmer are practically irreproachable, but Cranmer conducts the final divorce proceedings against the queen, and Katherine has the disadvantage of being a Spanish papist and perhaps an illegitimate wife. Not that papism is made a fault of character, and the religious issue is not brought into the open until the last act. But we must count a little on the bias of Shakespeare's audiences.

That bias is itself counteracted as it enters into the ambient vision of the play. Katherine appears in some of the best scenes: in three of them fighting Wolsey and in a fourth preparing for death. The play could well have been conceived as her tragedy, and one may fancy the prologue and epilogue reflecting a lingering-on of that conception. As it is, she becomes part of the human comedy, and her Catholicism one of the elements to be illuminated from opposite sides. There are obviously good and bad Catholics. Just as there are good and bad Englishmen. Just as England itself is viewed by the author's mature understanding—confirming what he knew since he wrote his first history play but never expressed so clearly as when he gave his sympathy to a foreign queen[34]—as imperfect in fact but perfect in potential.

NOTES

1. The pageantry has been emphasised by e.g. G. Wilson Knight in *The Crown of Life* (1947), Irving Ribner in *The English History Play in the Age of Shakespeare* (1957), and John D. Cox in "*Henry VIII* and the Masque," ELH, 45 (1978), 390–409; the mythic elements by e.g. Howard Felperin in "Shakespeare's *Henry VIII*: History as Myth," SEL, 6 (1966), 225–46, and Ronald Berman in "King Henry the Eighth: History and Romance," ES, 48, 2 (1967), 112–21; the looseness of plot by e.g. Ribner, op. cit., and A. R. Humphreys in his Introduction to the New Penguin *H8* (1971).
2. *Op. cit.*, p. 290.
3. Cf. Lee Bliss: "This is a rather bleak picture of an England where double-dealing seems the norm rather than the exception, where the king's 'pleasure' may be derived from appetite but is understood as law, and where men hardly dare discuss—much less act upon—matters of national concern" ("The Wheel of Fortune and the Maiden Phoenix of Shakespeare's *King Henry the Eighth*," *ELH* 42 (1975), 1–25. See p. 10).
4. *Op. cit.*, pp. 245–6.
5. See R. A. Foakes, "Introduction" to the New Arden H8 (1957, UP 1968), p. xlix. Foakes particularly refers to Hardin Craig's *An Interpretation of Shakespeare* (1948).
6. Felperin, pp. 243–4.
7. Frederick O. Waage, "*Henry VIII* and the Crisis of the English History Play," SSt, 8 (1975) 297–309; see p. 297 and cf. Lee Bliss, *op. cit.*, esp. p. 19.
8. Berman, *op. cit.*, p. 118
9. New Penguin *H8*, p. 19. Humphreys (p. 18) allies himself with Aldis Wright and David Nichol Smith and quotes Wright's opinion of *H8*: "without plot, without development, without any character on which the interest can be concentrated throughout."
10. A. R. Humphreys in the main defends the division of the play between Shakespeare and Fletcher suggested by James Spedding in 1850—see the New Penguin *H8*, pp. 21ff. He also provides a useful critical list of the main contenders for and against the collaboration theory pp. 50–54. To the supporters of collaboration may be added Cyrus Hoy and to the defenders

of Shakespeare's sole authorship Irving Ribner, Howard Felperin, H. M. Richmond, and Lee Bliss.

11. Ribner, p. 291. See also Humphreys, new Penguin *H8*, pp. 35–39.
12. R. A. Law, "The Double Authorship of *Henry VIII*," SP, 56 (1959), 471–88. See p. 488.
13. Spedding is quoted by Foakes, Arden *H8*, p. xlvii; Law, *op. cit.*, p. 486; Waage, *op. cit.*, p. 297.
14. Foakes, Arden *H8*, p. xlviii. Foakes does not endorse this view but refers it to a number of adverse critics of the play's structure whom he lists in the footnote: W. A. Wright, D. Nichol Smith, A. A. Parker, Eugene M. Waith, and R. Boyle.
15. Buckingham's valedictory speeches in II.i are inconsistent (see my introductory chapter and pp. 155–56 below) but not so as to create any major problems outside that scene.
16. See especially I.ii.132–35 and II.iv.168–79. It is interesting to notice that the question of legitimacy, so much at the centre of the early plays, is alto present in *H8*. The links with *KJ* are especially strong in this respect.
17. See V.i.129–33. The king now admits that "such things have been done."
18. Arden *H8*, p. lii.
19. G. Wilson Knight, *The Crown of Life*, p. 306.
20. Arden *H8*, pp. liii–liv.
21. Knight, pp. 334–36.
22. Arden *H8* p. lviii.
23. See note 3 above.
24. Bliss, *op.cit.*, p. 20.
25. Knight, pp. 306–15.
26. Arden *H8*, pp. lxi, lxiii. Cf. Bullough, *Sources*, IV, p. 448.
27. Henry's daughter Mary is mentioned by the king in II.iv.172–79 and by Katherine in IV.ii.131–38.
28. That human individuals could be both good and bad at the same time was always a part of Shakespeare's psychological and moral insight. That they could be greatly good and greatly bad at the same time was demonstrated in *R2*. A more penetrating character analysis is found in *Julius Caesar*. To quote Geoffrey Bullough (*Sources*, v, p. 57):

    > what Shakespeare learned from Plutarch was to represent more clearly than before the paradoxes of human motive, the mixture of good and evil in the same person.[...] In *Julius Caesar* the dramatist achieves a somewhat detached tolerance in his attitude towards historical figures, and at the same time a critical attitude towards politics and those who take part in it.

    At least one critic has also found a psychological relativism in *Julius Caesar* similar to that which I find to be central in *H8*: see Rene E. Fortin, "*Julius Caesar*: An Experiment in Point of View," *SQ*, xix.4 (Autumn 1968) 341–47.
29. For Katherine's judgment of Henry see also Bliss, *op. cit.*, p. 11.
30. Buckingham's warning against false friends may even be seen to be directed against the king. Wolsey's famous last words (". . . he would not

in mine age / Have left me naked to mine enemies") are certainly a veiled accusation of the king for his ingratitude. And Katherine cannot entirely conceal her bitterness. Is there a little of Webster's political radicalism in Shakespeare's last play?

31. See also Bliss, *op. cit.*, pp. 5–6: "Shakespeare capitalizes on the inconsistencies of the chronicles and with them enhances his use of multiple sympathetic perspectives."
32. Humphreys, Penguin *H8*, p. 8: "The title as Wotton cites it—*All is True*—was perhaps an alternative to that using the King's name, and meant to draw attention, as the Prologue also does, to the play's unusual care to be historically authentic." Contrast Felperin's view, *op. cit.*, p. 227: "*Henry VIII* departs from history, that is, from Holinshed, more radically than any of the earlier dramas—so much so, that the subtitle of the play, 'All is True,' makes one wonder whether Shakespeare is not ironically hinting that we revise our conventional notions of historical truth, even of mimetic truth itself."
33. Bliss, *op. cit.*, p.3
34. There remains an anti-foreign bias which finds an explicit outlet in the proclamation against French manners in I.iii. It must be supposed that the proclamation is issued by the king and is designed to set him in a favourable light. It has no other dramatic significance.

Bibliography

Ball, William T. W. Review of Henry Irving's *Henry VIII*. *The Boston Traveller*, January 10, 1894.

Bliss, Lee. "The Wheel of Fortune and the Maiden Phoenix of Shakespeare's *King Henry the Eight*." *ELH: A Journal of English Literary History*, XLII (1975), 1–25.

Bonjour, Adrien. "The Road to Swinstead Abbey: A Study of the Sense and Structure of *King John*." *ELH: A Journal of English Literary History*, XVIII (1951), 253–74.

Brownlow, F. W. *Two Shakespearian Sequences: Henry VI to Richard II and Pericles to Timon of Athens*. London: The Macmillan Press, 1977, pp. 185–201.

Byrne, Muriel St. Clare. "A Stratford Production: *Henry VIII*." *Shakespeare Survey*, 3 (1950), 1920–29.

Byrne, Muriel St. Clare. "Dramatic Intention and Theatrical Realization." *The Triple Bond*. Ed. Joseph Price. University Park, Pa.: The Pennsylvania State University Press, 1975, pp. 40–49.

Calderwood, James L. "Commodity and Honour in *King John*." *University of Toronto Quarterly*, XXIX (1960), 341–56.

Clapp, H. A. Review of Henry Irving's *Henry VIII*. *The Boston Advertiser*, January 9, 1894.

Davies, Thomas. *Memoirs of the Life of David Garrick, Esq*. Vol. 1. London, 1784, pp. 304–09.

[Gentleman, Francis]. *The Dramatic Censor or Critical Companion*. London: J. Bell, 1770, pp. 155–73.

Hazlitt, William. *Characters of Shakespeare's Plays*. London: Derby & Jackson, 1859, pp. 155–63.

Hazlitt, William. *A View of the English Stage*. London: Robert Stodart, 1818, pp. 382–86.

Jameson, Anna. *Characteristics of Women, Moral, Political and Historical*. Boston: Ticknor and Fields, 1866, pp. 407–37.

Nicholson, Marjorie H. "The Authorship of Henry the Eighth." *PMLA*, XXXVII (1922), 484–502.

Reese, M. M. *The Cease of Majesty*. London: Edward Arnold, 1961, pp. 260–86.

————. Review of Henry Irving's *Henry VIII*. *The Boston Evening Transcript*, January 9, 1894.

Smallwood, Robert. Introduction to *The New Penguin Shakespeare: King John*. London: Penguin Books, 1974, pp. 7–46.

Smidt, Kristian. *Unconformities in Shakespeare's History Plays*. Atlantic Highlands, N.J.: Humanities Press International, 1982, pp. 145–58.

Spedding, James. "On the Several Shares of Shakespeare and Fletcher in the Play of *Henry VIII*." *New Shakespeare Society Transactions*, Series I, Part I (1874), Appendix, pp. 1–18.

Sprague, Arthur Colby. *Shakespeare's Histories: Plays for the Stage*. London: The Society for Theatre Research, 1964, pp. 12–28.

Spurgeon, Caroline. *Shakespeare's Imagery and What it Tells Us*. Cambridge: Cambridge University Press, 1935, pp. 245–58.

Tillyard, E. M. W. *Shakespeare's History Plays*. New York: Macmillan Publishing Co., 1946, pp. 215–33.

Waith, Eugene M. "King John and the Drama of History." *Shakespeare Quarterly*, XXIX (1978), 192–211.